The Shell Channel Pilot

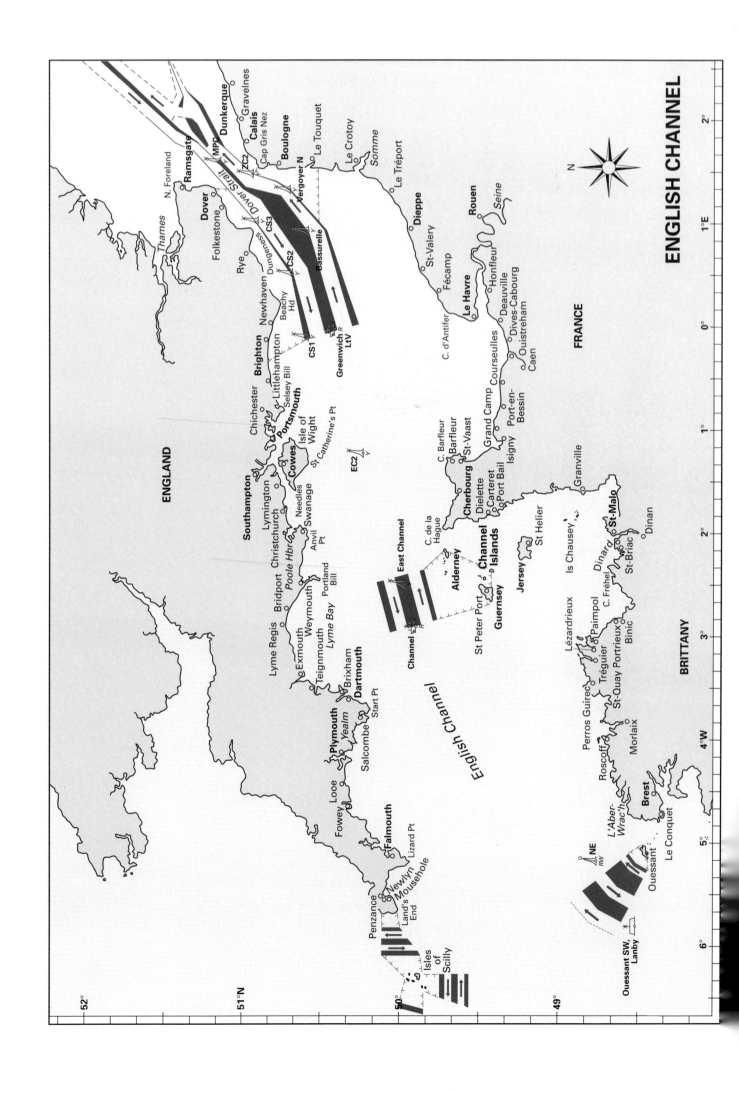

ENGLISH CHANNEL

The Shell Channel Pilot

The South Coast of England & the North Coast of France

TOM CUNLIFFE
Aerial photography by
Patrick Roach

Imray Laurie Norie & Wilson Ltd
St Ives Cambridgeshire England

Published by
Imray Laurie Norie & Wilson Ltd
Wych House St Ives Huntingdon,
Cambridgeshire PE27 5BT England
☎ +44 (0)1480 462114
Fax +44 (0)1480 496109
E-mail ilnw@imray.com
Web site www.imray.com
2000

First edition 1995
Reprint with revisions 1996
Second edition 1997
Third edition 2000

The plans and details of tidal streams are based on
information published by the United Kingdom
Hydrographic Office and Service Hydrographique et
Océanographique de la Marine with permission.

British Library Cataloguing in Publication Data.

A catalogue record for this book is available from the
British Library.

ISBN 0 85288 421 4

The Shell trademark is used under licence from
Shell International Petroleum Company Ltd.

CAUTION
Every effort has been made to ensure the accuracy of
this book. It contains selected information and thus
is not definitive and does not include all known
information on the subject in hand; this is
particularly relevant to the plans, which should not
be used for navigation. The publisher and author
believe that its selection is a useful aid to prudent
navigation, but the safety of a vessel depends
ultimately on the judgement of the navigator, who
should assess all information, published or
unpublished, available to him/her.

PLANS
The plans in this guide are not to be used for
navigation. They are designed to support the text
and should at all times be used with navigational
charts.

CORRECTIONS
The editors would be glad to receive any
corrections, information or suggestions which
readers may consider would improve the book, as
new impressions will be required from time to time.
Letters should be addressed to the Editor, *The Shell
Channel Pilot*, care of the publishers. The more
precise the information the better, but even partial
or doubtful information is helpful, if it is made clear
what the doubts are. Supplementary information is
published on our web site www.imray.com

The last input of technical information was
February 2000.

Printed in Great Britain by
Butler & Tanner Ltd, Frome, Somerset

Contents

Foreword

Dedication

The Shell Channel Pilot is dedicated to the memory of Captain John Coote RN, a great man of the sea.

The English Channel is one of the world's finest yacht cruising grounds. It has varying coastal topography, from the granite shores of Brittany to the Solent harbour mud-flats and the chalk cliffs of Sussex. Resorts, cities, naval bases and great commercial ports line its waters, but it also offers islands and quiet anchorages. For British or French sailors there is the added spice of foreign shores anything from a few hours to a day away, while for visitors from further afield two great nations are here to be explored by yacht, which, as all cruising people know, is the best way to discover any country.

Channel tides are of major significance to any sailing or low-powered motor craft. In parts of Brittany ranges climb up to a mind-bending 12m, with streams to match. Yet this very feature, which can easily alarm, is what makes the place so exciting to work in a small boat. A yacht might sail 30 miles through the water during a 6-hour period while receiving an extra 15 miles free by courtesy of the tide. This increases the range of an average daytime passage and makes more ambitious plans possible.

Coupled with the tides, our ever-changing weather generates such a massive variation in conditions that it is true to say that for those who sail our waters no two days are ever the same.

Since 1937 *The Shell Pilot* and its immediate progenitor, *Sailing on the South Coast*, by the redoubtable K. Adlard Coles, have been guiding yachtsmen into a greater enjoyment of Channel waters. The book started in the famous 'dumpy' format, and Shell soon took up the sponsorship. The work passed through various editions with its original publishers, Faber and Faber. In due course *The Shell Pilot*, as it was now known, came under the editorship of Captain John Coote RN, a famous submariner who became equally notable as an ocean-racing navigator. Johnnie Coote was a friend to all who loved the sea. He had great influence, and yachtsmen in all areas of the sport benefited from his work. Among cruising sailors, however, he will be mainly remembered for his tireless efforts on *The Shell Pilot*. In 1985 he expanded its horizons by including a new volume (in the traditional format) which covered selected French Channel ports. In addition to the usual pilotage notes, it contained swashbuckling commentaries on the World War II

Normandy landings, as well as many a useful tip on where to eat and where not to.

Johnnie Coote died in 1993, deeply mourned by his family and a host of friends, just as the old *Shell Pilot* was coming due for a new edition. Shortly before his death he handed the tiller over to me. At the same time, Faber and Faber were arranging to pass this, their one nautical title, over to Imray, who are, of course, nautical specialists. The scene was thus set for a major change in the book. People's sailing habits have altered since Adlard Coles' day and far more yachts now cross and recross the Channel as a matter of course. It was therefore decided that while *The Shell Channel Pilot* would retain its traditional feel of uncomplicated sailing directions, clear plans and useful photographs, the original two-volume, small-sized format would be brought into line with the standard A4 publication. Both sides of the Channel are now combined in one book; an exciting development which still generates the only yachting pilot for the whole of the English Channel cruising ground. I am sure Adlard Coles would have approved.

Whilst the text is constantly developing with each new edition, it is based on Johnnie Coote's work, which in turn drew its inspiration from Adlard Coles. Thus, the circle remains unbroken. Every effort has been made, both by myself and by Imray, to ensure that the information is up to date at the time of publishing. The notes on every harbour on the English side have been checked by the harbourmasters concerned or, in the absence of harbour authorities, with the local yacht club. Both official and unofficial sources have been extremely cooperative, and we acknowledge their assistance most warmly. French harbour staff have been personally visited wherever possible and, as with England, I have drawn heavily on my own experience of navigating Channel waters.

The Coote initiative of mentioning notable restaurants and other points of interest has been maintained. I have also tried to indicate the proximity of laundry facilities because, as a family yachtsman myself, I have found these of great use on trips of more than a few days' duration.

The new *Shell Channel Pilot* has aerial photographs ably taken mostly by Patrick Roach which will provide invaluable assistance when attempting to make sense of a two-dimensional chart. Most of the black-and-white photographs were shot by Johnnie Coote and have been generously made available by Mrs Coote and Faber and Faber.

I cannot end this foreword without recommending all yacht skippers to make maximum use of binoculars and to secure the services of a sharp-eyed mate. My own pilotage is frequently rendered free of impending drama by the presence of my wife, Ros, whose father was a fighter pilot and who has inherited his gimlet vision. Not content with this practical contribution, she also runs a tight ship in my study. Without her and that most equable of publishers, Willie Wilson, this third edition of the new-style *Shell Channel Pilot* might have been blown overboard off the Needles, or missed stays somewhere in the depths of cyberspace.

No small thanks is also due to the steady input of positive information from users of the pilot. Each year, we receive letters from sailors who have found details that have either changed since my most recent visit, or circumstances under which their experience has varied from mine. Correspondence now comes not only from Britain, but also increasingly from Dutch, German and sometimes Scandinavian seafarers who are enjoying our waters in ever-increasing numbers. We welcome these comrades to our 'Channel Fleet', and are grateful that a number have felt sufficiently a part of our scene to offer their comments. Keep this feed back coming please. The more of us who take part in the project, the more we all benefit.

Tom Cunliffe
February 2000

Acknowledgenents

The majority of the aerial photographs in colour were taken by Patrick Roach. Pat Blenkinsopp piloted the aircraft. The publishers are also grateful to Linda Dawes and Alison Walton who drew the plans. The index has been compiled by Elizabeth Cook.

Key to symbols

⚓	Visitors' moorings
Ⓥ	Visitors' berths
⚓	Yacht marina
⚓	Yacht berth
⬎	Public landing
➤	Slipway for small craft
⚒	Water tap
🛢	Fuel
▮	Gas
➘	Public telephone
⊖	Customs
Ⓖ	Chandlery
🍺	Public house, inn, bar
✕	Restaurant
⚑	Yacht or sailing club
WC	Toilets
🄿	Public car park
⛵	Parking for boats
⊚	Laundrette
🚐	Caravan site
Δ	Camping site
➤	Nature reserve
⚓	Harbour master
✉	Post office

Introduction

Warning

Users of this pilot book should be constantly aware that while every reasonable effort has been made to ensure its accuracy, experience shows that, as with all pilot books, there will remain the occasional error in the information. These generally arise due to changes in harbour arrangements and navigational aids subsequent to the date of compilation, but it is not unknown for a bearing or course either to be noted incorrectly in the first instance, or to become incorrect through errors in the typesetting or editing process. When a ship takes on a human pilot, the captain retains full responsibility for her safe passage. The same applies to yachtsmen using this book. Make sure your charts are up to date and proceed with caution.

Sailing directions

Charts

It cannot be over-stressed that, like all yachting pilots, *The Shell Channel Pilot* exists largely to expand and clarify the information on official navigational charts; these may be British Admiralty, SHOM, Imray or the Carte Guide de Navigation Cotière (Navicarte). The plans in this book are included in order to illustrate the text and are not to be used for chartwork navigation.

For planning and passage-making purposes you will require an overall Channel chart, which will cost the same as a dozen oysters and a bottle of Muscadet on the quay at St Vaast. What you buy after that will depend on how adventurous you want to be and the depth of your pocket. Some people find Admiralty charts the easiest to read. I am inclined to concur with this, but it must be said that the harbour plans and other information included on Imray's passage charts can represent a substantial saving in the number of charts to buy. French Navicarte charts are unusual in presentation, but once you are used to them they are an excellent pilotage tool. French (SHOM) charts are beautiful – some would say they are works of art. Unless you have seen them often, however, the British Admiralty offerings, while more prosaic, are far easier to read.

Datum

With the advent of accurate electronic fixing systems, it should be noted that the position reading from your GPS set may differ from that on the chart you are using. Always check the *datum* of the chart (usually given near the title, the cautions and any other such information), compare it with that on your computer and be ready to make any necessary alterations to your apparent position. Such changes may be insignificant in terms of pre-electronic navigation, but for a navigator who takes full advantage of the pinpoint accuracy sometimes now available, they may be important.

The term 'datum' in this context should not be confused with the 'Chart Datum' from which soundings are measured.

Waypoints

The Shell Channel Pilot has resisted the temptation to give waypoints. The reason for this is that in the experience of the compiler, the position of the desired waypoint may change from day to day, depending on wind and tide. Furthermore, if the waypoint were, for example, a landfall buoy and this were moved, confusion could be doubled. It is therefore recommended that users select their own waypoints where required.

Depths

Depths are given in metres at Lowest Astronomical Tide (LAT), which is also Chart Datum level. Thus, except in exceptional circumstances, you are unlikely to experience anything less than the depth stated.

Heights

Heights of lighthouses etc. are expressed in metres above sea level at mean high water springs. They will therefore only be less than this at times of unusually high tides.

Distances

Distances at sea are stated in nautical miles and cables. A cable's length is 200 yards, one tenth of a mile or, if you prefer, one tenth of a minute of latitude. Should you be of the metric persuasion, it represents something under 200 metres.

Tidal height information

This is given for every port by reference to Dover as the standard port. The heights thus computed will sometimes perforce be approximate and skippers are strongly recommended to calculate more accurate information from the *Admiralty Tide Tables* or the almanacs. The information given in this book will prove useful for planning purposes, however.

Always bear in mind that published tidal data are only predictions. The facts on the day may be affected significantly by wind and weather.

The *double high water* phenomenon in and around the Solent is notoriously difficult to predict. The above cautions should be particularly noted in this area.

Leading lines
While leading lines are theoretically safe, they sometimes pass a danger in close proximity to the channel. Examine the chart, therefore, and be ready to 'borrow' to one side or the other to give a safety margin.

Bearings and courses
Bearings and courses are given in degrees True, to which any necessary corrections must be made for Variation and Deviation. Unless otherwise stated, all bearings of shore objects, or headings up approach channels, are given as True from seaward.

Symbols
Symbols in the text for lights, sound signals and any other charted information are generally lifted straight from the chart and apply the same conventions, thus: 'Fort Gilkicker (Oc.G.10s7M)' is read as 'Fort Gilkicker, green light, occulting once every 10 seconds, 7 miles nominal range'. The attention of readers using French charts is drawn to the English/French glossary in the Appendix.

The anchorage symbol ⚓ is used on the plans to indicate a general anchorage. Its precise location does not necessarily recommend the ideal place to let go. Skippers are expected to apply the principles of good seamanship to selecting a precise location to lay their anchors.

Buoyage
IALA System A buoyage applies throughout the English Channel.

Customs
Since the rise of the EU, few formalities have been required of yachts passing between member states. Vessels arriving in the Channel from outside the EU are, of course, subject to the usual customs and immigration requirements. They should accordingly report at a major port as soon as practicable.

Unfortunately for us Europeans, there still exists a nonsense to encumber our local cruising. British yachts bound for the Channel Islands are required to fill out *Part I* of form *C1328*, obtainable from any customs house and many harbour offices. Hand in the remaining parts as directed on your return. If you have made an unscheduled call at the Channel Islands on your way home from France, you must clear into the UK by reporting your arrival to the nearest customs house by telephone. You will then be directed as to your correct course of action. In the islands themselves, ask the harbour staff for clearance advice.

On arrival at or from the Channel Islands, you must wear a yellow 'Q' flag as soon as you are within 12 miles of the coast, keeping it up until you are cleared.

Traffic signals

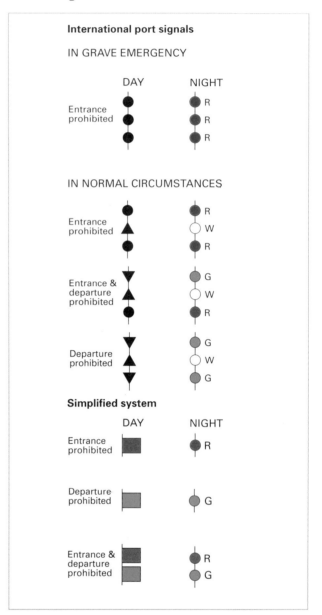

Checklist for cross-Channel departure
Always carry:
- a British ensign, a French courtesy ensign and a 'Q' flag.
- ship's papers – originals, not copies
- radio licence
- passports
- certificates of competence

Remember to clear customs to and from the Channel Islands. It is important to carry boat papers and passports when entering French waters. You will in all probability never be asked for them, but if you are and do not have them, you may be fined. The French customs carry out random checks and will not accept photocopies.

If you have a certificate of competence, such as *Yachtmaster Offshore*, show them this as well. You may also be visited by the *gendarmerie maritime*, who are the Naval Police, among whose duties is to check small boats. They will note everything on board, but it should be understood that they are only doing this in case the boat is lost. The information is filed on a computer. The *affaires maritimes* also have the power to board you, and here there is some overlap. They will sometimes check for VAT payment, so receipts are useful.

You must also have a current radio licence on board, lack of which may incur an on-the-spot fine. It is better to pay this immediately because to do so is cheaper than having to return later to brass up.

Never forget that many French officials have the power to seize your boat, so be polite and pleasant, even if a boarding party appears officious. If you cannot talk to them in French, try English. They may well understand.

Don't be alarmed by the appearance of French officials. They wear guns, which we Brits are generally unused to, but this doesn't mean they are about to shoot up your boat. It is merely a part of their everyday uniform.

VHF

It is now normal practice on approaching a British yacht harbour to call ahead on VHF to arrange a berth. Radio channels are given in the text. This may not always be convenient in France – it takes a very confident linguist to chance his arm on the radio with a French harbourmaster. Indeed, while the majority of English yacht harbours now maintain a VHF watch, at least in working hours, many French ones do not. If in doubt, tie up on the visitors' berths or reception pontoon and go to the harbour office for instructions.

French time

French time operates from the basis of 'Zone −1'. This means that you must subtract 1 hour from a French time as given in a tide table to convert that time to UT. Since an hour must then be added to UT to correct it to what a British watch says, you will realise that British Summer Time is the same as Zone −1. This simple device works for published tide times in France. It does not help you with restaurant opening times and the rest, which add an hour to Zone −1 and thus step away from the British once more.

Navigating the English Channel

I remember once returning home from a long cruise to foreign parts. I had enjoyed some excellent tropical sailing, yet as the old boat came onto soundings and I reached for my tidal stream atlas my heart gave a small skip of joy. At long last there would be more to passage-making than just pointing the boat in the right direction. I would be challenged once more, and my satisfaction would be in proportion to my success in meeting the demands of the ocean's own breathing, for in the Channel, the tide is king.

Winds can be from any quarter in the summer months, but are often westerly. This makes life easy for the south-coast sailor wanting to visit France, but highly inconvenient for a Dutchman who has it in mind to cruise the Isles of Scilly. We cannot change the weather, and where we end up in relation to the wind direction will always contain an element of lottery, but the tides are a different matter. Heights and streams are predicted years in advance to a surprising degree of accuracy, so that we have all the necessary information to allow us to work the fair stream wherever possible and avoid the worst excesses of foul tide. Occasionally there is no advantage either way, but even then the stream remains important, for without understanding its movements we cannot estimate our position. This leaves us with no hope save electronics, which, should our volts pour away down an electrical plughole, will be no hope at all.

Tidal streams

The tidal stream charts included in this book relate to the time of high water at Dover. The arrows indicating stream direction are self-explanatory. The speeds are given as two figures with a dot between them: for example, 21.42. This indicates that the neap rate at that point is 2·1 knots while the mean spring rate is 4·2. Tables are available for computing intermediate rates, but for most practical purposes an interpolation 'in your head' will prove satisfactory.

Study of the various tidal charts reveals a number of useful phenomena:

- Tides are strongest round headlands.
- In general, tides are weaker in the southwest of England than elsewhere.
- Tides run savagely around Cap de la Hague between Alderney and France (the Race of Alderney), and are generally strong on the French side of the Channel from Barfleur right down to Ouessant.
- Solent tides run hard, particularly in the West Solent and at the western entrance. They also turn an hour or so before the main Channel stream.
- Vicious tides may be encountered in the vicinity of Portland Bill. For information about these, see the chapter on 'Principal headlands'.

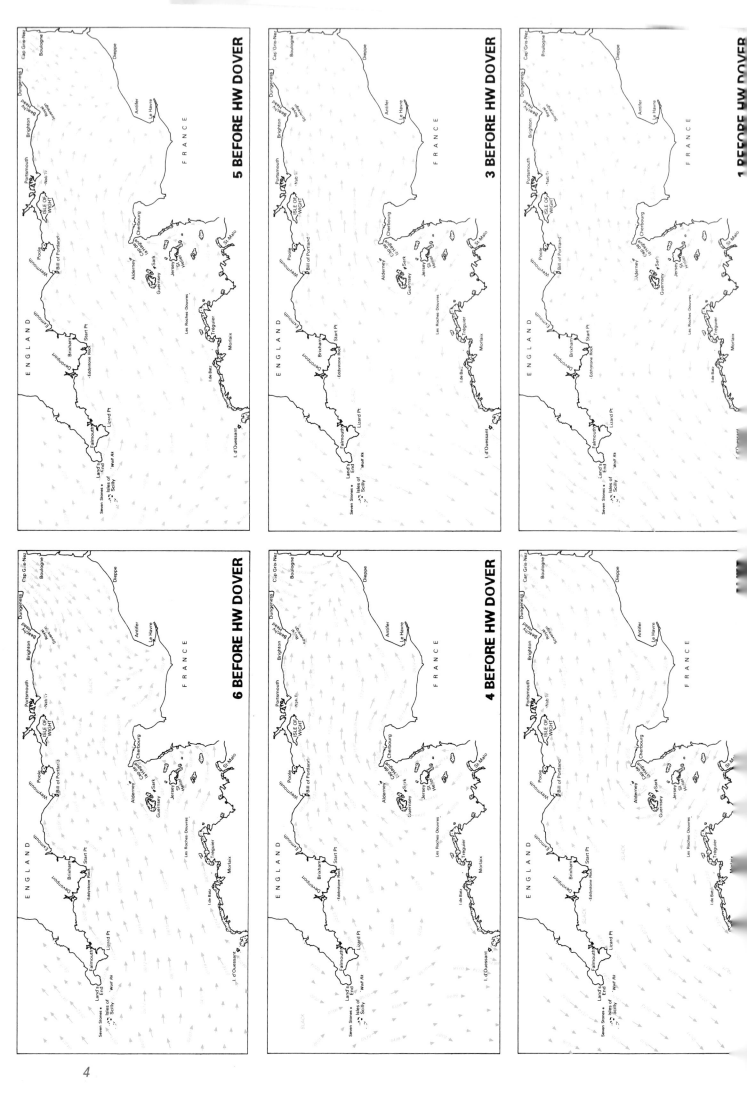

5 BEFORE HW DOVER

6 BEFORE HW DOVER

3 BEFORE HW DOVER

4 BEFORE HW DOVER

1 BEFORE HW DOVER

4

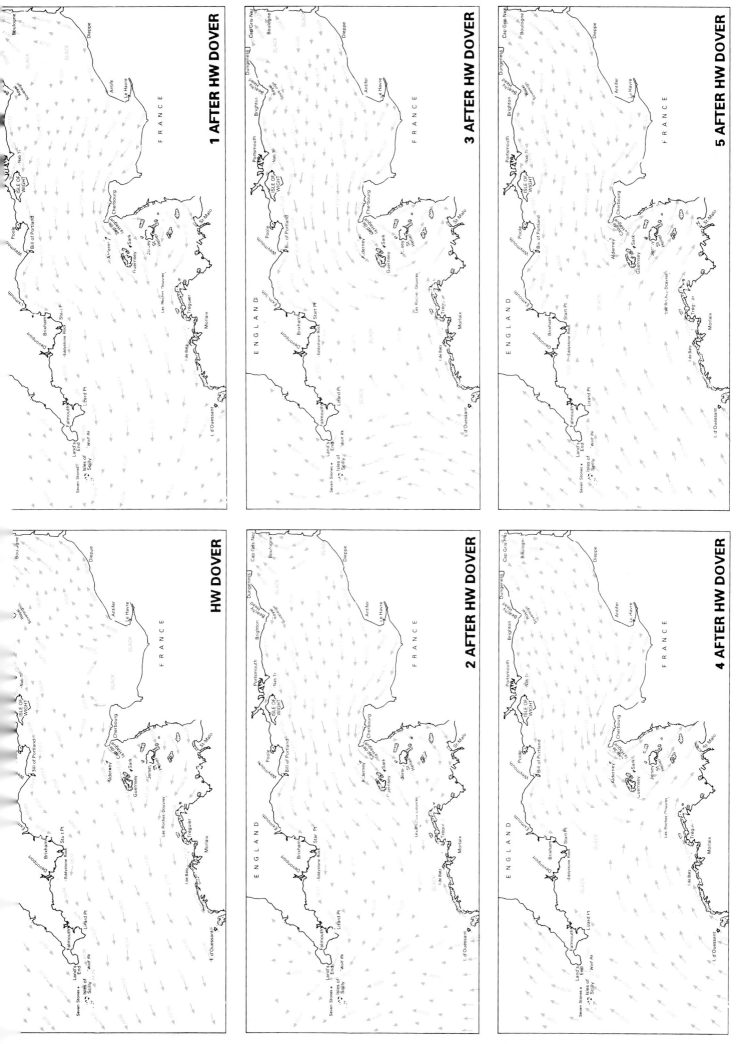

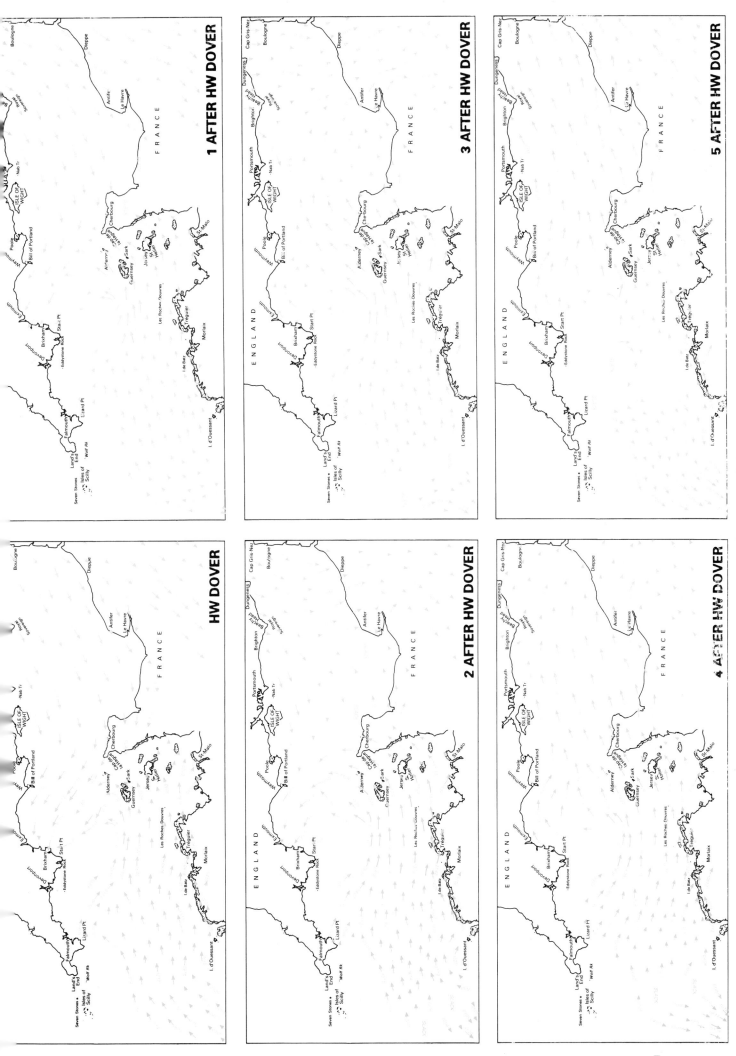

HW DOVER

1 AFTER HW DOVER

2 AFTER HW DOVER

3 AFTER HW DOVER

4 AFTER HW DOVER

5 AFTER HW DOVER

5

- As the tide floods up-Channel, with high waters progressively later the further east you go, it is possible to carry fair tide all the way from the Hamble River to Dover, given a boat speed of 7 or 8 knots, depending upon the tide. You must work the eddy down the Solent north shore, then step onto the 'gravy train' once past the Looe channel at Selsey Bill.
- Carrying a fair or neutral stream from the west Solent to Guernsey is easy, despite a distance of up to 90 miles. Take the last of the ebb down to the Needles, then make sure you arrive at the Alderney Race (60 miles on) at, or an hour or two after, HW Dover. You will then receive a push of anything from 3 to 7 knots all the way to St Peter Port. Get it wrong, and you might just as well stop off in Alderney for a night in The Diver's Bar.
- Always use your tidal atlas or charts creatively. They are your lifeline to happiness.

Tidal heights

Whilst many of the ports dealt with in *The Shell Channel Pilot* can be entered in most weathers and at any state of tide, others are tidally sensitive. These are marked * on the Contents page so that if the reader needs a decision at sea in a hurry in bad weather, he or she can see at a glance if a harbour is likely to present a problem. Those with a * will need more careful study.

A number of harbours on both sides of the Channel quite literally dry out at low water, or are only accessible via lock gates at half-tide or above. Drying harbours offer great satisfaction to boats able to take the ground conveniently, but for any strangers, all tidal harbours require great care.

In general, because the tide floods eastwards, it is better to approach such a port from the west, carrying fair tide. This raises its own problems when you leave, because from high water onwards the stream should be running away to the west again. Happily, this is not always so clear cut, with high water not coinciding perfectly with the end of the east-going stream. Careful planning with this question in mind can yield satisfying results.

Channel crossings

Various challenges and problems attach themselves to crossing the Channel, depending upon how far east or west you happen to be. These generally revolve around large cross-tide effects, shipping and the desirability of making a dawn landfall. The last factor is less important in the narrow waters at the east end of the Channel, while for many people, electronic navigation is rendering the attraction of a look at the lighthouses before they are switched off less of a consideration on the longer passages than once it was.

Traffic Separation Schemes

These are clearly marked on the passage charts. Their purpose is to prevent big-ship collisions in areas of heavy traffic. If navigating within such a scheme, yachts must proceed in the direction indicated for traffic flow, but you are generally better advised to stay out of them if you can. You may not navigate in the separation zone which lies between the lanes. You may only cross it at right angles. If you need to cross the whole scheme, you must do so at your best speed at right angles to the flow of traffic. When the tide is strong, this means that you do not try to plot a vector course in order to traverse the zone on a ground track at right angles to the lanes. You will cross more quickly if you *steer* at right angles. You will also be complying with the regulations.

Should you require to enter a traffic lane in such a scheme, do so at a shallow angle.

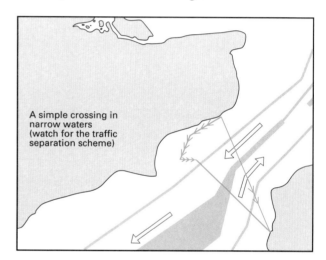

A simple crossing in narrow waters (watch for the traffic separation scheme)

Diagram 1

In the Dover Strait, these schemes are enforced rigorously and yachts must comply on pain of considerable fines. Fortunately, if you are proceeding from one local port to another, or otherwise along the coast, you may make use of the Inshore Traffic Zones. These are set up specifically to accommodate coastal shipping and small craft. You may pass in either direction, paying particular heed to the Colregs, being always aware of the presence of the main event going on in mid-Channel.

There is a further Traffic Separation Scheme off the Casquets to the northwest of Alderney. This must be considered if your passage plan leads you into its vicinity. Although the area seems well clear of danger, it has proved to be a pressure point and you must take heed.

The only other such zone of interest to Channel yachtsmen lies between Land's End and the Isles of Scilly. This one is less crowded and you cross it at right angles anyway, unless you are going to windward, in which case, watch out!

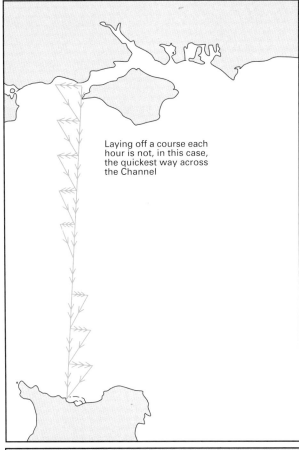

Laying off a course each hour is not, in this case, the quickest way across the Channel

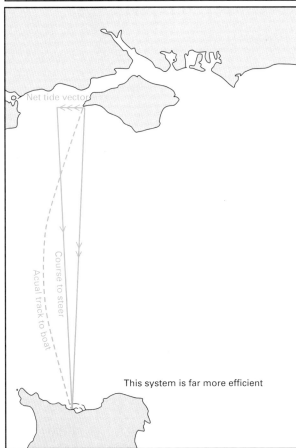

Net tide vector

Course to steer

Acual track to boat

This system is far more efficient

Diagram 2

Tidal vectors

When you are crossing the narrow part of the Channel – a trip of 4 or 5 hours perhaps – you can safely lay off a tidal offset for the whole period (diagram 1), given that you are not falling foul of a Traffic Separation Scheme. If you are crossing the central Channel, however, you must be careful. Unless your boat is extremely fast, your trip will be of over one tide's duration. You will thus be set east and west during the passage. It is a grave error to try to offset each hour's tide as in diagram 2, because if you do, you will sail considerably further each hour than you need. You may end up putting as much as 15 miles onto a 60-mile passage.

Instead, add up the total east going and the total west-going streams for your projected time at sea. Subtract the lesser from the greater and what is left is your *net tidal vector*. Apply this to your course to steer (see plan) and you will make your fastest possible crossing. The yacht will drift off the rhumb line, but this does not matter at all, for the tide will surely drift her back again before your arrival. You must bear this in mind if using a navigation computer and, unless you are prepared to steam or sail further than you need through the water, have nothing to do with 'cross track error' until you are nearly there.

Up-tide arrivals

Always steer for a point up-tide of your destination, even if this is somewhat to leeward, except in the heaviest weather. It is the easiest thing in the world to make up a couple of miles downtide after you have identified your position. Trying to claw back from a downtide situation can be tedious in the extreme.

Sea state

Bear in mind that in windy conditions, the 'chops of the Channel' become far more boisterous when the tide is running to windward. This can be dramatic at times. I recall coming out of Cherbourg at midnight in a northeasterly gale as a man young enough to know no better. We organised our departure to give us a full 6 hours' east-going spring tide.

By the time we were an hour out from Fort de l'Ouest every oil-lamp glass on board had jumped off its brackets (which shows how long ago it was) and we had thoroughly frightened ourselves. We made ground to windward, but it was never worth it.

For all these dire warnings, however, the Channel is the most satisfying place to sail that I can imagine. Take time to plan, work wind and tide, and the rewards are beyond price.

Weather services

BBC Radio 4

Shipping forecasts are broadcast on BBC Radio 4 on 198kHz (1515m) 92·4-94·6MHz, and on local MF frequencies daily at 0048, 0535 (clock times). The broadcast after the first news buletin after receipt includes area Trafalgar and is followed by a forecast, valid until 1800, for coastal waters of Great Britain up to 12M offshore, and reports from selected stations.

The bulletins include a summary of gale warnings in force; a general synopsis of the weather for the next 24 hours and expected changes within that period; forecasts for each sea area for the next 24 hours, giving wind direction and speed, weather and visibility; and the latest reports from selected stations. For each station are given wind direction and Beaufort force, present weather, visibility, and (if available) sea-level pressure and tendency.

Gale warnings are broadcast at the earliest juncture in the BBC Radio 4 programme after receipt, and also after the next news bulletin.

BBC Radio 3 & 4 Inshore forecasts

Forecasts are given for inshore waters (12 miles) until 1800 the next day at the end of Radio 4 programmes at about 0038. The forecast is followed by the 2200 reports from stations including St Catherine's (Isle of Wight) and Land's End.

On BBC Radio 3 a forecast for Great Britain is given at 0655 on 90·2-92·4MHz.

Weather centres

To arrange a forecast ring:

Plymouth	01752 251860
Southampton	02380 228844
London	020 7696 0573 or 020 7405 4356
Birmingham	0121-717 0570
Bristol	0117 9279298
Jersey	01534 46111 Ext 2229

Marine Call

Automatic telephone forecasts are available as follows at a peak rate (and more by VHF).

In each case dial 0891 500 then the three figures as follows:

450	3/5 day UK
992	2/5 day English Channel (Dover to Land's End)
458	South West (Hartland Pt to Lyme Regis)
457	Mid-Channel (Lyme Regis to Selsey Bill)
456	Channel East (Selsey Bill to North Foreland)
455	Anglia (North Foreland to The Wash)
432	Channel Islands

MetFAX

Weather maps and forecasts by FAX are available as follows:

0336-400 401	MetFAX Marine Index
01344-854 435	MetFAX ☎ helpline
01344-854 018	MetFAX facsimile helpline
0336-400 443	Beaufort scale
0336-400 442	Map of Shipping Areas
0336-400 441	24 hour Shipping forecast
0336-400 450	3/5 day Inshore Waters forecast UK
0336-400 444	Surface analysis chart
0336-400 445	25 hour Surface pressure forecast
0336 400 458	2 day SW Channel coastal forecast
0336 400 457	2 day Mid-Channel coastal forecast
0336-400 471	2/5 day Channel Waters forecast
0336-400 456	2 day E Channel coastal forecast
0336-400 470	2/5 day Biscay area forecast
0336-400 470	Channel Islands 2 day forecast

NAVTEX

NAVTEX services are available from Niton (S), Corsen (CROSS) (A), and Oostende (T).

FRENCH RADIO

France Inter 162kHz 1005 (Mon-Fri) 0650 (Sat-Sun) 2005 (daily)
Storm warnings, synopsis, 24 hour forecast for all French areas.
For English channel only
Brest 711kHz, 1404kHz 0655
Paris 864kHz, 0655
Lille 1377kHz 0655

Coast radio stations

United Kingdom Stations

Dover (Coastguard MRCC) 50°08'N 01°20'E
Note This station does not accept public correspondence; accepting distress, urgent and safety traffic only
RT (MF) Transmits and receives on 2182kHz
VHF Ch 16, 69[1], 10, 11, 67, 73, 80
1. Dover Coastguard operate the Channel Navigation Information Service (CNIS) in conjunction with Gris Nez Traffic. Primary working frequency for routine CNIS traffic. CNIS information bcsts are made on Ch 11.

Storm warnings
VHF CG District Ch 10 or 73 on receipt and at the following bcsts until cancelled 0105, 0505, 0905, 1305, 1705, 2105

Weather messages
VHF CG District Ch 10 or 73 at 0105, 0505, 0905, 1305, 1705, 2105. Inshore fcst for the area from North Foreland to Land's End. 0905, 2105 Shipping fcst, gale warnings, synopsis, 24h fcst for areas Thames, Dover and Wight

Navigational warnings
VHF North Foreland and Fairlight VHF Ch 10 or 73 on receipt and at the following bcsts until cancelled 0105, 0505, 0905, 1305, 1705, 2105

Thames (Coastguard MRSC)
Note This station does not accept public correspondence; accepting distress, urgent and safety traffic only
RT (MF) Transmits and receives on 2182kHz
VHF Transmits and receives on Ch 16, 10, 67, 73

Niton (S) (K)
RT (MF) Transmits and receives on 518kHz
Storm warnings
(S) 518kHz on receipt and at 0300, 0700, 1100, 1500, 1900, 2300
Weather messages
(S) 518kHz 0700, 1900
Navigational warnings
(S) 518kHz on receipt. Warnings of negative tidal surges in the Dover Strait. 0300, 0700, 1100, 1500, 1900, 2300
(K) 518kHz at 0140, 0540, 0940, 1340, 1740, 2140
Submarine exercises & Gunnery exercises
(S) 518kHz at 0700, 1900

Solent (Coastguard MRSC)
Note this station does not accept public correspondence; accepting distress, urgent and safety traffic only.
RT (MF) Transmits and receives on 2182, 2596, 1641kHz
VHF facilities located at: Newhaven, Selsey, Boniface, Isle of Wight, Lee-on-Solent, Needles, Isle of Wight Ch 16, 67, 06, 10, 73

Note VHF Ch 67 may not be monitored during MSI bcsts

Storm warnings

VHF CG District Ch 10 or 73 on receipt and at the following bcsts until cancelled 0040, 0440, 0840, 1240, 1640, 2040

RT (MF) 1641kHz on receipt and at the following bcsts until cancelled 0040, 0440, 0840, 1240, 1640, 2040

Weather messages

VHF CG District Ch 10 or 73 at 0040, 0440, 0840, 1240, 1640, 2040

RT (MF) 1641kHz and CG District VHF Ch 10 or 73 at 0840, 2040

Navigational warnings

VHF Boniface Ch 10 or 73 on receipt and at the following bcsts until cancelled 0040, 0440, 0840, 1240, 1640, 2040

RT (MF) 1641kHz on receipt and at the following bcsts until cancelled 0040, 0440, 0840, 1240, 1640, 2040

Falmouth (Coastguard MRCC)

Note this station does not accept public correspondence; accepting distress, urgent and safety traffic only.

RT (MF) Transmits and receives on 2182, 2226, 2670kHz

VHF Transmits and receives on Ch 16, 10, 67, 73

Storm warnings

VHF CG District Ch 10 or 73 on receipt and at the following bcsts until cancelled 0140, 0540, 0940, 1340, 1740, 2140

RT (MF) 2226kHz on receipt and at the following bcsts until cancelled 0140, 0540, 0940, 1340, 1740, 2140

Weather messages

VHF CG District Ch 10 or 73 at 0140, 0540, 0940, 1340, 1740, 2140

RT (MF) 2226kHz and VHF CG District Ch 10 or 73 at 0940, 2140

RT (MF) 2226kHz at 0950, 2150 (1 Oct–31 Mar)

Navigational warnings

VHF Falmouth, Land's End Ch 10 or 73 on receipt and at the following bcsts until cancelled 0140, 0540, 0940, 1340, 1740, 2140

RT (MF) 2226kHz on receipt and at the following bcsts until cancelled 0140, 0540, 0940, 1340, 1740, 2140

Brixham (Coastguard MRSC)

Note this station does not accept public correspondence; accepting distress, urgent and safety traffic only.

RT (MF) Transmits and receives on 2182kHz.

VHF Transmits and receives on Ch 16, 10, 67, 83

Storm warnings

VHF CG District Ch 10 or 73 on receipt and at the following bcsts until cancelled 0050, 0450, 0850, 1250, 1650, 2050

Weather messages

VHF CG District Ch 10 or 73 at 0050, 0450, 0850, 1250, 1650, 2050

VHF CG District Ch 10 or 73 at 0850, 2050

Navigational warnings

VHF East Prawle, Rame Head Ch 10 or 73 on receipt and at the following bcsts until cancelled 0050, 0450, 0850, 1250, 1650, 2050

Submarine/Gunnery Exercises

VHF East Prawle, Rame Head Ch 10 or 73 on receipt and at the following bcsts until cancelled 0050, 0450, 0850, 1250, 1650, 2050

St Peter Port

Note that with the exception of VHF Ch 62, service is restricted to messages concerning the navigation, pilotage, cargo and passengers of ships, exchanged with ships' captains and officials of the shipping companies concerned, and is not available for radio telephone link calls.

RT (MF) Transmits on 1662·5[1], 1764, 2182kHz. Receives on 1662·5[1], 2049, 2056, 2182, 2381[2]kHz

Traffic lists – Vessels for which traffic is held are called individually on 2182kHz. Traffic lists are broadcast on 1764kHz after the Navigational warnings at 0133, 0533, 0933, 1333, 1733, 2133

1. For Trinity House and Search and Rescue use only
2. Listening watch on 2381kHz is only maintained when distress working at adjacent coast stations is in progress

VHF Transmits and receives on Ch 16, 20, 62[1], 67[2]

Traffic lists – Vessles for which traffic is held are called individually on Ch 16. Traffic lists are broadcast on Ch 20 after the Navigational warnings at 0133, 0533, 0933, 1333, 1733, 2133

1. Available for link calls
2. Available on request for yacht safety messages

Navigational warnings

1764kHz, VHF Ch 20, 62 at 0133, 0533, 0933, 1333, 1733, 2133

Jersey

RT (MF)[1] Transmits on 1659, 2182kHz. Receives on 2045[2], 2048[2], 2084[3], 2534[3], 2182, 2191[4]kHz

Traffic lists – Vessels for which traffic is held are called individually on 2182kHz. Traffic lists are broadcast on 1659kHz after the Weather messages at 0645, 0745, 1245, 1845, 2245

1. Not available to radiotelephone link calls
2. For foreign registered vessels
3. For UK registered vessels
4. During distress working on 2182kHz, vessels may call on 2191kHz and listen for a reply on 1659kHz

VHF Transmits on Ch 16, 62, 25, 67[3]. Receives on Ch 16, 82[1], 25[2], 67[3]

Traffic lists – Vessels for which traffic is held are called individually on Ch 16. Traffic lists are broadcast on Ch 25 and 82 after the Weather messages at 0645[1], 0745[1], 1245, 1845, 2245

1. Direct calling on for UK registered vessels
2. Available for link calls
3. For small craft distress and safety working. Call on Ch 16

Storm warnings

1659kHz, VHF Ch 25, 82 on receipt. At the end of the next silence period. 0307, 0907, 1507, 2107

Weather messages

1659kHz, VHF Ch 25, 82 at 0645[1], 0745[1], 0845[1,2], 1245, 1845, 2245 and on request

1. Bcst given 1h earlier when DST is in force
2. 1 May to 31 August only

Navigational warnings

1659kHz, VHF Ch 25, 82 on receipt. At the end of the next silence period. 0433, 0645[1], 0745[1], 0833, 1245, 1633, 1845, 2033, 2245

1. Bcst given 1h earlier when DST is in force

Centres Regionaux Operationnels de Surveillance et de Sauvetage (CROSS)

The Centres Régionaux Opérationnels de Surveillance et de Sauvetage (CROSS) are centres for marine rescue co-ordination (a CROSS is an MRCC: Maritime Rescue Co-ordination Centre; a Sous-CROSS is an MRSC: Maritime Rescue Sub-Centre).

CROSS stations broadcast weather information in French or English after a call on VHF Ch 16.

Gris-Nez (CROSS) (MRCC)

Facilities are located at:
Dunkerque (51°03'N 2°21'E)
Gris-Nez (50°52'N 1°35'E)
Saint Frieux (50°37'N 1°36'E)
L'Ailly (49°55'N 0°58'E)

RT (MF) Transmits on 2182, 2677, 1650kHz. Receives on 2182, 2677kHz

VHF Transmits and receives on on Ch 16, 67, 68, 73

Storm warnings

RT (MF) 1650kHz on receipt and every odd H+03 in French.

VHF Ch 79. Dunkerque on receipt and every H+04. Saint Frieux on receipt and every H+10. In French and English

Weather messages

RT (MF) 1650kHz at 0833, 2033. VHF Ch 79. L'Ailly at 0703, 1533, 1903 LT. Gris-Nez at 0710, 1545, 1910 LT. Dunkerque at 0720 1603, 1920 LT. In French

Navigational warnings

RT (MF) 1650kHz at 0833, 2033 LT

VHF Ch 79 every H+10 in French and English

Jobourg (CROSS) (MRCC)

Facilities are located at:
Antifer (49°41'N 0°10'E)
Ver-sur-Mer 49°20'N 0°34'E
Port-en-Bessin (49°21'N 0°45'W)
Gatteville (49°42'N 1°16'W)
Jobourg (49°41'N 1°54'W)
Granville (48°50'N 1°36'W)
Roches-Douvres (49°06'N 2°49'W)

RT (MF) 1650kHz

VHF Transmits and receives on Ch 80

Storm warnings

VHF Ch 80 on receipt. Every H+03. On request in French. Jobourg on receipt. Every H+20, H+50. On request. In French and English

Weather messages

VHF Ch 80 Granville at 0703, 1533, 1903 LT. Jobourg at 0715, 1545, 1915 and 0733, 1603, 1933 LT. Port-en-Bessin at 0745, 1615, 1945. Antifer at 0803, 1633, 2003 LT. In French

Navigational warnings

RT (MF) 1650kHz at 0915, 2115 LT In French and English

VHF Ch 80 (Jobourg) every H+20, H+50 and on request

Corsen (CROSS) (MRCC)

Facilities are located at:
Cap Fréhel (48°41'N 2°19'W)
Bodic (48°48'N 3°05'W)
Ile de Batz (48°54'N 4°02'W)
Le Stiff (48°28'N 5°03'W)
Corsen (48°24'N 4°47'W)
Pointe du Raz (48°03'N 4°52'W)

RT (MF) Transmits and receives on 1650, 2677kHz

VHF Transmits and receives on Ch 79

Storm warnings

RT (MF) 1650, 2677kHz on receipt and every even H+03 in French. VHF Ch 79 on receipt and every H+03. In French. Le Stiff on receipt and every H+10, H+40 in French and English

Weather messages

RT (MF) 1650, 2677kHz at 0815, 2015 LT. In French

VHF Ch 79. Le Stiff at 0150, 0450, 0750, 1050, 1350, 1650, 1950, 2250 in French and English.

Pointe du Raz at 0445, 0703, 1103[1], 1533, 1903 LT
Le Stiff 0503, 0715, 1115[1], 1545, 1915 LT
Ile de Batz 0505, 0733, 1133[1], 1603, 1933 LT
Bodic 0533, 0745, 1145[1], 1615, 1945 LT
Cap Fréhel 0545, 0803, 1203[1], 1633, 2003 LT
In French

1. 1 May–30 Sep

Navigational warnings

2677kHz at 0735, 1935 LT

VHF Ch 79 every H+10, H+40 in French and English

I. The English coast
Ramsgate to the Isles of Scilly

Principal headlands

NORTH FORELAND

Tidal streams 3·2 miles 141° from headland
North-going −0120 Dover
South-going +0440 Dover
Spring rate 2¾ knots

Conspicuous 26m white eight-sided light tower (Fl(5)WR.20s57m19/15M) set on dramatic, nearly perpendicular chalk cliffs.

SOUTH FORELAND

Tidal streams between South Foreland and Deal
North-going approx −0145 Dover
South-going approx +0415 Dover
Spring rate 2¼ knots

The headland is an irregular chalk cliff over 90m high with two disused lighthouses at its summit. The western structure is a 21m square white castellated tower, 114m above sea level.

DUNGENESS

Tidal stream at position 2·4M 140° from Dungeness High lighthouse
East-going stream begins −2000 Dover
West-going stream +0400 Dover

Spring rate up to 2 knots, maybe more close inshore. These stream times are approximate as Dungeness is a sort of tidal watershed, experiencing some confusion as North Sea tides slop through into the Channel via Dover Strait.

A low promontory with a redundant lighthouse, and a nuclear power station to its west. There is a steep beach at its southeast end. The prominent lighthouse (Fl.10s40m27M Horn(3)60s) is a black round tower with white bands. The light also shows F.R sectors indicating comparatively shoal water inshore, but these are of little interest to the average small vessel.

Uneasy anchorage can be found in the roads on either side of Dungeness, according to direction of wind.

BEACHY HEAD

Tidal streams 2 miles south of the lighthouse
East-going begins −0520 Dover; spring rate 2·6 knots
West-going begins +0015 Dover; spring rate 2 knots

An extremely prominent chalk headland with a disused lighthouse about a mile west of the head. The current lighthouse (Fl(2)20s31m25M Horn 30s) is immediately to seaward of Beachy Head on a shelf of rock. To the southeast of Beachy Head are the rocks known as Head Ledge extending some half a mile from the cliffs. The white lighthouse has a broad red band and an elevation of 43m. Beachy

North Foreland

Beachy Head. White tower with red band and lantern 31m high, seen from the southwest

11

Head should be given a berth of 2 miles in heavy weather as there are overfalls and rough water to the south of it.

7 miles east of Beachy Head are the Royal Sovereign shoals with 3·5m least water. They can create a nasty sea, and are marked on the south side by a very conspicuous light tower (Fl.20s28m12M Horn(2)30s).

SELSEY BILL AND THE OWERS

Tidal streams in the Looe channel
East +0445 Dover
West −0120 Dover

Spring rate 2·6 knots, but faster between the Malt Owers and the Boulder bank. There are local variations in the directions of the streams 3 miles south of the Owers light buoy:

East-northeast +0540 Dover
West-southwest −0050 Dover
2½ to 3 knots at springs

Selsey Bill is a low point which is difficult to locate in poor visibility. There is a conspicuous hotel on the west side of the point. South of the Bill lie groups of rocks and ledges, between which passes the Looe Channel. The Owers pillar light buoy with ⚑ topmark (Q(6)+LFL.15s Whis) 7 miles southeast of Selsey Bill. By keeping south of the light buoy danger is avoided, but in clear weather and moderate winds the Looe channel, which is marked by buoys, affords a short cut, with the aid of a large-scale chart. The buoys are not easy to spot from a distance, so proceed with caution and do not lose heart too soon.

ST CATHERINE'S POINT

Tidal streams between St Catherine's Point and Dunnose
East +0515 Dover
West −0015 Dover

Maximum spring rate can achieve 5 knots immediately off the point, but is somewhat weaker to seaward.

St Catherine's Point is at the southern extremity of the Isle of Wight. It stands low at the foot of the hill which forms one of the highest parts of the island. The lighthouse is a 26m octagonal castellated tower standing at the back of a very low cliff; its light is

Fl.5s41m27M. It also has a F.R light (099°-vis-116°) shining over Rocken End which lurks only 2 cables west of the Point.

Owing to the uneven bottom and the strong streams there are significant tidal overfalls off St Catherine's. These should be avoided, particularly under wind-against-tide conditions, and may be dangerous in bad weather. The race varies according to wind, tide and swell and is sometimes rougher or calmer than may be anticipated from the conditions.

There are also lesser overfalls to the east of St Catherine's off Dunnose, with a number of isolated tide rips and whirlpools which may be almost as rough as St Catherine's race in small areas.

THE NEEDLES ROCKS

It is important to refer to tidal stream charts as you approach the Solent from the west, as streams are strong.

Tidal streams off Hurst Point
Northeast begins +0505 Dover
Southwest −0055 Dover
4 to 5 knots at springs

Off the Needles the streams tend to be earlier.

In the Needles Channel streams set strongly in both directions across the Shingles, so care is needed not to be set into danger.

Main flood stream divides at the Needles. The stronger flood stream runs northeast into the Needles Channel, while further south the stream runs east to southeast off the Isle of Wight coast. Conversely, on the ebb the local streams join west of the Needles and set west-southwest towards Durlston Head.

The sharp, white Needles stacks, with the lighthouse (white tower with red band, Oc(2)WRG.20s24m17/14M Horn(2)30s) at their seaward end, are unmistakable, but they are by no means conspicuous from west or southwest in hazy weather. From these directions, the high white cliffs above Scratchell's Bay, immediately southeast of the Needles, appear first, together with the high down 3 miles east on which stands Tennyson's Cross.

In heavy weather or fog, the western end of the Isle of Wight should be avoided if possible. Southwest winds make matters worse, if late on the tide with the ebb well underway. Entry to the Solent

The Needles from the entrance to the Channel

St Catherine's Point. White octagonal castellated tower 36m above sea level. Not very conspicuous by day

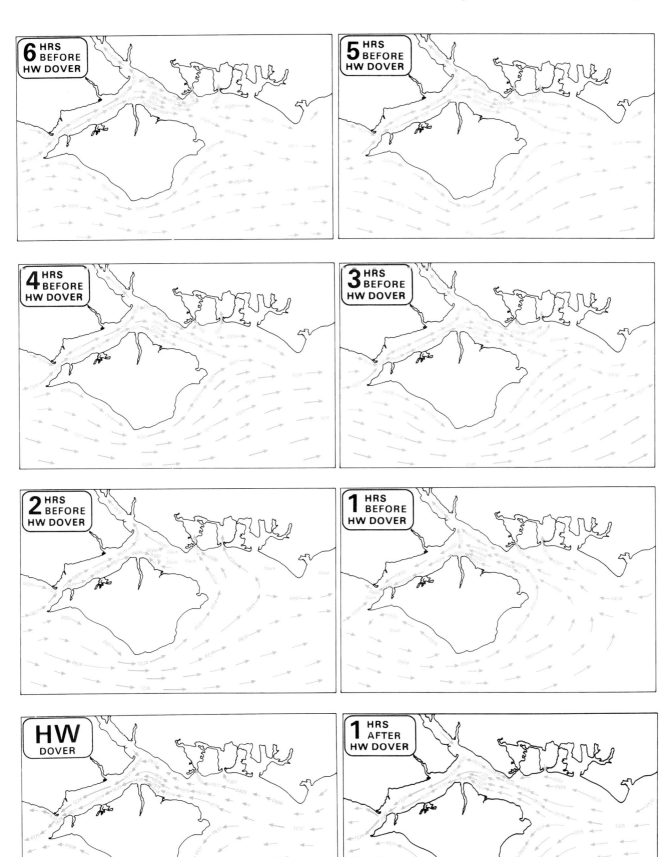

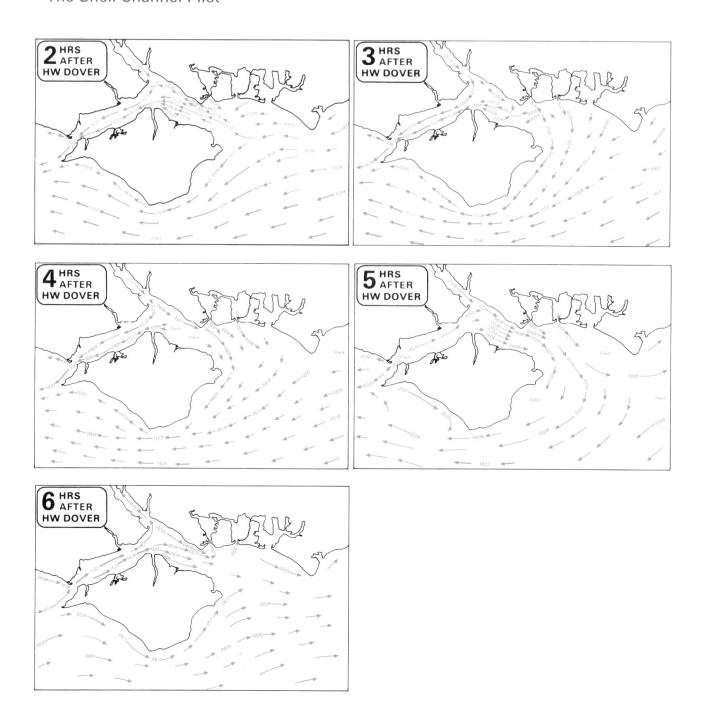

under such conditions should only be attempted via the North Channel, which lies north of the Shingles. If you must, this is a realistic option despite the proximity of the lee shore approaching Hurst Castle, but in gales it is safer to make for Poole or remain in harbour.

HENGISTBURY HEAD

Tidal streams are fairly strong at springs in the vicinity, and there are modest overfalls on the ebb tide over the ledges. The streams within Christchurch Bay itself are comparatively weak.

This unlit point, shaped like a long, low wedge of cheese, 5 miles east of Bournemouth pier and 1 mile southwest of the entrance to Christchurch harbour is the only headland between the Needles and Handfast Point south of Poole. It is conspicuous from seaward, being dark, reddish ironstone, though it may look yellowish from seaward.

There are ledges off the headland, and comparatively shoal water as far as Christchurch Ledge, which runs out to 2½ miles southeast. Watch out for pots in this vicinity, particularly after dark. One way and another, you are better off passing to the south of it.

PEVERIL POINT TO ST ALBAN'S HEAD

There are two official tidal races in this area: a small but vicious one off Peveril Point, and the larger race off St Alban's Head. There are also local tide rips,

Hengistbury Head from southeast. Entrance to Christchurch on right

Anvil Point lighthouse. White tower and squat building 12m high, set 45m above sea level. Durlstone Head to the right

and under certain conditions patches of broken water may be found practically the whole way from Handfast Point and Old Harry Rocks to St Alban's.

PEVERIL LEDGES

Tidal streams 3 cables east of Peveril Point
North-northeast +0500 Dover <1½ knots
South-southwest −0215 Dover <3 knots
Rates of tide may be greater on a spring ebb.

In bad weather, Peveril Race extends from the Point to seaward of its buoy, especially to the southeast of it during the west-going stream.

The Ledges extend about 3 cables from the low, rocky Peveril Point on the south side of Swanage Bay. The depths on the ledges gradually deepen to seaward and the end of the reefs is marked by an unlit red can buoy.

DURLSTON HEAD

Tidal streams
Northeast-going begins +0530 Dover
Southwest −0030 Dover
Up to 3 knots at springs

A rough, steep-sided headland of a characteristic shape, readily identified by the castellated building on its summit.

Inshore eddy
Extending westward from Durlston Head along the Dorset coast to beyond Lulworth there is an early turn of the tide – sometimes up to 90 minutes early – close inshore contrary to the main stream further seaward.

ANVIL POINT

Just half a mile or so southwest of Durlston, Anvil Point is easily located by the conspicuous white lighthouse and white wall round its enclosure, which stands in the green grass above the headland (Fl.10s45m24M). It also has a VHF lighthouse.

ST ALBAN'S HEAD

Tidal streams 1½ miles off the Head
East-going begins approx +0545 Dover
West-going −0015 Dover
Over 3 knots at springs

Instantly recognisable by its 'hanging cliff', where the near-vertical seaward face near the summit is falling steadily away onto rocks at its base.

There is a considerable tidal race which lies eastward of the Head on the flood and westward on the ebb. The race varies considerably in its position and its severity. It extends some 3 miles seaward except during southerly winds when it lies closer inshore. It may be avoided by giving the land a berth of 3 miles. There is a passage of nearly half a mile between St Alban's Head and the race, but it varies and may be less during onshore winds, and is not entirely immune from tidal disturbance. After prolonged heavy onshore winds the whole area can be 'wall-to-wall breakers', but in reasonable weather vessels can avoid the worst of the overfalls by keeping inshore in the deep water close to the headland. The inshore passage enjoys the early fair eddy, and it should be noted that a local eddy runs to the southeast nearly continuously down the west side of St Alban's promontory.

St Alban's Head from SSE. No conspicuous buildings, except a tiny lookout hut

PORTLAND BILL AND RACE

From the east or the west, Portland looks like an island, high on its northern end against the low Chesil Beach, sloping down towards the southern extremity, where the round lighthouse tower with a white and red band (Fl(4)20s43m25M Dia 30s) is situated. A F.R.13M (271°-vis-291°) covers the Shambles shoals for vessels approaching from the east. There is also a disused light tower standing 4 cables to the north-northeast.

Portland Race is the most dangerous extended area of broken water in the English Channel. Quite substantial vessels drawn into it have been known to disappear without trace. It lies south of Portland Bill, a little to the west during the ebb, and to the east during the flood, occurring as a result of an uneven bottom in conjunction with two strong south-going streams which roar down either side of the Bill for 10 hours out of every 12, to hit each other at the Race. Here, they meet the main east or west-going Channel tide. In bad weather there is confused and dangerous water as far as the eastern end of the Shambles.

The worst part of the Race extends over 2 miles from the Bill and is well defined by the overfalls. At spring tides the Race can exceed 7 knots, but for

Portland Bill lighthouse from the southwest. White tower, red band, 43m high

details of the speed and probable direction of the stream, consult the Admiralty tidal charts.

During the west-going stream there is a northerly set into West Bay from southwest of the Bill, which at times is strong.

When rounding Portland Bill the navigator has two principal options to choose between. The easier one is to pass outside the Race, about 3 miles off the Bill in calm weather or 5 miles off in bad, especially at spring tides if the wind is against streams. Even out here you will experience rough water.

The alternative is to use the 'inside passage'. This is a channel about a quarter of a mile wide (varying with direction of wind) lying between the Bill and the Race. This channel should not be used at night, and by day only under suitable conditions, for although the water is comparatively smooth, the streams are strong and the overfalls are not entirely avoided either off Grove Point or immediately west of the Bill, according to wind direction. There are also numerous lobster pots close inshore, some of whose buoys can be towed under by the stream. The correct timing of the passage is a matter of the utmost importance.

When bound westward, round the Bill between 1 hour before and 2 hours after HW Dover. When bound eastward, round the Bill between 5 hours after and 4 hours before HW Dover, though towards the end of this period you will find a foul set down the east side of the Bill.

Whether bound west or east through the inside passage, it is important to close with Portland at least a mile to the north of the Bill to be sure of not being set south into the Race. You can then work southward with a fair tide to arrive off the Bill at the correct time.

GOLDEN CAP

A useful landmark 3½ miles east of Lyme Regis and 3 miles west of Bridport. The point rises to Golden Cap, a conical hill 187m high which has pronounced yellow cliffs at its summit. With the sun on them, these can be conspicuous from a long distance even in hazy weather. Inshore streams are weak.

Portland Bill from the east. Note wedge shape. The Varne at right. At great range, Portland appears as an island, separated from the mainland

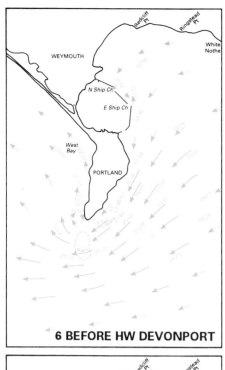

6 BEFORE HW DEVONPORT

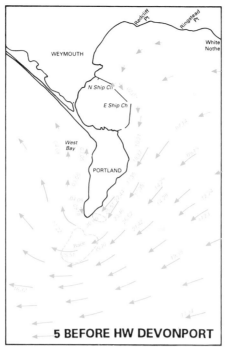

5 BEFORE HW DEVONPORT

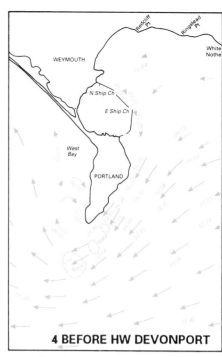

4 BEFORE HW DEVONPORT

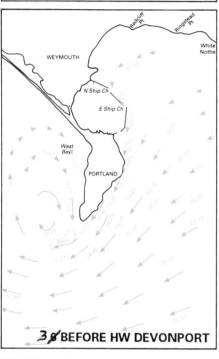

3 BEFORE HW DEVONPORT

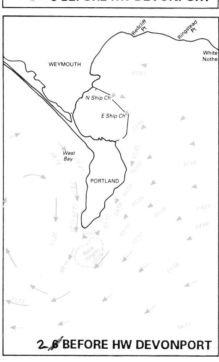

2 BEFORE HW DEVONPORT

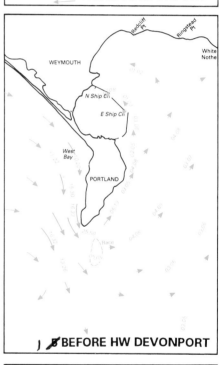

1 BEFORE HW DEVONPORT

HW DEVONPORT

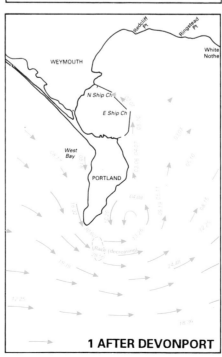

1 AFTER DEVONPORT

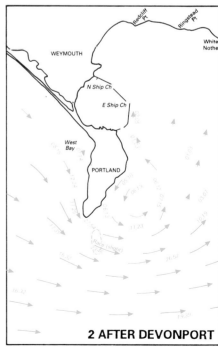

2 AFTER DEVONPORT

17

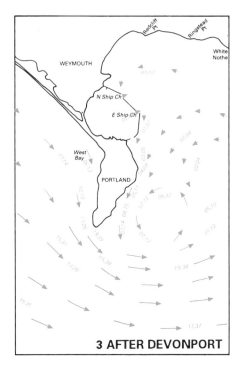

3 AFTER DEVONPORT

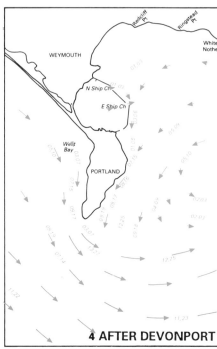

4 AFTER DEVONPORT

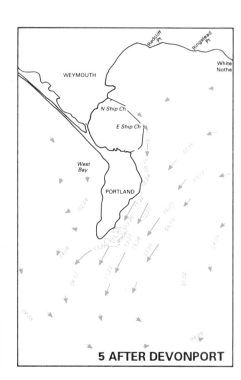

5 AFTER DEVONPORT

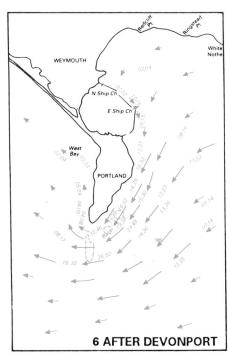

6 AFTER DEVONPORT

BEER HEAD

Tidal streams

East-going approx +0600 Dover
West-going begins at HW Dover
Inshore streams are weak.

This 130m-high chalk headland is the last white cliff on the coast before chalk gives way to the red cliffs of Devon. It is surprisingly conspicuous when one is crossing Lyme Bay well offshore.

BERRY HEAD

Tidal streams

North +0540 Dover
South −0100 Dover
1½ knots maximum

Bold, steep-ended limestone headland with a long, flat top, falling at about 45° to the sea. White lighthouse on summit with an elevation of 58m (Fl(2)15s58m14M).

START POINT

Tidal streams 3 miles south of the Point

East-northeast +0455 Dover
West-southwest −0120 Dover
2 knots at springs
Inshore, the streams are about an hour earlier, reaching 4 knots at springs, irregular at neaps.

A long, sharp-ridged headland, with 28m round white lighthouse (Fl(3)10s62m25M Horn 60s) which is unmistakable. A F.R.55m light covers the Skerries bank on 210° to 255°. There are rocks off the Start which are awash at HW and extend nearly 3 cables south of the Point. The Start race extends nearly a mile seaward of the Point; its severity depends much on the conditions of wind, tide and swell. The overfalls can be avoided in daylight by passing close to the rocks, but there is an outlying one to the south, so care is needed. It is safer for strangers to give the Point a berth of at least a mile.

PRAWLE POINT

Lies 3½ miles west of Start Point to the southeast of Salcombe Bar and has a prominent white coastguard station at its summit.

Berry Head from the south. Note coastguard station near right-hand edge

Start Point from the southwest with unmarked off-lying rocks and Berry Head beyond. White tower 28m high, 62m above sea level

Prawle Point from the southeast. Prominent old coastguard hut on cliff top 50m above sea level. Bolt Head beyond (left)

Bolt Head from the east

BOLT HEAD AND BOLT TAIL

Bolt Head stands on the west side of the entrance to Salcombe. Its spiky outline is unique in the Channel, and the ridge of dark, rugged cliffs extending to Bolt Tail is conspicuous. The sea is often rough between the two heads up to a mile or two offshore.

RAME HEAD

This is a classic, breast-shaped hill with a ruined chapel on the summit, conspicuous when one is approaching Plymouth Sound.

DODMAN POINT

This is a notable unlit headland standing about half-way between Fowey and Falmouth. It is 110m high,

Bolt Tail from the southwest with Hope Cove on left

Rame Head from the southeast outside Plymouth Sound, 102m high with ruined chapel on summit. Rame Head is conspicuous from well out at sea because of its symmetrical shape

Dodman Point from SSW. Stone cross on summit 111m above sea level. No lighthouse. The Dodman often appears dark from seawards

St Anthony Head marking the eastern side of the entrance to Falmouth. White octagonal tower 19m high

and precipitous, with a stone cross near its southwest extremity. The off-lying bottom is irregular, and as a result tide rips may extend 1½ miles to seaward.

ST ANTHONY HEAD

Lies 9 miles southwest of the Dodman, at the western side of the entrance to Falmouth. Its white octagonal tower light is Oc.WR.15s22m22/20M, and its horn sounds every 30s in fog. Immediately east-southeast of the headland stands Zone Point where there is a disused coastguard station.

LIZARD POINT

The Lizard is the most westerly of the conspicuous headlands on the south coast of England. It is a dividing line in the sense that west of it there is only limited shelter in Penzance Bay, but eastward there are many harbours available in bad weather.

Tidal streams at the Lizard
East-going starts at +0330 Dover
West-going starts at −0245 Dover
Spring rates are 2 and 3 knots respectively, and at times stronger.

The Lizard is a bold headland with a classically conspicuous lighthouse compound near its summit. This consists of white buildings with a white wall round their enclosure. The octagonal tower of the white lighthouse (Fl.3s70m25M Horn 30s) is situated at the eastern end of the buildings. Six cables eastward there is a coastguard station and Lloyd's signal station.

The group of rocks known as Stag Rocks, some of which are above water while others dry 4 to 5m, extends over half a mile south of the Lizard. These are visible at most states of the tide in daylight, but a mile east of Lizard Point off Bass Point lie the Vrogue Rocks, which have less than 2m over them at LW. The Craggan Rocks, with 1·5m over them, lie north-northeast of Bass Point, but these dangers will be avoided by vessels proceeding east or west. The Lizard Race extends 2 to 3 miles to seaward, and at times there is a race southeast of the head. The state of the seas varies considerably according to tide and wind direction, and things may get very rough with strong westerly winds against the down-Channel stream. In rough weather, or when a swell is running, especially with wind against a spring tide, vessels should keep at least 3 miles off Lizard Point.

The Boa race, which also breaks in bad weather, lies about 3 miles west-northwest of Lizard Point.

LAND'S END

Tidal streams
The ebb tide sets northwest immediately off the point for 9½ hours, starting at HW Dover −0300, and runs at up to 2½ knots. The east-going flood turns 6 hours before HW Dover and only runs for 3 hours.

Situated 20 miles west-northwest of the Lizard, Land's End is higher but less conspicuous, having no lighthouse. The unlit Gwennap Head is at its southernmost extension, with the dangerous Runnel

Lizard Point lighthouse. Octagonal white tower 19m high at eastern end of buildings, 70m above sea level with off-lying dangers unmarked

Stone Rocks a mile offshore. These are marked by a lit south cardinal buoy which has been known to drag off-station in severe weather. In calm weather and with local knowledge it is said to be possible to cut inside, but the distance saved will not be worth the ulcers.

The Longships lighthouse, a mile or so to the west of Land's End (Iso.WR.10s35m18/14M Horn 10s), marks the westernmost point of England, excepting the Scilly Isles 20 miles further west. There are always confused seas around the menacing group of rocks marked by Longships, and yachts on passage should keep at least a mile to seaward.

Harbour pilotage

Ramsgate

Tides

HW +0020 Dover

MHWS	MLWS	MHWN	MLWN
4·9m	0·4m	3·8m	1·2m

Streams

Streams run fast across Ramsgate entrance channel. North-northeast set runs from an hour before HW Dover for 6 hours; south-southwest set from 5 hours after HW Dover until 1 hour before the next HW. The lighthouse on the end of West Pier at the entrance to Royal Harbour shows a fixed red light when depth in the entrance is more than 3m above chart datum. When less than 3m, the light turns green.

Depths

The entrance channel is dredged to 7·5m, the outer ferry harbour to 6·5m. There is a least depth of 2·5m in the dredged entrance to Royal Harbour, though the best water is usually to the west side. West Gully (visitors' pontoons) has 2·1m LAT, which is also the dredged depth of Royal Harbour (see plan) and its visitors' pontoons near the east side of the lock. The 'temporary marina' outside the lock gates is generally dredged to 2m. The locked-in Inner Harbour has a maintained depth of 3m, except in certain corners.

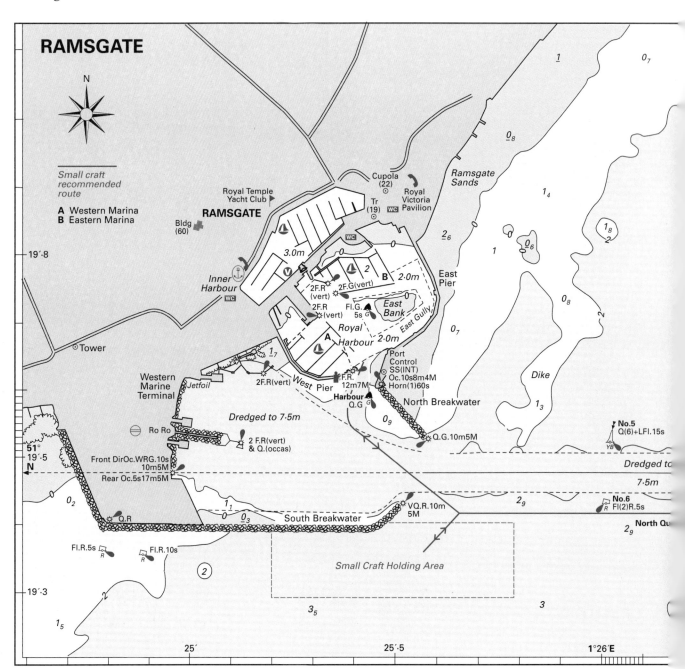

General

Ramsgate is a tactically important harbour of refuge for all vessels on passage from the English Channel to the Thames, or the North Sea. Royal Harbour is well sheltered, though not always comfortable, and can be entered in almost any weather short of storms from the east. Unusually for this corner of Britain, entry for most yachts is not subject to tidal restrictions. Ramsgate's history is colourful, and includes being a major port for the evacuation of Dunkerque in 1940 and the embarkation of Wellington's army before Waterloo. The artificial harbour was built in recognition of the site's importance to the fleets of sailing ships which used to lie up in the Downs awaiting fair winds for either 'Down Channel' or 'Up Thames'.

Today Ramsgate's importance centres on the frequent movements of ferries and jetfoils, as a result of which mariners are advised to proceed with caution at all times. Notwithstanding this, yachts are welcomed actively by the harbour authorities.

Approach

The crucial feature of approaching Ramsgate is that at some stage you must join the dredged entry channel which leads in due west from the *Gull* east cardinal buoy (VQ(3)5s), 3·7 miles slightly north of east from the harbour entrance. This channel is clearly marked with buoys (see plan), and is made entirely unambiguous by the leading lights (rear Oc.5s, front DirOc.WRG.10s5M). By day, the leading marks are: rear – black and white ▾; front – black ▲ with white stripe.

Ramsgate. (A) East breakwater head with entrance to Royal Harbour. (B) RoRo berth

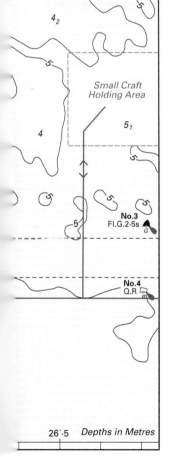

Ramsgate Harbour. Additional pontoons have been laid against the West Pier to form the West Marina. See plan

Ramsgate. Entrance to Inner Harbour. A - Entrance, lock gate shut. B - Lock master

A recommended yacht track has been established immediately to the south of the main channel, running parallel to it and passing north of Quern Bank and its guarding north cardinal buoy (Q).

Arriving from the north, you should cross the main channel at right angles west of *No.3* green buoy (Fl.G.2·5s), then turn to starboard and follow the recommended yacht track, entering the harbour as shown on the plan.

Approach from the east presents no difficulty, as the recommended yacht track may be joined in the vicinity of the fourth red can out (Fl.R.5s).

Coming up from the south, you will be in the proximity of the Gull Stream buoys. There is no need to follow these as far as *Brake* (red can, Fl(4)R.15s Bell), but so long as you pass within half a mile or so of it, you will be comfortably clear of Brake shoal. From here you can shape a course towards Ramsgate entrance channel, taking care to leave the unlit beacon tower to the east of Quern Bank well to port. This can safely be achieved by keeping the third red buoy out from the entrance (Fl(2)R.10s) in transit with North Foreland lighthouse (Fl(5)WR.20s), which shows white from this bearing.

Entrance

If you are equipped with VHF, always call Ramsgate Port Control on Ch 14 when in the offing, to receive authority to proceed either to the holding area (see below) or to the Royal Harbour. There are traffic lights exhibited on East Pier. Three vertical green lights – enter or leave port, or enter channel from seaward. Three vertical reds – no entry to channel, nobody to enter or leave port.

There is a small-craft holding area (see plan) to the south of the eastern part of the South Breakwater and another north of *No.3* green buoy.

There is enough space in the outer harbour for any yacht under 27·4m (90ft) to round up and lower her canvas. This can be useful, as there is often a lumpy sea outside.

The outer breakwaters have a red and white and a green and white beacon, each 10m high, lit with a VQ.R to port, Q.G to starboard. Enter between these beacons, keeping to the north side of the channel, then look for the small green buoy (Q.G) situated one cable west-northwest of the North Breakwater head. Leave this to starboard and swing round to about 015° to enter Royal Harbour. Note the East and West Banks, indicated on the plan.

Berthing

Once inside Royal Harbour, your choice of three marinas will usually be resolved by a call to the harbour office on VHF Ch 80 (Ramsgate Marina). Pontoon berths are available to visitors in either of the two outer facilities – the Eastern Marina immediately eastwards of the lock gates to the Inner Marina, or the new Western Marina immediately to port on rounding the West Pier.

Yachts staying more than week or so are welcome to berth inside the lock in total shelter. The 'flap gate' and lifting bridge open at ±2 hours. Very large yachts can be accommodated here by arrangement. Traffic lights operate the same code as the East Pier.

Charges are realistic in Ramsgate Marina, and it is perfectly sheltered, so it is an excellent place to leave a boat for a few weeks. Do not expect quiet nights on board, however. The trucks of all Europe thunder by through the night, bound for the ferries and exotic destinations. Their exhausts and undercarriages roar and crash to the echo from the high brick walls.

Facilities

Fuel from a barge by West Pier, seven days a week, 0830–1730. If unattended, call *Foy Boat* on VHF Ch 14, or ☎ 01843 592662. Fresh water in marina and on pontoons outside. Chandlery and full technical back-up (*Camping Gaz* and *Calor Gas*). Repairs and engineers. Diver. Showers, toilets and launderette close by marina are open to all. Old hands will rejoice to learn that a modern shower black is now to be found just west of the inner harbour lock. This finally banishes memories of the adventures enjoyed by some and feared by many which once waited under the railway viaduct for sailors in search of a clean-up. The finale demise of this colourful facility will be mourned by few. The Harbour Board maintain a number of slipways. Full domestic and entertainment facilities at hand as the harbour is right in the town centre.

Royal Temple Yacht Club has a fine view overlooking the harbour (☎ 01843 591766).

Rabies control

Note that the harbour will not tolerate animals aboard yachts at any price, even if they stay aboard.

Sandwich

Tides

HW at Bar +0015 Dover
HW at Sandwich +0100 Dover

Tidal heights for the lower River Stour are:

MHWS	MLWS	MHWN	MLWN
3·3m	0·1m	2·6m	0·3m

Streams

These can be very strong in the river at springs.
Note that HW at Sandwich comes 45 minutes later
than at the bar. The end of the flood can be
surprisingly vigorous, perhaps because its duration
is between 3 and 5 hours, depending upon the tide
and the fresh water content of the river. The ebb,
correspondingly, runs for anything up to 9 hours.

Depths

Bar dries 0·3 to 0·9m LAT. Depths in the river are
variable, generally between 0·5 and 1m LAT. Craft
of 2m draught can certainly reach Sandwich on
mean spring tides.

General

Sandwich, one of the original Cinque Ports charged
with the defence of the realm against invaders since

The River Stour

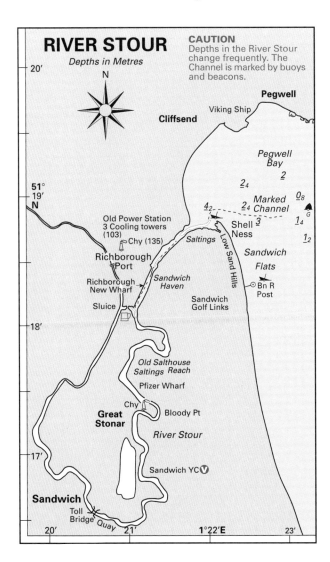

Norman times, lies 4½ miles from the mouth of the
meandering River Stour. Before it silted up, it was
the jump-off point for great fleets of warships.
Nowadays yachts lie alongside the Town Quay.

In the 18th century the local earl launched the
fast-food business with sandwiches devoured during
nonstop sessions at the gaming tables. In our times,
Sandwich's golf links gave Ian Fleming the
inspiration for some of James Bond's rougher
matches.

Approach

The approach to the River Stour and Sandwich
really begins some distance offshore on an
approximate transit of the 135m chimney inland in
Pegwell Bay with the left hand one of the three
adjacent cooling towers. These items are all so
conspicuous that in any visibility worthy of the name
they cannot be missed. Stay on this transit on a
course of around 260° until you arrive in the vicinity
of the first pair of channel buoys which are a red and
green conical. Pass between these and follow the
next pairs down to the southwest until you come to
the only lit channel mark. This is a spindly structure
bearing a Fl.R.10s light. Its opposite number is a
post with a lattice green triangular topmark. From
here to the mouth of the river at Shell Ness, the
channel is marked by posts – red square topmarks to
port, green triangles to starboard. It is now trending
in a westerly direction and the best water tends to lie
on its northern side. In due course you will discern
Shell Ness, but it is not conspicuous, so this may
seem a long time coming.

Follow the posts into the river; when in doubt,
keep central until the upper end of Richborough
New Wharf. Thereafter, the best water is usually to
be found nearer the west bank, when the river is

wide enough to offer a realistic choice. Pass the tiny Sandwich Marina and press on the final half-mile to Sandwich.

It cannot be over-stressed that, for the stranger, it is prudent to navigate the Stour on a rising tide, and that night entry without local knowledge is not recommended.

Berthing

Anchoring in the Stour is impractical. Berth alongside the quay at Sandwich.

Deep-keeled yachts should dry against the wall (thin layer of mud over chalk), towards the upper end of the quay. Bilgekeelers can settle into soft mud at the downstream end. Further downstream, Sandwich Marina (max LOA 18m, draught 2·1m) may have room for visitors.

Facilities

Fresh water and toilets at Sandwich Quay. Fuel in cans from nearby garage. Yacht yard above bridge with chandlery, *Calor Gas* and engineering facilities. Other utilities, such as pubs, restaurants and banks, in the town. Yacht club: Sandwich Sailing and Motor Boat Club.

Dover

Tides

MHWS	MLWS	MHWN	MLWN
6·7m	0·8m	5·3m	2m

Note Irregular, depending on wind conditions.

Streams

Streams off the harbour vary considerably, with a maximum spring rate of 3 knots. The flood sets northeast at HW−1hr to HW+3hr.

Depths

The outer harbour is generally deep, but shoals gradually to its landward boundary. Note the large, isolated bank just north of centre. Depths in the Inner Harbour are generally 9m, shoaling to 4m on the west side of Prince of Wales Pier and to 3m on close approach to the Hoverport ramp. The approach channel from the Inner Harbour to the Tidal Basin between the North and South Piers has an average dredged depth of 5m below chart datum. A dredged channel (1·5m) leads from here up to Wellington Dock and its waiting pontoon. The marina in Wellington dock has 4·5m at springs and 3·3m at neaps. Granville dock, now also a locked marina, has more. Its sill is 2·5m above chart datum. Depths vary in the dredged tidal marina, but are generally more than adequate. Enquire if you are

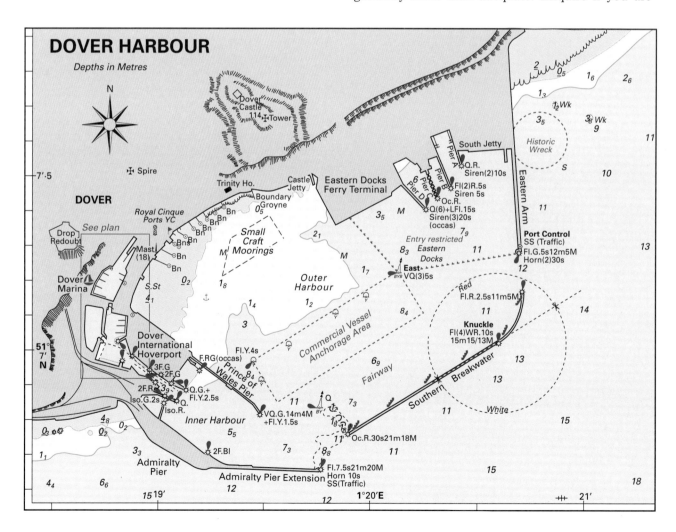

directed there should the nature of the neighbouring yachts give you any cause for doubt. The extreme eastern end of this harbour is foul, so do not manoeuvre too close to this wall.

General

Dover is the busiest port in England and its primary commercial importance is known to every mariner. Despite this, in recent years Dover Harbour has gone out of its way to become a yacht-friendly port. It offers an all-tide dredged marina and an even more attractive locked-in facility for visitors in the Granville Dock. Both are realistic propositions with easy access to the town's facilities. The strategic value of Dover to the low-powered vessel needs no underlining and the fact that berthing is now an uncomplicated affair in perfect shelter makes it a useful overnight stop. The Granville or the Wellington Docks might also be an option for leaving a boat in mid-cruise.

Approach and entrance

Dover Harbour is some two miles southwest of the South Foreland. By day, the long breakwaters overlooked by the famous castle make the harbour easy to identify. At night, the breakwater lights are as follows: the west entrance has Oc.R.30s21m18M on the south breakwater and Fl.7·5s21m20M Horn 10s at the seaward end of Admiralty Pier; this also displays the port movement lights. Towards the east

entrance, the Knuckle light on the southern breakwater is Fl(4)WR.10s15m15/13M, with a Fl.R.2·5s11m5M at the entrance.

The Eastern Arm has Port Control, Horn(2)30s and a Fl.G.5s12m5M light. Lights inside the harbour are shown on the plan.

In southwesterly gales a very confused and steep swell may develop off the western entrance. Exercise extreme caution during these periods, especially if they coincide with HW springs.

Yachts may use either entrance, although a careful lookout should be kept for the entry signals. Permission to enter should be requested from Dover Port Control on VHF Ch 74. If you do not have VHF, the authorities ask you to contact Port Control with an Aldis lamp or some similar signalling device. Use 'SV' (I wish to enter port) or 'SW' (I wish to leave port). A 'Q' flashing light from the office or the HM's launch means 'Keep clear of the entrance you are approaching'. Small or slow craft are not normally cleared for entry until within a cable of the entrance. A series of short flashes from Port Control at the end of the Eastern Arm, or from the Harbour Patrol launch, indicates 'STOP. WAIT'.

In order to leave room for bigger ships to manoeuvre, yachts should keep well clear of the entrances until they receive their entry or exit signals.

Dover in 1996. Wellington Dock lies beyond the bridge. Note the dredged marina centre picture, and Granville Dock inside the lock immediately left of it. This is now fully equipped with marina pontoons available to visitors.

Dover. Waiting area outside Wellington Dock.
(A) Dockmaster's office. (B) Waiting pontoon. (C) Lock open,
bridge lowered

Dover. Granville Dock in the centre with lock closed. Tidal
harbour on right-hand side. Fuel dock on left. Note the three
unlit green beacons on your starboard hand. Photo from 1999.
New harbour office not yet built

Enter under power if possible and look out for the Harbour Patrol launches, which are always ready with friendly advice for yachts. Do not hesitate to call Dover Port Control on VHF if you are in any doubt, or need advice on movement in or near the port.

Traffic signals

Lights covering both entrances are exhibited at the ends of the Eastern Arm and Admiralty Pier. All traffic is regulated by day or night by IALA port signals, using directional high intensity lights beamed to seaward or inshore as relevant. Signals are vertically displayed as follows:

RRR flashing – Emergency; entrance closed

RRR fixed – Entry or exit prohibited from the direction indicated

GWG – Ships may proceed to or from direction indicated

Navigation in Outer Harbour

If in doubt, call Harbour Control, or speak with the Harbour Patrol launch (flashing blue light at night), which will advise you.

Yachts should beware of hovercraft and Seacats which may use either entrance at 40 knots. They must also keep well clear of Channel ferries and cargo ships manoeuvring in the fairway.

The best anchorage for yachts lies east of Prince of Wales Pier, and west or northwest of the Fl.Y spherical buoy marking the western limit of the dredged anchorage for commercial craft (see plan). There is plenty of room here, and the shelter is the best you'll get, but be ready with earplugs for the hovercraft limbering up on the other side of the pier. Alternatively, small visitors' boats may use a trot of orange mooring buoys. These have one or two-ton sinkers, but are considered inadequate for 40-footers and above, which should therefore anchor if not going in alongside. Craft may remain unattended on the moorings, but anchored craft are not to be left under any circumstances.

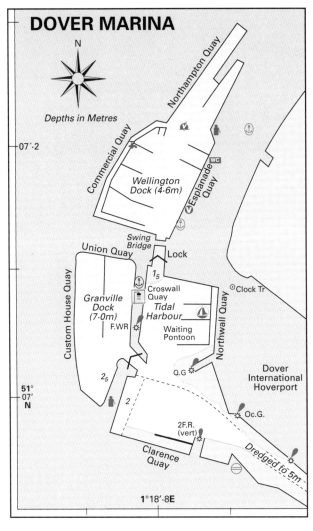

DOVER MARINA

N

Depths in Metres

-07'.2

Northampton Quay

Commercial Quay

WC

Esplanade Quay

Wellington Dock (4·6m)

Swing Bridge

Union Quay

Lock

1₅

Croswall Quay

Custom House Quay

Granville Dock (7·0m)

F.WR

Clock Tr

Tidal Harbour

Northwall Quay

Waiting Pontoon

2₅

Q.G

Dover International Hoverport

51° -07' N

2

Oc.G.

2F.R. (vert)

Clarence Quay

Dredged to 5m

1°18'·8E

Inner Harbour

Having been given permission to enter, call the marina on VHF Ch 80. The inner harbour is straightforward and well lit (for lights, see plan), but note that anchoring is strictly prohibited within its walls. As noted above, there is a dredged channel to the reception pontoon outside Wellington Dock (3 unlit green beacons to leave to starboard before making the turn into the waiting berth or the tidal harbour). At LW, it is important to head straight for the Granville Dock gates. There is a sectored leading light (324°-330°) which affords safe access from the main channel to the waiting pontoon.

Depending on your expected future movements, you will be allocated a berth either in the tidal marina or the Granville Dock which has 9-hour access. To reassure you, there is a depth gauge beside the Granville Dock entrance. It reads out in metres for the modern-minded, but those who do not wish to forget Dover's past may prefer to use the alternative, more artistically presented Roman numerals which, of course, measure in British feet. For Wellington Dock, an amber flashing light and a bell warn of the opening of the lock. Traffic lights now control your movements, with 3F.R stopping traffic and GWG giving the all-clear. Generally, outbound traffic clears the lock first.

Departures

All yachts must report to marina staff prior to departure. Whether bound east or west, you can rely on being given every assistance with locking times, etc. so that you can make the most of your tide. Whichever way you intend to turn at the breakwater entrance, you must report to Harbour Control for instructions before leaving the Inner Harbour. As likely as not, you will then be escorted seawards by the patrol launch.

Facilities

Water and power on the pontoons by the marina office. Toilets, showers and a launderette below the new marina office by the Wellington Dock lock. Telephones outside. Fuel in Wellington Dock during normal working hours. 24-hour fuel opposite the marina in the tidal harbour, west of the Granville Dock entrance VHF Ch 80 or ☎ 01304 201073 for Wellington Dock – 206809 for outer harbour, or contact marina office. Scrubbing or minor underwater repairs on the Dolphin Hard in the tidal marina by arrangement with the office. Full repairs from Dover Yacht Company in the Wellington Dock, electronics from Smye Rumsby ☎ 01304 201525. 50-ton boat hoist in Granville Dock. Facilities for disabled, customs box on dock near Granville, a waste oil dump, divers; indeed, everything you could wish for in the way of services.

All real sailors must make a pilgrimage to the chandlery of Sharp and Enright, just across the road from Wellington Dock. Here, time has stood still and the world is a better place. Where staff who fully understand their business purvey proper gear for real vessels actually going to sea. Almost next door, on the same side of the road, is another jewel; the 7-day, all-day (6am to 7pm) breakfast from the Happy Chef. Here, grown-up ladies who know what a man needs after a rough night at sea, serve up the goods at popular prices.

Meanwhile, back in the harbour, a water taxi is available to anchored yachts via Harbour Patrol (contact Port Control, VHF Ch 74). All town facilities, are to be found close by, including provisions, banks, fine restaurants, and fish and chips.

Folkestone

Tides
HW −0010 Dover

MHWS	MLWS	MHWN	MLWN
7·1m	0·7m	5·7m	2m

Streams

Tidal streams run at up to 2 knots off the pier head as follows: east-northeast from 2 hours before HW Dover; setting west-southwest from 3½ hours after HW Dover. There is an eddy on the east-going stream.

Depths
The Outer Harbour is dredged to a least depth of 4·5m and is formed by the breakwater, which extends into deep water. In the entrance to the Inner Harbour there is 5·5m at MHWS; there is 3·3m to 4·2m MHWS within the harbour. At neaps there is at least 1m less. At LW it dries everywhere.

General
Folkestone is a busy commercial port, operating a freight and Seacat service to Boulogne. The Inner Harbour is only suitable for yachts which can conveniently dry out, either on legs, bilge keels, or their multiple hulls. It was at one time recommended that deep-keeled yachts dry out against the South Quay but this is no longer advised. In the first placc there is an enormous Russian submarine, now derelict, against the wall, and even if this is towed away in due course, the wall itself is very high and beset with piling. For any but the boldest to dry out alongside would be asking for trouble, unless you happen to be driving a coaster. Yachts are only welcome for overnight stops as the inner harbour is well stocked with local moorings. There is, however, room to dry out a moderate-sized yacht near the entrance, and there would be nothing to stop a quick visit an hour or two either side of HW.

Folkestone is not a good refuge in bad weather from east or southeast, as the inner harbour faces east, but the entrance itself receives extra protection from the west from a long breakwater (built for railway ferries) which forms the Outer Harbour. The tiny harbour behind the inner wall is mostly used by fishing boats equipped with legs. The town itself has all the usual urban facilities.

Approach and entrance
The Port of Folkestone operates on VHF Ch 15, and should at all times be contacted before entering or leaving. The harbour is busier than ever and Port Control emphasises the importance of this requirement.

Folkestone is about 5½ miles west of Dover. It is a large town and is thus easy to recognise. The harbour lies nearer its eastern end, behind the conspicuous outer breakwater.

There are rocky ledges to the west of the breakwater and east of the Inner Harbour entrance. Of these, the Mole Head Rocks less than two cables east of the inner end of the outer breakwater,

Folkestone Harbour

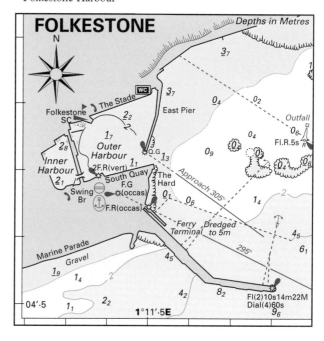

together with the ledges off Copt Point, are the more dangerous. A mark (Fl.R.5s) is sited at the seaward end of an outfall which passes through Mole Head Rocks. To clear all these when approaching from the east, keep the South Foreland well open of the Dover cliffs. When the south end of the East Pier of the Inner Harbour (Q.G) bears 305°, alter course leaving the outer breakwater close to port.

Make allowance for the fact that the bottom begins to shoal about 2 cables off the Inner Harbour, shelving gradually to 1m drying at the entrance. For depths within the harbour, see 'Anchorage and harbour', below.

Traffic signals

Leading lights (occasional) F.G behind F.R at 295° on ferry terminal.

Entry and leaving signals are exhibited as follows from a trellis mast adjacent to the lighthouse at the pier head: three vertical green lights indicate permission to enter and three vertical red lights show that the port is closed.

When leaving, three vertical green lights give permission to leave, and three vertical red lights indicate that departure is prohibited.

For entry to the Inner Harbour, a single red light indicates that the Inner Harbour is closed while a single green light shows permission to enter. For departure, green is 'go' and red means that the harbour entrance is closed.

Anchorage and harbour

Anchoring outside the Inner Harbour is inadvisable owing to the ferry traffic and the risk of fouling the ground moorings used for winching off the ferries. It is also exposed and has indifferent holding ground. No yacht may ever moor alongside the ferry pier except in the direst emergency.

Yachts may lie in the Inner Harbour if there is room, arranging their own ground tackle. Do not attempt to dry out immediately in front of the toilets which are on the seaward end of the Stade in a black clapboard building with ice-cream kiosk attached. There are several rocks in front of here, but all is clear 15m west of the extrapolated line of the west wall of this building. At LAT the harbour dries 1m at the entrance, about 2·2m in the centre and up to 3·7m at the northern end of East Pier. Yachtsmen must calculate the tide level by reference to the heights above datum (see under 'Tides', above), but boats of up to 2·5m draught can enter 3 hours either side of HW.

The swing bridge at the western end of the Inner Harbour is permanently fixed, and the shallow inner basin can be entered only by boats able to pass below it.

Wherever you berth, if you have not already contacted the harbour authorities on VHF Ch 15 you should check with them that your selection is suitable.

Facilities

Folkestone has good pubs and restaurants and is much more than a mere ferry terminal. Water at quay. Good shopping centre. Station. Buses to all parts. Yacht club: Folkestone Yacht and Motor Boat Club (☎ 01303 251574) near slipway in Inner Harbour offers showers when clubhouse is open. Bosun's Locker chandlery. Harbourmaster's ☎ 01303 220544. Diesel by pump from the Stade at HW.

Rye

Tides

HW +0002 Dover

Rye Harbour

MHWS	MLWS	MHWN	MLWN
5·3m	Dries	3·6m	Dries

Approaches

MHWS	MHWN	No LW data
7·7m	6·0m	

Depths

The bar dries 1·5m LAT, and the River Rother has little more than a foot of fresh water at MLWS, though this may increase after heavy rain. Tides are big, however, and the visitors' berths at Strand Quay have around 4m at MHWS, and 2·3m at MHWN.

General

Rye is an ancient harbour whose history dates back to the Iron Age. Shingle drift along the coast has moved its entrance many times, but the harbour has not lost its commercial significance, even in the face of a drying bar and a river channel now reduced to half a metre of fresh water at LW springs. An average of 50 vessel visits per year maintains the harbour's vitality. There is also a fishing fleet of moderate proportions, and a number of yachts sail from here on a regular basis.

Shelter is superb, once inside, and although all the berths dry, there is a warm welcome for visitors. The town, which is a Cinque Port, is picturesque in the extreme, standing proudly on its hill and beckoning the brave, as it has done for a very long time indeed.

Given an offshore wind, fair weather and the right state of tide, strangers should not find the well marked entrance difficult. An onshore breeze of Force 5 is uncomfortable, however, and probably too much for a first attempt. Power is desirable, as the tide runs very hard in the narrow channel – the flood is stronger than the ebb, which is unusual in rivers.

Approach and entrance

Rye Harbour entrance lies at the apex of Rye Bay, which is a shoal bight to the west of Dungeness. Apart from Tower Knoll 2½ miles to the west (2·2m), and Boulder Banks (3m), there are no dangers in the offing, save the generally shoal nature of the bay. Its sand bottom holds no shocks, however, so a prudent eye on depth will suffice to keep you out of danger.

The *Rye Fairway* buoy (LFl.10s) lies about 5° south of west from Dungeness, distance 7 miles. From the west the most prominent landmark, around 5 miles down the coast, is Fairlight Church, which (under its older name) has the distinction of a mention in the great sea song *Spanish Ladies*: 'We bore away up-Channel past Fairlee and Dungeness . . .' From here you may have to take note of Boulder Banks or Tower Knoll (see above).

From the fairway buoy it is 1·8 miles on a track of 329° to the conspicuous west pier with its

Rye Harbour approach. Note training walls which cover at HW

characteristic red-painted tripod beacon (Fl.R.5s7m 6M). Note that the three horizontal timbers of this beacon form a unique tide gauge. The central one shows 3m; the upper member gives you 4·5m above datum.

The entrance to the channel, which is from 30m to 45m wide, lies between the east and west piers. On the west side a long training wall has a groyne which extends to seaward of the entrance. This training wall is covered between half-tide and high water (depths above 2·4m). It is marked by a series of pole beacons with red cage topmarks, some on top of dolphins; there are three Q.R lights at irregular intervals along the walls as far as Rye Harbour, and further lights at the bend beyond it.

The east pier is also long, though it does not extend as far seaward as its counterpart; at its end there is an unusual square, four-legged green tower (Q(9)15s5M). Two cables northwest, where the east bank begins, is a Q.G light. At MHWS the upper parts of this east pier are awash, but it is marked by posts with green conical topmarks.

Vessels making for Rye should head up towards the *Rye Fairway* buoy, then alter course to around 329° so as to leave the tripod of the west pier open on the port bow. There is always an easterly set across the harbour entrance, especially on the flood tide. Once inside, a mid-channel course is generally best, although the deeper water is on the west side. Care must be taken on the flood, when side currents

flowing across the training wall may affect steering. The cage beacons marking the training wall are fixed to its inside edge, except for one off the harbourmaster's office. This is a prominent solitary house on the east bank of the Rother opposite the lifeboat slip. The harbour office is adjacent the harbourmaster's house with timber constructed moorings below. Visiting vessels are requested to stop at these reception moorings and report to the harbourmaster who will provide up-river chartlets and berthing instructions for Rye.

The entrance should not be approached by vessels with a draught of 2m earlier than 3 hours before HW; the best time to enter is around 1 hour before HW. The best time to leave is not later than 1 hour after HW, but for yachts of moderate draught 2½ hours either side is possible with care at springs. A conventional tide gauge is fitted to the seaward end of the eastern training wall.

By night, a directional Oc.WG indicates the safe water into the inner channel. White is on 326° through 331°. Green is on either side. The eastern pier end has a fog horn (7s).

Just below the village of Rye Harbour the well marked training wall on the west side of the entrance channel gives way to the River Rother, which is also clearly marked all the way up to the town of Rye.

A mile upstream of Rye Harbour village, the Rock Channel branches off to the west. North of here, the river is navigable for a short distance only. Watch

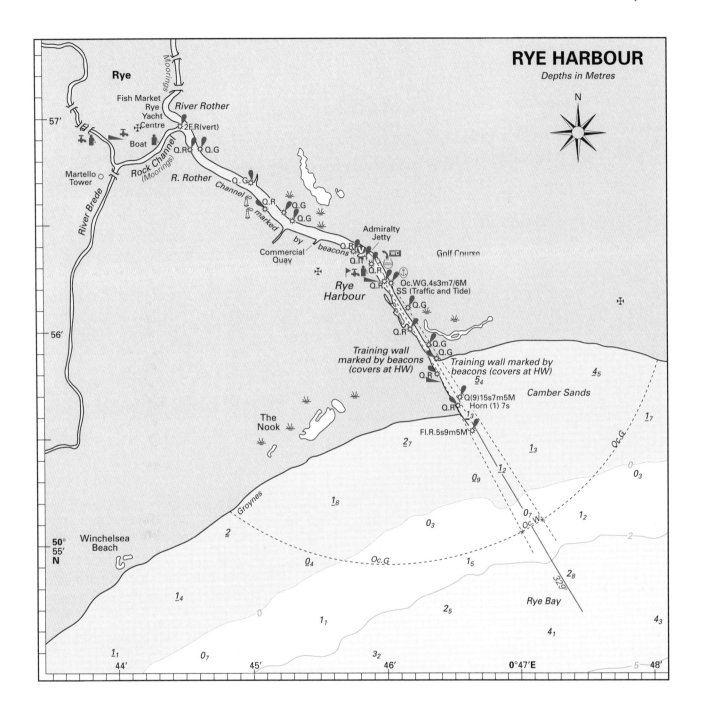

RYE HARBOUR

Depths in Metres

N

Rye

Fish Market
Rye
Yacht
Centre

River Rother

River Rother

2F.R(vert)

Q.R Q.G

Boat

Martello
Tower

Rock Channel
(Moorings)

R. Rother

River Brede

Q.G

Channel

Q.R

Q.G

Q.G

57′

marked

Admiralty
Jetty

Q.R

Golf Course

by

Commercial
Quay

beacons

Q.R

WC

Q.R

Q.R

Oc.WG.4s3m7/6M
SS (Traffic and Tide)

*Rye
Harbour*

Q.G

Q.R

56′

*Training wall
marked by beacons
(covers at HW)*

Q.G

Q.G

*Training wall marked by
beacons (covers at HW)*

Q.R

5̲4

Camber Sands

4̲5

The
Nook

Q.R

Q(9)15s7m5M
Horn (1) 7s

1̲7

Fl.R.5s9m5M

1̲3

2̲7

1̲3

1̲2

0̲9

Oc.G

0₃

1̲8

0₃

1̲2

Groynes

2

0₇

Oc.W

1̲2

2

50°
55′
N

Winchelsea
Beach

0̲4

Oc.G

1₅

329

2₈

Rye Bay

1̲4

0

1₁

2₅

4₁

4₃

1̲1

0₇

3₂

44′   45′   46′   0°47′E   48′

Rye. West pier and tripod beacon from the southeast at low
water

Rye. The tripod beacon at the breakwater end

Rye. The fairway buoy

Rye Harbour village. Admiralty Jetty on right

out for the 2F.R lights which you will see unexpectedly on the north side of the Rock Channel entrance. Look for the small red and green buoys in the channel, but do not turn to port until they are well open, as the inside of the bend shoals. Now maintain a course in the centre of the channel for almost ½ mile until you reach the sluicegate of the River Brede on your port hand. Keep very close to the moored yachts to port of you in this vicinity, as the opposite side of the river is very shallow indeed. After completing your starboard turn, go back to the centre of the channel up to Strand Quay and choose a berth on the town side, on your starboard hand. Some of the bottom is deep, soft mud, but other areas have a layer of mud over shingle. In the absence of advice, be prepared to lean on the pilings if you have a deep keel.

Firing range

The army firing range at Lydd has a Sea Danger Area extending 2M offshore and stretching east from *Rye Fairway* buoy to a north/south line approximately 1½M west of Dungeness lighthouse. Firing takes place on about 300 days per annum from 0830–1630 LT (occasionally to 2300). Red flags or red lights are displayed ashore when the range is in use, and a range safety craft may be on station.

Further details via VHF Ch 13 or 73 (☎ 01679 20203 or 01303 249541 ext 8518).

Traffic signals

International three-light traffic signals are exhibited from the harbour office during times of commercial shipping movement, usually at or near HW. These must be obeyed.

Berthing procedure

With sufficient rise of tide, all visiting yachts should moor initially at special berths provided alongside the piles at Rye Harbour village, about a mile from the entrance on the east side of the river, just beyond the harbourmaster's office. This is about 2 miles from Rye town. The berths are lighted at night. Double mooring is not allowed. Care should be taken when turning at Rye Harbour village at springs.

The large range of tide calls for careful mooring, but yachts will lie afloat for about 4 hours, then take the bottom, which is hard muddy shingle. Always consult the harbourmaster, who can be contacted on VHF Ch 14 or 16, or at the harbour office.

Lying at Admiralty Jetty holds little potential for a long stay. Up-river the charms of Rye await, but first you must report to the harbour office, where you will be instructed in how to work up to Strand Quay. You will also be invited to pay your dues, and will be given a most useful and informative booklet about the port and town of Rye. If you are in a multihull, you may be denied access to Strand Quay.

Facilities

Showers and toilets at Strand Quay and at the

harbour office by Admiralty Jetty. Diesel from Sandrock Marina in Rock Channel at HW. Diesel is now also available from a 24-hour unmanned pontoon, tide permitting. Discs for pump operation may be purchased from the harbourmaster. Garage at Strand Quay. There is a bunkering barge on the west bank of the river.

Fresh water by hose at Admiralty Jetty and Strand Quay or by can from taps at Strand Quay. Chandlery at Rye (Rock Channel) with *Calor Gas/Camping Gaz* exchange. Repairs from Phillips Yard in Rock Channel, including electronics. There is a slipway (HW±2/3hr) at Rye Harbour village, with road access. Excellent town facilities of all types in Rye itself.

Communications

Rye Harbour (a dinghy trip from Admiralty Jetty) connects by regular buses to Rye itself, whence rail and bus connections to all parts.

Eastbourne (Sovereign Yacht Harbour)

Tides

HW −0005 Dover

MHWS	MLWS	MHWN	MLWN
7·4m	0·7m	5·5m	2·2m

Depths

2m, dredged twice annually. This channel is subject to some post-gale disturbance, so deep-draught boats are well advised to enquire about depths by VHF on approach, if near to LWS. Normally, there is no problem, but the operators take a sensible attitude and will provide a guard boat to guide you should the unlikely occur and there be less water than you would want.

General

Sovereign Harbour is a modern, artificial development of large proportions situated at the southwest end of Pevensey Bay, about two miles northeast of Eastbourne Pier. An even greater acreage of enclosed docks is promised early in the

new millennium. Visitors are welcome. All berths are inside the locked inner harbour and are thus perfectly sheltered. The entrance channel is dredged and well marked so that in most conditions it presents no difficulties. In a hard blow from east-northeast through to east-southeast, however, it could be unwise for a stranger to attempt it.

The pleasures of Eastbourne, a short cab ride away, are many and varied, but for pure relaxation a stroll along the Edwardian promenade followed by an hour's snooze in a deckchair by the bandstand is hard to beat. The gulls cry, the sun seems always to shine, while elderly gentlemen in panama hats and linen jackets tap their fingers gently to the stirring strains of *Soldiers of the Queen*.

Approach and entrance

From east or southeast the only dangers, except the inshore rocks of Bexhill Reef, Oyster Reef and Codheath Shoals, 4 miles up-Channel, are the tide rips set up under certain conditions on Royal Sovereign Shoals and the Horse of Willingdon. Fortunately, these can readily be given a wide berth with sensible pilotage.

From the west, clear the shore by a mile or so after rounding Beachy Head. This will keep you outside Holywell Bank and any small craft or swimmers ambitious enough to cross your track.

Call *Sovereign Harbour* on Ch 15 (or 16) from a mile or two out if you have VHF.

The Martello tower at Langney Point now serves as a lighthouse indicating the position of Sovereign Harbour. The xenon light (Fl(3)15s) is visible in daylight, so identification is easy.

The start of the entrance channel is marked by a red and white vertically striped fairway buoy (LFl.10s) about 4·5 cables east-northeast of the breakwaters. The outside channel is clearly buoyed and is crystal clear at night by virtue of the single point leading light (DirFl.WRG.3s) whose white sector leads in on 258°. If it shows red turn to starboard, if green swing to port. There are two lit green buoys (Fl.G.3s) to starboard marking a wreck.

Come off the leading line once inside the outer harbour with its white-painted jetty ends (Fl(4)R.12s and Fl.G.5s), and follow the lit buoyed channel up to the lock. There is room for all but the largest boats to round up here to drop sails if required. Bear in mind, however, that this area is not officially dredged and depths cannot be guaranteed. Watch out around LW if you stray from the straight and not too narrow.

The locks monitor VHF Ch 17 24 hours a day. They open on the hour and the half-hour. Call them for instructions once inside the outer harbour, and note the international traffic signals. Rig fenders on both sides and stand by with warps before entering. Inside the locks, which are 150ft long by 50ft wide, secure to the convenient floating pontoons as far down the lock as possible. Spring lines are advisable and be prepared for the fact that the lock pontoons have 1·2m freeboard. Once inside the harbour, you will be allocated a berth via a computerised

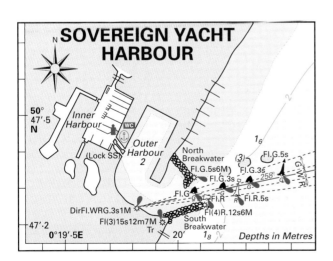

Eastbourne. Sovereign Harbour as seen in 1996. The entrance remains effectively unchanged, but considerable residential and leisure business development has now taken place. Also, further dredged basins are opening up inside the locks – see plan.

management system. Report to the harbourmaster's office once tied up to receive security access cards, etc.

Facilities

Langney Marine Services can deal with repairs of most sorts on site. There is a 50-ton lift. DIY fuel pontoon (1·2m freeboard) open 24 hours a day, with discounts available for bulk purchases of diesel. Fresh water at berths. Excellent showers, toilets and launderettes. Bottle banks. Asda Superstore with breakfast bar and cashpoint so you can pay for your coddled eggs. This spectacular is a ten-minute walk, but you can trundle back aboard with your shopping trolley. Ice from supermarket. The yacht club serves food, as of course do the growing number of restaurants appearing in the bijou dockside locations.

Bicycle hire under HM office. You can walk or ride the bikes along a path on the shingle ridge towards town. It is about 1 mile to the swimming pool, fitness centre and go-carts, and approximately two to the start of Eastbourne promenade with its striped deckchairs, tidy gardens, shopping centre and the best traditional bandstand (see 'General') in Blighty – performances on many summer afternoons after lunch.

It should be understood that in 1999, the time of the *Shell Pilots's* last visit, this whole development was far from fully grown. Mammoth investment is taking place and there is an inevitable air of the building site pervading behind the immediate façade of the marina. This will undoubtedly change in time, and we can look forward to an ever-improving

atmosphere to go along with the already excellent technical facilities.

Communications

Cab to Eastbourne, thence by train to London Victoria (85 mins) via Gatwick Airport (45 mins).

Newhaven

Tides

HW +0004 Dover

MHWS	MLWS	MHWN	MLWN
6·7m	0·4m	5·1m	2·0m

Depths

Entrance and harbour dredged to 5·5m as far as Sleeper's Hole. Water is limited alongside the visitors' berths on the inside long pontoon. 2½ hours either side of LWS there can be problems entering the marina, although once inside the bottom is soft mud. 2m draught is said to be dubious at springs and yachts have been seen to fall over. Dredging is promised soon (1999).

General

Newhaven is a traditional port of refuge about half-way between the Solent and Dover, but facilities for visiting small pleasure craft have not moved on with time. The only officially recommended berth is now the marina in Sleepers Hole, but this does not have all-tide availability for boats drawing more than 1·5m, and even for them, things may be tight at LWS. Fortunately for the sailor in need of respite from the rigours of a tough passage up or down channel, Brighton is close to the west, and Sovereign Harbour now welcomes visitors a few miles east of Beachy Head. The circumstances which made Newhaven important did not include these two comparatively new harbours which have now all but taken over from it as a port of passage. Nevertheless, Newhaven can still be approached when needs must.

Approach and entrance

The town of Seaford is 5 miles west of Beachy Head; at the western end of the low and shingly Seaford Bay stands Burrow Head. Immediately to the east, at the foot of this, lies Newhaven. The big breakwater at the entrance, with its fine classic lighthouse, is conspicuous and makes an easily recognisable landmark.

From the east, stand well away from Seaford Head and steer for a position off Burrow Head. Alter course for the entrance when it bears north, steering in towards the eastern pier, which is some 3 cables inshore of its western partner. In bad weather, with an onshore wind, there is an awkward sea off the entrance south of the breakwater. Steer mid-channel, noting signals as described below.

From the west, keep at least half a mile off Burrow Head. Do not come close to the end of the breakwater in strong onshore winds, for very rough conditions may be experienced.

Within half a mile of the shore, a weak west-going stream starts about 1½ to 2 hours before HW. In the entrance the stream reaches 2 knots at springs, running with ebb and flood into the harbour.

Signals

Harbour Control is located inside the breakwater at the western entrance to the port. Traffic is controlled by signals:

Entry permitted
By day Red triangle over red ball
By night Green all-round

Departure permitted
By day Red ball over red triangle
By night Red all-round

Vessels under 15m free to move in or out
By day Red ball
By night Green light over red

No movement permitted
By day Red ball over red triangle over red ball
By night Lights RGR(vertical)

River Ouse Swing Bridge traffic signals
Fl.G Bridge moving
F.R Ships may proceed downstream
F.G Ships may proceed upstream

Berthing

All yachts entering the harbour should seek instructions from Harbour Control on VHF Ch 16 or 12. Space is limited.

Berthing is usually available in the 355-berth marina in Sleeper's Hole, 3 cables within entrance on port-hand side. Visitors secure inside the long outer pontoon. Call the marina on Ch 37 or 80. The

former is to be preferred as Dover coastguard operates on Ch 80. The marina prefers a day's notice of a visitor, so call them on ☎ 01273 513881 (*Fax* 01273 517990) if you can.

Facilities

Yacht yard, grid-irons and scrubbing hard. Divers (contact marina). Hauling-out facilities at marina, which operates a bar/restaurant. Chandlery. A useful provisions store is situated immediately under the marina office, fronting onto the street. A large pub of grim aspect stands opposite, but the tiny café looks more promising, offering breakfast from 0700–1700.

Good selection of restaurants, from fish and chips upwards. Café by marina patronised by fishermen. Launching site at Sleeper's Hole on application to marina office. Yacht club: Newhaven and Seaford Sailing Club. Customs. A convenient port for opera-lovers on course for Glyndebourne.

Communications

Railway station and numerous buses to all parts.

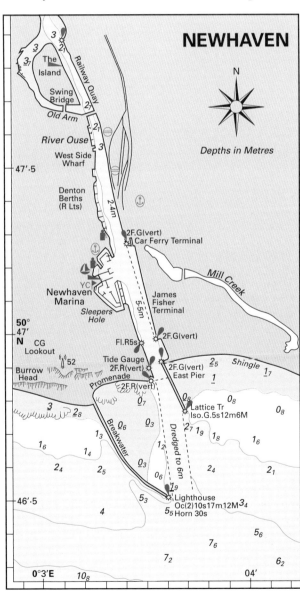

Newhaven Harbour. Marina at left centre in Sleepers Hole.
Note shoal area in bight of east breakwater (see plan)

Brighton

Tides
HW approx +0004 Dover

MHWS	MLWS	MHWN	MLWN
6·6m	0·5m	5·0m	2·0m

Depths
At least 2·7m in the immediate offing. The entrance
is dredged to 2m. Inside the tidal basin berths vary
from 3m to 0·5m on some of the inner pontoons.
The locked inner harbour has 2·7m. Storms
sometimes pile up shingle immediately south of the
end of the East Breakwater. This is regularly
dredged but it you are in any doubt, especially near
LW, call the office for the latest information.

General
Brighton Marina, situated approximately 1 mile east
of Palace Pier, is a most useful stop-over for yachts
on passage up or down the Channel. The harbour is
entirely artificial, and was built to seaward of what
had always been known as Black Rock. It was
opened by HM The Queen in 1979, and for some
years had a chequered business history. This has
finally been resolved, with the marina removed as a
unit from the property development side of the site.
It is now well run by a dedicated team of
experienced hands who are so well organised that
the vital harbour wall has a hundred-year
maintenance programme already in operation.
Divers work every January to check the walls. Berth
numbers are stable at 1200 for residents, with
potential for more. Visitors can always be
accommodated, even vessels over 150ft, depending
on draught.

The harbour is formed by a long, curving eastern
breakwater and a shorter western one, extending to
seaward. Together with a wave screen and Spending
Beach, they form a double entrance which kills the
sea almost completely. Shelter inside is excellent.

Approach and entrance
When coming from the west there are no notable
dangers except for Palace Pier (2F.R) itself, which
would be hard not to see in any but the thickest
visibility. From the east, if you are well inshore,
watch out for the heavily used lobster grounds to the
north of the Fl.Y.5s buoy marking the sewer outfall

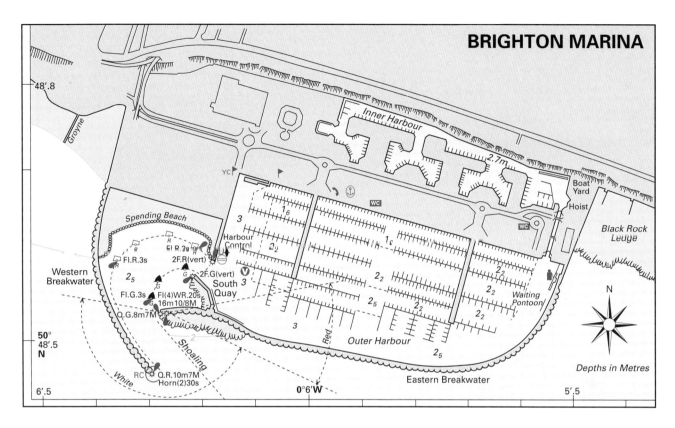

off Portobello. These are particularly insidious at night under power.

The best final approach from offshore is to line up a white high-rise building on the cliff road with the light (Q.R.7M) on the red and white horizontally striped beacon at the head of the western breakwater. These form a transit of 330°. Do not come too close to either breakwater as you enter, because wave backlash can be considerable and there may be shoaling. On the eastern breakwater is a white and green pillar (Fl(4)WR.20s10/8M) with a smaller pillar (Q.G) at the extreme end. The sectored light shows white from 100°–295°. Coming from the east, if you see the red you are closer inshore than you might care to be.

Immediately inside the eastern breakwater the channel swings to starboard, well marked with 4 red and 3 green buoys. The first and last red buoys flash every 3 seconds, the first green likewise. The inner breakwaters have 2F.R and 2F.G marking their positions at night. There is room inside for all but the largest craft to round up and lower canvas.

The reception pontoon lies to port. If you have not been allocated a berth, tie up here and enquire with the berthing master. It is preferable, however, to telephone (☎ 01273 693636) or to call on VHF Ch 11, 37 or 80 shortly before you arrive. Ch 37 is preferred. The harbour office is manned 24 hours. There are berths with depths from 1·6 to 3·0m for vessels up to 30m long (even longer by arrangement). There is always room for visitors.

Brighton. Approach from the southeast. Note vertical white stripe on high-rise hospital building and red-and-white light structure on western breakwater (extreme left)

Brighton Marina

Brighton Marina entrance is difficult in strong onshore winds and can be virtually impassable in a southeasterly gale. If you have no choice in what may seem marginal conditions, the port suggests entering from the east, avoiding the backlash of the harbour wall, or from the west and skirting the outer arm. Once inside the outer westerly arm, the sea subsides quickly and sails can be dropped safely. In a strong SE wind, waves run right into the outer harbour. In such going, however, you should make every effort to put in somewhere else, with Newhaven (subject to its restrictions), a possible alternative.

Fog signal
The western breakwater has an excellent fog signal (Horn(2)30s), and the 10M range radiobeacon can be a great comfort (*BM* 294·50kHz) for those lacking GPS.

Facilities
Fresh water and power on the pontoons. Sheltered, easy 24-hour facility on fuelling pontoon for diesel, not petrol. Travel-hoist and boatyard with rigging facilities. Full repair facilities including a diver. *Calor Gas*, *Camping Gaz* and LPG.

On-site cinema, David Lloyd fitness centre, 24-lane bowling alley, various boutique shops. Restaurants vary from Macdonalds to Italian and include good fish bistros. Pubs. Bicycles for hire near marina office, plus a hypermarket where you could provision for a world voyage. There is a cash-point at the hypermarket which opens seven days a week in season.

Waste oil disposal tank behind the services workshop.

Brighton Marina Yacht Club ☎ 01273 697049 welcomes visitors, both to its shore-based facilities and to its competitive racing.

The town centre of Brighton with its numerous attractions is a mile or so along the front. The main line station has regular fast trains to London and connects with other South Coast stations.

Shoreham

Tides

HW +0010 Dover

MHWS	MLWS	MHWN	MLWN
6·3m	0·6m	4·9m	2·0m

Streams

Off the entrance the west-going stream starts about 2hr before HW and the east-going 6hr later. During the west-going stream there is a southwest set across the entrance from the east breakwater towards the west breakwater, where part of it is deflected into the entrance. This run of tide bends round to the northeast towards the end of the east pier. The eddy is strongest ±1hr HW.

The maximum rate of the main stream at the harbour entrance is about 3 knots, but the river which makes up the Western Arm of the harbour can attain 4 knots at the flood, with an ebb of 5 knots in some parts at springs. In the Eastern Arm there is practically no stream, but a yacht should be piloted with caution in the vicinity of the division off the middle pier.

Depths

The approach shoals to a least depth of 1·7m, with 2·1m in the entrance. The harbour is mostly dredged, with depths shown on the plan. Note that any berths available to visitors in the Western Arm of the harbour dry. The Eastern Arm of the harbour has 2m.

Inside the lock, Southwick Canal is deep enough for commercial coasting vessels, with depths in the order of 5 to 7m.

General

Shoreham Harbour consists of the well sheltered Western Arm, which is the mouth of the River Adur, and the short Eastern Arm leading through lock gates to the Southwick Canal. Shoreham has few attractions for visiting yachtsmen unless a berth inside the locks is available. This is best arranged by calling the harbourmaster on VHF Ch 16 or 14, or ☎ 01273 592366. There is considerable commercial traffic (timber, seaborne aggregates, stone and steel) whose movements take priority and which uses up most of the wharf frontage along the north bank of the River Adur.

Approach and entrance

Shoreham Harbour entrance is about 4 miles west of Brighton Palace Pier. An unlit south cardinal buoy nearly 3 cables east-southeast of the entrance marks the outer end of a sewer outfall.

The shallowing water in the approach off the entrance can be very rough in strong onshore winds and may be dangerous, particularly on the ebb tide. Newhaven is generally a better port of refuge, as is Brighton in suitable conditions.

The entrance lies between the two concrete breakwaters (Fl.R.5s7M and Fl.G.5s8M), within which are the west and east piers (F.WR.6m and F.WG). Further north is the 'middle pier', on the fork of the Western and Eastern arms of the harbour.

The leading lights consist of a lower light (Oc.5s10M) on the watch hut at the end of the middle pier and a higher one (Fl.10s13m15M) from a grey lighthouse beyond. The structures are conspicuous by day, and approach to the harbour is

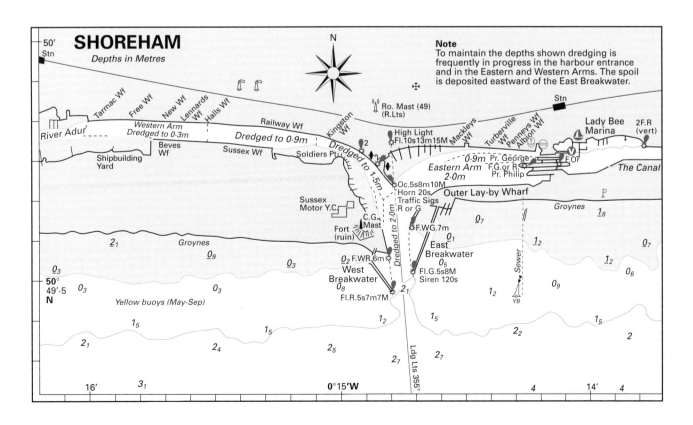

Shoreham entrance from the southwest.

best made on their transit at 355°. A radio mast (red lights, 49m) is just to the left of the transit.

The Western Arm is unsuitable for visiting yachts unless they have a prior arrangement, perhaps with the yacht club. All berths dry. The channel in the Eastern Arm is dredged, and leads via locks into the Southwick Canal. Traffic signals, given below, must be observed. The locks are manned 24 hours per day and will open on request. Use VHF Ch 14. Lock keepers are sympathetic to small craft, despite the lack of instant availability of berths inside (see below, under 'berthing').

A small-craft lock has been established, employing a single sector gate at either end of the Prince George Lock. It offers improved access for small craft, but is restricted to vessels of less than 20ft beam.

Traffic control Signals

From lock
3F.R(vert) – do not approach lock entrance
GWG(vert) – vessels may approach lock

Middle Pier Control Station
Oc.Or.3s – No vessel shall enter the port for the purpose of proceeding to the Eastern or Western Arm, and no vessel outside the port entrance shall be navigated in such a way as to hinder the passage of vessels leaving the port.

Lifeboat House (focusing over Eastern Arm)
Oc.R.3s – No vessel shall proceed along the Eastern Arm for the purpose of leaving the port, moving to another berth in the Eastern Arm, or passing into the Western Arm of the port.

Lifeboat House (focusing over Western Arm)
Oc.R.3s – No vessel shall proceed along the Western Arm for the purpose of leaving the port, moving to another berth in the Western Arm, or passing into the Eastern Arm of the port.

Fog Signals
East breakwater – Siren 120s.
Middle pier – Horn 20s. This is only sounded when ships are approaching.

Berthing

Directions for berthing inside the harbour may be obtained from the duty officer at the locks, where the Port Control building is situated.

All the available berths along the Western Arm (River Adur) dry out and there are many houseboats already there. The Shoreham clubhouse of the Sussex Yacht Club will be found on the N side.

Waiting for the locks: yachts are usually directed to secure temporarily to the north of the fairway.

Berthing in Shoreham, except by prior arrangement, is somewhat hit-and-miss. The Lady Bee Marina (VHF Ch 80 ☎ 01273 593801) is fully subscribed, but will make available any berths free as a result of their usual incumbents being away. The same goes for the hospitable Sussex Yacht Club immediately east of Lady Bee which also has a small marina. You cannot rely on any of these berths, however, particularly away from high season, so it really does pay to pre-arrange, or at least call before committing to an entry. Further east, up the 'canal', is the so-called Aldrington Quay marina. This consists of a single pontoon running along the harbour wall (north side) backing onto a small industrial estate. There is no discernible security, but there is often space, so if you arrive during the night and cannot find another berth, it is a safe resting place until you could make other arrangements. You will recognise it by keeping going along the harbour until you arrive at one or two yachts on your port hand. Beyond them is what appears to be a fishing boat mortuary.

Facilities

Basic toilets and showers at both marinas and the Sussex YC.

Water at marinas. Diesel from a pump at Corrall's (Mon–Fri 0700–1730 −3hr to +2hr HW). Chandlery, *Gas* and *Gaz* from Lady Bee. Repairs through Lady Bee or yacht club. Fine Tapas bar at Lady Bee and yacht club. Various pubs. No shops, short of a cab ride or a less than pleasant hike along the main road.

Aldrington Marina is in reach of a launderette, a few shops and one or two pubs over the same busy highway. The charming Shoreham clubhouse of the Sussex Yacht Club serves lunches through the week, except Mondays, and dinners on Friday and Saturday nights.

Communications

Shoreham has excellent communications by rail or bus to Brighton and London. It also has the distinction of having its own airport, with scheduled flights to France and the Channel Islands as well as charter services.

Littlehampton

Tides

HW at entrance +0015 Dover

Height at entrance

MHWS	MLWS	MHWN	MLWN
5·9m	0·4m	4·5m	1·8m

(MLWS 0·8m at Norfolk Wharf)

Streams

These can be fierce in the entrance, up to 6 knots on the spring ebb. In the offing, the stream turns west nearly 2 hours before HW. Be prepared for a strong contrary eddy inside the training wall.

Depths

The bar dries 1m in the vicinity of the pier head, and thereafter deepens gradually to sea, so tidal height calculations should be worked from this figure. Inside, depths in the river vary between a metre or so and 2·4m as far as the opening footbridge. This has a height of 3·6m at MHWS, and only opens for visitors who 'book' it by 1630 the previous day. If you can pass under this, however, there are only two further low bridges (the old road bridge in the town has a clearance of only 1·7m at MHWS) between you and Arundel, with depths of at least 1·3m at MLWS the whole way. The new road bridge just short of Arundel is considerably higher, and exceedingly satisfactory dinghy trips into the hinterland above this historic town have been reported (1994).

General

Littlehampton is a convenient harbour for yachts, with a relaxed, friendly atmosphere and berthing facilities handy for all the pleasures of the town. It is the home of the famous building yard of Hillyard and, at the right state of tide, can offer a realistic stop-over for yachts bound either up or down the Channel. Shelter is good except in strong southerly and southeasterly weather, which can send a swell up the harbour.

Approach and entrance

When approaching Littlehampton, be aware that it is a small commercial port and that coasters or dredgers may be under way. See 'Bylaws' below, and monitor the port frequency, VHF Ch 71. Littlehampton is readily identifiable from seaward, but if in doubt note the isolated high-rise building with a white structure on top at its western end. Look also for the funfair immediately to the east of the entrance. Approaching from the west through the Looe channel, do not turn to port too soon after the *Mixon* beacon. There is grief aplenty still available inshore. It is therefore prudent to stand on for a mile or so, then steer a track of 065° until you either pick up the leading marks for Littlehampton or bring the head of the 275m-long West Pier onto a bearing of 346°. The West Pier head consists of a large 'cage' of piles. Closer in, the structures supporting its 2F.R lights will be seen.

The bar extends 3 cables to seaward of West Pier. Leading marks for the best water across it on 346° are as follows: a white pepper-mill-shaped lighthouse (Oc.WY.7·5s9m10M) at the inshore end of the east breakwater, and in front of it a black steel column (F.G.6m7M) at the seaward end of the breakwater. The black column is hard to spot by day until it comes 'on' with the white lighthouse, but for all practical purposes you will be safe if you steer across the bar on this sort of heading, then between the West Pier head and the East Beacon on the end of the eastern training wall. This covers at 3m height of tide, but is marked by seven black and white perches every 100m with radar reflectors inshore of the green East Beacon with its light (Q.G.2M).

A tide gauge on the Pier Head reads tide height, so don't forget to subtract the drying height of 1m to arrive at the present depth. It is clearly painted and can be read from seaward by sharp eyes equipped with decent binoculars. Be conservative about the readings on the ebb, because what is literally a gradient created by the stream is reported by the harbourmaster as delivering a level of as much as 0·6m less at the West Pier Head.

If approaching from the east, maintain a sensible offing until the bar is reached.

Littlehampton entrance can be dangerous in strong onshore winds, and should not be attempted in these conditions when the tide is ebbing hard.

Byelaws

Keep clear of all commercial traffic, particularly if a ship signals one long and two short blasts. Traffic passing up and down the harbour has right of way over anything crossing the river, with the exception of the ferry, which takes precedence over everyone. Vessels proceeding against the stream keep clear of those moving with the tide. Ships coming up or down the harbour simply cannot alter course, so it is up to you to monitor the VHF and not be there when they are or, if you are, to keep clear as best you may.

Berthing

Anchoring is prohibited inside the harbour. Regardless of your ultimate berth, you are obliged on arrival to report to the harbourmaster and pay modest harbour dues. Contact the office on VHF Ch 71, ☎ 01903 721215, or mobile 07775 743078. Secure to the clearly marked 'visitors' floating pontoon alongside the Town Quay. This is on your starboard hand opposite the yacht club marina, and is unambiguous because of a blue crane in the yard adjacent. If nobody contacts you, report to the harbour office in a portacabin on the dock above the pontoon. Alternatively, try your luck berthing at the friendly Arun Yacht Club where visiting yachts (bilgekeelers only) are welcome on any spare marina berths. Call on Ch 37.

It is important for visitors to understand that while rafting up to three deep may often be permissible on the harbourmaster's pontoons, this is a privilege not a right. Any more boats can lead to difficulties for commercial access, so if the harbour staff ask you to move, be ready to comply willingly. They will do their best to arrange an alternative. Notwithstanding this, Littlehampton is a friendly place keen to encourage callers and there is rarely a problem.

Further upriver is the fully equipped, modern Littlehampton Marina (VHF Ch 37 and 80, ☎ 01903 713553. To access this, it is necessary to have a footbridge raised, unless you are a motor boat. 24 hours notice is required to the harbourmaster, but this does not mean he is unwilling to comply. If you want to stay for a few days, call in advance and make the arrangements. The marina has all you need and would be a tranquil and safe place to leave a boat for a while. Depths are up to 2·5m, lengths up to 18m.

Littlehampton entrance

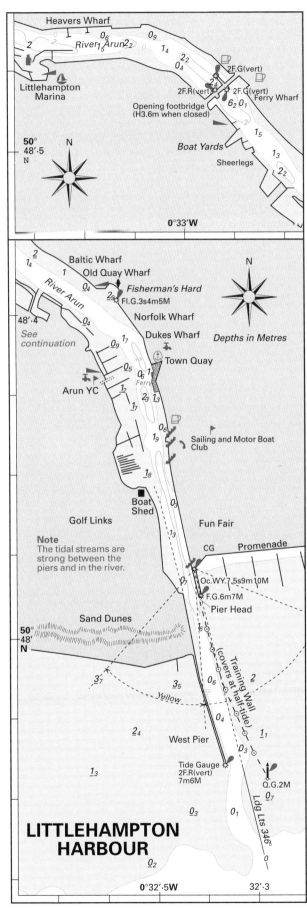

Facilities

Water on all docks. Power also (ask if you are on the Town Quay). Littlehampton Marina has fuel, a slipway, a travel-hoist, a chandlery, washing machines, tumble driers and clean smart loos.

Shingly sand bathing beach on eastern side. If at the Town Quay, use the ferry (£1 adults 50p for children) to go to the more beautiful west beach with its miles of open sand. Walk through the dunes to see many rare plants and birds. Remains of Napoleanic fort, café and toilets there also.

Dinky-Doo Diner for your breakfast just across the street from the Town Quay, open 0630–1400, closed Sundays. Market Friday and Saturday 0900–1600.

Short walk of 1½ cables from the Town Quay to the old-fashioned town centre.

Chichester

Tides

HW +0027 Dover

Entrance

MHWS	MLWS	MHWN	MLWN
4·9m	0·9m	4·0m	1·9m

Minor differences inside the harbour, but none are greater than the LW figures for Itchenor, where neaps are 0·2m lower than at the entrance.

Depths

Various shoal areas in the approaches to the bar, with the least depth of 0·2m half a mile southeast of West Pole beacon. Drying areas to east and west. The bar is dredged to 1·5m, though depths may vary after severe weather. Further in, depths increase rapidly into the entrance where there is a pool of 26m. Thereafter, there is at least 2·4m as far as Emsworth south cardinal beacon and the same up to Itchenor. Further up the harbour depths diminish in both channels – see plan for details. It should be understood that Chichester Bar, like many others on this coast from here on eastwards, is subject to shoaling and general change as the shingle shifts. A tide gauge on the bar beacon gives heights of tide.

General

Chichester Harbour is an ideal dinghy-sailing area, with extensive deep-water channels usable by deep-draughted yachts. Over 10,000 craft upwards of 3m LOA are based here, with 2,000 yachts on marina berths. Bosham, Emsworth, Birdham and Itchenor are all attractive villages, and the anchorage at East Head is a delight when not too crowded. Generally speaking, the area is low-lying and the shores are muddy and reedy, though there are also some beautiful sand and shingle beaches. The harbour's commercial past goes back to Roman times but is now almost completely consigned to the history books. As a leisure centre, however, these waters have few equals.

The *Bar* beacon

The harbour is controlled by Chichester Harbour Conservancy through a manager/harbourmaster based at Itchenor (☎ 01243 512301). His call sign is *Chichester Harbour Radio* on VHF Ch 14; his two RIB patrol boats (*Chichester Harbour Patrol*) on the same channel. Watch is kept during office hours; his staff will be pleased to advise you about berthing or any other problems you may have.

Policing is strict on the 8-knot speed limit and also on Rule of the Road. If you are motorsailing, even motoring with a sail idling in calm weather, hoist your motorsailing cone, point downwards.

Approach and entrance

Chichester Harbour entrance lies some 7 miles west of Selsey Bill. Sands extend seaward on both sides of the approach, namely the West Pole, the Middle Pole and the East Pole. Chichester Bar claims victims nearly every year from amongst those foolish enough to chance their luck. The ebb runs hard, the waters are shoal and exposed from southwest through to southeast, with southeast being the worst wind direction. Do not even think of entering the harbour after half-ebb in a strong onshore wind. In an onshore gale, don't do it at all. These cautions cannot be over-stressed.

Chichester harbour entrance

Approaching from the east, either from the Looe channel or from the Outer Owers, do not turn in too soon. The conspicuous, lit, red West Pole Beacon stands out to seaward of the older *Bar* dolphin surmounted by its white lattice tower. The safest approach is to put this on a bearing of around 005° from a mile or more offshore, then shape up to leave it a few boat's-lengths to port. As you pass the *Bar* beacon to port three hundred or so yards further in, note the height of *tide* on the gauge on one of its legs (add 1·5m to find the *depth* on the bar).

If you cannot discern West Pole and the *Bar* beacons from the offing, it is a good policy to place the very conspicuous Nab Tower on a back bearing of 184° and run in on this until you pick them up.

The East Pole Sands stretch well to seaward of the beacons and are only really cleared by a bearing on the West Pole beacon of 321° or more, so if you head in early and find your course for the beacon is less than this, clear out, steer to seawards and think again. This bearing is covered by the red sector of the West Pole light Fl.WR.5s7/5M.

Approaching from the southwest, you may find yourself seeing the Fl(2)R instead of the safe white sector of the bar light. Steer to starboard until the red goes out on a bearing of 081°.

A track of 013° from a point about half a cable east of the beacon will now lead you to the harbour

Hayling Island Sailing Club and Sandy Point, beyond which the channel to Sparke's Yacht Harbour leads westwards

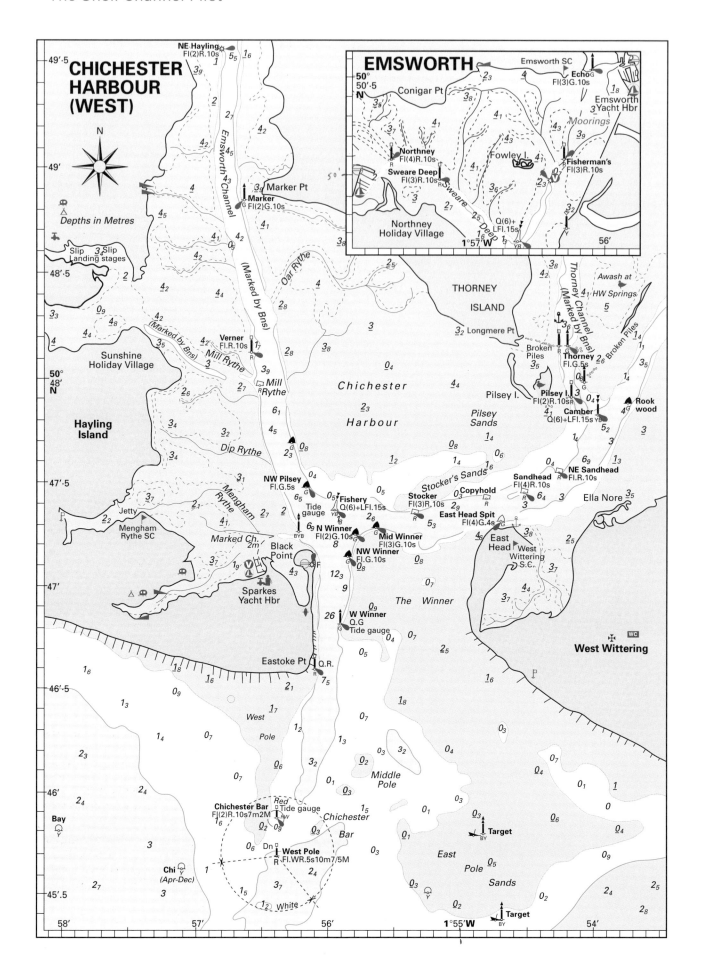

CHICHESTER HARBOUR (WEST)

NE Hayling
Fl(2)R.10s

N

Depths in Metres

Emsworth Channel

(Marked by Bns)

Marker Pt

Marker
Fl(2)G.10s

Oar Rythe

Verner
Fl.R.10s

(Marked by Bns)

Mill Rythe

Sunshine
Holiday Village

Mill
Rythe

Hayling
Island

Dip Rythe

Chichester

Harbour

50°
48'
N

Mengham
Rythe

NW Pilsey
Fl.G.5s

Jetty

Mengham
Rythe SC

Marked Ch.

Black
Point

Fishery
Q(6)+LFl.15s

Tide
gauge

N Winner
Fl(2)G.10s

NW Winner
Fl.G.10s

Mid Winner
Fl(3)G.10s

Stocker's Sands

Stocker
Fl(3)R.10s

Copyhold

East Head Spit
Fl(4)G.4s

Pilsey
Sands

Pilsey I.

Sandhead
Fl(4)R.10s

NE Sandhead
Fl.R.10s

Ella Nore

East
Head

West
Wittering
S.C.

Sparkes
Yacht Hbr

The   Winner

W Winner
Q.G
Tide gauge

Eastoke Pt

Q.R.

West Wittering

West

Pole

Middle
Pole

Chichester Bar
Fl(2)R.10s7m2M

Red
Tide gauge

Chichester
Bar

Dn

West Pole
Fl.WR.5s10m7/5M

Chi
(Apr-Dec)

White

East

Pole

Sands

Target

Target

Bay

EMSWORTH

Emsworth SC

Echo
Fl(3)G.10s

Conigar Pt

50°
50'·5
N

Emsworth
Yacht Hbr

Moorings

Northney
Fl(4)R.10s

Fowley I.

Fisherman's
Fl(3)R.10s

Sweare Deep
Fl(3)R.10s

Sweare Deep

Q(6)+
LFl.15s

Northney
Holiday Village

1°57'W

56'

THORNEY

ISLAND

Longmere Pt

Awash at
HW Springs

Thorney Channel
(Marked by Bns)

Broken Piles

Broken
Piles

Thorney
Fl.G.5s

Pilsey I.
Fl(2)R.10s

Camber
Q(6)+LFl.15s

Rook
wood

1°55'W

entrance in rapidly deepening water. Leave the red *Eastoke* beacon (Q.R) to port and, 2½ cables further on, the *W Winner* green beacon (Q.G) to starboard, taking care to leave the small unlit red posts on the ends of the groynes round Eastoke Point to port. Streams in this channel can reach extremes of over 6 knots on a big spring ebb. Run in parallel with the steep shingle beach on your port hand until you are between the Hayling Island Sailing Club clubhouse on Black Point to port and the green *NW Winner* buoy (Fl.G.10s) to starboard. You now have two choices: Emsworth Channel to the north and Chichester Channel to the east.

Emsworth Channel

Steering about 335° from the Black Point/*NW Winner* entrance, leave the lit *Fishery* south cardinal well to starboard, followed by the *NW Pilsey* (Fl.G.5s) green buoy. The channel is now well marked and adequately lit up the almost straight 2-mile leg northward which culminates in the lit south cardinal *Emsworth* beacon and the red (Fl(2)R.10s) *NE Hayling* beacon. If you are bound up Sweare Deep towards Northney Marina, you will leave *NE Hayling* to port and follow red piles up the channel, keeping them on your port hand on a northwesterly heading as far as *Sweare Deep* beacon (Fl(3)R.10s). Leave this to port and a heading of around 290° will take you up to *Northney* (Fl(4)R.10s) beacon. Swing round this, noting its depth gauge, and to the southwest you will see the red and green piles at the marina entrance. Boats drawing up to 2m can work into the marina on a mean tide.

The other channel from *Emsworth* beacon leads up to the village itself and Emsworth Yacht Harbour. The lower part of the channel as far as the red *Fisherman's* beacon (Fl(3)R.10s) is set with pile moorings. Above here, a series of red piles is left to port, following the drying (0·5m) channel a little east of north until at the first lit green pile (Fl(3)G.10s) the channel swings to starboard between a second green and further red piles up to the marina, where a sill maintains a depth of 1·5m. This marina is only accessible to shoal-draught boats for an hour or two either side of HW.

There are various other channels in the vicinity of Emsworth, all of which dry, some being marked with piles and withies.

Chichester Channel

This leads to Thorney Channel, Bosham Channel, Itchenor and thence to Birdham Pool, Chichester Yacht Basin, and drying 'points beyond'.

After passing Hayling Island Sailing Club, bear to the east to leave to starboard the green conical *NW Winner*, *N Winner* and *Mid Winner*. The small *Stocker* red buoy is now ahead and to port. Look out on your starboard bow for *East Head Spit*, now a G conical buoy which has replaced the age-old beacon left silted up by changing times. This is sometimes obscured by myriad yachts anchored off East Head on summer days, but will be readily spotted in sterner weather. Leave to port *Copyhold* and *Sandhead*, also red cans.

Do not take any chances with the *Winner*. Cutting corners here can lead to long and gravelly waits for the tide. If the wind kicks in hard while you are stranded, your position may become hazardous. The bank is well marked, so there should be no difficulty.

After leaving *NE Sandhead* (Fl.R.10s) to port, the channel bears to the northeast, onto the distant *Roman Transit* beacon (red port-hand daymark) in line with the so-called *Main Channel* beacon (white rectangular daymark) on the shore at 032°. Both line up with Stoke Clump, a conspicuous group of trees on the distant downs. If visibility shuts out these markers, do not concern yourself, for the channel is clearly marked on the port hand by the lit south cardinal *Camber* beacon at the entrance of the Thorney Channel, and by the unlit green *Rookwood* buoy (leave to starboard). There are also a number of perches, but these are situated high up on the mud and should be given a wide berth near low water.

After passing the *Chalkdock* beacon (Fl(2)G.10s), come to starboard and shape up for the green conical starboard-hand *Fairway* buoy (Fl(3)G.10s) at the junction of the Bosham and Chichester Channels. Close to the northeast is the *Deep End* south cardinal beacon, which is an unlit starboard-hand mark for the Bosham Channel and a port-hand one for Itchenor Reach. The chart suggests that you can leave fairway on either hand, but there are two unlit G buoys between it and the southern shore, so it would seem prudent for strangers bound for Itchenor to pass between fairway and *Deep End*. Itchenor Reach is deep almost to Longmore Point, getting on for a mile east of Itchenor. Hereafter the channel shallows, but is marked by buoys. Access to Birdham Pool and the Chichester Yacht Basin is dependent on some rise of tide.

Birdham Pool is entered by following a series of green piles, after rounding *Birdham* beacon (Fl(4)G.10s), then passing through a lock manned for 3 hours either side of HW in winter and from 0700 to 2200 in season. Yachts of up to 2m draught can get there, tide permitting, but the approaches dry at least one metre, so proceed with caution.

Chichester Yacht Basin's beacon (CM Fl.G.5s) lies a couple of cables east-northeast of Birdham's. From it, a line of green piles leads east-southeast down a channel which has approximately half a metre of water (LAT) up to the locks. These are manned in summer from 0700 to 2359 weekends and 0700 to 2100 Mondays to Thursdays; in winter, from 0800 to 1700.

Bosham Channel carries 1·8m to within 2 cables of the quay at the village and is marked by red and green perches. It is possible for craft drawing 1·8m to lie alongside the quay, and to dry out at moderate spring tides.

Thorney Channel is entered by leaving the lit south cardinal *Camber* beacon to starboard, and then leaving *Pilsey Island* red beacon (Fl(2)R.10s) to port

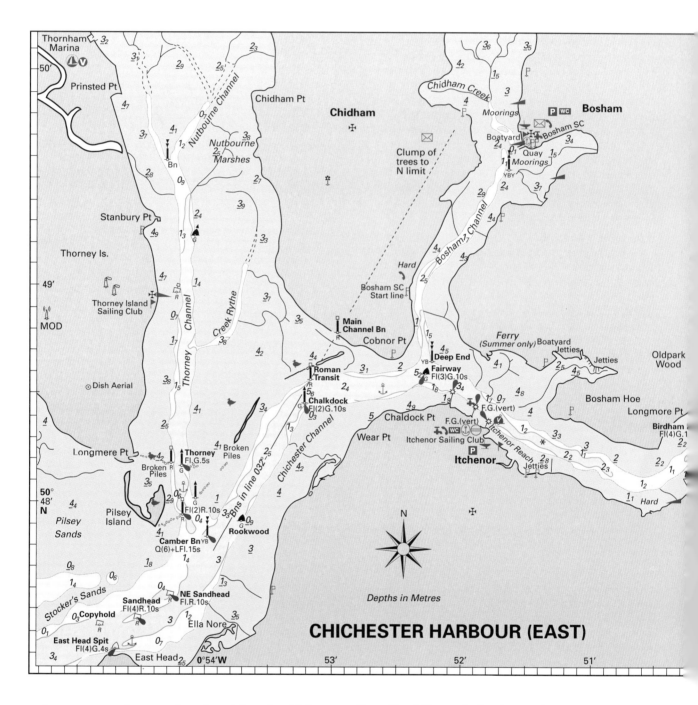

CHICHESTER HARBOUR (EAST)

Depths in Metres

and a green perch to starboard; neither should be passed close to. Now pass between a pair of beacons, beyond which the channel is straight and marked by red and green perches. Depths range from 3·7m down to 1·8m to the northeast of Stanbury Point. The upper channel contains moorings.

Anchorages and berthing

North of Sandy Point, just inside the entrance on the west side, there is a large clutch of moorings. The occasional one may be free for a lunch stop. Hayling Island Sailing Club maintain a jetty to the west of their dinghy launching area whose outer end is fully intertidal. This is available for 'picking-up and putting-down' stays up to a maximum of twenty minutes.

East Head Beyond the buoy there is a pleasant anchorage on a sandy bottom. It is fine in settled weather, but very crowded in summer and rather exposed except from south and east. A shallow creek marked by perches leads to the Roman Landing and West Wittering Sailing Club.

Itchenor There is a pontoon at the end of a long low jetty below the harbour office. Lie here for 15 minutes *only* to take on water and load stores or bodies. Upstream are 6 large visitors' moorings where you may be invited to raft up to six abreast. Still further upstream is a visitors' pontoon on the south side of the channel. If in doubt, call the harbourmaster on VHF Ch 14, although you may well be met on arrival. A pretty village with few domestic facilities save The Ship Inn, where good

Itchenor

seafood is served these days, joyously replacing a very long-gone unpleasant landlord. To anyone upset here in the past, it is now safe to enter. A fine pint and a good welcome awaits you. There is also a boatyard and a small chandlery. Rubbish disposal and oil dumping facilities on the pontoon. Scrubbing piles for moderate draught vessels on the foreshore. Enquire of the harbourmaster.

Birdham Pool Approach as described above (see 'Approach and entrance'). Birdham can accommodate yachts up to 15m long and 2m draught. The place has great charm, a shipyard with full repair facilities, showers, toilets, fuel, sailmaker, chandler and electrical engineer. Shops are a 25-minute walk. Do not call on VHF. They are not listening. Just come up on the tide.

Chichester Marina Call VHF Ch 80. Lock available 24 hours year round. Free flow at ±1½hrs HW in summer. Traffic lights.

Lock signals
R – wait
G – enter

Take care in the lock during free flow periods. The tide can swirl in and out at great speed. Visitors are welcome up to 20m LOA and 1·8m draught. The surroundings are pleasant and the facilities all you would expect in a major modern marina, including a launderette, fuel (plus LPG). Provisions/newsagent, chandler, bar/restaurant, riggers, sailmakers and engineers are all on site. The Chichester Yacht Club welcomes visitors to all its facilities.

Thorney Channel is a beautiful and well sheltered anchorage when you can find space, of which there is often plenty off Pilsey Island. You can 'dinghy' ashore onto a spit but, thankfully some would say, there are no facilities.

51

Birdham Pool

Northney Marina usually has space for visitors drawing up to 2m. Call on VHF Ch 80, or ☎ 01705 466321. All facilities, but shops are 15 minutes' walk.

Emsworth Yacht Harbour maintains only four visitors' berths, but may have more due to berth-holders' absence.

Call on VHF Ch 37 or 80; this is highly advisable as space is limited. Facilities are water, toilets, showers and a payphone, but Emsworth Shipyard next door can solve most problems. 10 minutes' walk brings you to the town of Emsworth with shops, pubs, bistros, etc. Emsworth Slipper Sailing Club and Emsworth Sailing Club welcome visitors.

Emsworth Channel South of Emsworth you will find a couple of visitors' pontoons slung between piles for boats theoretically up to LOA 12m. These are in 2m LAT. Boats can be left unmanned here and here only within the channel. The dinghy ride can be a

tough one, but in summer a water taxi (Sid Kennett) plies his trade. Call VHF Ch 14 or *Emsworth Mobile*.

The Emsworth service pontoon with fresh water (for tanks only – no washing down), rubbish disposal is available to all-comers for 2 hours free of charge. 1m draught can lie here at HW ±4 hours. A penalty of £30 per hour hits you if you overstay your welcome. Scrubbing piles also available through Itchenor harbour office.

Sparkes Yacht Harbour, with 150 berths, plus 30 for visitors and all the facilities of an active yacht yard, lies immediately west of Sandy Point, the home of the Hayling Island Sailing Club, at the end of its own 2m dredged channel. Leave the unlit east cardinal beacon to starboard, swinging to port out of the main channel, and follow the yellow 'x' leading marks to the westward until the red and green channel posts leading to the conveniently sited marina open up on your port hand. Berths have

Bosham

Dell Quay.

depth up to 2·5m afloat at MLWS. Contact on VHF Ch 37 or ☎ 02392 463572. Excellent facilities including fuel, repairs, showers, laundry room, bar/restaurant, chandler with *Calor Gas/Camping Gaz* exchange, and some provisions.

Bosham It is possible to dry out alongside Bosham quay, in depths/heights noted above (see 'Approach and entrance – Chichester Channel'). Village facilities only, with pleasant walks, two pubs and a yacht club. This is an excellent scrubbing berth, with a firm bottom and a freshwater stream running beneath the wall to sluice off with. It is also one of the prettiest berths on the South Coast. Leave the west cardinal beacon below the quay well to starboard. There is a south cardinal mark by the end of a wooden breakwater/training wall which runs parallel and close to the quay. Leave the mark to starboard and keep close to the piled quay wall. Tie up and enjoy the summer's day.

Launching sites in Chichester The harbour is a small-craft paradise, so it is not surprising that it is well equipped with launching places. Some are as follows:

1. From public hards at the ends of roads at Itchenor, Bosham, Dell Quay, Thornham and Emsworth, with car parks nearby.

Approach to Emsworth Yacht Harbour

Emsworth Yacht Harbour

2. Near HW on the northeast side of Hayling Bridge at the slipway administered by the Langstone Sailing Club, and also at Birdham Yacht Club and Dell Quay.
3. At Sandy Point, with the permission of the Hayling Island Sailing Club.
4. At Emsworth, from the public hard or Emsworth Yacht Harbour.

Yacht clubs

Birdham Yacht Club, Bosham Sailing Club, Chichester Cruising Club (Itchenor), Chichester Yacht Club (Birdham), Dell Quay Sailing Club, Emsworth Sailing Club, Hayling Island Sailing Club, Itchenor Sailing Club, Langstone Sailing Club, Mengham Rythe Sailing Club, West Wittering Sailing Club, Thorney Island Sailing Club.

Langstone Harbour

Tides

Similar to Portsmouth
HW +0014 Dover

MHWS	MLWS	MHWN	MLWN
4·8m	0·8m	3·9m	1·9m

Streams

Streams run extremely strongly at springs in the vicinity of the entrance – beware of mooring buoys towed under by the tide.

Depths

With prudent pilotage, a least depth of 2·1m LAT may be found on the bar. A large proportion of the harbour dries, but the main channels offer well over 2m for much of their length. The short channel up to Langstone Marina virtually dries. The automatic sill 'opens' when there is 1·6m of water above it, giving access to the marina where 2·4m is available in its deepest part. The waiting pontoon outside has 2·5m at LAT.

General

It could be said that Langstone Harbour lacks the natural beauty of Chichester to the east, or the historic fascination of Portsmouth on its western

Langstone Harbour entrance.

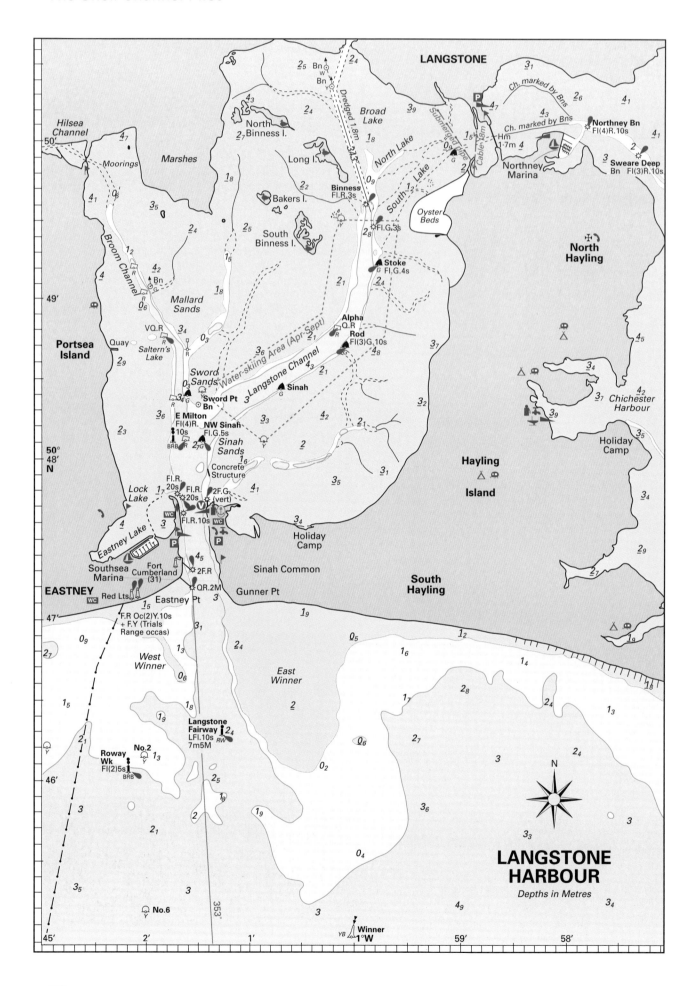

LANGSTONE

Hilsea Channel

North Binness I.

Marshes

Moorings

Broad Lake

North Lake

Submerged Pipe

Dredged 1.8m 3m3

South Lake

Cable 18m

Hm 1·7m

Northney Bn
Fl(4)R.10s

Northney Marina

Sweare Deep
Bn Fl(3)R.10s

Oyster Beds

North Hayling

Portsea Island

Broom Channel

Bn

Mallard Sands

Bakers I.

South Binness I.

Binness
Fl.R.3s

Fl.G.3s

Stoke
G Fl.G.4s

Long I.

VQ.R

Saltern's Lake

Quay

Sword Sands

Water-skiing Area (Apr–Sept)

Langstone Channel

Alpha
Q.R

Rod
Fl(3)G.10s

Sinah

Chichester Harbour

Holiday Camp

Sword Pt
Bn

E Milton
Fl(4)R.10s

NW Sinah
Fl.G.5s

Sinah Sands

Concrete Structure

Hayling

Island

Fl.R.20s

Fl.R.20s

2F.G (vert)

Fl.R.10s

Lock Lake

Eastney Lake

WC

P

WC

P

Holiday Camp

Sinah Common

Southsea Marina

Fort Cumberland (31)

2F.R

EASTNEY

WC Red Lts

QR.2M

Eastney Pt

Gunner Pt

South Hayling

F.R Oc(2)Y.10s
+ F.Y (Trials Range occas)

West Winner

East Winner

Langstone Fairway
LFl.10s
7m5M RW

Roway Wk
Fl(2)5s

No.2

No.6

353°

Winner
1°W YB

North

LANGSTONE
HARBOUR

Depths in Metres

Langstone fairway buoy

Eastney Cruising Association clubhouse on west side of entrance

East side of Langstone Harbour entrance

flank. Nonetheless, this large expanse of mud and tide-controlled water possesses a distinct charm of its own. It has been called bleak, but some enjoy its gutsy, outpost feel in a region where many places have been tooth-combed almost to the extinction of their natural character.

Approach and entrance
The entrance to Langstone Harbour is identified by a tall chimney on its west bank. As at Chichester, the channel into the harbour is bounded on both sides by dangerous banks of shingle and sand, in this case the West and East Winner.

If arriving from the east, it is prudent to leave the south cardinal *Winner* buoy (unlit) to starboard, then hold a course of due west until the red and white fairway beacon comes into transit with the inner end of the west side of the entrance. The beacon is set in the deepest available water, and even if the banks shift, this approach should keep you off them. From the fairway beacon steer for the entrance, taking note of the transit (353°) of the red entrance dolphin (with port-hand topmark on the end of an outfall) and the edge of the land on the west side of the entrance. As you approach the entrance itself, any cross set will be replaced by a potentially very strong stream running straight in or out. This can kick up a bad sea, especially towards the end of a spring ebb in strong onshore winds.

Coming from the southwest, bring Horse Sand Fort onto a stern transit (235°) with No Man's Land Fort. This will lead to the vicinity of the black/red/black isolated danger beacon with ⁞ topmark marking Roway Wreck. Before you reach the beacon, you will have identified the red and white *Langstone* fairway beacon fine on your starboard bow. Steer towards this, being mindful of a 1·3m (LAT) patch just to the north of your track. Outside the line of the two beacons is a least depth of 1·8m, which at MLWS gives you 2·6m of water.

Approaching from the west, you may opt for the gap in the submerged barrier joining Horse Sand Fort with the Hampshire shore. The passage lies almost a mile south of Lumps Fort on the beach and is marked by a dolphin (Q.R) on its south side, whose light is exceedingly feeble. Keep close to the dolphin, in 1·2m (LAT), then steer east until the two forts come in line as described above.

Once inside the harbour, navigate to your chosen berth, but be ready for powerful streams in the lower part of the main channel.

Fraser Gunnery Range
In occasional use Mon–Fri (0800–1800) as notified by Radio Solent, or by telephone (☎ 02392 822351). The range area is a circle of 1 mile radius centred on 50°47'·03N 01°01'·09W. There is also a sector 120°–155° ranging out to 9 miles. The range is marked when in use by two red flags, and at night by 2F.R and an Oc(2)Y.10s light exhibited just to the west of the harbour entrance.

Berthing
No anchoring is allowed in the harbour without the permission of the harbourmaster, who maintains a watch on VHF Ch 16 and 12. Call *Langstone Harbour Radio* during working hours, including weekends. The favoured anchorage for deep-draught craft is on the north side of Langstone Channel on a clean, sandy bottom. The berth is,

however, exposed and a long way from any shoreside comforts.

There are a number of visitors' moorings in the main run of the entrance. Those on the west side are maintained by the Eastney Cruising Association (☎ 01705 734103). To the east of the fairway are the Harbour Board moorings. The harbourmaster's office can be reached on ☎ 01705 463419, or call *Langstone Harbour Radio*. It should be noted that at springs the tide past these moorings reaches prodigious velocities, and that as a result the greatest care should be taken over dinghy work. Anyone unfortunate enough to fall from a moored yacht during the height of the ebb on a dark night could very well be lost. Despite these gloomy observations, should you opt for one of these berths, Hayling Ferry will provide a 'get-you-ashore' service. Call *Pride of Hayling* on VHF Ch 10.

The deep-water moorings inside the entrance are private, and those outside the channels mainly dry.

Southsea Marina has 30 visitors' berths. Enter the narrow channel by passing close north of the western pontoon and the point on your port hand, immediately inside the harbour entrance. Watch out for cross set. The channel is now marked with red and green piles, the salient ones being lit. It appears tortuous, but as you work along its half-mile length it becomes plain enough. There is a waiting pontoon with shore access immediately outside the sill. The sill itself is automatically operated by water pressure, so that when 1·6m stands above it a balance weight folds it down flat, allowing access. As this happens, the red lights turn to green and boats drawing 1·6m or less may enter. If your draught is greater, observe the gauge near the gate, which indicates depth on the sill. Vessels outward bound have right of way in the 7m-wide entrance.

Southsea Marina keeps a 24-hour watch on VHF Ch 80 and can be called on ☎ 02392 822719.

Facilities
Hayling Island These are situated in a cluster around the pub on the east side of the entrance to the harbour. Diesel and fresh water from Hayling pontoon near to the harbourmaster's office. Water here is deep, but this is a very busy berth, so no vessels should be left without sufficient crew to move them except with specific permission from the harbour office, and then only in the designated berth. If you ignore this warning, you are liable to be towed away and billed.

Ferry Boat Inn with bar meals, a café and a modest general store. Launching site at slip. Summer bus service to Hayling Island and Havant. Ferry to Eastney all year round, thence to Portsmouth by bus, or bracing walk.

Eastney Cruising Association situated in the entrance on the west side is a hospitable organisation whose fine clubhouse contains showers, a bar and a restaurant. Visitors are welcome and the members are a friendly, able group whose numbers have included none other than Sir Alec Rose.

Southsea Marina has fuel, water, good showers, laundry and a chandlery. Basic provisions. Visitors are granted access to the marina clubhouse with balcony, bar and good tasty meals. First-class provisions at caravan park after an easy walk.

Communications
Bus to Portsmouth.

Portsmouth

Tides
HW +0029 Dover

MHWS	MLWS	MHWN	MLWN
4·7m	0·8m	3·8m	1·9m

Depths
The entrance and main channels are deep, as are the approaches to Camper and Nicholson's Marina (Gosport) and Haslar Marina. Portchester Lake shoals towards the top, but is dredged 1·5m up to the Port Solent lock. The main branch of Fareham Lake has depths of over 5m for much of its length, but depths reduce to 3m off Wicor Hard. Above here the creek shoals up to Fareham, where it dries 0·9m off the Lower Quay, with greater drying heights towards the undeveloped edges. The outer Camber Dock has 2·2m, with around 1·6m on the Town Quay itself (but see 'Approach, entrance and navigation', below).

General
Portsmouth is inextricably tied up with the Royal Navy's history. Wherever you look, the Senior Service has made its mark. HMS *Victory* towers over the Royal Dockyard. HMS *Warrior* soars over HMS *Victory*, while the remains of Henry VIII's *Mary Rose* are no less important, for all their comparative modesty. Across the water at Haslar is a submarine museum, with HMS *Alliance* on blocks above the tide. Ships of today's navy are much in evidence, both active and mothballed, and naval buildings abound.

As the battle fleets decline, the economy of the town is bolstered to some extent by the cross-Channel ferries which berth in Fountain Lake, immediately off the M27 spur road.

The upper reaches of Portsmouth Harbour are a great place for dinghy sailors, or Yachtmaster Examiners in search of challenges for their customers on 'green' water. Many sailors will be pleased to learn that water-skiing is forbidden within the domain of QHM (Queen's Harbour Master) Portsmouth, who runs this great port with surprisingly little fuss.

Approach, entrance and navigation
Boat Channel
Vessels under 20m LOA entering harbour should either use the Boat Channel, on the west side of the entrance, or stay close inshore on the east side. Such craft should leave *only* by the Boat Channel. If you

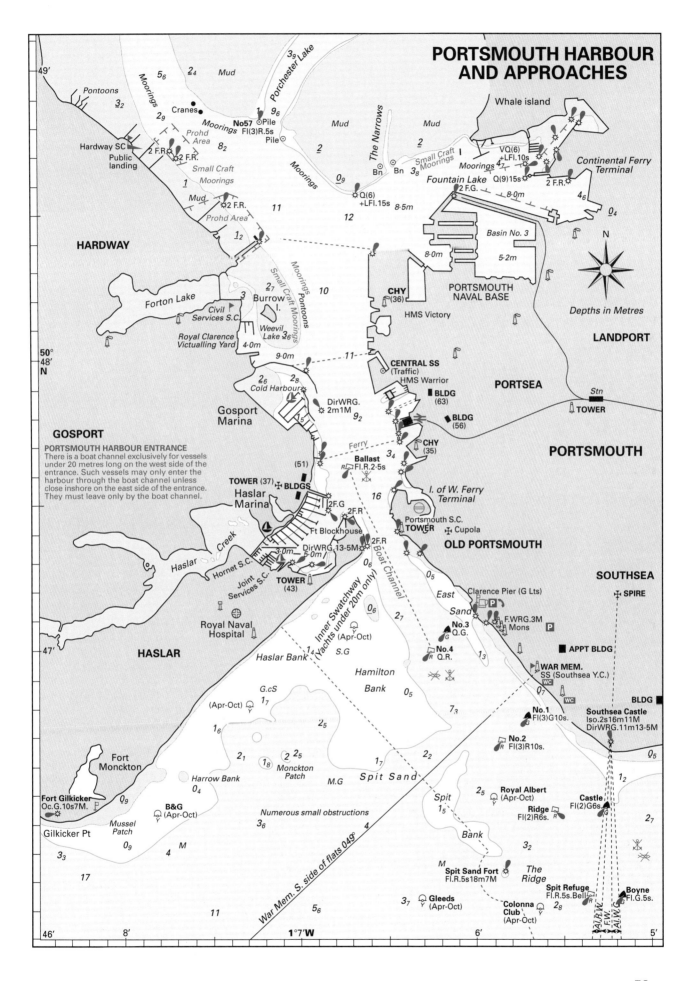

PORTSMOUTH HARBOUR AND APPROACHES

Whale island

Mud

Porchester Lake

Mud

Moorings

Cranes

Pontoons

3·9

2·4

5·6

3·2

2·9

No57 ⊙Pile
Fl(3)R.5s
Pile ⊙

Moorings

1

9·6

Prohd
Area

8·2

Hardway SC
Public
landing

2 F.R.

2 F.R.

Small Craft
Moorings

1

Mud

2 F.R.

Prohd Area

The Narrows

Mud

2

Small Craft
Moorings

2

3·8

Bn   Bn

Fountain Lake

Q(6)
+LFl.15s   8·5m

VQ(6)
+LFl.10s

4·7

Moorings

Q(9)15s   8·0m

N

2 F.G.

Continental Ferry
Terminal

2 F.R.

4·6

0·4

0·9

11

12

HARDWAY

1·2

Basin No. 3

8·0m   5·2m

8·0m

PORTSMOUTH
NAVAL BASE

Depths in Metres

LANDPORT

Forton Lake

3

Burrow
I.

2·7

Moorings Pontoons

10

Small Craft Moorings

CHY
(36)

HMS Victory

Civil
Services S.C.

Royal Clarence
Victualling Yard

Weevil
Lake   3·6

4·0m

2·6

9·0m

11

PORTSEA

Stn

TOWER

Cold Harbour

2·8

DirWRG.
2m1M

9·2

CENTRAL SS
(Traffic)
HMS Warrior

BLDG
(63)

BLDG
(56)

PORTSMOUTH

Gosport
Marina

2·6

2·8

5

Ferry

3·4

CHY
(35)

GOSPORT

PORTSMOUTH HARBOUR ENTRANCE

There is a boat channel exclusively for vessels
under 20 metres long on the west side of the
entrance. Such vessels may only enter the
harbour through the boat channel unless
close inshore on the east side of the entrance.
They must leave only by the boat channel.

TOWER (37)

Haslar
Marina

BLDGS

Ballast
Fl.R.2·5s

(51)

2F.G

2F.R

Ft Blockhouse

16

I. of W. Ferry
Terminal

Portsmouth S.C.
TOWER   Cupola

OLD PORTSMOUTH

SOUTHSEA

SPIRE

Haslar
Creek

Hornet S.C.

3·0m

DirWRG.13·5M
5·0m

2F.R

Joint
Services S.C.

TOWER
(43)

Boat Channel

East
Sand

Clarence Pier (G Lts)

F.WRG.3M
Mons

P

APPT BLDG

Royal Naval
Hospital

HASLAR

Inner Swatchway
(Yachts under 20m only)

0·6

0·6

S.G

Haslar Bank

(Apr-Oct)

1·4

2·7

0·5

No.3
Q.G.

No.4
Q.R.

1·3

WAR MEM.
SS (Southsea Y.C.)

WC

WC

BLDG

G.cS

(Apr-Oct)

1·7

Hamilton
Bank

0·5

0·7

7·3

No.1
Fl(3)G10s.

Southsea Castle
Iso.2s16m11M
DirWRG.11m13-5M

1·6

2·5

0·5

2·2

No.2
Fl(3)R10s.

Fort
Monckton

2·1

1·8

2   2·5

Monckton
Patch

M.G

Spit Sand

1·7

Spit

1·5

2·5

Royal Albert
(Apr-Oct)

Ridge
Fl(2)R6s.

Castle
Fl(2)G6s.

2·7

Fort Gilkicker
Oc.G.10s7M.

0·9

Harrow Bank

0·4

B&G
(Apr-Oct)

Numerous small obstructions

3·6

Bank

3·2

1·2

Gilkicker Pt

Mussel
Patch

0·9

4   M

4

War Mem. S. side of flats 049°

Spit Sand Fort
Fl.R.5s18m7M

The
Ridge

Spit Refuge
Fl.R.5s.Bell

Boyne
Fl.G.5s.

3·3

17

11

5·6

Gleeds
(Apr-Oct)

3·7

2·8

Colonna
Club
(Apr-Oct)

Al.R.W.

F.W.

Al.W.G.

War memorial transit 049°

In the Boat Channel: leaving *No. 4* buoy close to starboard heading to pass close to Fort Blockhouse

Portsmouth. Entrance between Fort Blockhouse on the left and Old Portsmouth on the right. Small Boat Channel is on the extreme left-hand side, leaving red beacons close to port

Red beacons off Fort Blockhouse which must be left close outside by small craft

Approach to Gosport Marina, with fuel barge at the end of wave baffles

Ballast buoy off entrance to Haslar Creek. Small craft must pass to the west of it

have an engine, you must use it between red *No. 4* buoy (Q.R, the last port-hand mark before the entrance) and the red *Ballast* buoy (Fl.R.2·5s), the first red you come to a cable or so inside. The Boat Channel is situated immediately outside the main channel until the entrance is reached, at which point vessels making use of it must stay as close as they dare to the two red posts with topmarks a few metres off the bank.

The approach from eastward simply follows the buoyed channel from Horse Sand and No Man's Land Forts past *Saddle* (VQ.G), *Horse Sand* (Fl.G.2·5s) and so on to the Boat Channel. It is important to maintain a good lookout. Yachts should be ready to leave the channel for the navigable water outside it well before the arrival of any commercial vessel. Approaching along the coast from the direction of Langstone and Chichester Harbour, you may opt for the passage through the Horse Sand submerged barrier, given a sufficient rise of tide.

From the west, leave Fort Gilkicker (Oc.G.10s7M) a cable to port. You now have 3 choices. You can steer about 110° towards *Outer Spit* south cardinal, and so join the main channel, turning to port south of Spit Sand Fort as your draught dictates, but bearing in mind that south of the fort there is always at least 2·1m of water. This route is, however, time-consuming and devious. The preferred course is to cross Spit Sand with a minimum of 1·8m on the transit (049°) of the War Memorial on Southsea front in line with the right-hand side of the yellow apartment building behind it. Watch your echo sounder as you cross the sand, and as soon as the bottom falls away to 5m or more, turn in towards the harbour entrance, keeping the red main channel buoys close to starboard.

To the northwest of this transit lies Hamilton Bank, the inshore end of which dries 0·6m. There is a channel inside the drying patch with a depth of 0·5m which is forbidden to vessels over 20m LOA and is only recommended to navigators with local knowledge. However, a yacht drawing 1·8m or less can make use of it subject to a sensible tide rise. Use the chart, and keep within a cable of the wall for the final 2 cables before the harbour mouth (once past the white tower 100m behind the wall), closing to 100m or less at the corner itself. This will keep you off Hamilton Bank. It should be noted that the bank does shift. A transit is being considered that will lead in through this channel. In the meantime, it should be used with the greatest caution.

Both these latter approaches are unlit, so should only be used at night with caution, or a more than ample rise of tide. If you do opt to cross Spit Sand or Hamilton Bank after dark, watch out for unlit buoys.

By night, note the sectored light on Fort Blockhouse, on the western entrance. Occulting white (fixed when on 320°) puts you squarely in the centre of the channel as far as *No.4* buoy. Oc.G says you are on the starboard side of the channel, red places you to port. If you see Al.WG, or Al.WR, it tells you that you are straying out to that side.

From *No.4* buoy, the lead in is taken over by a directional light set up half a mile inside the entrance by Gosport Marina. This takes you onto about 335° and shows isophase white in the central channel, with Al.WR to port, and Al.WG to starboard. If you see isophase white, you are neither in the Boat Channel nor close enough to the east side. Take action accordingly.

Tides in the entrance run very hard, up to a maximum of 5 knots on spring ebb. There may be counter-currents on the flood, particularly on the west edge of the channel just inside the entrance. Once inside, proceed as follows:

Old Portsmouth. Entrance to the Camber. Ferry terminal on left. Proceed ahead to where fishing boat is lying, then swing to starboard into dock

Some yachts berths are available on the right after rounding the Bridge Tavern

The Camber

The Camber entrance lies immediately north of the peninsula of Old Portsmouth, with its conspicuous pubs, which is on your starboard hand as you enter the harbour. Unless you have arrived along the east side, however, do not turn to starboard until you reach *Ballast* buoy. Leave the Isle of Wight ferry terminal to port and follow the dock round.

Haslar Creek

Haslar Creek, running southwest from the immediate vicinity of the main harbour entrance, has long been the home of HMS *Hornet* and the Joint Services Sailing Club. Their marina on the south side, well up the creek, is private. For the public Haslar Marina, see 'Marinas', below.

Fareham Lake

Fareham Lake is the western channel of the two into which the upper harbour divides about 1½ miles inside the entrance. The lower part of the channel is defined by big-ship moorings and moth-balled warships. These peter out above Bomb Ketch and Spider Lakes, which are largely filled with private moorings. From here on, the channel is marked by green and red posts, some of which are lit.

Do not be distracted by the red pile (*No.57*, Fl(3)R.5s) on your starboard hand at the lower end of the channel. This marks the entrance to Portchester Lake, for which it is a port-hand marker.

Yachts drawing 2m can navigate up to the drying Fareham Quay for two hours either side of HW, but note that you will have to pass under power cables with a height of 12m.

Portsmouth harbour entrance. Camber Dock immediately inside to starboard. Haslar Creek and Marina to port

Below Haslar Marina. Note green lightship on right-hand harbour head. This is very conspicuous as you enter

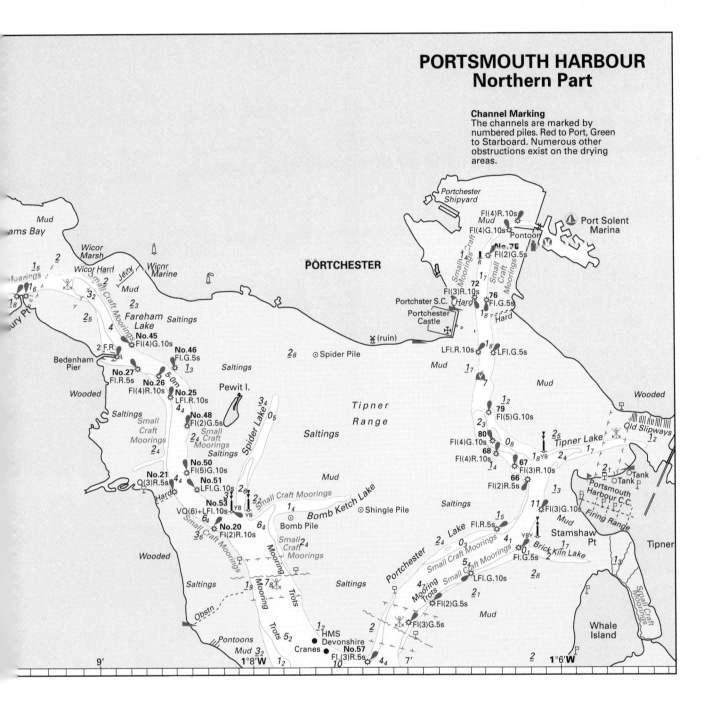

**PORTSMOUTH HARBOUR
Northern Part**

Channel Marking
The channels are marked by numbered piles. Red to Port, Green to Starboard. Numerous other obstructions exist on the drying areas.

Portchester Lake

This begins as described above, between red *No.57* pile and green *No.95*. The channel is sufficiently lit to permit night entry with care. By day it presents no problems until, after turning north-northeast at Brick Kiln Lake, the channel takes a dive to the northwest at green *No.85* pile. Do not confuse piles *No.83* (red) and *No.84* (green) with Portchester channel markers. They indicate the entrance to Tipner Lake.

When Portchester Castle comes abeam to port, you are entering the dredged (1·5m) channel which leads via lit green piles and unlit reds – except for *No.72*, which is Fl(3)R.10s – up to the lock at Port Solent Marina.

Fountain Lake

This is the main eastern arm of the big-ship harbour; the cross-Channel ferries operate from the eastern end. Yachting is discouraged except for boats bound to or from the Naval Sailing Centre at Whale Island.

Moorings and anchorages
Gosport Cruising Club, Weevil Lake
Some moorings may be temporarily available.

Hardway Sailing Club
Half a mile due west of the junction of Portchester and Fareham Lakes, Hardway Sailing Club has a number of piles painted red with orange tops which may be used by visitors whose length does not exceed 10·6m (35ft). The club is very active and has the usual shore facilities. Provisions can be bought

nearby, as can chandlery and *Calor Gas/Camping Gaz* refills. The club has a restaurant, and the streets behind hold further possibilities for the adventurous diner, including a Chinese takeaway.

Wicor Marine

Further up Fareham Lake, still in well over 3m LAT, is Wicor Marine. Here, a well equipped and friendly yard welcomes you to use any spare moorings and to avail yourself of the shower facilities. Chandlery with *Calor Gas/Camping Gaz* exchange. All repair services. Water and diesel (HW±3 hours).

The Camber

Tie up alongside the wall in the vicinity of the Bridge Tavern which, although face-lifted and given new furnishings, is far from being the pub it once was. The wall has a number of wicked girders and pilings, so berth with care.

Anchoring

Portsmouth Harbour presents an unattractive anchoring prospect, unless your yacht can dry out upright in mud. In this case, no doubt an independent spirit would find a quiet corner full of interest.

Marinas
Haslar Marina

Magnificent marina with excellent shelter and deep water. This is the company which started the move back to realistic marina prices on the central South Coast. Their big visitors' berths can accommodate anyone who turns up, even a 45m yacht.

Above Port Solent
Below Gosport Marina

Approach is easy up Haslar Creek in 8m of water and more. Call on VHF Ch 80 as you approach. The office is manned 24 hours a day. Facilities are first class, with toilet, wash basin and shower in each ensuite cubicle. Laundry, ice, public phone and a proper chandlery (not a boutique with a few small shackles) which will open at any hour in order to get you on your way. Divers on site, as well as diesel and outboard engineers.

The marina maintains a light vessel where the Royal Albert Yacht Club have a bar and restaurant to which visitors are welcome. But before committing yourself, see first 'The Castle' noted in 'Gosport Marina'. Well worth the ten minutes it may take you to walk it. After all, your legs need a stretch after a day's yachting, and your taste buds will be rewarded for the effort.

If not even this first-class establishment suits your fancy, the berthing masters are skilled in directing you to the better of the lesser-known pubs in the immediate vicinity. Gosport itself and the Portsmouth Ferry are ten minutes' walk.

Gosport Marina

No problem with pilotage here. Call them up on VHF Ch 37 or 80 (24-hour watch, call sign *Camper Base*). Beware of tides running through the berths. Depths vary, but there are plenty with deep draught. Advise the berthing master of your length and draught when you call.

Camper and Nicholson's, to which the marina is attached, can hoist 180 tons, and can cope with all repairs and emergencies. There is also a scrubbing grid, chandlery, diesel, fresh water, launderette and marina club with all the usual facilities.

The outer berths at Gosport Marina can be subject to wash and some surge. Immediately outside Camper's gates stands the Castle public house. Inside is a haven of joy, not too rough, but definitely ready, with the finest ales and food to suit all tastes. The wine list is realistic, the word is getting around (1999) and if you sit in there long enough, you will meet every serious sailor you ever knew.

Port Solent Marina

Large, modern locked marina development at the top of Portchester Creek, at the upper end of the 1·5m dredged channel. Call *Port Solent* VHF Ch 37, or 80, for the lock-keeper. The locks work 24 hours a day, with some free flow around HW. All the usual marina facilities await you inside, plus many shops and an on-site supermarket, open 0800–2200 every day. Yacht club open to visiting sailors. 40-ton hoist, various repair companies.

Communications

Isle of Wight car ferries. Cross-channel ferries. Railway station with trains to all parts.

Bembridge

Tides

Long stand at HW, the beginning of which is approx +0014 Dover

Range

MHWS	MLWS	MHWN	MLWN
3·1m	0·2m	2·3m	0·5m

Depths

The entrance channel may dry in the vicinity of red buoys *No.6* and *No.6a*, through to *No.10*, but the tide gauge beacon at its entrance indicates depth of water at its shallowest part. Much of the harbour itself also dries, but within the channels there is more than enough water to accommodate any craft which can pass the bar. Vessels drawing 1·8m can lie afloat on visitors' pontoons at LAT, while a minimum of 1·5m is promised at LAT on the marina. Deeper water than this exists in the pool just inside the entrance, where moorings may occasionally be available by arrangement with Attrill's or Coombes' boatyards.

General

Brading Haven, with Bembridge at its seaward end and St Helen's at the other, was once a busy Roman port. It has long since silted up, however, leaving only limited access and mooring areas for yachts. Since Elizabethan days St Helen's Roads outside have provided shelter, so long as westerlies predominate. This anchorage is still good today, though considerable quantities of kelp may necessitate more than one 'try' before you are confident your hook is holding.

St Helen's Fort, which stands ¾ mile northeast of the entrance, was built by Palmerston in 1860 to guard against a French invasion which never materialised. A second prominent navigational feature, which has even less social relevance nowadays, is the conspicuous whitewashed seamark on the Duver foreshore south of Node's Point. This is the remains of a 13th-century church, most of which slid into the sea in 1550. Stones from its ruins were widely used for scouring wooden decks, hence, according to local folklore, their being known as 'holystones'.

Bembridge beacon. Tide gauge shows depth at shallowest part of channel

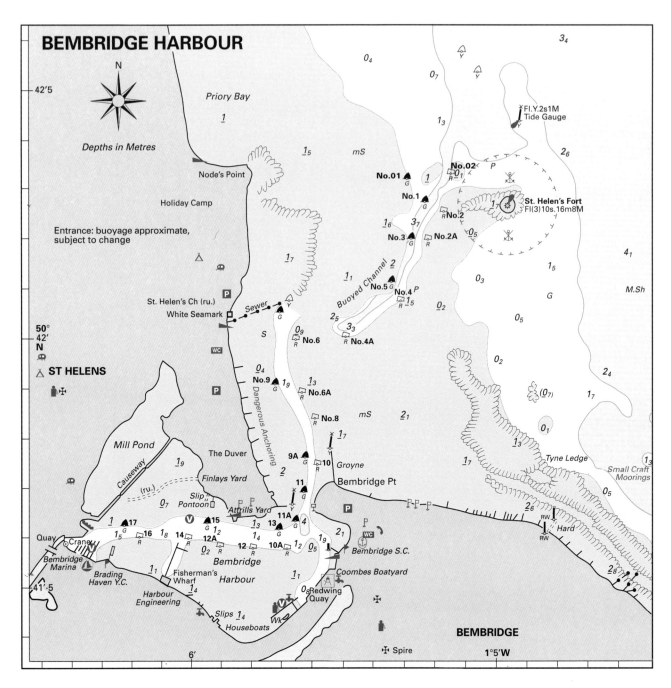

BEMBRIDGE HARBOUR

N

Depths in Metres

Priory Bay

Node's Point

Holiday Camp

Entrance: buoyage approximate,
subject to change

St. Helen's Ch (ru.)
White Seamark

ST HELENS

Mill Pond

The Duver

Causeway

Finlays Yard

(ru.)

Slip
Pontoon

Attrills Yard

Quay
Crane
Bembridge
Marina
Brading
Haven Y.C.

Fisherman's
Wharf
Harbour
Engineering

Slips

Houseboats

Bembridge
Harbour

Sewer

Dangerous Anchoring

Buoyed Channel

No.01
No.02
No.1
No.2
No.3
No.2A
No.5
No.4
No.4A
No.6
No.9
No.6A
No.8
9A
Groyne
Bembridge Pt
10
11
11A
13
12A
12
10A
4
15
16
14
17

Coombes Boatyard

Redwing
Quay

Bembridge S.C.

St. Helen's Fort
Fl(3)10s.16m8M

Fl.Y.2s1M
Tide Gauge

M.Sh

Tyne Ledge
Small Craft
Moorings

Hard

Spire

BEMBRIDGE

1°5'W

Access to Bembridge is limited by the nature of the entrance channel, whose depth and whereabouts are modified, apparently at random, by the shifting sands. Buoyage is maintained, however, so a stranger may enter with confidence, given a rising tide, a sensible clearance and seamanlike caution.

Approach and entrance
From the west, make for the yellow tide gauge beacon (Fl.Y.2s). Beware of the shoals and extending rocks off Nettlestone and Horestone Points. Coming from the east, leave St Helen's Fort at least a cable to port before heading up for the tide gauge. From the northeast, open the transit between the right-hand edge of St Helen's Fort and the white daymark, then steer for the yellow beacon. Night entry into Bembridge is not recommended without

local knowledge, as the channel itself is unlit and may be tortuous. The yellow light is also very feeble.

From the beacon, enter between green and red buoys Nos. 01 and 02. Now follow the buoys implicitly. On first seeing them from seaward they may present a confusing image, but so long as you work through the numbers in order and have read the tide gauge to your satisfaction, all will be well.

Once inside the entrance, look for Nos. 11A and 13 green cones. Swing round to starboard past the moorings, keeping red cans 10A and 12 to port. Now proceed in a westerly direction, past the visitors' pontoons to the east of green No.15, between buoys 16 (red) and 17 (green) until you reach Bembridge Marina.

Bembridge entrance

Berthing

No anchoring is allowed in the harbour (nor, incidentally, within 200m of St Helen's Fort), with the exception of the sandy beach in front of Bembridge Sailing Club and the harbourmaster's office. Here shoal-draught yachts may moor fore and aft and dry out.

Deep-water berthing (not less than 1·5m LAT) is available at Bembridge Marina (VHF Ch 80 at HW±3 hours during daylight). The visitors' berths are on the first and second pontoons (Nos. 5 and 6). Before departing, check the marina tide gauge which indicates the least depth in the entrance channel.

Berths are also available for visitors on the detached pontoons west of No. 15 buoy, up to three abreast on the south side.

Facilities

Brading Haven Yacht Club (☎ 01983 872289) immediately east of the marina is an active sailing club with 1,500 members. The club welcomes visiting yachtsmen and provides hot meals, generous bar hours, showers and toilet facilities. Its private pier can be used for landing by dinghy.

Bembridge Marina has its own car park, toilets, fresh water, showers and rubbish skips.

Bembridge Sailing Club, with its fleet on private moorings occupies the southwest corner of the harbour. Visitors by invitation.

Fuel and repairs at Attrill's Yard, opposite No. 13 buoy (☎ 01983 872319), or at Stratton's, near No. 17 buoy.

Chandlery, marine engineer and sailmaker near the Bembridge Sailing Club (☎ 01983 872686). Bembridge village has all facilities including two restaurants and a pub offering meals, but it is a long walk from the marina. A ten-minute stroll up to St Helen's Green brings you to The Vine, a village PO and stores, and two further restaurants.

Excellent swimming from the safe, sandy beach on the seaward side of the harbour. Many first-class walks. Fresh fish and lobster can be bought straight off the boats down at Fishermen's quay. Just be there around HW and ask the guys as they land the catch. Sadly, Captain Stan, who used to ply a colourful trade in fishmongery from his own doughty craft, has been closed down by the 'health and safety'.

Communications

Buses to Sandown and Ryde, whence you can cross to Southsea by catamaran or hovercraft. Taxis from Bembridge Harbour Taxis (☎ 01983 874132).

Bembridge Harbour

Ryde

Tides
Similar to Portsmouth
HW Dover + 0015

MHWS	MLWS	MHWN	MLWN
4·5m	0·9m	3·7m	1·9m

Depths
The harbour is charted as drying 1·3m, but there is definitely less water than that anywhere away from the entrance. The compiler of the *Shell Pilot* has been aground in a number of locations not too far inside at HWN while hunting for a berth with 2m draught. However, this should not deter the adventurous, and a colleague with the Laurent Giles-designed classic in the photograph had a fine time of it dried out alongside the wall in peace. He draws around 1·5m and found access ±1½ hours HW on a 4·1m tide at Portsmouth.

General
Ever since paddle-wheel ferries from Southsea linked the main railway network to all parts of the Isle of Wight, Ryde has been its largest town. The community's winter population is 34,000, swollen by swarms of summer visitors.

Ryde now has its own artificial 150-berth yacht harbour, enclosed by a substantial breakwater, approximately 2 cables east of Ryde pier. The harbour dries completely at LW, leaving a sandy bottom on which suitable craft may take the ground with confidence. It is well sheltered from all directions except northwest, when strong conditions may bring in some surge at the top of the tide.

Successful rallies have been organised at Ryde. These began in 1993; the harbourmaster will be pleased to supply details (☎ 01983 613879).

Approach
Ryde Harbour is identified from seaward by the ice rink and the ten-pin bowling building. It lies immediately east of these. Maintaining an awareness of the extent of Ryde Sands, proceed to a point 600m east of Ryde pier head. On the edge of the 1m contour, pick up the first of the small, unlit R and G channel buoys on course 197°. From here it is under half a mile to the small northwest-facing entrance. A single directional amber light shining seawards indicates 1m depths inside; a second light above it means not less than 1·5m. There is also a tide gauge. 2F.R are mounted on the breakwater, with 2F.G on your starboard side at the entrance. Night entry is assisted by a floodlight, directed shorewards, mounted on the end of the breakwater.

Visitors should realise that the buoyed channel is not dredged. It exists to keep yachts clear of hovercraft manoeuvring to and from their terminal close by. Keep in the channel and you have rights. Stray from it and you may be deemed responsible for any resulting difficulties involving hovercraft.

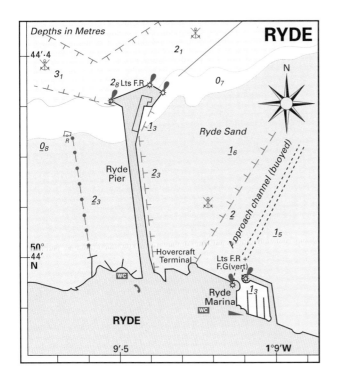

Berths

There are up to 70 visitors' berths in the harbour. Tie up either alongside the eastern arm of the breakwater or on the nearest pontoon to it. There is a slipway at the southwest corner. Deep-keeled yachts can dry out on firm sand against the wooden piles mounted on the inner side of the breakwater. The firmest sand is beside the fourth ladder in, which is the nearest one to the harbourmaster's office. Moor at ladders where piling is closest together. Fender boards provided. The harbourmaster's office is in a portacabin at the southeast corner. Contact him on ☎ 01983 613879, or on VHF Ch 80 – call sign *Ryde Harbour*. Be sure not to call 'Ryde Marina', as this has led to confusion with nearby 'Hythe Marina' in the past.

On no account pump heads or bilges whilst in the harbour.

Facilities

Fresh water, toilets, showers, car parking and garbage disposal.

No fuel or repair facilities at the harbour, and generally speaking, Ryde is light on technical support for yachts. Diesel and petrol are, however, available from a garage within walking distance, and there are numerous pubs, bars, restaurants, hotels, B&Bs, banks and all the other comforts of a large town.

Communications

By catamaran to Portsmouth Station and the main line, or hovercraft to Southsea. Buses to all parts of the Island. Railway to Shanklin.

Fishbourne - Wootton Creek

Tides

Long stand at HW
HW approx +0014 Dover
Range

MHWS	MLWS	MHWN	MLWN
4·5m	0·7m	3·7m	1·9m

Depths

3m in the dredged fairway as far as the ferry terminal. Thereafter the creek dries, except for a channel of 0·3–0·6m and a 2m dredged pool at Fishbourne Quay.

General

Fishbourne has considerable natural beauty and offers attractive amenities ashore. It has limited room for visiting deep-keeled yachts, although it provides excellent shelter for shoal-draught craft and those able to take the ground. The east bank of the entrance to Wootton Creek is largely given over to the busy terminal for RoRo ferries linking the Island to Old Portsmouth.

Approach and entrance

Whether you approach Wootton from east or west, watch for off-lying dangers. From the east, keep outside the line from Ryde pier head to the north cardinal *Wootton* beacon (Q.1M), which lies 1½ miles west of Ryde pier and ½ mile offshore, and marks the seaward end of the 3m dredged fairway. From the west, avoid Peel Wreck, marked by an unlit red can and, close to the entrance, Wootton Rocks, whose position is indicated by a post or withy with a topmark.

The 224° fairway is clearly marked by four beacons on its starboard hand and two to port: *No.1* Fl(2)G.5s, *No.2* Fl.R.5s, *No.3* Fl.G.3s, *No.4* Fl.R.2·5s, *No.5* Fl.G.2·5s and *No.7* Q.G. A directional Oc.WRG.10s light inshore of the ferry ramp shows a narrow 1·5° white sector when you are on course; green means you are off to starboard, red indicates straying port of the line. 2F.R lights are exhibited from the end of the jetty at the east side of the ferry berth. There is very little water either side of the fairway inshore of beacons 2 and 3, so do not use the channel during a ferry movement. In fog, a bell is rung from the ferry jetty.

Just beyond *No.7* beacon, work round to starboard onto a westerly heading, bringing the two triangular leading marks on the western bank into line. These indicate the run of the best water through the pool and into the creek, though it is also worth taking note of the lie of the moorings. Note the very tatty red and green unlit buoys, steer between these onto the transit. If continuing further, watch for a small green buoy off a jetty exhibiting a speed limit sign, and leave it very close to starboard. This will keep you clear of the gravel spit extending out into the creek on your port side. The small red buoy following it must be left to port, as must a line

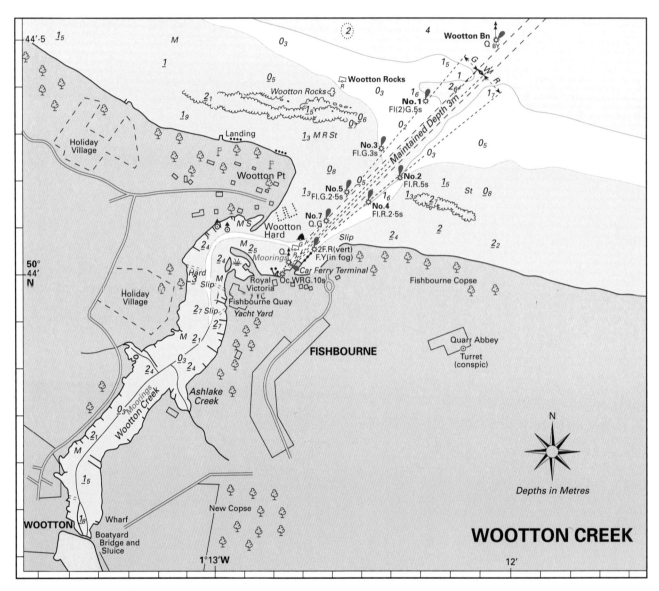

WOOTTON CREEK

Depths in Metres

of old piles, after which Fishbourne Quay is immediately at hand. To proceed beyond this point, keep to the starboard side and follow the line of moored boats for the best water in the fairway.

Berths and moorings

Anchorage (no charge) can be found on the north side of the fairway opposite the yacht club. You will probably dry out at half-ebb – as you will if you anchor further up the creek – but the bottom is soft mud. Do not anchor in the fairway. Wherever you bring up, an anchor buoy is advisable.

Apart from privately owned moorings, the Royal Victoria Yacht Club (☎ 01983 882325) has some buoys and four piles for visitors to secure between, fore and aft. These also dry. The boatyard at Fishbourne Quay makes available to visitors its own floating pontoons in a 2m dredged pool. These can be reached by deep-draught yachts around the top of the tide, but do not expect to arrive or leave at less than half-tide.

There is a public landing at Wootton Bridge, accessible to dinghies.

Facilities

Before the war the Royal Victoria Yacht Club had imposing premises on the front at Ryde, from which it conducted racing for all classes, including the J-boats. Its more modest clubhouse in Wootton Creek is still most hospitable to visitors from other clubs and offers full facilities. There are two pubs in the vicinity, both of which provide substantial food: The Fishbourne Inn, close to the ferry, and The Sloop, at Wootton Bridge.

The boatyard has full repair facilities as well as toilets, fuel, fresh water, telephone and a chandlery. In addition to the Sloop Inn, two supermarkets are located near Wootton Bridge. All of these are best visited by dinghy on the tide, unless you enjoy a long walk.

Communications

Depending upon season, the car ferry to Portsmouth leaves on the hour – sometimes the half-hour – from first light until midnight.

Buses from Wootton Bridge go to Ryde and Newport.

Taxis on ☎ 01983 884345 or 883421.

Wootton Creek

Cowes

Tides
Double HW at springs, otherwise a 2-hour stand.
HW approx +0021 Dover

MHWS	MLWS	MHWN	MLWN
4·2m	0·8m	5m	1·8m

Depths
A minimum of 2·2m (LAT) in the fairway, continuing to one cable south of the chain ferry (known locally as the floating bridge), though 2m has been reported (1997) immediately N of here. After a shallow patch which still leaves 1·5m at LAT, deeper water of at least 2·5m extends up-river to within half a mile of The Folly Inn. From this point, at least 1·2m LAT will be found as far as *Medham* beacon, with a minimum of approximately 1m as far as *South Folly* beacon, two cables above the pub. Thereafter, the river shoals gently into the 'drying mode', giving depths on the visitors' pontoons at Newport of at least 2·5m at MHWS, and a minimum of 1·7m at MHWN. It should be noted that the apparently shoal water leading up to The Folly Inn poses little problem in practice to most yachts; even at MLWS a vessel drawing 1·5m can creep up with caution. Deeper-draughted craft whose skippers have been over-ambitious will suffer little worse than a brief sojourn with their keels in soft mud.

General
Cowes lies at the mouth of the Medina River which, on favourable tides, is navigable for 4 miles up to the island's capital, Newport. Cowes itself is sheltered in all but north or northeast winds, but when the weather kicks in from these directions, visitors in the outer harbour can seek shelter above the chain ferry.

Cowes is justly known as England's leading yacht-racing centre. Clubs and facilities of all types abound, and the Castle at the western entrance has been the home of the Royal Yacht Squadron since mid-Victorian days. Full back-up facilities, but do not expect too much at weekends.

Cowes is a community of great character, but is not what the uninformed visitor generally expects. The main street was smartened up during the late 1980s, and fascinating sights abound for the observer with a sharp eye. Nonetheless, the town grew up around ship and yacht yards with a large working population. This meant streets lined with houses more suited to Victorian tradesmen than to the yachtsmen they ultimately served. Do not be dismayed by this. Spend time here and you will begin to discover the rich essence of the place. If you still can't cope with the workaday atmosphere, walk

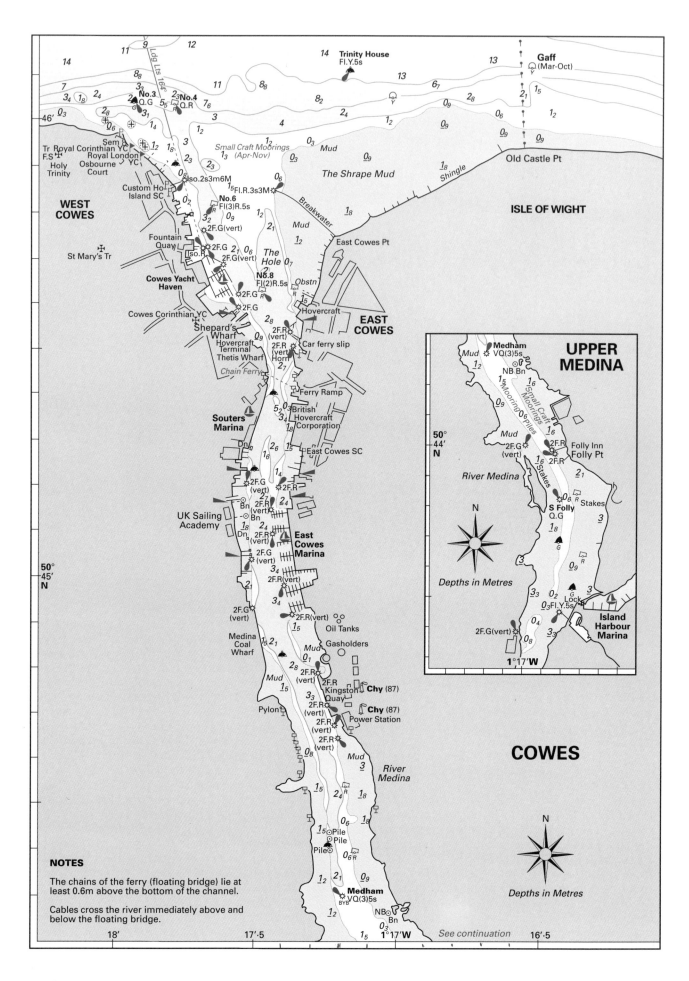

WEST COWES

ISLE OF WIGHT

EAST COWES

UPPER MEDINA

COWES

Depths in Metres

Trinity House
Fl.Y.5s

Gaff (Mar-Oct)

Old Castle Pt

The Shrape Mud

Shingle

Breakwater

Mud

East Cowes Pt

Obstn

The Hole

Hovercraft

Car ferry slip
Horn

Ferry Ramp

British Hovercraft Corporation

East Cowes SC

UK Sailing Academy

East Cowes Marina

Oil Tanks

Gasholders

Medina Coal Wharf

Mud

Kingston Quay
Chy (87)

Power Station
Chy (87)

Pylon

River Medina

Pile
Pile
Pile

Medham
VQ(3)5s

NB Bn

Tr Royal Corinthian YC
F.S
Holy Trinity
Royal London YC
Osbourne Court
Sem
Iso.2s3m6M
Custom Ho
Island SC
No.6
Fl(3)R.5s
St Mary's Tr
Fountain Quay
2F.G
2F.G(vert)
Cowes Yacht Haven
Cowes Corinthian YC
Shepard's Wharf
Hovercraft Terminal
Thetis Wharf
Chain Ferry
Souters Marina
Dn
2F.R (vert)
Bn
Bn
Dn
2F.G (vert)
2F.G (vert)

No.3
Q.G
No.4
Q.R
1.5 Fl.R.3s3M

Medham
VQ(3)5s
NB Bn

Mud
VQ(3)5s
Small Craft Moorings
Mooring Piles
2F.G (vert)
2F.R
2F.R
Folly Inn
Folly Pt
Stakes
Stakes
S Folly
Q.G
River Medina
Lock
Fl.Y.5s
Island Harbour Marina
2F.G(vert)

Depths in Metres

50°
44'
N

1°17'W

COWES

Depths in Metres

50°
45'
N

50°
46'

NOTES

The chains of the ferry (floating bridge) lie at least 0.6m above the bottom of the channel.

Cables cross the river immediately above and below the floating bridge.

Small Craft Moorings (Apr-Nov)

18'   17'·5   1°17'W   *See continuation*   16'·5

round past the Castle to Cowes Green, where the gentlemen had their villas. It is a different world, and you might run into the ghost of Uffa Fox, watching critically as a latecomer barges on the Squadron Line.

Approach

From whichever direction you head for Cowes, remember that the Solent tides run fast in this vicinity. Coming from the west, rocks lurk close offshore either side of Egypt Point. The Shrape mud-flats catch many a navigator taking the most direct course from Old Castle Point in the east, and whatever the state of the tide, never cut through the closely packed moorings for racing keelboats which extend both sides of the breakwater.

One of Britain's busiest shipping lanes runs past Cowes Harbour entrance. Solent bylaws give commercial craft right of way over all yachts at all times, besides which, to impede the progress of a supertanker setting up to make the tight turn round the Bramble Bank could have the gravest ecological consequences. The harbour itself is also subject to commercial traffic, with coasters running up to Medina Wharf and beyond. Add car ferries to this, as well as high-speed passenger transport, and the necessity of keeping a good lookout both ahead and astern will be clear. Listen on VHF Ch 69 – the port working frequency.

The most prominent seamark off Cowes is the north cardinal *Prince Consort* buoy (VQ) 4 cables northeast of the red can *No.4* fairway buoy (Q.R). This pairs with the green conical *No.3* buoy (Q.G), and between them lies the 164° leading line with its two Iso.2s lights. The front one is white, on a pile off the slip by the customs watch-house, downstream from the Island Sailing Club pontoon; the rear one is red, on another pile by the Jubilee ferry pontoon. Each has a tide gauge showing water above chart datum in the fairway. You may not notice these during a daytime entry, but the river is so straightforward in daylight that failing to spot them will not trouble you.

Proceeding up the fairway, there are two red can buoys on the port hand. *No.6* (Fl(3)R.5s) is followed, close to the East Cowes ferry terminal, by *No.8* (Fl(2)R.5s). Jubilee Pier, the West Cowes catamaran terminal, next to the Old Town Quay, is marked by 2F.G(vert) at each end, as are the limits of the Cowes Yacht Haven. The breakwater off East Cowes Point has a Fl.R.3s3M light.

The river above *No.8* buoy has plenty of water (subject to depths given above) as far as Folly Inn. If in doubt, stay in the middle. Although there is not a great deal in the way of lit navigational marks above the chain ferry, night entry is easy enough because of the essentially straightforward character of the

Cowes, East and West and the River Medina. Note moorings to the east of the channel. Stay inside these when approaching from the east. There may be less water amongst them than you imagine

The Castle is the home of the Royal Yacht Squadron

Cowes looking downstream. East Cowes Marina far right. UK Sailing Academy at left. The floating bridge (chain ferry) is at the narrows immediately below the ferry

river and the ambient light from shore establishments, though these peter out above Medina Wharf.

Note that tides run very hard through the chain ferry, particularly the spring ebb. Large yachts which may experience difficulty manoeuvring under these circumstances should call the chain ferry on Ch 69 and advise.

The speed limit is 6 knots over the ground.

Berths and moorings

Cowes is well stocked with berthing facilities, as it needs to be during Cowes Week or on the weekend set aside in early June for the Round the Island Race, which often sees 1,500 yachts on the starting line.

Berths may be allocated by the harbourmaster from his launch or his office, situated between the Jubilee Pier and Cowes Yacht Haven. Contact him on VHF Ch 69 or by phone (☎ 01983 293952), manned during working hours. There are five visitors' buoys just downstream of the Island Sailing Club, and a shore-access pontoon for visitors at Thetis Wharf, near the chain ferry, with walkway access to the shore. The harbourmaster also has fore-and-aft pontoon berths further upstream. There is talk (1999) of a new basin for short stays by the Town Quay. Moorings which are owned by clubs are clearly marked. Other moorings are privately controlled.

Anchoring is prohibited in Cowes Harbour itself. It is permitted out of the fairway up-river south of the last of the moorings, but is likely to be impractical unless you want to dry out.

Visitors are also accommodated on a selection of berths off the Folly Inn, 1½M upstream of the Chain Ferry. Here, you may lie on midstream deepwater pontoons strung between piles, or try your luck in the orchestra stalls alongside a step-ashore pontoon beside the long, narrow jetty along which those dignifying ashore from the river berths must teeter at closing time. If you draw more than 1½m or so, you may poke your keel into the mud at LWS, but this does not create problems as the mud is very soft. If you are deep draughted, wait until

±1½ hours LW before moving into the berth. The Folly may not be everyone's ideal of a bijou pub but, like Cowes itself, the place grows upon those who frequent it. Now renovated and extended, the establishment retains its unique character and offers good facilities as well as fine ales to the weary sailor.

The Cowes harbourmaster's jurisdiction extends two miles upstream as far as the Folly Inn. Beyond that, Medina Borough Council's Marine Authority controls all the berths in the river. There is a small harbour office at the head of the pier next to The Folly Inn. Call *Folly Launch* on Ch 69, or ☎ 01983 295722 for berthing assistance if nobody has approached you. After hours, use your initiative and relax. The staff here are very laid back.

Newport offers alongside drying-out berths at the Odessa Yard on the west bank, and at the Town Quay opposite, close to the end of navigable water. The harbourmaster listens on Ch 69, or can be reached on ☎ 01983 525994.

Marinas

Cowes Yacht Haven (formerly Groves and Gutteridge, Ancasta and West Cowes Marina) is now dredged to 3m near the fairway and 2·5m close inshore within the south basin. It has 220 pontoon berths, a high proportion of them for visitors. During peak periods you may find yourself rafted up on the river side of the long pontoon, exposed to the wash of passing traffic and onshore winds. Call *Cowes Yacht Haven* on VHF Ch 80.

Shepard's Wharf, downstream from the chain ferry, has some pontoon berths. Contact ☎ 01983 297821.

UK Sailing Academy (the old National Sailing Centre) maintains a small marina on the west bank a little under 3 cables above the chain ferry. A limited number of visitors' berths are available on a first-come, first-served basis. No VHF watch is kept, but the berth is a snug one in all conditions. Showers and toilets. Shore access via Arctic Road, with a 15-minute walk to Cowes centre.

East Cowes Marina has 300 berths for boats drawing up to 4m. Contact on Ch 80, or ☎ 01983 293983. Excellent shelter, but shoreside amenities are limited and less accessible than those in West Cowes. Showers, chandlery, riggers on site, and if you want to hit the flesh-pots in preference to the more pedestrian pubs over this side, you can either walk to the floating bridge (chain ferry) or take the regular water taxi.

Island Harbour (formerly Medina Marina), half a mile upstream from the Folly, is a 180-berth locked harbour for boats up to 15·2m (50ft) LOA. It is accessible at the top half of the tide by way of a clearly marked buoyed channel off the fairway. Movements through the locks are ordered from a prominent white control tower by red or green traffic lights. Full marina facilities include the Skipper licensed restaurant and the nearby converted paddle-wheel ferry *Ryde Queen*. Contact on VHF Ch 80, or ☎ 01983 526020. There is a waiting pontoon immediately outside the lock-gate.

The town quay, Newport, Isle of Wight   *John Cole*

Facilities

Cowes offers yachtsmen every facility they may require. There are cranes at Thetis Wharf and Souter's, and a travel-hoist at Cowes Yacht Haven, whilst Lallow's slip can handle all but the largest boats. Cowes Yacht Haven and Shepard's Wharf are amongst several who can tackle most engineering, electronic and structural problems. The latter hires tools for owners to carry out their own work.

Yacht clubs: Island Sailing Club, Cowes Corinthian, Royal Corinthian, Royal London and the Royal Yacht Squadron.

There are restaurants and pubs to suit all tastes and pockets.

Fuel is available 24 hours at the yacht haven, at Lallow's pier and from the bunkering barge operated by Marine Support Bunkering off Souter's; they also have *Calor Gas*. Island Harbour has its own fuelling point inside.

Various chandlers, including Pascall Atkey right in the middle of town.

Customs are in the watch-house next to the Island Sailing Club. ☎ 01983 293132. Out of hours ☎ 02380 827350.

Communications

Car ferries run regularly from East Cowes terminal. Catamarans to Southampton from Jubilee Pier, every half-hour from 0630–2230 (2330 Fri/Sat). Both have connecting bus services to Southampton main line railway station with services to Waterloo and the West.

Frequent buses to Newport with connections to the rest of the Island.

Taxi stands at each ferry terminal, or call Tony's Taxi on ☎ 01836 248679 or Russell's on 01983 292083.

Island Harbour ½ miles upstream from Folly Inn. (A) Harbour office. (B) Fuel berth. (C) Medway Queen restaurant

Hamble River

Tides

Double HW
First HW springs approx Dover −0020

MHWS	MLWS	MHWN	MLWN
4·5m	0·8m	3·8m	2·0m

Depths

Over 3m LAT as far as Port Hamble. At least 2·8m from there up to *Crableck* beacon above Mercury Yacht Harbour. Half a cable above *Crableck* beacon, depths fall fractionally below 2m for a few yards, then 2m and more will be encountered as far as the Elephant Boatyard. Between the Elephant and Bursledon Bridge, depths may shoal to 1·5m LAT.

General

The Hamble offers all-weather shelter except to vessels moored close to the entrance in strong winds from south through southwest. Enough visitors' berths are available to encourage an interesting stop-over. The density of the Hamble's private moorings and marinas and the diversity of craft occupying them make the river a must for the sailing enthusiast. Night entry is possible with care on a first visit, at least as far as Port Hamble.

The charm that the river and its banks must have exhibited before the yachting revolution is not now always easy to spot, though extensive mud-flats and sedge still contrive to avoid the developers' dredgers. Hamble village itself has a tumbly main street with pubs and other temptations. Warsash offers little to the pleasure-seeker. At Old Bursledon, however, connoisseurs of great yards will discover the Elephant Boatyard still purveying traditional skills alongside the best of the modern. They will also discover interesting walks, good pubs and fascinating views. The mighty Swanwick Marina across the river gives inspiration to those who would bring nature under control, but down-river on the east bank the Crableck supplies a haven of unspoilt delight. No shareholders' group has ever contrived to concrete these meadows by floating a new share issue. Here, the birds still sing, and a poor man may yet moor his yacht in the ancient, accommodating mud of Hampshire.

Approach and entrance

Coming in from the West Solent, make tracks for *Hamble Point* south cardinal buoy (Q(6)+LFl.15s), taking care not to impede commercial traffic passing up and down from Southampton and the huge Fawley oil jetties. From the East Solent, head for the same point, watching out for anchored coasters lying between *Hook* (green) and *Coronation* (yellow) buoys. Despite the generally shoal water on your starboard hand, the bottom is as flat as a billiard table in this vicinity, so you can avoid unpleasantness by reading your chart, then keeping an eye on your echo sounder in the confidence that at least nothing sudden will happen.

Approaching from Southampton, do not cut inside the 'spit pile' (*No.2* east cardinal Q(3)10s3M). There is a least depth of 0·8m between here and *Hamble Point* buoy, with over 2·5m for the 100m nearest the buoy, so time your turn accordingly.

Once inside the entrance, follow the channel, clearly marked with red and green piles (noting that *No.6* (red) is marking a dogleg), as far as Warsash and Hamble Point Marina. Above here, although there are a number of lit navigational piles, you will do best by sticking to the centre of the river between the moorings. The density of the mooring piles suddenly thins out above Mercury Marina, and here it is important to identify *Crableck* beacon with its tide gauge, and give it a robust clearance to starboard. To the east of it, the river shoals rapidly.

Now follow between the piles once more in a northeasterly direction past Crableck and Universal yards on your starboard hand. At the head of this reach, take care to keep the red pile to port and the green to starboard as you swing to port towards Bursledon. After making the turn you will see two sets of trots ahead. Pass between these and the marina, then follow the centre of the river up to the Jolly Sailor and the Elephant Boatyard pontoons on your port hand.

Bursledon Bridge is the effective head of navigation of sailing craft, though if your air draught enables you to pass under its 4m height you will also clear the railway and motorway bridges immediately upstream of it. You then enter a different world, where fields and woodland hold sway, and the water off the Horse and Jockey at Curbridge may float the shoalest of craft for long enough to permit a swift lunch-time session on a brewer's (in this case, spring) tide.

By night, enter the river on a northerly heading in the white sector of the occulting light (Oc(2)WRG.12s5m4M) on Hamble Common. You will find this by arriving at the lit *Hamble Point* south cardinal buoy and leaving it close to port. If the light goes G thereafter, turn to port; if R, swing to starboard. You will now pass three lit G piles to starboard and the lit E cardinal *Spit Pile* plus a lit R (Q), before arriving in the W sector of the second leading light which is situated on the Warsash shore. Steer to starboard onto this line, making the same corrections for red and green sectors as before, and keep going past the various lit piles indicated on the plan until Warsash Jetty is abeam. You can't miss this even in the dark. It is operated by a merchant Navy training establishment and features ship's lifeboats hoisted on davits as well as F.G lights at either end. Now steer a touch west of north, leaving the Fl(2+1)R.10s pile to port. Thereafter, follow the various red and green lights and look out for moored craft. If you are proposing to venture north of Port Hamble, moonlight and caution are strongly recommended if you have not seen the river in daylight.

Berthing

Anchoring in the river is impractical except for shoal-draught craft prepared to dry out beyond the fairway.

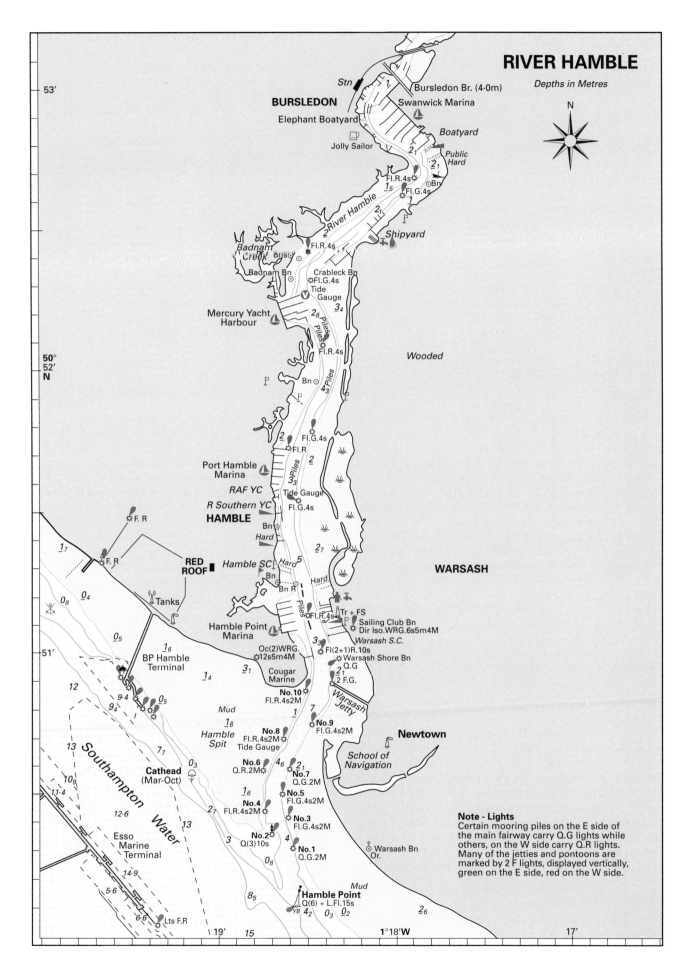

RIVER HAMBLE

Depths in Metres

N

BURSLEDON

Stn

Bursledon Br. (4·0m)

Swanwick Marina

Elephant Boatyard

Boatyard

Jolly Sailor

Public Hard

Fl.R.4s

Bn

River Hamble

Fl.G.4s

Shipyard

Fl.R.4s

Badnam Creek

Bn

Badnam Bn

Crableck Bn
Fl.G.4s
Tide Gauge

Mercury Yacht Harbour

Piles
Piles

Fl.R.4s

Wooded

Bn

Piles

Fl.G.4s
Fl.R

Port Hamble Marina

Piles

RAF YC

R Southern YC

Tide Gauge
Fl.G.4s

HAMBLE

Bn
Hard

F. R

F. R

WARSASH

RED ROOF

Hamble SC
Hard

Bn

Bn R
Hard

Tanks

Piles

Fl.R.4s

Tr + FS
Sailing Club Bn
Dir Iso.WRG.6s5m4M

Hamble Point Marina

Oc(2)WRG.
12s5m4M

Cougar Marine

Warsash S.C.

Fl(2+1)R.10s

Warsash Shore Bn
Q.G
2 F.G.

BP Hamble Terminal

No.10
Fl.R.4s2M

Warsash Jetty

Mud

Hamble Spit

No.8
Fl.R.4s2M
Tide Gauge

No.9
Fl.G.4s2M

Newtown

School of Navigation

12

Southampton Water

Cathead
(Mar-Oct)

No.6
Q.R.2M

No.7
Q.G.2M

No.5
Fl.G.4s2M

No.4
Fl.R.4s2M

No.3
Fl.G.4s2M

No.2
Q(3)10s

Warsash Bn
Or.

No.1
Q.G.2M

Esso Marine Terminal

Mud

Hamble Point
Q(6) + L.Fl.15s

Lts F.R

1°18'W

Note - Lights
Certain mooring piles on the E side of the main fairway carry Q.G lights while others, on the W side carry Q.R lights. Many of the jetties and pontoons are marked by 2 F lights, displayed vertically, green on the E side, red on the W side.

The River Hamble entrance

For the harbourmaster's visitors' berths apply to his launch, or call him at Warsash on VHF Ch 68, or ☎ 01489 576387. Visitors may land at his pontoon in front of the Rising Sun at Warsash for advice, or at the public landing at Hamble, which is administered in a similar way to the pontoon at Warsash. You may be directed to the mid-stream pontoons, clearly marked 'visitors', in deep water just upstream of the harbourmaster's pontoon. Further upstream, just above Port Hamble, are more well marked visitors' piles (Nos. 9–16), with 2·0m LAT. These are comparatively convenient for Hamble village.

It is also sometimes possible to find a berth at The Elephant Boatyard or at Universal Shipyard, on the east bank above Crableck, both by arrangement.

Marinas
Much of the Hamble River berthing is now given over to large marinas which offer the usual facilities. All maintain a number of visitors' berths and monitor VHF Ch 80.

Hamble Point Marina Some depth restrictions here for deeper-draught vessels. If in doubt, check with berthing master. Not the easiest marina for the visiting yachtsman anxious to sample the fleshpots but unwilling to take a cab.

Port Hamble Deep water. Well situated for Hamble village.

Mercury Yacht Harbour Quiet marina a considerable distance from the village.

Swanwick Marina Large marina attached to Moody's Yard. Launderette. Direct access to railway and to the main A27 road where you will find a selection of pubs, none of them what they once were, and an up-market Chinese restaurant. A very short dinghy trip to the Jolly Sailor pub on the waterfront at Old Bursledon. If you don't want to launch your boat, you can walk round in about 20 minutes.

Facilities
All possible facilities are available around the river. Numerous repair yards, some with travel-hoists capable of lifting maxis. Pump-out at the harbourmaster's pontoon at Warsash. Also safe disposal of dead batteries, waste oil, etc. Most marinas support chandlery shops. Fuel at various obvious sites, fresh water from marinas or harbourmaster's pontoon. Customs office at Port Hamble. Warsash Nautical Bookshop, one of the nation's finest, is sited up the hill by the crossroads, 10 minutes' walk from the Public Hard. Pubs in Warsash are disappointing, though the Rising Sun can be a godsend to the mariner who, having dried out his yacht on the piles at Warsash Public Hard, discovers himself faint from his labours. Hamble, on the other hand, is well supplied. Go right up the street past the square to find the White Hart. The King and Queen halfway up the High Street has a launderette in the basement especially for yachtsmen.

At Bursledon, the famous Jolly Sailor sells excellent beer and good pub food. Eat on the terrace when you can.

Scrubbing berths on piles at Warsash Public Hard below the Rising Sun Inn. Also at Land's End Hard opposite Swanwick Marina and at Mercury. Launching ramps at Warsash Public Hard, Hamble Public Hard, Swanwick Shore Public Hard, and Land's End Hard (no car park) at Bursledon.

Banks at Warsash and Hamble.

The Royal Southern Yacht Club, RAF Yacht Club, Hamble River Sailing Club and Warsash Sailing Club are all based in the river.

Communications
The Hamble River is not notably well served by public transport, but it is by no means cut off. Buses run from Hamble, Warsash and Swanwick. There is a railway station at Bursledon, with trains to Southampton or Portsmouth. Hamble Station (same line as Bursledon) is a cab ride from the village or the marinas.

Southampton

Tides
Double HW
First HW springs approx −0013 Dover
Stand halfway up the flood (the 'young flood stand') beginning at approximately LW+1½ hours and ending at approximately LW+3 hours.

MHWS	MLWS	MHWN	MLWN
4·5m	0·5m	3·7m	1·8m

Depths
Southampton Water main fairway is dredged to 10m.

The River Itchen has 6m or more as far as Ocean Village, then shoals to a minimum of 2m (LAT) up to Shamrock Quay.

There is at least 2·5m up to and inside Town Quay Marina, with greater depths on the Town Quay Pier itself.

Apart from shoaling areas on its southern bank, and the well marked shoal off Marchwood, the River Test is dredged to 10·2m as far as the swinging ground at the top end of the container berths. Above this point the river shoals rapidly and dries up to Eling Channel and the well sheltered Eling Basin.

General
Southampton lies at the head of the 6-mile-long Southampton Water. The port could be said to have been founded by the Roman Emperor Vespasian in AD50, when he ordered a fortified settlement on the River Itchen. After Rome fell, the town pursued the usual track of prosperity followed by minor sackings until the French did a thorough job on the place in 1338. Some say that this deplorable event occurred while the inhabitants were in church instead of watching their backs. The Pilgrim Fathers sailed from here aboard the *Mayflower* in 1620. The great ocean liners saw their finest hours along Southampton's wharves, and in 1944 over 3 million troops were embarked for the Normandy landings.

So long as there has been popular yachting, Southampton has been a centre for local enthusiasts, but only in recent years has this great port really opened up for visitors. It now boasts four major marinas, providing excellent shelter, all-tide access and full though varying facilities.

The city of Southampton, like many other ports, lost much of its innate character to the bombing in World War II, but the local watermen were not blitzed out and the essential spirit of the place lives on in the yards and creeks of the Test and Itchen. There is literally nothing that you cannot have done for your boat in this buzzing hive of seafaring.

Approaches
At all times, yachts navigating within the Port of Southampton, which includes Southampton Water and its approaches, should be aware of the priority given to any commercial traffic. Whenever possible, it is good policy to operate in the mainly navigable waters outside the buoyed shipping channels. Pay particular note to the manoeuvring requirements of large vessels approaching Southampton from the east and leaving the Bramble Bank in mid-Solent to starboard. The need to keep very well clear of these ships in the area between *Prince Consort* north cardinal buoy (off Cowes) and Calshot cannot be over-stated. Do not insist on your right of way under sail. Under local bylaws you do not have any.

Traffic is controlled by Vessel Traffic Services (*VTS*, VHF Ch 12). They will be pleased to help with any problems you may experience in general navigation of Southampton Harbour. Look out for their blue harbour launches with a yellow strip across the bows (blue light at night). If you are manoeuvring too close to a ship, you may receive a visit from a harbour launch, which will invite you to clear the way.

Southampton Water is entered between *Calshot Spit* light float (Fl.5s) and *Calshot* north cardinal (VQ) bell buoy. Note Calshot Castle and its radar tower 2 cables WNW of Black Jack buoy.

Running up Southampton Water there are good depths available on both sides of the dredged fairway as far as Western Shelf. Above the two conspicuous beacons 6 cables northwest of Hamble bunkering jetty the northeast shore is generally shoal, but this presents no difficulties to the navigator because a series of green buoys is established in the vicinity of the 5m contour, outside the main channel. If you are on this side of the

Port Signal and Radar Station at the division of Southampton Water. River Test to left, Itchen to right

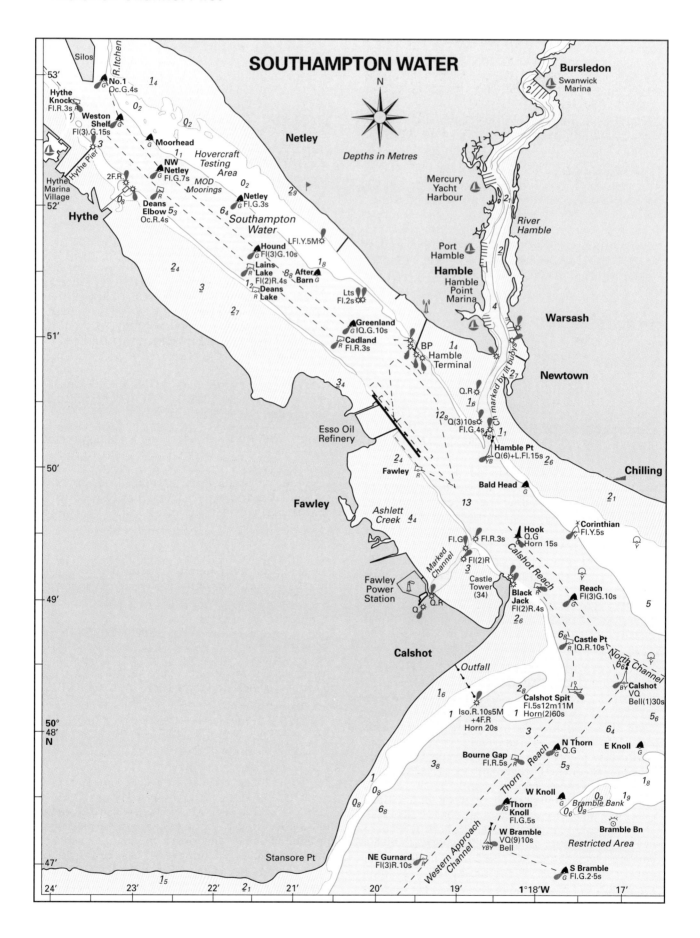

SOUTHAMPTON WATER

N

Depths in Metres

Approach to Hythe Marina Village. Lock gate shut

River Itchen leading towards entrance to Ocean Village Marina just right of yacht under sail

Entrance to Ocean Village Marina from River Itchen. Signals: RRR – Stop; GGW – Free flow

fairway, care is needed as you approach *Western Shelf* (Fl(3)G.15s) and *No.1* (Oc.G.4s) buoys. Shoal water extends much closer to these than to the green main channel buoys lower down Southampton Water.

Entrance
River Itchen
The Itchen is clearly marked. Enter between the conspicuous Port Signal and Radar Station, at the junction of the two channels, and the *Swinging Ground No.1* green buoy (Oc.G.4s). Now keep the docks (steep-to) to port and the series of large lit green beacons to starboard. Ocean Village Marina is opposite *No.4* beacon (Q.G) and is clearly identified by its new, red-roofed 'developer houses'. Above Ocean Village, favour the east side of the river until you have passed under the Itchen Bridge (height 24·4m), then swing back to the middle, leaving the green *Chapel* beacon (Fl.G.3s) to starboard.

The east bank is now shoal, but presents no problems if you keep to the west of the numerous mid-stream moorings. The wharves on the west side are mainly steep-to until you reach Shamrock Quay Marina opposite *No.5* pile (Fl.G.3s). Above Shamrock Quay depths continue in the region of 2m to Northam Bridge (height 4·7m), which may be regarded as the head of normal yacht navigation.

River Test
Leave the Port Signal and Radar Station to starboard, then steer about 325°, keeping the dock walls to starboard and the large red navigation buoys to port.

Pass Town Quay (white building complex with grey roofs) and Royal Pier (Red Funnel Terminal for Isle of Wight car ferries) on your starboard hand. The main channel continues with plenty of water up to the head of the container berths.

If you are proceeding to Marchwood Basin, enter Marchwood Channel between *No.2* red buoy (Oc.R.4s) and *Crackmore* buoy (Oc.R.8s). Steer towards a daymark triangle on a dolphin (Q.Y) (labelled 'Marchwood YC') on 298°. This forms the front mark of a transit, the back marker being a yellow beacon (Y) 1½ cables behind it. The depth on this bearing is 2·4m to within half a cable of the dolphin. Close to starboard is a shoal. On the port hand, the water shoals almost as far as Husband's Jetty, after which it deepens to at least 2m for 3

cables. Observing a north cardinal buoy (Q) close southwest of *No.2* buoy will keep you in channel.

Moorings abound hereabouts. Note the shoal water in the Marchwood Channel from about ½ cable southeast of the first beacon nearly as far as the rear beacon; both beacons should be left close to port. There are many small-craft moorings in the area, in depths of 0·5m to 0·9m. Immediately after passing the rear beacon a vessel is back in the deep water of the main channel, dredged to 10·2m. This now leads past the container berths and Swinging Ground.

The Eling Channel, which is very narrow and dries out, is entered close south of the northwest *Swinging Ground* (Eling) buoy. It is marked by beacons with triangle topmarks on the starboard hand, except at the junction with the Redbridge Channel, which is marked by a south cardinal beacon. Near the entrance of Eling Channel there are two port-hand beacons, south of which are small-craft moorings in 0·3m. Power cables cross the channel; height 36m.

Anchorage and moorings
Because of the scale of the area, anchoring or mooring may be less than comfortable in all but the fairest weather. Nonetheless, it is possible to anchor in Southampton Water so long as one keeps clear of prohibited areas, moorings, fairways, docks and their approaches. Moorings may also be found and used by arrangement in a number of places.

Behind Calshot Castle Occasionally, a mooring may be available here. Good shelter from the southwest. If you anchor, use a tripping line.

Hythe Large yachts can anchor south of Hythe pier. Smaller craft apply at the yacht yard or club for

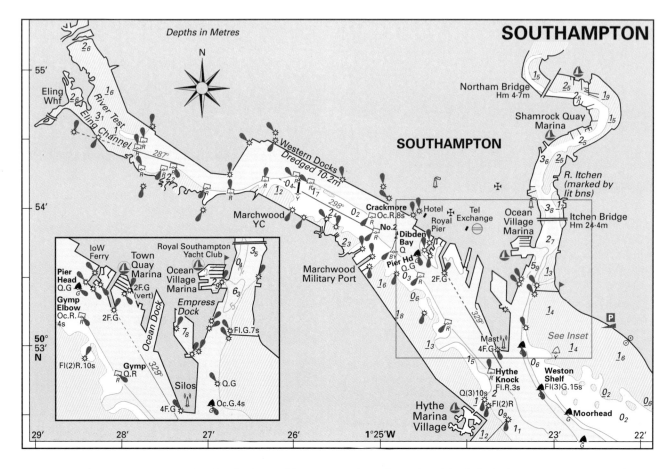

moorings. Yacht yard, shops, banks, fuel, etc. Ferry to Southampton from Hythe Pier.

Southampton Off Royal Pier are one or two Harbour Board moorings for large yachts.

Marchwood Moorings south of Marchwood Channel. Enquire at the hospitable Marchwood Yacht Club if open, otherwise help yourself and ask later. Launch service to Southampton Town Quay.

Eling Channel Anchorage possible just outside the container-ship swinging ground at neaps.

River Itchen A few Harbour Board large yacht moorings. It is possible to anchor on the east side of the river, out of the fairway, giving due care to the depth of water.

Netley Anchorage in calm weather only, or offshore (northeast) winds.

Marinas

By far the most usual way to visit Southampton is to make use of one of its excellent marinas.

Town Quay Marina Town Quay Marina will be found, after Ocean Dock, by leaving the end of the Quay itself (F.Y) to port. You will now see a wave breaker ahead, with an overlapping entrance near its eastern end.

The marina is relatively small, but visitors are welcome and the place is certainly convenient for Southampton city centre and all its facilities. You can phone to reserve a berth (☎ 02380 234397) or try Ch 80, but except at peak times you will often be lucky if you just turn up. Yachts over 15m, or 2·5m

draught, should definitely make contact first, however. Town Quay has showers, toilet, launderette and 24-hour security.

Hythe Marina Village This is entered via a short, straight channel, dredged to 2m and well marked by red and green piles. The outer beacon, to be left to starboard, is an east cardinal (Q(3)10s), while on your port hand is a beacon with a red ■ topmark. Like Ocean Village, Hythe Marina Village is made conspicuous by the characteristic nature of its architecture. Visitors are welcome, and can lock in at any state of the tide into a dredged basin with control depth of 2·5m. Call on VHF Ch 80, or ☎ 02380 207073, especially if your boat is over 16m LOA.

Fuel, water, electricity, showers, toilets, launderette, etc. Also restaurant and on-site pub. Hythe is close by, with further excellent facilities, as well as the regular ferry service to Southampton Town Quay.

The lock works 24 hours a day. It exhibits 2F.R lights to port and 2F.G to starboard. Note the following traffic signals at the control tower:

3 fixed red – wait

3 flashing red – all traffic stop

3 fixed green – go ahead

2 fixed green over one white – free flow in the lock (around HW except dead neaps).

There is a useful waiting pontoon (2F.R at outer end) outside the lock which is linked to the shore.

Shamrock Quay on west bank of Itchen River – shot from the southeast

Ocean Village Marina

Conspicuous by its houses and its large sign. Ocean Village Marina welcomes visitors, but try to book ahead at peak times as it gets very busy (VHF Ch 80 or ☎ 02380 229385). Toilets and showers, plus the Royal Southampton Yacht Club. Convenient for city centre, well sheltered and excellently staffed by people who care about you and your boat. Note the traffic lights on the northern approach wall: 3F.R – all stop, 2 greens over a white – free flow.

Shamrock Quay

Named after *Shamrock V*, one of the Lipton America's Cup challengers built by Camper and Nicholson's, whose yard this once was, Shamrock Quay has every repair facility. Major yachts are still refitted here, as are small ones and everything in between. Visitors' berths are available, but if the tide is running dock with the greatest care if you are allotted an inside berth. The streams can be vicious, particularly on the spring ebb. Good chandlery and toilets, showers and laundry. Excellent 'transport-style' café, the Yellow Welly. If the on-site pub doesn't suit your taste, walk a hundred yards outside the gate to fetch the Cooper's Arms, a fine traditional dock-side watering hole. Central Southampton is a cab-ride away.

Launching sites

- Foreshore north of Hythe pier
- Ramp at head of Ashlett Creek, south of oil refineries
- Hard on north shore of Eling Creek
- Itchen River: at Woolston hard on east side, or at either marina
- Public hard, Netley

Yacht clubs

Royal Southampton Yacht Club, Southampton Sailing Club, Eling Sailing Club, Weston Sailing Club, Hythe Sailing Club, Marchwood Yacht Club, Esso Sailing Club, Netley Cliff Sailing Club.

Communications

Car ferries or fast catamaran to Cowes, Isle of Wight.

Main line trains to Waterloo and the West (70 minutes to London).

The Beaulieu River

Tides

Double HW. First HW springs at entrance approximately −0030 Dover

Range

MHWS	MLWS	MHWN	MLWN
3·7m	0·6m	3·1m	1·6m

Streams

There is a general slackening of the flood stream from 2 hours after LW lasting until about 4 hours after. This is more noticeable at springs, and is known as the 'young flood stand'. The usual mid-Solent HW stand is also experienced, and the ebb does not run hard until its final 3½ hours. All these effects are much gentler during neap tides.

Depths

The Beaulieu River has a bar, on which the depth varies from year to year, but 0·9m at LAT is a good assumption, always bearing in mind that prolonged winds from the north or east can depress Solent tidal heights. Allow generous clearance two hours either side of LWS, particularly in a strong southeasterly. Neaps are obviously more accommodating, but even so, take care around LW. Inside, a least depth of 1·8m will be found as far as Buckler's Hard, except for a 1·2m patch opposite a small boathouse 3 cables downstream of the marina. Navigable water exists up to Beaulieu at HW, but drying heights of up to 2·6m may be found in the upper reaches, outside the stream bed.

General

The Beaulieu River runs up into the New Forest and is undoubtedly the most beautiful harbour on the mainland side of the Solent. Anchoring inside Gull Island on a moonlit night offers an intimacy with nature not easy to discover in these crowded waters. Above Gins Farm oak woods close in, from which ships of Nelson's navy were built, many of them at the upstream village of Buckler's Hard. The whole river, including its bed, is owned by Lord Montagu, whose careful custody has made it pay while avoiding any hint of over-exploitation.

Approach and entrance

On a quiet summer's day, the Beaulieu River entrance is a tranquil place, but in gale conditions from any southerly point, it can be dangerous if taken for granted. Arriving from the southwest in a following gale, the situation as you round up in the entrance can be a nasty surprise, even at HW. Once, taking his chances in 50kts of wind, the *Shell Pilot* compiler was faced with 'wall-to-wall' breakers and found his boat unable to 'punch' up the sea reach. He had to turn to run for Cowes instead.

The old passage across the bar is marked by the transit of two orange lattice boards in line on 341°. The front one has a triangular top and is sited on the first port-hand pile (*No.2*) inside the entrance dolphin. The rear board, which has a vertical black bar in its centre, is sited high in the pine trees on the low cliff to the north of the river. At the time of writing (2000), as for some years prior to this, the deepest water lies on the transit of the right-hand side of Lepe House (a rambling 'pile' to the west of the old rear transit board) and R pile No. 2. There are no surprises here, with the bottom shoaling fairly smoothly.

Approaching from the east, keep the large south cardinal mark off Stansore Point to starboard, then steer about WSW until in the vicinity of a yellow spherical racing buoy which lies conveniently to the east of the old transit before turning in to the mouth of the river. If the buoy, which is seasonal, is not there, make your turn well before the transit closes, bringing the bathing huts on Gurnard (IoW) beach right aft. The shallowest part of the bar lies in the area up to 2 cables to seaward of the RW dolphin. Thereafter, if you have succeeded in getting this far without touching, you will float up to Buckler's Hard, unless you are proceeding very slowly against the last of a strong ebb. In these circumstances you may get caught by the shallows mentioned in 'Depths' opposite the boathouse before Buckler's Hard. This 100-yard-long shoal extends from the bank on your starboard hand right across to the

moorings. It is firm if you hit it, but not rocky. If soundings are looking 'thin', work in as close to the moorings as is prudent. It doesn't help much, but it might just see you through. On a flooding tide, if you clear the bar, you'll clear the shoal as well.

From the west, keep well off the mudbanks of Beaulieu Spit and Warren Flat. You will recognise the entrance by the conspicuous white boathouse and a cottage, also picked out in white, at the west end of a row of old coastguard houses. As when coming from the east, place yourself east of the old transit before turning in and look for the Lepe House guide line. At night, keep the dolphin (Fl.R.5s3M) bearing about 315° until you are in the entrance.

Once in the river, proceed between the red and green beacons until they run out above Needs Ore Point. Thereafter, the channel is marked by withies which stand at or near the low water mark. The moorings make the channel easy to spot, but a first-time entry at night requires plenty of moon and the greatest caution if you are not to suffer an expensive collision with a moored yacht. After dark, the lit piles provide an adequate safe passage as far as the first moorings; all the piles carry reflectors. Thereafter you

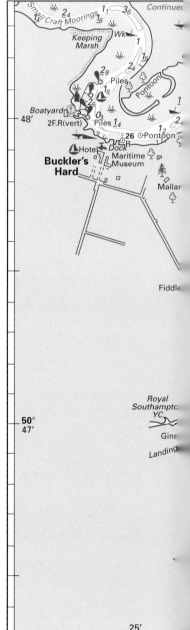

Entrance to Beaulieu River. Note dolphin 'bar' beacon and dogleg course around Beaulieu Spit. Shoals off Stone Point in the foreground

are on your own, except for a lit green pile marking a mudbank opposite the marina.

Take note of the shoals charted on the north side of the long 'sea reach'. They have temporarily stopped many a homeward bounder creeping into the river near the bottom of the tide.

Berthing

Anchoring is welcomed in the lower reaches below Needs Ore. Small yachts can bring up in the bight formed by the causeway linking Gull Island to the mainland, otherwise anchor on the south side of the channel. Holding is good in mud, with fine shelter in westerly weather. You will lie safely enough in an easterly, but strong winds from this quarter can bring in a send which disagrees with a spring ebb. Anchoring elsewhere is impractical for all but the smallest yacht because of the danger of foul-berthing moored craft.

The river is well stocked with harbour moorings, both above and below Buckler's Hard, which are let to berth holders. Any suitable buoy can be picked up, given the usual regard to courtesies if the owner should return. Visitors' berths off the village are between piles. When these are full, a further group of trots is available just above the marina. The marina itself welcomes visitors when berths are clear, and vessels of up to 23m (75ft) can be accommodated. Whoever you are and wherever you berth, the harbour staff will come to direct you and to gather dues. The harbourmaster does not monitor any public radio channel.

Facilities

Beaulieu may not be cheap, but its facilities are top class. Water and fuel, telephone, showers and a launderette are available at the yacht harbour, with the Agamemnon Boatyard and Chandlery close by.

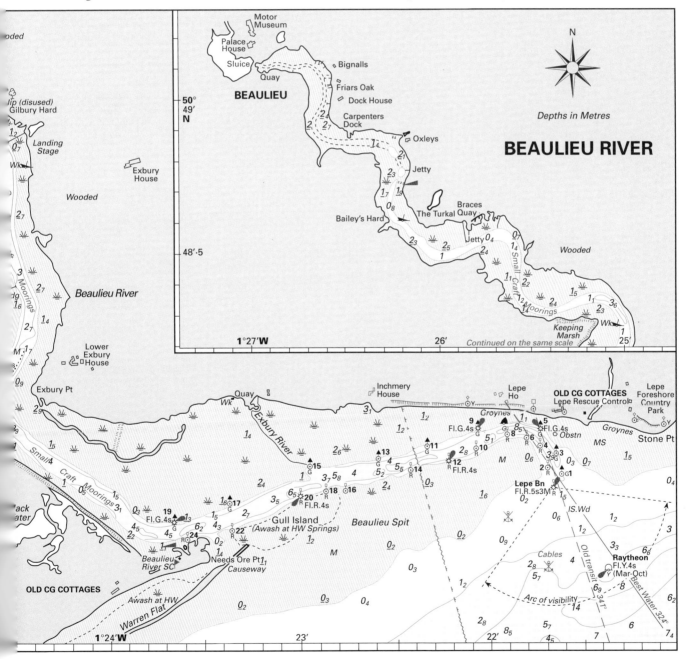

Buckler's Hard Garage offers excellent outboard repair facilities, open seven days a week in summer. There is a scrubbing pad at Buckler's Hard capable of floating boats up to 2m draught at MHWS. There is also a launching site and car parking facilities. Enquire with the HM.

The Royal Southampton YC maintains a station at Gins Farm, welcoming members of affiliated clubs when open.

Customs visit regularly. There are excellent walks from the marina up to Beaulieu for tea and sticky buns in the proper tea shop. Here you will also find the National Motor Museum. Buckler's Hard has a useful licensed village store, open daily in season, and the Master Builder's House provides both public bar and restaurant services. Taxis are available, but otherwise public transport is poor, with Beaulieu Road and Brockenhurst rail stations six miles distant.

Newtown River

Tides
Double HW. First HW springs approximately −0030 Dover

Range

MHWS	MLWS	MHWN	MLWN
3·4m	0·5m	2·8m	1·5m

Streams
7 hours flood tide. Approximately 2-hour stand at HW. A vigorous ebb for the remainder of the period.

Depths
1·5m LAT on the bar. Deep water in entrance. Up to 2·5m on visitors' moorings in Newtown River, depending upon swing. 1·8m anchoring depths at lower end of Clamerkin Lake.

General
The uninformed visitor to Newtown River would never for a moment imagine the depth and length of its history. Said to date back to Roman times, the port of Newtown was sufficiently prosperous in 1001 to warrant sacking by Vikings. By the mid-14th century the borough was assessed at twice the value of Newport, and in 1377 the French took full advantage by helping themselves to its riches, leaving the town in flames.

Newtown River with Shalfleet Quay in clear view. The dozen or so yachts immediately inside the entrance are on visitors' moorings

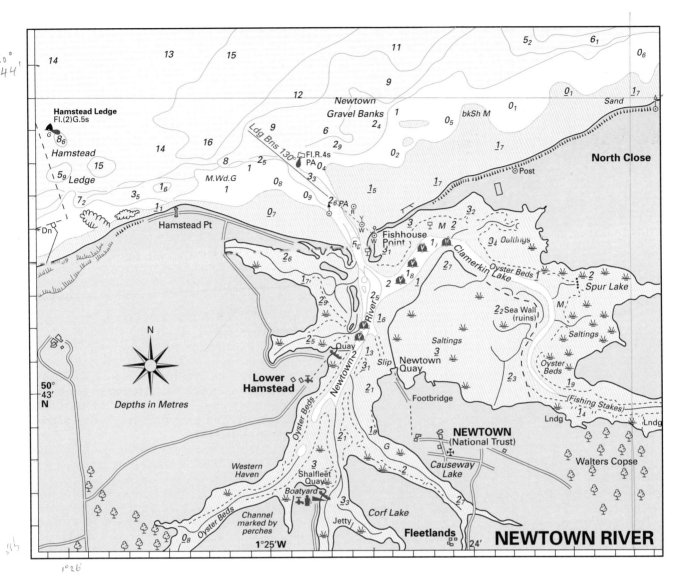

NEWTOWN RIVER

Now, overgrown tracks are all that remain of busy streets, and nature with her oak woods and saltings reigns unchallenged. Over 150 species of bird pass here as the year turns, including rare little terns and migrant ospreys.

Newtown River is owned and administered by the National Trust. A visit out of season reveals a paradise for those who love the wild foreshore. On summer weekends, you may occasionally find your patience stretched by the proximity of your fellow-humans.

Approach and entrance

The entrance to Newtown River is narrow and not conspicuous from seaward. Coming in from the west, however, if you look carefully east-southeast from the green conical *Hamstead Ledge* buoy you should make out its buoys and leading marks. From the east, keep roughly on a line joining the green buoys *Salt Mead* and *Hamstead Ledge* until the Rowridge TV mast bears about 150°. This mast is the closer of the two you may see well inshore on the Island. Look below it with your binoculars and you will discern the entry marks.

There is shoal water on both sides of the approach, but if you keep to the excellent leading marks (a white and black circular 'target' kept snug in the 'V' of the 'Y'-shaped marker in front of it) on 130° you will find a least depth of 1·5m LAT. The transit will carry you close to a small lit red buoy Fl.R.4s, difficult to spot from the offing. This must be left to port unless there is a suitable rise of tide. Continue down the transit until approaching a red pile, by which time you will have a green beacon on the west side of the entrance in clear view. Steer between these through the middle of the entrance, which is a clear break in the shingle and sand beach, scoured out to a considerable depth by the strong stream. To starboard the shingle bank is steep-to with mud beyond. To port, Fishhouse Point also shoals rapidly.

Once inside, note carefully the colour and rough-hewn topmarks of the many withies. It is easy to go astray, particularly as the weather can do away with the colours on the woodwork. It is therefore important to familiarise yourself with the lie of the water before entering.

The channel's first swing is to port. Do not make the turn into Clamerkin Lake too soon; or if you are proceeding up Newtown River, watch out for the drying bank to starboard. Once these dangers have been negotiated, a careful eye on marks, moorings and echo sounder will reveal the rest.

Anchorage and moorings
Any vacant mooring that appears to be of suitable size may be picked up by a visitor. The large white buoys in the main run-up to Newtown River, as well as those inside Clamerkin Lake, are official. All others are private, but this need not mean they are unavailable. The berthing master will advise, if on duty.

Now that most of the best water is taken up with moorings, the principal anchorages are to be found in Clamerkin Lake. You can lie in 1·8m LAT between the entrance and the first moorings. Subject to tide and swinging room, it is also possible to find a snug berth between the moorings and the oyster beds further up. These latter are clearly marked and must on no account be disturbed.

Holding ground is good in mud, and the whole complex of creeks is well sheltered, save for the outer regions, which become uncomfortable in strong northerlies. If the anchorage is crowded, the weather unsettled and spring tides upon you, be ready to take the Newtown Pyjama Party in jovial spirit...

Landing
Newtown Quay (tidal) gives access to the ancient town hall and numerous fine walks. Shalfleet Quay is found at the boatyard in the creek of the same name. The yard is served by an unmetalled lane leading to the village, about 10 minutes' walk away. Do not land on the spit leading to Fish House Point (April to September). It is a bird sanctuary.

Facilities
Water from tap at the south end of the footbridge by Newtown Quay; also at Lower Hamstead Farm. Fuel from Shalfleet Service Station, just to the east of the village on the main road. Provisions from Eddy's Farm Shop at Shalfleet (up lane beside church and left turn at Warlands Lane) – closed Sunday pm, Wednesday pm and every lunchtime. Excellent seafood and good beer at the New Inn, Shalfleet, but organise your run ashore so that if your dinghy is going to dry out, you have another pint or two as it re-floats.

Yarmouth Harbour

Tides
Long stand at HW. First HW springs approximately −0050 Dover

Range

MHWS	MLWS	MHWN	MLWN
3·1m	0·8m	2·5m	1·5m

Streams
Streams in the harbour run with the state of tide, and this must be borne in mind when manoeuvring. Pay particular attention to the spring ebb in the vicinity of the entrance.

Depths
The harbour is dredged to 2m below chart datum from the entrance to the bridge, though draughts in excess of this figure can be accommodated in places. There is a minimum of 2m in the entrance, and more on the transit in the approach.

General
Yarmouth is an extremely useful passage port, lying as it does immediately inside the tide-swept Needles Channel. It is also a favoured destination for many of the numerous yachts enjoying the sheltered Solent scene. It is well equipped with convivial hostelries, pretty, and snugly sheltered from all but northeasterly weather.

The town is a car ferry port for the Isle of Wight, but this has not spoiled its atmosphere. Indeed, the bustle it lends to the summer months adds to the fun of what can be a very busy little harbour. Do not be disappointed to be turned away if you arrive in late afternoon during a holiday weekend. Berthing is plentiful, but not endless which, alas, sometimes seems to be the condition of the stream of yachts.

Approach and entrance
Yarmouth is easy to spot from seaward. By day its pier and church tower are unmistakable, while by night the lights of the town, the ferry dock, and specifically the 2F.R lights on the end of the pier, show the way. Approaching from the west, keep outside the only danger, Black Rock, with its lit buoy (Fl.G.5s). If you are arriving from east of the pier, look out for the large, unlit mooring buoys which, fortunately, are clearly charted. In the more immediate offing is a further mooring buoy lit Fl.Y, but whose light is readily missed.

Tides run very hard in the Solent outside Yarmouth, so care is needed not to become disorientated, particularly on night approaches.

Yarmouth entrance lies immediately west of the pier. Note the leading marks on 187° (white diamonds with two horizontal black lines, each with F.G light). These are not always clear on a first entry. If you are unable to discern them, keep ½ cable or so west of the pier head and steer in towards the centre of the entrance on about 185°. There you will see a dolphin (Q.G.3M) on the end of the breakwater. On the port hand is the short ferry jetty (2F.R at end). Immediately inside this are public steps (for landing only – no dinghies to be left here) used by the water taxi. The steps are followed by the Town Quay wall, against which yachts may lie. Note the tide gauges on Town Quay and on pile *A1*. These indicate the height of tide above chart datum. In the entrance, beware of the wash from ferry propellers which may turn constantly, even when the ship is loading.

Once clear of the dolphin, bear to starboard towards the rows of mooring piles, unless you are intending to berth on the Town Quay. The piles can present a bewildering spectacle to the inexperienced, but the harbourmaster or his staff are usually on hand in a dory to direct visitors to a berth. Be aware that Yarmouth is an important lifeboat station, and take care not to berth so as to impede the boat.

Do not even consider sailing into Yarmouth in any but the smallest and handiest of yachts. There is no room to manoeuvre under canvas.

If the harbour is full, a red flag is flown at the pier head, and an illuminated board is shown at the entrance, bearing the dismal legend, 'Harbour Full'.

At night, after the 2F.R on the end of Yarmouth pier, where an additional high intensity F is shown in fog, look for the green light on the dolphin and the 2F.R on the car ferry terminal. When this latter is abeam, you can begin swinging to starboard. Note that the jetty on the east side of the ferry terminal carries F.R.4m2M and an additional high intensity F.Y in fog. The entrance is brightly lit by the arc lights from the terminal, which helps a lot, but always remember the cross set in the offing. After dark, it can be especially deceptive.

Berthing

Yarmouth Harbour is blessed with unusually understanding and philosophical staff. You will almost certainly be met by a dory on entry. Be assured that the man driving it will understand your needs. He will help you secure to piles if necessary and generally do all he can to get you into the right place.

Berthing is first come, first served. The harbourmaster does not keep a VHF watch, but vessels over 15m LOA or 2·4m draught should telephone before arrival (☎ 01983 760321).

Berth between piles (all numbered and lettered), as directed by the harbourmaster. Increasing numbers of the old piles are being replaced by pontoon berths, especially round the edge of the harbour, so if you arrive late at night, these may prove more than useful. Raft up as necessary, always leaving room in the 'fairways' between the trots. Berthing is also possible alongside the Town Quay, which is dredged for its entire length as an emergency ferry berth, but in northeasterly winds this can become uncomfortable. The road bridge to the upper Yar opens, but visitors are not allowed above it.

When the harbour is full, you may pick up one of the thirty-six visitors' moorings laid on the 3m contour outside the breakwater. Here, rafting is not permitted owing to the surge and occasional wash from shipping. A riding light is a sensible precaution.

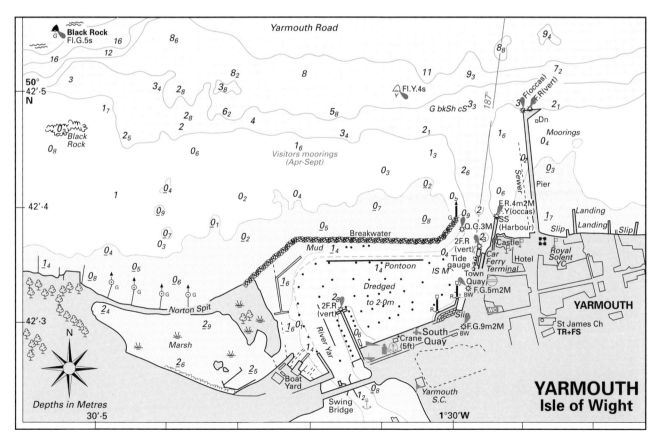

Yarmouth Harbour. Road bridge on extreme right-hand side.
Ferry moored at terminal. Visitors' moorings this side of pier
head. More visitors' inside

Anchorage for deep-draught yachts is possible to seaward of the visitors' moorings, but it is an uncomfortable berth in all but the fairest weather. Inside the moorings, depths shoal rapidly.

Facilities
Three yacht yards, including Harold Hayles, who have a slipway, an engineer, and where most jobs can be undertaken. The harbourmaster maintains a DIY 5-ton crane on the South Quay. His staff will assist visitors to lift their yachts at a modest price and for a few pounds more will hire them a pressure washer. Many yachts of up to 9·7m (32ft) fall within the weight limit and can make use of this unusual facility.

First-class showers with launderette on the South Quay.

Excellent chandlery in the town square. First-class pubs, a good hotel and the finest puff pastry in the West at The Wheatsheaf (reported 1993). Provisions from various sources. 24hr fuel and water from South Quay. Water only on Town Quay. Launching from slips at quay or from ferry slip by arrangement with the harbourmaster. Water taxi from 0800–0000 all year round. Royal Solent YC is a pleasure to visit with its magnificent Solent views and true sailing membership. Buses to Newport,

and the best website on the central South Coast. Find them on www.harbours.co.uk. The other harbours covered are no great shakes, but Yarmouth have shown the way ahead.

Lymington

Tides
Double HW at springs, otherwise a long HW stand
HW approx Dover −0045 springs, +0010 neaps

MHWS	MLWS	MHWN	MLWN
3·0m	0·7m	2·6m	1·4m

Depths
2·4m minimum at chart datum up to Lymington Yacht Haven. 2·2m minimum to Berthon's Lymington Marina. Thereafter, no less than 1·1m up to the Town Quay, which has alongside depth of 1·5m.

General
Lymington is an attractive town on the edge of the New Forest. Its 1½-mile river is dominated by frequent car ferries to Yarmouth, operating from the railhead on the east bank, and by two of the largest marinas in the Solent area, on the west bank. It

boasts a comprehensive back-up for yachts and powerboats: designers, electronic and marine engineers, sailmakers, builders and repair yards.

The river mouth is only 2½ miles from the Needles Channel, gateway to the open sea.

Approach

There are no dangers in the immediate vicinity of the Lymington River. Note, however, that shoal waters extend on both sides. From a distance the first landmark you will see, apart from the veritable forest of masts up-river, is the club starting platform. This takes the form of a shed on stilts, standing immediately to the east of the channel.

On closer approach, identify the red *Jack in the Basket* beacon (Fl.R.2s9m). This is highly conspicuous by virtue of its black 'basket' topmark. Its name, according to one source, comes from fishermen's wives leaving their hard-worked husbands' jack, or lunch, in a basket attached to the outer pile. I prefer the more robust explanation that malefactors were once immured in a cage on the pile as an alternative to the town stocks. There they could be pelted with fish offal, or other suitable reminders of their misdemeanours. Leave *Jack* to port, and pick up the 319° leading line. This is marked by two metal columns. Their F.R.8M lights are readily identifiable by night, but entry in daylight is simply a matter of following the prominent red and green beacons marking the channel from its seaward end between *No.2* (Fl.R.2s) with a rectangular red topmark and *No.1* (Fl.G.2s) with a triangular green topmark. Do not confuse the latter with the nearby starting platform.

Half a mile upstream, with the green *Tar Barrel* beacon (Fl.G.2s) abeam, alter to starboard to 007° and pick up the black and white leading marks (DirF) for inward-bound ferries at the end of the next short reach. When departing, the corresponding red and white leading marks (DirF) on 187° are in the mud-flats south of the red *Seymour's Post* beacon (Fl.R.2s).

At *No.10* red beacon, opposite the green *No.9 Cage Boom* mark (Fl.G.2s), the fairway swings to the left, facing the clearly marked entrance to Lymington Yacht Haven on a heading of about 282°.

From the east cardinal *Harper's Post* beacon (Q(3)10s), carry on past the prominent Royal Lymington Yacht Club (with its own landing and pontoon berths) towards the ferry terminal, leaving the Lymington Marina and Berthon yard to port. In addition to all the pontoons, there are pile berths opposite the marina fuel dock. These can be safely negotiated on either hand. Thereafter, the river shoals gradually as you approach the Town Quay.

At night, the dogleg in the outer river has led to many a moonlit tryst on the mud. Note that all the lit piles show similar light characteristics (Fl.R.2s or Fl.G.2s). Keep your wits about you to avoid an early end to your entry.

The speed limit is 6 knots, and the ferries have absolute right of way. There is nearly always room to give the ferries clear water and stay afloat yourself. Bear in mind, however, that at LW springs, the ferry's displacement wave may leave a deep-draught yacht temporarily embarrassed – fortunately in soft mud.

Berths and moorings

Anchoring anywhere in the river is prohibited.

The Harbour Commissioners have in their gift 200 berths, mostly up-river. Under favourable tidal conditions, boats drawing less than 2m should head for the Town Quay if marina prices fail to appeal. (At peak holiday periods it could well be full, even though it is permissible to lie six abreast on the pontoon.) Alternatively, the harbourmaster (☎ 01590 672014), who is usually on hand in his launch, may direct a visitor to a buoy. Not only is berthing at the Town Quay about half the price of the marinas, but you step off the boat into a cobbled lane between traditional waterfront cottages and shops leading straight to the High Street.

Be sure all the boats lying outside you are aware of your intended ETD well in advance.

Lymington Yacht Haven has 600 pontoon berths. Call Ch 80 or 37 (M), or ☎ 01590 677071. To enter, leave the east cardinal *Harper's Post* beacon close to starboard and an artificial breakwater to port. The leading transit is on 244°: by day two red triangles on poles, by night a F.Y on each. Follow the 'visitors' signs to C pontoon, near the fuelling point and marina office. Berthing here entitles one to access to the hospitable Lymington Town Sailing Club nearby.

Berthon's Lymington Marina is opposite the car ferry terminal and can handle boats of all sizes. Call on VHF Ch 80 or 37 (M), or ☎ 01590 673312.

Both marinas have full facilities.

In the entrance to the river upstream of *Seymours Post* are a number of moorings on the west side. Some of these are sometimes vacant and are useful to yachts arriving in the middle of the night with no wish for an immediate run ashore. They are also handy for yachts of up to 40ft or so arriving from far afield who have missed their tide when bound eastwards up the Solent. To these they offer an opportunity for rest in safety. At spring tides, deep draught vessels may swing onto the mud at LW, particularly as ferries go by, but this need be no special hardship as the bottom here has a gentle touch.

Facilities

The Royal Lymington Yacht Club welcomes guests by invitation. Lymington Town Sailing Club is open to all bona fide yachtsmen. Both provide hospitality and views across the Solent of a high order.

Numerous pubs and restaurants to suit all tastes, nationalities and pockets. New showers promised for 2000 at the Town Quay, from which a high standard is hoped following a 5% rise in harbour dues to pay for them.

The High Street has all the shops, banks, etc. you would expect to find in a prosperous country town

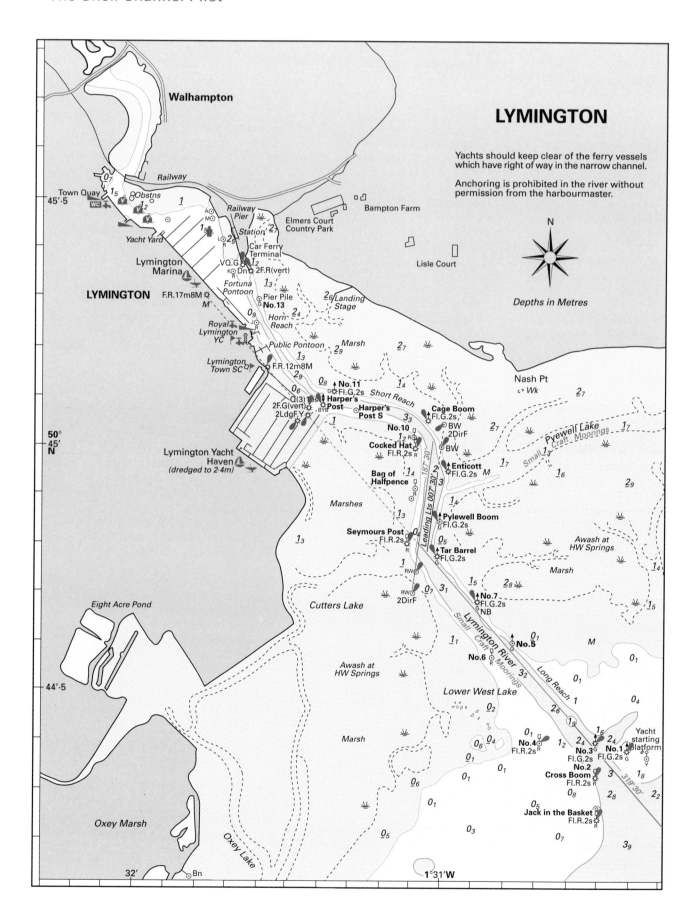

LYMINGTON

Walhampton

Yachts should keep clear of the ferry vessels which have right of way in the narrow channel.

Anchoring is prohibited in the river without permission from the harbourmaster.

N

Depths in Metres

Railway

Town Quay
45'·5
Obstns
WC
Yacht Yard

Lymington Marina

LYMINGTON

F.R.17m8M

Royal Lymington YC

Lymington Town SC

Public Pontoon

F.R.12m8M

Lymington Yacht Haven
(dredged to 2·4m)

Railway Pier

Station

Car Ferry Terminal

VQ.G

Dn   2F.R(vert)

Fortuna Pontoon

Pier Pile
No.13

Horn Reach

Elmers Court Country Park

Bampton Farm

Lisle Court

Landing Stage

Marsh

Nash Pt
Wk

Pyewell Lake
Small Craft Moorings

No.11
Fl.G.2s
Harper's Post

2F.G(vert)
2LdgF

Q(3)

Harper's Post S

Short Reach

Cage Boom
Fl.G.2s
BW
2DirF

BW

No.10
Fl.R.2s

Cocked Hat
Fl.R.2s

Enticott
Fl.G.2s

Bag of Halfpence

Marshes

Pylewell Boom
Fl.G.2s

Seymours Post
Fl.R.2s

Tar Barrel
Fl.G.2s

Awash at HW Springs

Marsh

Eight Acre Pond

Cutters Lake

Awash at HW Springs

Lower West Lake

Marsh

2DirF

No.7
Fl.G.2s
NB

Lymington River

Long Reach

No.5

No.6

No.4
Fl.R.2s

No.3
Fl.G.2s

No.2
Cross Boom
Fl.R.2s

No.1
Fl.G.2s

Yacht starting platform

44'·5

Oxey Marsh

Oxey Lake

Bn

Jack in the Basket
Fl.R.2s

50°
45'
N

1°31'W

32'

Lymington

of 36,000 inhabitants. First-class market in the High Street on Saturdays.

Lymington can fill every possible technical back-up requirement. First-class chandleries, yards, electronics, sails, the lot. Fuel and fresh water at both marinas. Fresh water only at the Town Quay, where a public scrubbing berth for shoal draught craft is situated.

Communications

The ferry to Yarmouth sails at regular intervals from early morning until late evening, depending upon the time of year.

Trains to Brockenhurst, where there are main line connections.

Keyhaven

Tides

Long stand at HW (double HW at springs)
First HW springs −0055 Dover
HW neaps +10m Dover

MHWS	MLWS	MHWN	MLWN
2·7m	0·7m	2·3m	1·4m

Depths

0·3m LAT in the shallowest part of the entrance, in the vicinity of the red buoy. 6m immediately inside the entrance, then just under 3m in the anchorage west of the main part of North Point. About 1·5m off Mount Lake. Thereafter the water shoals to 0·2m at the quay, with much of the creek drying outside the stream bed.

General

Keyhaven entrance is exposed to easterly winds, but in normal conditions the creek gives a pleasant though somewhat crowded haven for small craft.

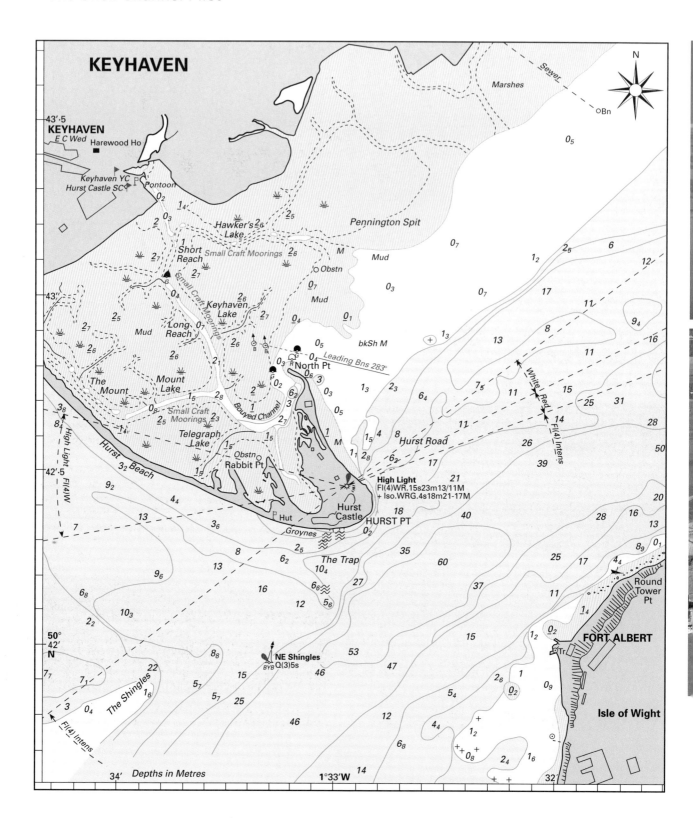

KEYHAVEN

KEYHAVEN
E C Wed Harewood Ho

Keyhaven YC
Hurst Castle SC Pontoon

Hawker's Lake

Short Reach

Small Craft Moorings

Pennington Spit

Mud

Obstn

Mud

Keyhaven Lake

Long Reach

Mud

bkSh M

Leading Bns 283°

North Pt

Small Craft Moorings

The Mount

Mount Lake

Bouyed Channel

Telegraph Lake

Hurst Beach

Obstn

Rabbit Pt

Hurst Road

High Light
Fl(4)WR.15s23m13/11M
+ Iso.WRG.4s18m21-17M

Hurst Castle

HURST PT

Hut

Groynes

The Trap

White Red

Fl(4) Intens

High Light Fl(4)W

Round Tower Pt

FORT ALBERT

Isle of Wight

NE Shingles
BYB Q(3)5s

The Shingles

Fl(4) Intens

Depths in Metres

1°33'W

43'·5

43'

42'·5

50°
42'
N

34'

Keyhaven entrance

Approach and entrance

Keyhaven lies on the north side of the Solent, 4 cables north-northwest of Hurst Point. On your approach, allow for strong tidal streams. These run southerly from −1hr to +5hr HW Dover, at a maximum of 2½ knots.

The entrance to Keyhaven lies at North Point, which is conspicuous, standing out as a low sand and shingle promontory against a background of mud-flats. There are two rather inconspicuous leading marks on the flats, each with a red and white vertical topmark. They form a transit of 283°. There are no lights. Do not take the above information regarding the transit as gospel. The channel silts and shifts on a regular basis and any of the markers, including the buoys, may be moved. The topmarks of the transit also have been changed from time to time.

Shape a course for a position something over a quarter of a mile northeast of the old pier near Hurst High Light, then pick up the leading marks. A little under a cable east of the entrance there is a small green buoy to be left to starboard, and a red buoy to port. Proceed from this pair to round a red port-hand buoy 15m north-northwest of North Point, after which you must leave the series of spherical green buoys to starboard, taking care to steer along the bows of the moored boats, the mooring buoys in a single line being in the deepest water.

The channel at first bears to the southwest, clearly marked by the starboard-hand buoys in the first reach, then continues around the bend to the northwest as far as Mount Lake. Above that, 3 cables short of Keyhaven where the channel turns

Top Keyhaven looking directly inwards up Hawkers Lake entrance and *above* Hurst Point High Light with North Point at extreme left

Leading marks on 283°. Shown bold on photograph but normally inconspicuous. Topmarks may vary from year to year

Keyhaven, looking eastwards out towards the Solent. (A) Hurst Point high light. (B) Watch hut. (C) North Point. (D) First of succession of green buoys

northwards, there is a green spherical buoy at the end of Long Reach. The trend of the channel can be judged by the line of yachts on moorings in the centre or, further upstream where it is very shallow, by a double line of smaller craft.

Near HW it is possible to enter through Hawkers Lake, keeping close to the line of boat moorings.

Anchorage

The only anchorage inside Keyhaven Lake lies between North Point and the first of the private moorings which occupy the whole river further up. Contact the river warden next to the yacht club (☎ 01590 645695) for temporary moorings.

Immediately outside Keyhaven, off the old pier near Hurst High Light, is an open roadstead which is sheltered in moderate SW–NE winds. The quietest water is found just S of the transit of Hurst High and Low Lights, 50yds or so off the beach. To the north of this the water soon begins to shoal. You may roll somewhat in disturbed conditions and a big tide, but you will be safe.

Facilities

Landing steps can be found at the end of Keyhaven Old Quay. There are others at New Quay, beyond the yacht club, but these are shallow at LWS. West Solent boat builders for repairs and laying-up services. There is a hard for scrubbing with 1·8m at MHWS.

Water, fuel and some chandlery from the boatyard. Hospitable Gun Inn at Keyhaven.

At the pleasant and lively village of Milford-on-Sea, 1 mile distant, are the usual facilities of a small seaside town.

Launching sites at Keyhaven hards with car park adjacent.

Yacht clubs: Hurst Castle Sailing Club on North Point; Keyhaven Yacht Club at the head of the lake is friendly (☎ 01590 642165).

Christchurch

Tides

HW springs −0210 Dover
HW neaps −0140 Dover

Entrance

MHWS	MLWS	MHWN	MLWN
1·8m	0·6m	1·4m	0·7m

Tuckton

MHWS	MLWS	MHWN	MLWN
1·7m	0·9m	1·3m	0·9m

Note that Christchurch has a double high water and that the heights predicted here relate to the highest rise. At neaps, the flood is a slow rise to second HW, which is the higher of the two. River water is a significant factor on depths inside, and the ebb stream can run up to 4½ knots at a high spring, particularly at the entrance.

Christchurch entrance

Depths

0·1m on the bar, but this may be less in prolonged easterly winds. 2m off Mudeford Quay. The channel up to Christchurch varies greatly in depth, from 0·1m to 3m. Generally speaking, boats drawing up to 1·37m can creep in at HW springs, but only shoal-draught yachts drawing 1·12m or less can proceed up the harbour.

General

Christchurch Harbour is an interesting place to visit, if your draught permits. Christchurch priory with its surrounding gardens and ruins is one of the most remarkable places of its kind in England. Not only is the building splendid, the artefacts and paintings are worthy of a day's study. If in doubt as to your place in life as years tick by, check out the inscription on Shelley's memorial (south side at the west end). The town has many facilities, and the environment of the harbour is surprisingly unspoilt, with salt marsh, reefs, dunes and woodland, and the river winding up to the confluence of the Stour and the Avon at Christchurch Quay.

Approach and entrance

Christchurch Harbour entrance lies about a mile north of the unmistakable promontory of Hengistbury Head. From the east, approach with the conspicuous priory tower well open to the right of Hengistbury on about 285° until, in steadily shoaling water, a series of small red and green entrance channel buoys appears ahead of you. It is impossible to be specific about these because their position changes frequently, as do the direction and depths of the channel itself.

These buoys, and those inside the harbour, are maintained by the local fishermen's association, supported by a voluntary group representing all those concerned with navigating these waters.

Proceed across the bar and up the channel, keeping red buoys to port, green to starboard, until you enter the Run. This is 250m wide and is formed by Mudeford Quay on the north side and a shingle spit to the south. Do not be alarmed if the entrance buoys take you very close to the wall of the quay before you turn sharply to port. Tides run so strongly here that this is well scoured out and remains steep-to. The channel is unlit, save for 2F.G (vertical) on the seaward end of Mudeford Quay.

Once inside the Run, turn to port and follow the sand spit (with a prominent black house and beach huts on it), leaving green buoys and some small boat moorings to starboard. Now follow the red and green buoys (reds to port, greens to starboard) as far up as you wish to proceed, all the way to Christchurch if required. The plan indicates the general lie of the channel which, like the entrance,

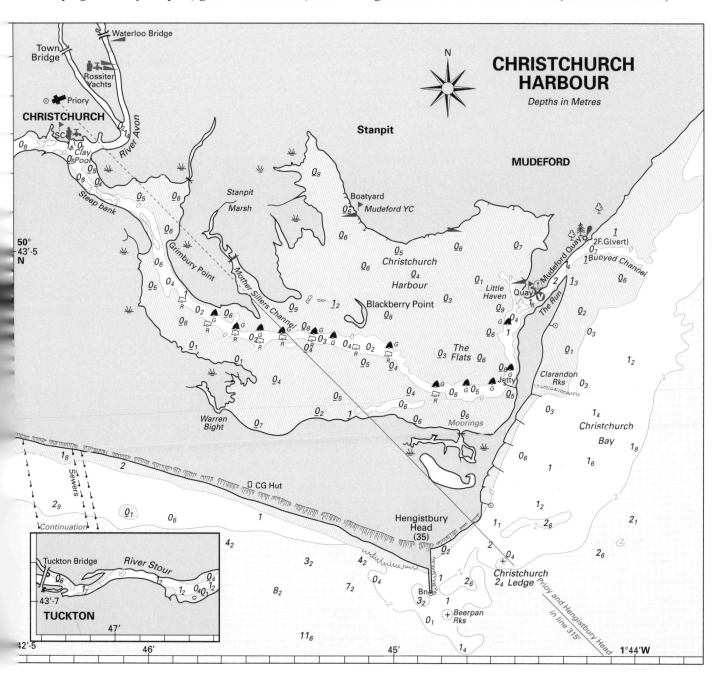

Christchurch approach from seaward. Initially course tends towards right-hand edge of Mudeford Heaven Quay – channel is now buoyed

Christchurch. The Run with Hengistbury Head beyond. Yachts at anchor inside

may be subject to shifting. Outside the buoys, the harbour mostly dries anything up to 1m.

The channel swings to starboard off a floating jetty 300 metres past the black house. Follow the green buoys to starboard, leaving a triple trot of moorings to port. From halfway up this reach you can feel your way with caution into the isolated hole with 0·5m which lies due north of Hengistbury Head.

Approach from the west is hampered by the unmarked Beerpan Rocks, which lie one cable to the south-southeast of the beacon immediately off Hengistbury Head, as well as by a further rock and various shoals of up to 1·2m further east and up to 6 cables offshore. In settled weather, with enough tide to cross Christchurch Bar, you may feel you can sail over all these except Beerpan, but with any sea running in from the southwest this would be imprudent. It is safer to give the headland at least a mile clearance until its left-hand edge bears south of west before working up towards the entrance.

Moorings and Anchorage

Anchor anywhere you can on the limit of the buoyed channel, but do not expect an easy ride. Finding space to anchor is not easy, owing to the narrowness of the channel and the closeness of the moorings.

Apart from the hole behind Hengistbury Head, where you should anchor inside the moorings (about 1m at low water neaps), there is another likely spot clear of the single visitor's mooring opposite Grimbury Point just to the north of the final port-hand buoy. Another is 200 metres to the northwest of Grimbury Point, close to the western bank.

Christchurch Sailing Club (☎ 01202 483150) maintain a pontoon where visitors may lie, and they may also have a buoy to spare. Rossiter Yachts in the right-hand arm of the River Avon keep a number of moorings available to visitors and may well prove your best bet. The yard is certainly handy for town.

Facilities

Three yacht yards. Fuel and fresh water available at Rossiter Yachts jetty. Christchurch is a thriving town with all shops, hotel and banking facilities.

Launching sites

Slipways At Christchurch Quay; at the Sailing Club by permission; at one of the yacht yards.

From the beach on the harbour side of Mudeford Quay, where there is convenient car parking.

Communications

Frequent buses and main line trains. Hurn Airport nearby.

Old Harry (Handfast Point)

Poole

Tides

Tides in Poole Harbour are small in range but highly significant to navigation. Streams run particularly fast in the narrow entrance, where an ebb rate of 4½ knots can be found at springs. Times are difficult to predict, and those using tide tables will note that only the times of LW are confirmed. The long double HW stand is best predicted by reference to its height (in the tide tables) and the tidal curve. Heights are approximately as follows:

Entrance

MHWS	MLWS	MHWN	MLWN
2·0m	0·3m	1·6m	1·1m

Town Quay

MHWS	MLWS	MHWN	MLWN
2·1m	0·6m	1·6m	1·2m

Wareham

MHWS	MLWS	MHWN	MLWN
2·2m	0·9m	1·7m	1·2m

Depths

The deep-water fairway from the bar up the Swash Channel, through the Middle Ship Channel and up to the ferry berths is dredged to 6·2m. The Middle Ship small-craft channel is dredged to 2·0m, but may be only 1·5m near the stakes. However, the old Main Channel (now the North Channel) is still available and is dredged to 4m. The least depth at Poole Quay is 3·5m and there is about 2·5m, plus tide, up to Poole Yacht Club Yacht Haven. The channel up to Wareham has a least depth of 0·1m below chart datum, giving over 1m of water at MLWN. Holes Bay has a minimum of 0·3m going up to Cobb's Quay.

General

Poole is a very large natural harbour which can be entered by day or night and at all states of tide. Much of its area is shoal, but there is nonetheless ample deep water for ships and yachts in great numbers. It is a main RoRo terminal for cross-channel ferries. There are a number of yacht clubs and every facility for the yachtsman. There is also a choice of berth types from marina, through the piled Town Quay, down to swinging moorings and anchorages. For the shoal-draught cruiser, the possibilities for taking the ground for a quiet night in an interesting spot are considerable, subject always to the ubiquitous small-craft moorings.

Approach and entrance

Swash Channel The Swash Channel is the main entry to Poole Harbour and runs largely between a training bank on its western side and the Hook Sand to the east. In reasonable conditions, most yachts arriving from the east can now enter the channel by leaving the unlit south cardinal buoy *South Hook* to starboard, thus cutting out a needless dog-leg. In hard going, however, the sands are known to shift and depths south of the buoy may not exceed 2·5m at LWS, so take care and be ready to join the channel further out if need be. Whether you are approaching from the east or the south, your most prominent landmark will be the white chalk stacks of Old Harry Rocks off Handfast Point, where the water cuts up in strong winds against the fast-flowing tide. First locate the bar buoys, which are a large red and a green. The channel is straightforward and well marked by lit buoys (see plan). Note the conspicuous hotel at the harbour entrance, and watch out for the chain ferry, which has a difficult time in a busy entrance where streams run extremely hard. It shows a white strobe light forward to indicate motion.

The channel divides inside the entrance, the main arm swinging to starboard around a lit west cardinal beacon off North Haven Point, and a second channel running off hard to port around *No. 18* red can buoy (Fl.R.5s). It should be noted that streams can be of major significance all up and down the Swash Channel and that on the ebb tide in southeasterly gales a bad sea is set up in the vicinity of Poole Bar. If there is any significant commercial traffic in the offing, small craft drawing up to 3m should use the small-craft channel which lies immediately west of the buoyed ship channel.

East Looe Channel

If arriving from the east, this is an attractive alternative to the long slog down to the bar and back, particularly if the tide is ebbing hard down the Swash Channel. There is a least depth of 0·8m a cable or so southeast of *East Looe* buoy (Q.R). This is situated 2·5 cables offshore and a little over 5 cables somewhat north of east of the Haven Hotel. To use the channel, approach the buoy so as to be well off Hook Sand, leave it close to port, then steer about 240°, leaving an unlit north cardinal beacon to port. Thereafter, you run parallel to the beach in deeper water until you join the Swash Channel at the harbour entrance. The East Looe is not recommended to strangers after dark. It should be noted that the amount of water in the East Looe Channel can be unreliable and a least depth of 1m was reported in 1998.

Channels within the harbour

If proceeding up towards the Town Quay, head first for the lit east cardinal *Brownsea* buoy, then alter north-northeast towards the lit south cardinal *No. 20* bell buoy. This marks the division of the two main channels.

The Middle Ship Channel

This well marked and well lit channel (see plan) takes you up to *Aunt Betty* east cardinal buoy, where you swing round into the straight mile run on 293° up to *Stakes* lit south cardinal buoy. Note the small-craft channel on your port side, which craft drawing 1·5m or less are obliged to use as necessary. From *Stakes*, if proceeding to the Quay, steer 343° up the Little Channel past two unlit green piles and *Oyster Bank* beacon (Q.G) until the Quay opens to the west. Berth on the north side.

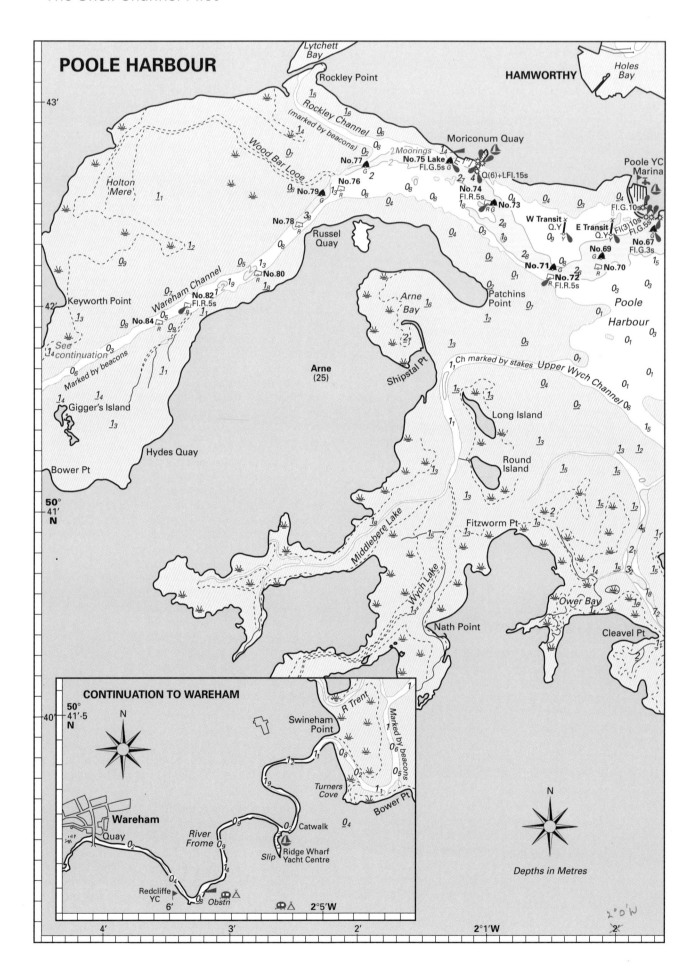

POOLE HARBOUR

HAMWORTHY

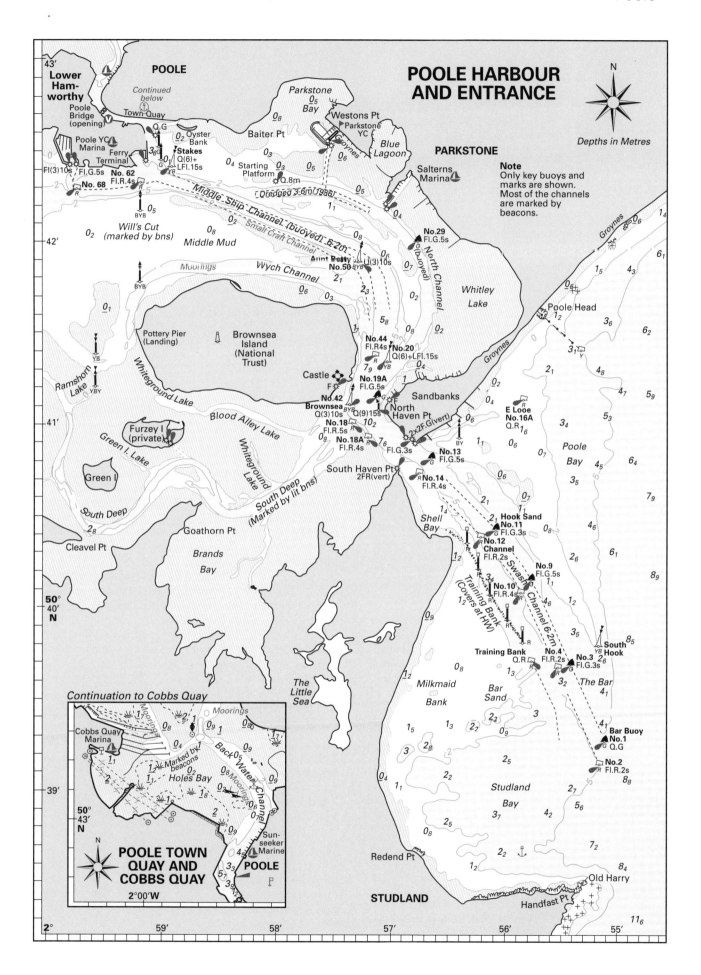

POOLE HARBOUR AND ENTRANCE

N

Depths in Metres

Note
Only key buoys and
marks are shown.
Most of the channels
are marked by
beacons.

POOLE

Lower Ham-worthy

Continued below

Town Quay

Poole Bridge (opening)

Poole YC Marina

Ferry Terminal

Fl(3)10s Fl.G.5s **No. 62**

No. 68 Fl.R.4s

BYB

Q.G

Stakes
Q(6)+LFl.15s

Oyster Bank

Parkstone Bay

Westons Pt

Parkstone YC

Blue Lagoon

PARKSTONE

Baiter Pt

Starting Platform

Q.8m

Dredged 3.6m (1988)

Will's Cut
(marked by bns)

Middle Mud

Middle Ship Channel (buoyed) 6.2m

Small Craft Channel

Wych Channel

Moorings

Salterns Marina

No.29
Fl.G.5s

North Channel (buoyed)

Groynes

Whitley Lake

Poole Head

BYB

Aunt Polly
No.50
BYB

Q(3)10s

Ramshorn Lake

YB

YBY

Whiteground Lake

Pottery Pier (Landing)

Brownsea Island (National Trust)

Blood Alley Lake

Whiteground Lake

Castle

No.42
Brownsea
Q(3)10s

F

No.44
Fl.R.4s

No.20
Q(6)+LFl.15s

No.19A
Fl.G.5s

Q(9)15s

North Haven Pt

Sandbanks

2×2F.G(vert)

E Looe
No.16A
Q.R

No.18
Fl.R.5s

No.18A
Fl.R.4s

Fl.G.3s

BY

No.13
Fl.G.5s

Furzey I (private)

Green I. Lake

Green I

South Deep

Cleavel Pt

South Deep
(Marked by lit bns)

South Haven Pt
2FR(vert)

No.14
Fl.R.4s

Poole Bay

Goathorn Pt

Brands Bay

Shell Bay

Hook Sand
No.11
Fl.G.3s

No.12
Channel
Fl.R.2s

Swash Channel 6.2m

No.9
Fl.G.5s

No.10
Fl.R.4s

Training Bank (Covers at HW)

Training Bank
Q.R

No.4
Fl.R.2s

No.3
Fl.G.3s

South Hook
YB

The Little Sea

Milkmaid Bank

Bar Sand

The Bar

Bar Buoy
No.1
Q.G

No.2
Fl.R.2s

Studland Bay

Redend Pt

STUDLAND

Old Harry

Handfast Pt

Continuation to Cobbs Quay

Moorings

Cobbs Quay Marina

Marked by beacons

Holes Bay

Moorings

Back Water Channel

Moorings

Sunseeker Marine

POOLE TOWN QUAY AND COBBS QUAY

N

2°00'W

POOLE

Poole approach. View from the vicinity of the outer end of the training bank

Poole entrance. (A) Chain ferry. (B) Brownsea Island.
(C) Sandbanks Hotel. East Looe Channel runs close inshore in front of this

The North Channel
Also well marked and lit, this was the main channel before the Middle Ship Channel was dredged in the late 1980s. It leads to Salterns Marina and Parkstone Bay. Salterns Marina is entered beyond *No.29* green buoy (Fl.G.5s) and the unlit *No.31* green buoy. The marina entrance channel runs at 033°, past a small unlit red buoy (leave to port) and three small green buoys to starboard. The entrance now opens on your port hand, with 2F.R lights to port and 2F.G lights to starboard. If continuing beyond the marina, stay in the buoyed North Channel until you rejoin the Ship Channel at *Diver* west cardinal buoy.

Wych Channel
The Wych begins in the vicinity of the fuel barge moored near *Aunt Betty* buoy and runs close parallel to the north shore of Brownsea Island. It is marked by red and green posts with topmarks. The channel swings round the west end of the island, carrying at least 2·2m of water as far as Pottery Pier. There is a shoal channel called Wills Cut marked by an east cardinal beacon on the north side of the Wych. This channel runs a degree or two west of north up to another east cardinal beacon, soon after which the deep water of the Little Channel (as the main channel is called as it turns north towards the quay) is regained. The Upper Wych Channel swings round a south cardinal beacon and winds away into the marshes behind Round Island. It is marked all the way and does not dry, though depths vary considerably.

South Deep
South Deep runs southwest from *No.18* red can (Fl.R.5s) and *No.1* green pile (Fl.G.5s). It is lit (see plan) as far as the oil workings on Furzey Island, above which it is marked by less ostentatious beacons and piles. South Deep connects up with the Wych Channel via Ramshorn Lake, joining it at the only west cardinal beacon in the vicinity.

Wareham Channel
To enter the channel, ignore the Little Channel at *Stakes* buoy and continue west past the ferry terminals (note the transit of two Q.Y lights), then proceed between red and green buoys as per the plan. Beyond Lake Pier there are a number of big-ship mooring buoys to be left to port. Upstream of these, there are a number of seasonal red buoys before the channel becomes defined by red and green posts with topmarks. These wind southwest, south, then swing around to the northwest past Bower Point. Here they peter out, but you should steer about 325° from the last one, heading immediately west of Swineham Point. As the point approaches and the river proper opens up, turn into it and keep in the middle, favouring the outside of the bends. The shallowest part (0·1m LAT) is off Redcliffe, where the bottom can be uncomfortably hard. Thence, on to Wareham.

Holes Bay
Access through Poole Town Bridge above the Quay, opening approximately every 2 hours from 0730 until 2130 at weekends and 0930 to 2130 weekdays. Light signals:

Red – bridge closed
Green – bridge open
Fl.G – bridge opening: proceed with caution

Keep to the east bank past the Sunseekers Marina until you reach Back Water Channel leading off to the northwest for 3 cables, marked by red and green piles. At the east cardinal post, swing sharply to port with the channel straight to Cobb's Quay Marina, leaving the post on your starboard hand.

Poole Harbour entrance looking northwest

Anchorages and berths

Studland Bay is an excellent anchorage with good holding and fine shelter in west and southwest winds. There are lovely views and a small village about ¼ mile inshore with a grocer's shop, a hotel and a post office. Studland is one of the south coast's most popular anchorages, and can be approached without difficulty. Sound in to find a suitable depth. The holding is good.

Off Brownsea Island Anchor in the entrance to South Deep clear of the fairway, or off Goathorn Point clear of moorings, or in one of the deep pools further up. Beware of the clearly marked oyster beds and do not anchor near these. There are some moorings off Goathorn Point which may be vacant. The best anchorage is probably in the pool to the southwest of Green Island in 3m, clear of underwater pipes, cables and oyster beds. Careful pilotage on a good rise of tide will be needed to get you there.

North of South Middle Ground buoy (No.20) to the east of the Middle Ship Channel are numerous moorings, some of which are sometimes vacant.

Salterns Marina (300 berths) usually has room for a visitor. Manoeuvring space is tight; if you have not called ahead on VHF Ch 80 or 37, tie up on the hammerhead of B pontoon for instructions. There are all marina facilities, including a laundry and use of the fine bar premises of the Poole Harbour Yacht Club. There is also a chandlery which changes *Calor Gas/Camping Gaz* bottles, but you are some distance from town, with little option save a cab ride.

Town Quay 100 berths rafted up. Call on VHF Ch 14, *Poole Quay*, or *Poole Harbour Control* out of hours. If less than 12·5m LOA, a call is unnecessary. Just stand off the conspicuous marina office until they notice, or tie up to a suitable berth, or raft up to a similar-sized boat. The quay wall is clearly marked to indicate berths allocated to craft of varying LOA. Rafting up to six deep is permitted. Beware of the strong current around the bridge.

There are pay showers near the bridge, with public toilets at the east and west ends of the quay.

A plan is now in operation for the construction of a breakwater to shelter the Town Quay from the southeast and to provide for 100 comforable, safe pontoon berths. This development has met with fierce resistance but has finally been admitted. It will be centred around a refurbished traditional coaster, where modern showers, toilets and other facilities will be sited. The harbourmaster will have an office on the bridge, from where he will administer the quay. This will mean a major improvement for visitors.

Cobb's Quay is a large marina in generally shoal water, though depths of up to 2m are promised. If you should end up with your keel in the mud at LW, it is very soft indeed and you won't feel a thing. Bridge openings are described above. Call the marina on VHF Ch 80, or ☎ 01202 674299. There are no visitors' berths as such, but the marina has a huge population and the helpful staff will frequently be able to accommodate you in a spare berth.

Poole Yacht Club Yacht Haven is private, but welcomes visiting yachtsmen from recognised clubs arriving by boat. The facilities are excellent, but the visitors' berths cannot be reserved, being allocated on a first-come basis. ☎ 01202 672687, or call *Pike* on VHF Ch 80 and 37 (May to September 0800–2200). Yachts up to 11·5m LOA and 2·5m draught can be accommodated.

River Frome Shallow berths at Wareham Quay (0·2m MLWS), where all town facilities are available. Ridge Wharf Yacht Centre, on the south bank a little over half a mile upstream of Swineham Point, has a surprising number of facilities and usually has room for visitors. Generally speaking, strangers whose yachts draw more than 1·3m are not recommended to attempt Wareham.

Facilities

Yacht yards with repair facilities at Sandbanks, Parkstone, Cobb's Quay, Salterns Marina and many other places. Fuel from barge by *Aunt Betty* buoy; call *Poole Bay Fuels*, VHF Ch 37 working hours. Diesel from Corral's (opposite Town Quay) during working hours. Fresh water from marinas, and at the Town Quay by hose on application to the berthing office.

Salterns Marina and Cobb's Quay have fuel facilities, as do Ridge Wharf Yacht Centre, Dorset Yacht Co. and Sandbanks Yacht Centre. There are a number of chandlers, including good ones at Poole Quay and Salterns Marina. Sundry pubs and restaurants, first-class shopping, various sailmakers,

Salterns Marina

Poole Town Quay from the southeast. Note *Stakes* S card
beacon opposite moored ship

Cobbs Quay Marina
Below Poole Yacht Club Yacht Haven

and numerous launching sites, including the slipway at Baites, east of Fishermen's Dock, Lilliput Yacht Services, Sandbanks Road, Cobb's Quay, Poole Harbour Yacht Club, Ridge Wharf Yacht Centre and Sunseekers Marina.

Communications
Main line trains to London Waterloo.

Wareham Quay

Swanage

Tides

HW springs −0235 Dover
HW neaps +0120 Dover
These time differences should be considered very approximate.

MHWS	MLWS	MHWN	MLWN
2·0m	0·5m	1·6m	1·2m

Streams

The tide swirls about in Swanage Bay, so expect to swing. Beware of the race at Peveril Point (up to 3 knots at springs) – see below.

General

Swanage offers a pleasant if somewhat insecure anchorage in the right weather conditions. The bay is sheltered from north-northwest to south-southwest, but if the wind blows in with any force it soon becomes untenable.

Holding is not good, with a thin layer of sand over rock, with some weed patches adding to the fun, but the aspect is amenable, and in settled weather the anchorage is an excellent afternoon-tea stop. Unless you are sure of your anchor and the wind direction, an easier overnight berth can be had in Studland Bay (see Poole), which has better shelter and superior holding, and is closer to Poole Harbour, your final bolt hole in the event of unexpected easterlies.

Entry from the east is simple. From the north, likewise, given that you clear Old Harry Rocks and Handfast Point by a couple of cables. From the south, you should resist any temptation to pass inshore of the unlit red buoy off Peveril Point. The tide runs over Peveril Ledge like a millrace. There is a rip outside the buoy as well, but it is not nearly so dangerous.

Sound in and anchor in the vicinity of the pier head, ideally about a cable to the west-northwest in about 2m, keeping to seaward of local moorings.

Facilities

Hotels and shops, although the pubs fall short of the standard sought by the true connoisseur. Good sailing club, launching site at a slipway near to the pier with car parking adjacent.

Swanage Bay. Note pier and Peveril Point with its associated ledge and tidal activity.

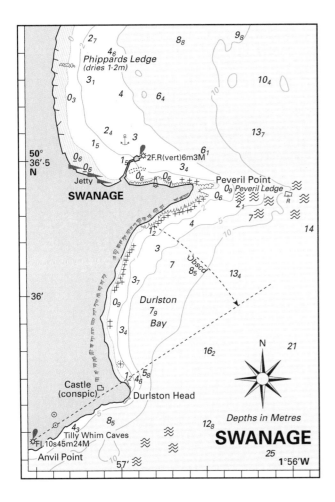

SWANAGE

Depths in Metres

SWANAGE

Lulworth Cove

Tides
HW approx −0450 Dover

MHWS	MLWS	MHWN	MLWN
2·3m	0·3m	1·5m	0·9m

Double LWs are experienced in Lulworth. Predictions attach to the first of these.

Depths
5m in the centre of the entrance, then the bottom shelves gradually, leaving 2m LAT to within 100m of the beach. There are rocks inside the entrance on the east side (see plan), and a ledge on the shore side of the 2m line to the west of the entrance.

General
Lulworth is a well publicised beauty spot, and is of great interest to students of geology. The stratified rocks are fascinating even to the nonspecialist observer. The cove looks very sheltered on the chart, and in settled northerly weather a quiet night can be enjoyed. However, if the wind takes an onshore turn you should clear out without delay. Cases are on record of anchored yachts rolling their rails down, and horror stories are in plentiful supply. Your problems will be exacerbated if you have not left at the first sign of trouble, because if it really comes on to blow from a southerly or southwesterly quarter you may not get out at all.

Approach and entrance
It is not easy to identify Lulworth from seaward, though there are characteristic cliffs on either side of the entrance, and immediately to the west is a sugar-loaf hill with an ex-coastguard hut. Fortunately, it is safe to steer fairly close to the cliff once in Lulworth's vicinity, and eyeball the gap in the rock walls. Keep slightly east of centre in the entrance to avoid the rocks off West Point (marked by an unlit red buoy in the summer months). The wind is fluky and squally, particularly in the desired northerlies, so sailing in may present something of a challenge. If you must beat in, remember the rocky shoals in the southeast corner inside East Point.

Anchorage
Anchor in around 2·5m about due north of East Point in clay with some sand and weed.

In southwesterly breezes use the northwest corner. Keep clear of local moorings, but try not to anchor in the fairway near the beach landing for Lulworth village, which is in this vicinity.

Facilities
Petrol and oil from garage. Small hotels, pub and simple shops. Launching site at the beach at the end of the road. Frequent buses in the summer.

Lulworth Gunnery Ranges
There are two danger areas for shipping to the south of Lulworth and Kimmeridge. The one normally in use extends 6 miles out to sea, while the outer, which is seldom utilised, reaches out to 13 miles. Times of firing are published in local papers and notified to neighbouring harbourmasters and yacht clubs, who can supply leaflets giving the details. These can also be obtained from the Range Office, ☎ 01929 462721 ext. 4819 or 4859, or by listening to Radio Solent (96·1kHz), who broadcast the information on their morning forecasts.

When firing is in progress, red flags are flown by day. After dark, red lights are shown at the huts immediately east of the cove on the summit of Bindon Hill, and on St Alban's Head. Vessels may pass through the areas, but passage must be made as

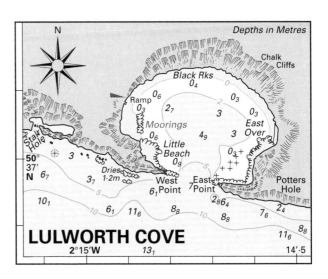

LULWORTH COVE

Lulworth Cove. View from the southeast. Lulworth village in
the centre

quickly as possible. Anchoring, fishing and stopping
are prohibited.

When the range is active, fast patrol boats are on
station to keep yachts clear of the area. Set watch on
Ch 8 during firings. Portland Naval Base gives firing
times on Ch 13 or 14 at 0945 and 1645. The ranges
are not used during August.

Lulworth Cove. Do not be deceived by the apparent spaciousness
on this view, when manoeuvring inside, you may find yourself
strapped for space

Weymouth

Tides

HW approx −0440 Dover

MHWS	MLWS	MHWN	MLWN
2·1m	0·4m	1·4m	0·8m

Tides in Weymouth are eccentric, with 4 hours
flood, 4 hours ebb and 4 hours slack around LW,
subject to a small rise of around 0·2m (the Gulder)
which creeps in around three quarters of an hour
after LW.

Depths

The entrance, the fairway and the ferry-terminal
area, including Berth No. 4 (adjacent to the Pavilion
Theatre), are dredged to 5·2m. Depths alongside
berths Nos 5 and 6 (opposite Weymouth lifeboat
and slipway) are 4·8m. Between No. 7 Berth (by the
yacht toilet facility at No. 13 Custom House Quay)
and the bridge, depths are in excess of 3m. Berths in
the Cove have at least 2m, and usually the best part
of 3m. Above the bridge there is 2·5m in the channel
and 2·5–1·75m in the marina.

General

Weymouth is a useful port for yachts bound east or
west. It is also a strategic point to leave a boat for a
week or two in the safety of the marina above the

Weymouth harbour. Berths for commercial traffic on right.
Note leading marks low on left bank, downstream of sailing
club. Proceed up-harbour leaving ships (if any) and 'large white
yacht' to starboard. Yachts over 13m berth in this vicinity

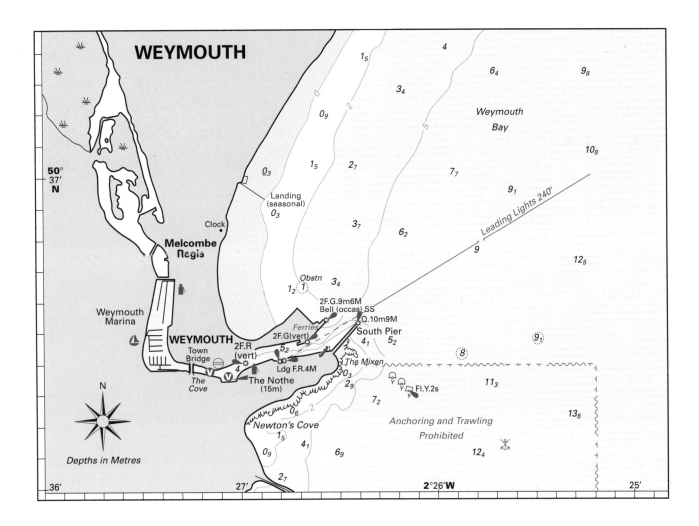

bridge as well as a practical destination for a weekend sail from the Solent. The pretty harbour is sheltered in all weathers and can be entered at any state of the tide, though easterly gales can make the entrance rough. The town itself is a delightful cameo of the English seaside holiday. As one strolls down the seafront, one expects to see Edwardian gentlemen in striped blazers and boaters escorting long-skirted beauties twirling parasols. Even in their absence, there are still real swingboats, donkey rides, a sand modeller and Punch-and-Judy shows. The town even puts on a serious firework display on most Monday evenings in high season. This is best watched from the promenade and it is well worth hurrying your dinner or turning your troops out of the pubs.

Approach and entrance

From the west, the question will arise as to whether you should pass inshore or offshore of the Portland Race (see 'Principal headlands'), but in either event you will ultimately find yourself approaching from the vicinity of Portland Harbour breakwaters. These are left to port, giving sensible consideration to any traffic which may be about to appear through the entrances, and a course shaped for the South Pier of Weymouth with its conspicuous white lighthouse (Q.10m9M).

From the east, you will first discern the high ground of the Isle of Portland; as you come closer the wooded hill of the Nothe will become apparent immediately south of the entrance, with the buildings backing the perfect crescent of the beach showing up rather later. Note the conspicuous Jubilee Clock about half a mile north of the harbour mouth.

Various buoys will be seen between Portland and Weymouth Harbour. Some are lighted, marking the Outer Degaussing Range, but none is of navigational significance to yachts. The Mixen rocks which lie to the south of the South Pier cover at half-tide.

Apart from generally shoaling rocky water in towards Newton's Cove, which has little relevance to passage navigators, there are no dangers in the offing.

Give the South Pier half a cable clearance, watching out for fishing lines, and enter the harbour between it and the North Pier (2F.G). By night there is a useful transit of F.R leading lights on 240°. These have white posts with open diamond markers for daytime recognition, but in practice these are little noted by yachts. The harbour supports an active fishing fleet and is used by commercial vessels up to 130m LOA.

Weymouth Harbour entrance

Attention to traffic signals shown from a mast midway along the South Pier is mandatory for safety reasons.

During normal working hours (summer 0700–2230) advice can be requested from *Weymouth Harbour Radio* on VHF Ch 16, working Ch 12.

RRR flashing – Emergency. Port closed
RRG – Entrance foul. Movement prohibited
RRR – Ship sailing. No entry
GGG – Ship entering. No departure
GWG – Move as directed by harbourmaster

If there are no signals, move at your own discretion.

Berthing

Call *Weymouth Harbour Radio* on Ch 12. If you do not hear a response and do not find a berthing master, berth in the cove as follows: on the south side where the harbour opens up, or on the north wall, now with its pontoon, before you get to the fishing boats. Larger yachts may raft up nearer the entrance on the north side oppposite the lifeboat station. The pontoons in Weymouth have sometimes been slippery, so beware if you are obliged to jump down onto them.

Alternatively, you can opt for the new marina. The bridge opens on even hours (0800–2000 +2100 in summer. Winter by arrangement which creates no problems in practice).

There is a clearly marked waiting pontoon immediately to seaward of the bridge on the north side of the harbour. Once through the bridge, turn to starboard and follow the signs. Call the marina on VHF Ch 80 and you will be met by berthing staff. The marina is run by the same firm as Haslar Marina in Portsmouth Harbour, whose showers and toilets have been described as the finest in the Channel. Similar facilities are available here.

Anchorage

In settled weather it is possible and economical to anchor northwest of the North Pier in varying depths. You must, however, lie to the east of a line joining St John's Church spire and the port signal station. There is a yellow can buoy marked 'foul' approximately 350m from the signal station and in line with the spire. Greater depths are available further to seaward. Sadly, this apparently excellent roadstead has given the *Shell Pilot* some uncomfortably rolly nights. However enticing it appears, it seems that on many occasions, a swell hooks round Portland and fetches up off Weymouth beach. Some people don't mind this, feeling it adds to the salty flavour of their cruising. Others find it abhorrent. Be warned, and hope you are lucky. Holding is good but, rolling or not, the anchorage becomes untenable in easterly winds.

Facilities

Repairs and chandlery of most descriptions at Kingfisher Marine, ☎ 01305 766595. Marine engineers at Rover Marine Services ☎ 781612, MPI Engineers ☎ 821862 and Cosens & Co ☎ 822922. Showers, toilets and launderette beneath the berthing master's office, 13 Custom House Quay, and at the back of the Royal Dorset Yacht Club bar on the North Quay – all welcome. Water on quays, but it is not always convenient to run a hose, and some electricity. Diesel from the fuelling jetty on the south side of the harbour. A small mobile road tanker also offers diesel service. Petrol from garages. Launching from Wyatt's Wharf, adjacent to Weymouth lifeboat station. All town facilities: banks, restaurants, etc. Excellent waterfront pubs, particularly on the cove side, with the King's Arms to be preferred by connoisseurs of the real thing.

Communications

Main line rail station with trains to London and Southampton. Buses also. High-speed passenger ferry to the Channel Islands.

Portland Harbour

Tides

HW approx −0430 Dover

MHWS	MLWS	MHWN	MLWN
2·1m	0·2m	1·4m	0·7m

Depths

Generally deep, but shelving towards its western boundaries – see plan.

General

Portland Harbour is far from ideal as a stopover for visiting yachts. It was built as a naval harbour in the mid-19th century of local stone using labour from the prison which still stands above it.

The Navy moved out in the mid-1990s, leaving the port facilities to commercial operators. There are some yacht moorings – all private – and limited anchoring possibilities. The harbour is large enough to be exposed in strong winds unless you are berthed under a weather shore. There have been numerous instances of yachts breaking free of their moorings and being wrecked on the stony breakwaters. A grim prospect.

Approach, entrance and berthing

There is no difficulty in identifying Portland, from whichever direction you approach. Note Portland Race (see 'Principal headlands') and the Shambles. Enter either at A head or between B and C heads. The lights are shown on the plan. Do not attempt the South Ship Channel. This is obstructed by the remains of the old HMS *Hood*, scuttled in 1914.

It may be possible to use a yacht mooring under the control of either the Castle Cove Sailing Club (☎ 01305 783708) or the Royal Dorset Yacht Club (☎ 01305 786258), but prior arrangement is strongly recommended. These moorings are in the Castle Cove area.

Alternatively, you could try anchoring to the east of Small Mouth, where a bridge joins the Isle of Portland to the mainland. Beyond Small Mouth is the East Fleet, the first of the lakes behind Chesil Beach. Depths to the east of the 2m line at this anchorage are adequate for all but the largest yachts; the recommended spot is likely to be 2 cables northeast of the *New Channel* beacon, which lies 4 cables east of Small Mouth Ferry bridge. There are no launching facilities here, and utilities are restricted, but you can walk to Weymouth from Castle Cove. Whatever your intentions in Portland Harbour, you should contact Port Control on VHF Ch 13 between the hours of 0900 and 1700 when the office is manned. Outside these times, you are on your own, but don't be tempted to seek an alongside berth.

Portland Harbour looking towards Portland

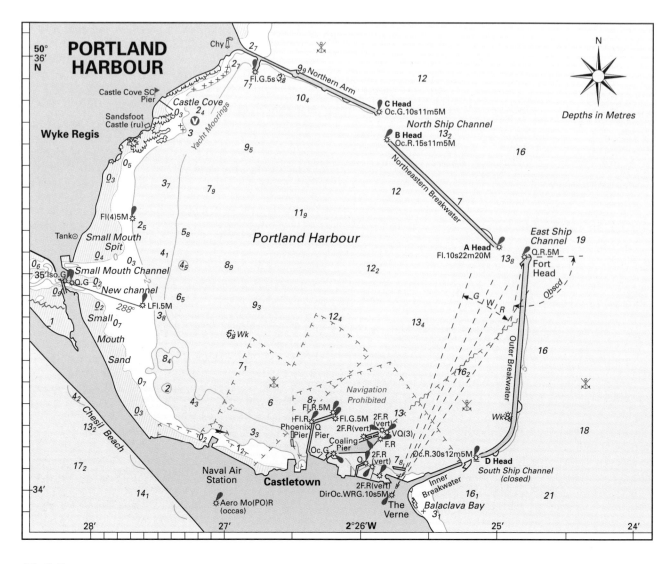

Bridport

Tides
HW −0500 Dover

MHWS	MLWS	MHWN	MLWN
4·1m	0·6m	3·0m	1·6m

The flood slackens after the first hour, then resumes its normal rapidity about 90 minutes later. HW stands for 1½ hours.

Depths
1·2m in the immediate offing, but the entrance channel dries up to 0·6m about halfway in. The eastern section of the harbour dries about 0·9m. The western varies from drying 0·7m in the centre to a drying height of 2·7m beside West Quay. There is a deep pool of about 3·3m at the coaster berth on the east side of the main run of the channel alongside the Quay.

General
West Bay, the port for Bridport, has little to offer yachtsmen. The entrance can be highly dangerous in strong onshore winds and there are few berths at which yachts may lie afloat. Nonetheless, the harbour has a strong character of its own, so for the brave and the adventurous it may prove worth a visit.

Approach and entrance
Apart from a 4m patch (the Pollock) about 7 cables south-southwest of the entrance, and a 3·7m patch inside this, there are no dangers in the offing. There is a lit yellow buoy (Fl.Y.5s) a cable southeast of the Pollock, marking a sewer outfall. Entry is only recommended within 2 hours of HW.

The best approach line is on a transit of 011°, which lines up the west pier head with Bridport town hall tower and flagstaff a mile or so inland. Enter between the pier heads. Beware of backwash from the walls and do not be surprised by the exceedingly narrow channel between the piers. It is around 12m wide.

Do not even think of sailing in, unless you are operating a quarter tonner with a following wind. Under power, do not be afraid to keep way on until you are well up the channel. If there is a surge, you will be glad of all the steerageway you can get.

Note that the harbour lights shown on the plan are only exhibited when a coaster is expected, so that night entry for strangers in small craft is a non-starter.

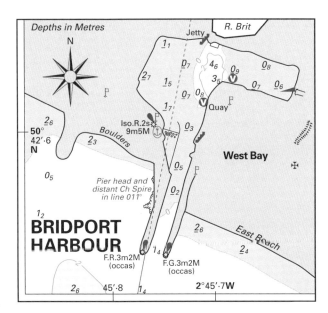

A black ball signal from the harbourmaster's office indicates that the harbour is closed.

Berthing

Consult the harbourmaster (*Bridport Radio*) on VHF Ch 16 or 11, or ☎ 01308 423222. A call in good time seems prudent in order to secure a berth in this tight little port.

Small yachts can dry out in mud at the west end of the harbour, or lean on the walls with their keels in mud, but the area is full of local moorings so space is severely limited. There is also a coaster berth, which is by the visitors' symbol indicated on the plan. This is scoured out by the river, which is released periodically through sluicegates. You may be given permission to lie here if the berth is unoccupied.

Bridport

Bridport Harbour entrance near high tide

Facilities

Fresh water near the quay. There are shops and stores, but no notable repair facilities for yachts. There is a good slipway with a convenient car park.

Regular buses run to Bridport, a pretty West Country town 1½ miles distant.

Lyme Regis

Tides

HW −0455 Dover

MHWS	MLWS	MHWN	MLWN
4·3m	0·6m	3·1m	1·7m

The rate of rise is similar to that experienced at Bridport (page 112).

Depths

The whole harbour dries up to 2m, with around 0·3m drying height in the entrance. Berths along the sailing club wall dry from 0·3m to 1·3m. There is 1–2m of deep water a cable and more to the east of the harbour entrance, where the anchorage is to be found.

General

Lyme Regis is a fascinating town whose atmosphere derives from a unique mixture of fine old West Country buildings, which somehow do not quite dispel an exciting sort of 'outpost' feeling. This is particularly noticeable during periods of hard weather blowing in from the sea, when the harbour entrance becomes dangerous, and those drying out within its walls may experience prolonged heavy bumping. In settled weather, however, the anchorage outside makes for an attractive visit, and a berth inside by the warmly welcoming sailing club can be an experience to cherish.

Approach and entrance

Lyme Regis is to be found some 22 miles west of Portland Bill; the approach is straightforward. The harbour lies immediately south of a conspicuous green park, marking the scene of a landslip. It is protected from the west by a long stone pier known as the Cobb, which is forked at its eastern end. To seaward of the outer fork stands a post with a red can topmark marking a pile of large Portland stones covered at half flood. There is also rocky debris and shelves along the west and south sides of the Cobb.

The narrow harbour entrance lies between the inner fork of the Cobb and the southern end of the North Wall, a breakwater which affords partial protection to the harbour from the east.

Having done your tidal sums, steer for the post and topmark off the outer fork of the Cobb, leaving it about 50m to port, then stand on until the harbour entrance is open. Now steer in.

Leading lights

A transit of 296° leads up to the harbour entrance. It is formed by a rear F.G and an Oc.WR on the north arm of the Cobb, or south breakwater. Note that the cut-off point of the white and the red comes exactly on the transit, so if the light shows red and you are having trouble locating the F.G, come to starboard until the white sector hints at its presence. You are now on line. 'Too much white' at the inner end of the approach could place you uncomfortably close to the rocks.

Lyme Regis. Note the Cobb, lying to seaward of the true harbour entrance

Anchorage and berthing

If you decide to anchor outside, which is a fair proposition in calm weather with no onshore component in the breeze, sound in on a northwesterly heading towards a point to the north of the pier heads until you find a suitable depth. Shoal-draught craft can work well in, particularly on neap tides. Deeper boats may feel rather far out to seaward if proposing to pass a low water springs in their berth. The quality of the bottom varies, so be prepared to try again if your hook fails to hold at the first attempt.

There are 5 red buoys for visitors in the anchorage. They are clearly marked.

Vacant drying berths inside the harbour are likely to be few, as the harbour is much used, but there is room for a dozen or so visiting yachts to dry out on clean sand alongside the wall beside the sailing club (see 'Depths').

Whatever berth you may fancy, it makes sense to call the harbourmaster in advance on VHF Ch 16 (working Ch 14), or ☎ 01297 442137.

Facilities

Lyme Regis Sailing Club (☎ 01297 442800) is very hospitable, with showers and a bar which is open when a green light is shown.

Water at shoreward end of the Cobb. Fuel can be delivered for a small fee. Hotels and shops.

Scrubbing can be arranged, and small yacht repairs. Launching site, slip and car park adjacent. Dinghy park.

Communications

Buses to all parts. Axminster station is 6 miles distant by road.

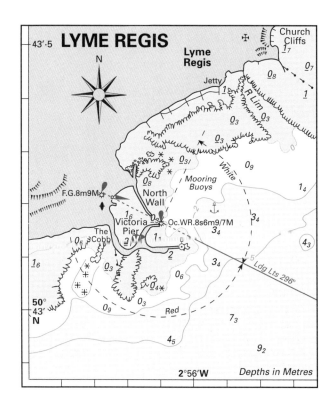

Below top Lyme Regis. Entrance from eastward
Bottom Close to entrance. Sailing club on upper floor of building nearest entrance

Axmouth and Beer

Beer

Beer is an open anchorage which should only be used in settled, offshore weather. In the right conditions it can be a delightful place. The nearest all-weather refuges are Torquay and Brixham.

The cove in which yachts may lie offers a little more protection than the chart might imply, and is first identified from seaward by Beer Head. This mighty, 130m headland is the last white cliff on the coast before chalk gives way to the red cliffs of Devon. The cove lies east of the headland.

Approaching from the west, round Beer Head then follow the cliffs northwards, skirting the rocks at their base, until abeam of the road running down from the village to the beach. The village church is conspicuous. The fixed white light nearby is not.

If you are coming from the east, give the headland to the east of the cove a wide berth as it has off-lying rocks extending for a cable to seawards.

Sound in and anchor as close to the shore as you reasonably can, clear of the fishing boat moorings. Landing is by dinghy on the steep beach.

Beer has the usual facilities of a moderate-sized village, plus Beer SC, an active club with both dinghy and lugger sailing.

Axmouth

Eastward from Beer Roads, 1½ miles across Seaton Bay, lies the interesting haven of Axmouth. Axmouth was a flourishing small port until, after the advent of the railway which killed its trade, the harbour entrance works were destroyed in storms between 1869 and 1875. Inside, shelter is still excellent for bilgekeelers, yachts with lifting keels, or those equipped with legs. Visitors are welcomed, but the entrance is dangerous in more than moderate onshore winds.

The entrance is found at the end of a shingle spit where the Axe River runs out to sea, close to the west of Haven Cliff. The bar dries 1m and the unmarked channel shifts, though it normally runs east-northeasterly. Strangers are therefore recommended to anchor 2 cables west of the entrance, then either take local advice or sound the channel by dinghy. Enter half an hour either side of HW (Dover −0433), and note that the spring ebb, once running at full spate, can achieve 6 knots. The flood also runs harder than you would expect right up to the last, so if entering even thirty minutes before HW, watch out as you make the turn inside.

The channel is very narrow, but craft of up to 8·5m LOA and 1·5m draught which can take the ground can enter safely. Its position is denoted by a starboard-hand beacon (Fl.5s) on the pier. Immediately inside you must make a sharp turn to

Axmouth. Steer towards the end of the pier, then swing to port close to the wall, where the fairway is found

port, then keep over towards the wall, where the fairway is to be found.

The Axe YC ☎ 01297 20742 has fore-and-aft moorings where boats up to 28ft raft in pairs to dry out. Larger craft may find space along the wall. The club also has a boat-house and slipway, also a bar and showers in the clubhouse. Boat builder and general marine services. Four hundred metres above the entrance, low bridges (2m) form an effective head of navigation.

The adjacent town of Seaton has most domestic facilities.

Exmouth

Tides

HW Exmouth Dock −0455 Dover
HW Topsham about ¼ hour later

Exmouth approaches

MHWS	MLWS	MHWN	MLWN
4·6m	0·5m	3·4m	1·7m

Streams

Streams run strongly in the entrance, with up to 5 knots past Exmouth dock gates on a spring ebb.

Depths

The sands around the approaches are liable to change, but the bar is often as little as 1m or less at LAT, giving a dubious 1·5m at MLWS unless you can be sure of the best route by virtue of local knowledge. Inside the river the bottom is uneven, with deep areas as well as the shoal patches which are notable to the west and north of Bull Hill Bank, where 1·5m LAT may be encountered.

Further up, the channel shoals intermittently to Topsham Lock, but you should not find less than 0·4m anywhere within its boundaries.

Above this lock, the river dries completely. The canal is very deep, but height is limited to 11m by the motorway bridge.

General

The River Exe is well worth a diversion during a West Country cruise. While the small tidal dock at Exmouth itself is closed to yachts, there are a number of useful anchorages, and there is the possibility of locking into the Exeter Canal at Turf Lock for complete shelter and a good pub. In shoal-draught craft, or others at the right tides, a visit to Topsham is fascinating for bird-watchers, or anyone who cares that galleons were built here that stood out to face the Spanish Armada.

The bar is not always easy to cross, with its shifting sands. Indeed, in the wrong conditions it is not a nice place to be. Nonetheless, on a reasonable day it presents no serious problems, being well buoyed.

Approach and entrance

The outer fairway buoy (east cardinal *East Exe* Q(3)10s) is to be found 6 cables southwest of Straight Point. This is a low promontory with two flagpoles on it, backed by red cliffs. It is not to be confused with Orcombe Point a mile to the west. Between these points there are high, red cliffs with rocky shelves at their feet.

Make for the *East Exe* buoy whatever your direction of approach, but if you are coming from Torbay be sure to give a good offing to the dangerous Pole Sands, which form the south side of the entrance channel by extending well to seaward. Do not attempt the entrance with strong onshore winds against the ebb. Ideally, a half-flood approach is recommended, but do not forget the powerful streams.

Because of the shifting sands, it is vital to follow the sequentially numbered red (even numbers) and green (odd numbers) buoys. These are rather homespun in form, but are nonetheless clear enough. Once in the vicinity of *No.6* (red) you may come onto the leading marks on 305° (flagstaff on customs house at rear, black post on the sea wall in front), but they are difficult to spot. By night, the two leading lights tend to become lost in the town lighting. The port-hand buoys should be given a wide berth as they are often close to the dangers. The tide really picks up after *No.10* buoy (Fl.R.3s) marking the treacherous Checkstone Ledge has been passed.

The River Exe

The channel takes a sharp turn to the southwest off Exmouth Dock immediately after *No.12* unlit red buoy. This avoids the shoals extending east from Bull Hill Bank and takes you down past the Warren Sands. The main flood sweeps on northwesterly, so you must turn well before the dock opens, and make due allowance for cross-set, so as to get into the stream between Bull Hill Bank and Warren Point. This part of the river is called the Bight. It has two green buoys (Q.G *No.13* and Fl.G.5s *No.15*) to leave to starboard. On your port hand are moorings.

The channel now bends round northwards, past *No.17* green (Q.G), left to starboard.

If you wish to anchor off Starcross you must pass west of Shaggles Sand, leaving the red *No.16* buoy well to starboard, shaping up for the jetty as soon as green *No.17* buoy is a cable or so abaft the beam, with depths of 0·9m to 2·1m as far as Starcross. The channel is unmarked save for a red beacon on your port side, but it can be readily discerned by following the line of deep-draught yachts on moorings.

From red buoy *No.16* (Fl.R.5s) and unlit green buoy *No.19* the main channel now trends north-northwesterly, past an unlit green buoy to starboard, with more moorings on your port hand.

St Clement's Church tower appears ahead as you pass Q.R buoy *No.18* close to port and shape up towards *No.25* (Fl.G) buoy. Leave this and Fl.G *No.27* to starboard before the channel bears round to the northeast, with *No.29* (Q.G) buoy to starboard. Markers continue green (see plan) until the river curves round northwesterly once more

Exe approach looking to Straight Point

River Exe approach. Note extensive shoaling to port inside estuary.

RIVER EXE

Powderham Castle

N

Depths in Metres

50°
38'
N

37'

36'

28'   27'

Starcross
Tr

Landing at HW
Cockwood

Dawlis

towards the Q.R *No.20* buoy. Follow the buoys to Turf Lock, and thereafter the buoys and perches up to Topsham.

Shelley Gut

There is an unmarked shallow channel on the east side of Bull Hill Bank, which offers considerable time savings to yachts bound up-river from Exmouth. The sands are steep-to on either side and the channel is intricate, so it is not recommended without local knowledge.

Anchorage and moorings
Exmouth

Exmouth Marina (VHF Ch 14 or ☎ 01395 269314) is happy to accommodate visitors in berths vacated by absent berth-holders. Beware cross sets

at the entrance and do call first to enquire. Alternatively, anchor clear of the moorings (there is not much room) beyond the entrance to Exmouth Dock off the Point in 3m LAT if required, keeping clear of the lifeboat. This may be a rough berth when the wind blows against the tide, which can run at up to 5 knots.

Bull Hill

Four yellow visitors' moorings have been established by Exe Harbour Authority, upstream of *No.13* buoy south of Bull Hill Bank. If you don't fancy what can be a strenuous dinghy trip to either Exmouth or Starcross call the water taxi in season from 0600 to 2000 (*Conveyance* VHF Ch 37).

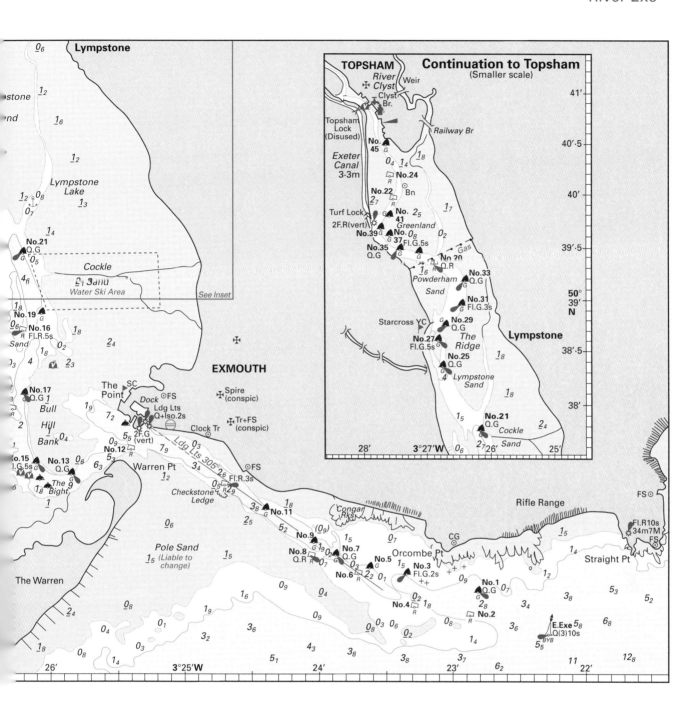

Inset: **TOPSHAM** — **Continuation to Topsham** (Smaller scale)

River Clyst · Weir · Clyst Br. · Railway Br · Topsham Lock (Disused) · No.45 · Exeter Canal 3·3m · No.24 · No.22 · Bn · Turf Lock 2F.R(vert) · No.39 · No.41 · Greenland · No.37 Fl.G.5s · No.35 Q.G · No.20 Q.R · Gas · Powderham Sand · No.33 Q.G · No.31 Fl.G.3s · Starcross YC · No.29 Q.G · No.27 Fl.G.5s · The Ridge · No.25 Q.G · Lympstone Sand · Lympstone · No.21 Q.G · Cockle Sand

Lympstone · Lympstone Lake · Cockle Sand · Water Ski Area · See Inset · No.21 Q.G · No.19 · No.16 Fl.R.5s · **EXMOUTH** · The Point SC · Spire (conspic) · No.17 Q.G · Bull Hill Bank · Dock FS · Ldg Lts Q+Iso.2s · Tr+FS (conspic) · Clock Tr · 2F.G (vert) · No.12 · No.13 Q.G · No.15 Fl.G.5s · The Bight · Warren Pt · Ldg Lts 305° 2·6 · Checkstone Ledge · Fl.R.3s · No.11 · No.9 · Congar Rks · Rifle Range · Pole Sand (Liable to change) · No.8 Q.R · No.7 Q.G · No.5 · No.3 Fl.G.2s · Orcombe Pt · CG · Straight Pt · No.1 Q.G · No.6 · No.4 · No.2 · E.Exe Q(3)10s · The Warren · Fl.R10s 34m7M · FS

Exe approach. Passing *Checkstone* buoy with Exmouth seafront on right

Inside the Exe estuary. Exmouth on right, looking up-river. Main channel passes close round Warren Point (lower centre). Moored yachts in centre are *not* in channel

Exmouth Harbour

Starcross

Anchor southeast of the pier in 0·6 to 2·1m as required. The best positions are taken up with moorings; apply at the club if you see a vacant one you fancy. Starcross is well sheltered from the west and has a few facilities, such as a main line station.

Turf Lock

Pick up a spare mooring south of the landing stage. Alternatively, anchor in 1·5m clear of the channel. The pub is a wonderful place with no public road access. It features a beautiful lawn with views over the river and a characterful interior for nasty days. Food is first class, as are the beer and wine. The landlord really cares. He has a pontoon to welcome you ashore.

Topsham

Anchor on the edge of the fairway north of the quay, opposite Trout's Boatyard. Here there is a landing which may be used by arrangement. Holding is poor, the bottom gravel, and there is 1m at LAT, so the berth may not suit you down to the ground. A happier solution may be Trout's outer berths (alongside) which are often available to visitors with up to 2m depth at neaps.

It is possible to lie alongside Topsham Quay drying out in soft mud. You are then conveniently sited for the ten or more pubs favoured by Exeter University students, (the 'Topsham Ten' pub-crawl) the excellent fish restaurant, the best cream tea around at the Georgian House Tea Rooms, or just to sift through the antique shops in search of something useful. If an on-board soirée is more in your line, fish and chips can be carried out from a nearby frier.

Exeter Canal

This excellent facility is being steadily run down by a short-sighted council. It is still possible to enter the lock for a peaceful stay at the Turf Lock hotel, but since the traditional daily sludge barge was axed by a health-conscious EU in 1999, openings are no longer encouraged. The price was reasonable when the *Shell Pilot* managed to locate a lock keeper in 1998 (a jolly and accommodating fellow he turned out to be, despite his bosses), but trying to get an answer to your calls to arrange entry will require persistence ☎ 013392 74306, or call *Port of Exeter* on VHF Ch 12. Give it a go, though. It's well worth it if you can sidestep the forces of darkness.

Facilities

Mainly at Exmouth and Topsham. Boat builders and repairs. Showers at yacht clubs. The usual town benefits.

Yacht clubs: Exeter Sailing Club. Starcross Yacht Club at Powderham Point. Starcross Fishing and Cruising Club. Topsham Sailing Club. Lympstone Sailing Club.

Water taxi at Exmouth. Call *Conveyance* on Ch 37.

Fuel from The Retreat Boatyard (☎ 01392 874 720) near the M5. Accessible around HW.

Rail and bus services on both sides of the river, with Exeter Airport near at hand.

Topsham with Exe Canal in foreground
Below River Exe. Time for some real yachting, safely tucked away inside Turf Lock

Teignmouth

Tides

HW −0450 Dover

Heights in the approaches

MHWS	MLWS	MHWN	MLWN
4·8m	0·6m	3·6m	1·9m

Depths

0·3m on the bar, but this is easily missed, and a drying height of 0·3m surrounds both passages. Inside there is at least 2·7m as far as Old Quay. Thereafter, gradual shoaling to an LAT depth of 1·5m just below the road bridge.

General

Teignmouth is a working port with coaster traffic as well as fishing boats. There is only one designated trot for visitors in deep water, so if you want to stay over a tide and this is full, you will have to dry out on 'The Salty'. Shelter is good inside the harbour, but the bar can be nasty with onshore winds and a swell, particularly on the ebb. Daylight entry is easy enough with a good rise of tide, but night entry is not recommended for strangers, even though the river is lit. The town is pretty. Shaldon is notably so, and quieter as well.

Approach and entrance

The Ness is easy to identify. It is a red cliff with pine trees at its summit. The point is much lower. It is wise to approach the entrance from well offshore, taking up a line of around 254° on the distinctive white Philip Lucette Beacon (Oc.R.5·5s2M) on the north side of the Ness. Cross the shallow water, which changes frequently, with the greatest caution because without local knowledge you may find less water than you had hoped. When the beacon is 50m or so ahead of you, come slowly round to starboard and head for the green beacon with triangular topmark (Oc.G.5s and F.G(vert)) off The Point. The stream runs hard here. After leaving the green beacon clear to starboard, you should alter course to 021° and head for New Quay (2F.G(vert)), leaving the three red buoys to port. These mark the Salty, a

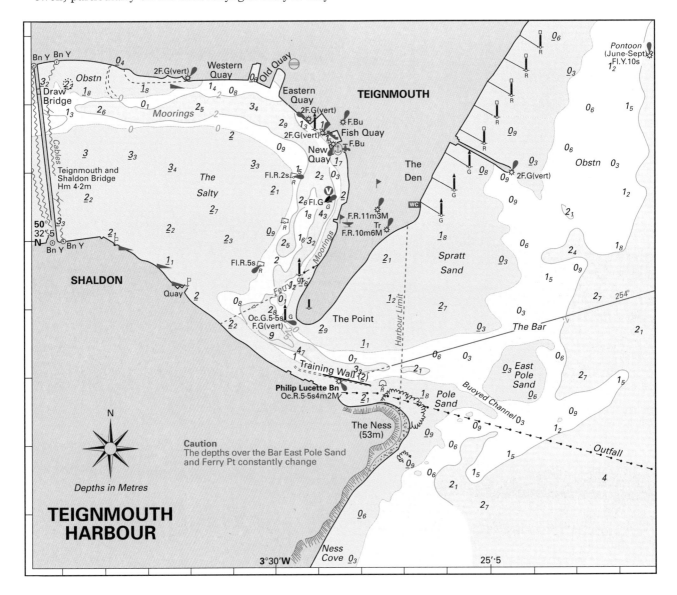

Caution
The depths over the Bar East Pole Sand and Ferry Pt constantly change

Depths in Metres

TEIGNMOUTH HARBOUR

Teignmouth at low water, with the bar clearly showing. The
Ness at the extreme left-hand side

Teignmouth. Close to the Bar on west-southwesterly course. *Philip Lucette* beacon centre. Shaldon to its right. Cliff to the left is the
Ness

Rounding up to the moorings of Teignmouth. Note green beacon off the Point and pier to seaward

drying bank which occupies much of the harbour. The starboard side of the channel is largely steep-to. Once round the corner into the east-west part of the channel, the deep water is best found by observation of the moorings.

You may notice a number of small orange buoys with ■ topmarks in the vicinity of the bar. These are used by pilots, but you will not be privy to their meaning unless you are lucky enough to be able to follow a ship or a pilot boat in. (Beware if your draught is deep. You may need more water than the pilot boat.)

Anchorage and mooring
There is a pair of large red mooring buoys with a 15m spread, in front of the town before the channel swings westward, to which visitors secure fore and aft, up to four abreast. The harbour office (VHF Ch 12 when a ship movement is expected) can advise as to availability. Otherwise, tie up and report to the office (☎ 01626 773165). The only viable alternative, short of picking up a vacant private mooring, is to sound in through the moorings off Shaldon, anchor (indifferent holding) and dry out in front of the village on sandy shingle. A ferry runs from the village to Teignmouth.

Upper reaches
The road bridge is so low that it is effectively the head of navigation for most craft. Dinghies can pass it, however, or cruisers able to negotiate its 3·5m clearance. It is then possible to reach Newton Abbot, given knowledge of where the channel may lie.

Facilities
Fresh water from New Quay. Fuel from garages. *Calor Gas* exchange at chandlery in Shaldon. No showers. Launderette in Teignmouth. Engineers and electronic repairs. Plenty of pubs, restaurants, fish and chips, etc. Good shops. Teign Corinthian Yacht Club in Dawlish Road, Teignmouth.

Communications
Buses. Main line railway.

Torquay

Tides
HW −0500 Dover

MHWS	MLWS	MHWN	MLWN
4·9m	0·7m	3·7m	2·0m

Depths
4·2m inside the entrance. For other depths, see plan, but note that visitors' berths have at least 2m LAT. The inner harbour mostly dries up to 1·5m.

General
Torbay is a fine big-ship anchorage in westerly weather. Indeed, it was the favoured bolt hole for the fleets blockading Brest during the Napoleonic Wars. In strong easterlies it was never the place to be. Today the new marina in Torquay gives all-

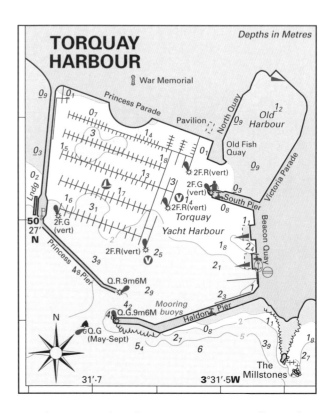

weather protection, but even now some discomfort may be felt in southeasterly gales. The town is well known for its riviera atmosphere. It is, it must be said, overcrowded at the height of the season, but many will enjoy a visit here nonetheless.

Approach and entrance
As it was in Nelson's day, Torbay is still easy to

Torquay Marina

approach. Torquay itself presents no difficulties either, except in strong southeasterly winds, when backwash from the harbour wall may render the entrance dangerous. During the summer months, a green conical buoy (Q.G) is established 75m west-southwest of Haldon Pier head. Leave this to starboard and enter between Haldon Pier (Q.G.9m6M) on your starboard hand and Princess Pier (Q.R.9m 6M) to port. It is only 80m or so from Princess Pier head to the marina, so there is less room than you might imagine, but there is still enough space for most yachts to be able to drop their sails in the sheltered water inside.

Each of the eastern pontoons of the marina, which are the visitors' berths, show 2F.R lights from the seaward ends.

Marina

There are berths for 60 visitors, clearly indicated by notice boards.

As you approach the port, call *Torquay Port* on VHF Ch 14. Then call the marina on VHF Ch 37, or tie up and report to the office.

Alternatively, telephone the harbour authority on ☎ 01803 292429 (out of hours ☎ 01803 550405), then the marina on ☎ 01803 214624. Subject to circumstances, pontoon berthing may be available on Haldon Pier.

Those more interested in historical authenticity than in present luxury may choose to anchor outside in westerly weather. The holding is good off Princess Pier in at least 3·6m. Do not be put off after dark by the creaking of ghostly oars and the muffled sound of 4in-diameter hempen cables running out after the splash of a wooden-stocked anchor.

Facilities

The marina (☎ 01803 214624/5) has water, showers, and launderette. Water on marina berths. Fuel and water are conveniently obtainable alongside South Pier of the old harbour. Repairs, with lifts up to 20 tons can be organised. Chandler, and all the facilities of a major seaside town. Customs, if required, on ☎ 01752 662091.

The main line railway station has frequent Intercity services.

The Royal Torbay Yacht Club (☎ 01803 292 006) welcomes visitors to its bar, restaurant and showers.

Paignton

Tides

As Torquay.

Depths

The approaches dry progressively to a height of 1·8m on the visitors' berths alongside the East Quay, giving up to 3m at MHWS, 1·9m at MHWN.

General

Once a fishing and small commercial harbour, Paignton, with the exception of one crabber who

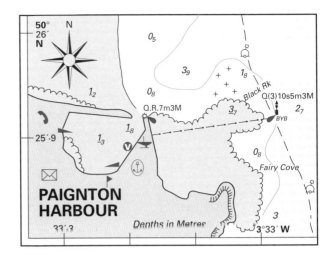

will not give up, is now officially designated a leisure port. The town is part of the Torbay resort complex. It is quieter than Torquay, but still bustles with summer activity.

Approach and berthing

Paignton harbour stands on the north side of Roundham Head with its prominent red cliffs. A rocky outcrop extends to the east from the entrance, so approach from the northeast is best. The East Quay outer end exhibits a light Q.R.3M.

Berth inside the East Quay, drying out if required on firm sand. The quay is not lit as such, but the street lighting is bright, illuminating the scene clearly. There are three drying visitors' moorings in the harbour, but whether lying on these or alongside, a maximum LOA of 8·2m (27ft) is adhered to.

Facilities

Fresh water at either end of the East Quay slipway. Toilets at the northwest corner of the harbour. Good beaches and the usual range of summer resort activities.

Brixham

Tides

HW −0505 Dover

MHWS	MLWS	MHWN	MLWN
4·9m	0·7m	3·7m	2·0m

Depths

Up to 6m in the outer harbour (see plan), with 3m and more in the Prince William Marina. The deep-water fishing harbour is prohibited to yachts, and the inner harbour with its scrubbing grids dries 0·6m (plus the height of the grid sleepers).

General

Brixham's fame and fortune rest firmly on its fishing fleet. From the days of its innovative and highly successful sailing trawlers, the town has fed the nation with its deep-water catches. Today, after a serious recession in the early 1970s, the port is once again one of England's foremost fishing stations.

Brixham showing the docks

Brixham Marina and Inner Harbour. Note YC pontoons under
the cliff immediately left of the white building outside the
covered fish quay.

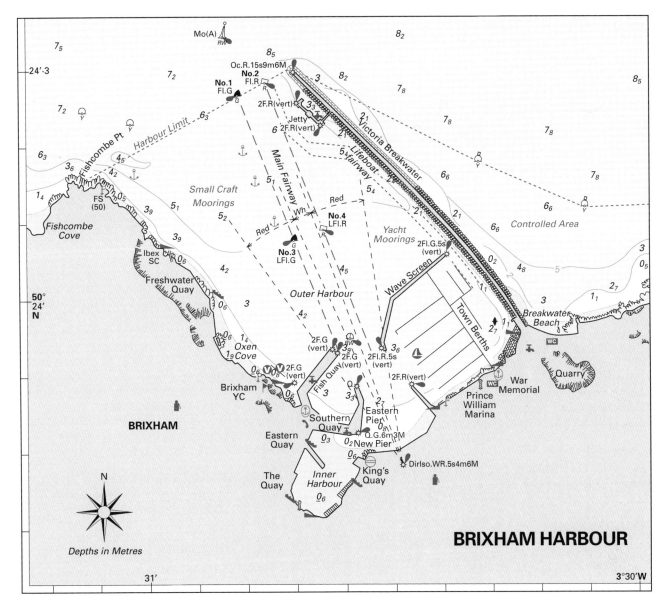

BRIXHAM HARBOUR

Depths in Metres

With fish come the incontinent Brixham seagulls, infamous throughout the West Channel for their gross behaviour. Never mind. Brixham remains a pretty town and an exciting port of call.

The port is also an important station for the Channel pilots who embark and disembark from here. So long as you stay out of their way and do not impede the fishing fleet, you will be little troubled by the business of the town.

The outer harbour and the marina are accessible at all states of tide and in virtually any weather, though northwesterlies can make things uncomfortable.

Approach and entrance

The long Victorian breakwater with its white lighthouse (Oc.R.15s9m6M) lies just over a mile west of the prominent silhouette of Berry Head. There is a safe water red and white vertically striped lit buoy (Morse code A) a cable off the end of the breakwater. For safety, this should be left to port, unless the harbour entrance is very quiet. Proceed up the fairway, keeping green buoys close to starboard and the reds well off to port. Entry into the marina is straightforward, but you are recommended to call ahead (*Prince William Marina*) on VHF Ch 16, 37 or 80, or ☎ 01803 882929.

Berthing, mooring and anchorage

Anchoring

Do not anchor in the fairway, or close under the breakwater, as this is an unmarked fairway for the lifeboat.

In offshore winds, a better bet is to anchor in Fishcombe Cove, immediately west of the outer harbour. It is a pleasant spot, and lack of dues will suit the yachtsmen of frugal pocket.

Mooring

There are three pontoons moored off the delightful Brixham Yacht Club. These are for members' convenience and can readily accommodate visitors. Great views from the club house high above on the cliff, welcoming members, attractive bar and helpful staff. The pontoons even have their own ancient dinghies to save you launching your own. The row to the private club landing is a very short one.

Drying berths

In the inner harbour there are a number of scrubbing berths for craft drawing up to 3m. These are available by arrangement with the harbourmaster ☎ 01803 853321, or VHF Ch 14 or 16.

Prince William Marina

Brixham's marina, named after William of Orange, who landed here to take over his new kingdom in 1688, is a large, modern establishment protected from the northwest by a wave screen. There are 30 visitors' berths. The reception berth is immediately inside on your port hand, but ideally you should call ahead on VHF Ch 37 or 80.

Facilities

All town facilities. Banks, pubs, restaurants, etc. General repairs and a sailmaker. Fresh water at the marina or from New Pier (see plan) where diesel is also available.

Launching sites can be found at public slipways on both west and east sides of the outer harbour.

Brixham Yacht Club welcomes visitors. It has an excellent restaurant, as well as showers, etc. Launderette in town and at the marina, where you can, of course, also have a shower.

Communication

Buses to Torquay and Paignton; thence main line trains.

Dartmouth

Tides

HW −0510 Dover

MHWS	MLWS	MHWN	MLWN
4·8m	0·4m	3·6m	1·8m

Depths

Deep water up to Dittisham, with the exception of a 4·5m patch a cable southwest of Higher Noss Point. Thereafter depths are variable, with only one drying patch to cross before Totnes.

General

Dartmouth is the archetypal West Country harbour. The lower reaches of the river are dominated by the pretty town of Dartmouth itself, with Kingswear climbing up the hill opposite on the east bank. The Royal Naval College stands proudly overlooking the anchorage. Further up lies the idyllic village of Dittisham, readily reached by yacht at all states of the tide. Beyond, a number of interesting creeks and villages are passed before fetching up at the fascinating town of Totnes – on the tide.

Dartmouth harbour is remarkably beautiful; it is well sheltered and can be entered by day or night at any state of tide. There is always room for visitors.

Approach and entrance

Dartmouth entrance is by no means obvious from seaward, but the 24m daymark (elevation 170m) on the hill behind Froward Point east of the entrance is unmistakable, as is the craggy Mewstone Rock (35m).

The entrance is deep and well marked, but there are a number of dangers. Rocks lie to the west of the Mewstone as follows: the Verticals (dry 1·8m), and the West Rock (with a depth over it of only 0·9m) is nearly 3 cables west-southwest of the Mewstone. The Bear's Tail (dries 0·6m) is 175m off Inner Froward Point, while 2¼ cables west is Old Castle Rock (with 1·8m over it), marked by the green conical *Castle Ledge* buoy (Fl.G.5s). For about three hours either side of HW the stream sets towards these dangers, which should be given a wide berth.

Approaching from the east, keep the East Blackstone Rock (a smaller version of the Mewstone half a mile east of it) well open of the Mewstone, until *Castle Ledge* buoy comes in line with Blackstone Point on the west side of the entrance.

On the west side there are drying rocks a cable off Combe Point; three cables east of this point is the Homestone (with 0·9m) with its red can buoy. Further in are the Meg Rocks, which dry 3m, and the 2m-high Western Blackstone Rock.

Between these dangers the approach is easy, except when strong south or southeast winds send a heavy swell into the harbour, sometimes as far up as the lower ferry. This can give rise to an ugly sea for small vessels, particularly on the ebb.

In the narrows you must avoid the Checkstone (0·3m over it) and the Kitten rock (1·8m), west-southwest of the red can *Checkstone* buoy (Fl(2)R. 5s), which lies off the ledges on the western side. Both rocks lie opposite Kingswear Castle. The Kitten rock is on the edge of the fairway, so when approaching the narrows keep east of it and give a good berth to the *Checkstone* buoy.

In the dark, stay in the white sector of the Iso.WRG.3s9m8M light shown from a squat white tower on the Kingswear side. Past the two castles and a cable beyond the *Checkstone* buoy, come round to 293° in the middle of the river in the white sector of the Bayard's Cove light (Fl.WRG.2s5m6M), on the Dartmouth side. The light's position is emphasised by day with a white stripe on the foreshore.

When the river is well open, proceed up the harbour in mid-stream. Note that there is a directional fixed white light just up-river of Kingswear Castle, shining across the deep water between it and Bayard's Cove, which is of assistance to outward-bound traffic.

Berthing in Dartmouth and Kingswear

All berthing is controlled by the DHNA (Dart Harbour and Navigation Authority). Wherever you berth, you will have to pay them dues.

Anchorage

Anchor off Kingswear between the row of large free-floating pontoons occupied mainly by fishing boats, and the line of big-ship moorings in mid-stream. The holding is pretty good, but wind against tide can cause some notoriously chaotic situations with dissimilar craft lying too close to one another. The aspect pleases, however, and it is a beautiful spot in good weather. It is also perfectly safe in all weathers for vessels properly equipped with good ground tackle. Just keep an eye on the neighbours and beware fouling the bracing chains and anchors stretching E–W from the big-ship buoys. The harbourmaster does not like yachts to be left unattended in this anchorage except for short periods, and never while the stream is on the turn.

Anchoring is also possible on the edge of a deep pool immediately below the Anchor Stone and the first of the moorings downstream of it. The Anchor Stone is just south of Dittisham.

Pontoons and moorings

DHNA maintain a number of useful visitors' pontoons. A long one is on the Kingswear side just below the position of the Dart Marina, once again inshore of a trot of big-ship mooring buoys. This provides a snug berth, from which you must take the dinghy or the water taxi ashore. There are also pontoons on the Dartmouth waterfront (max. LOA 35ft) clearly marked 'Visitors'. Larger vessels can berth on the Town Jetty pontoon by arrangement between 1700 and 0900, when the tripper boats go off watch. It may be possible to lie on the inside of this pontoon over the full 24-hour period.

There are also a number of visitors' buoys. DHNA can be called on VHF Ch 11, or ☎ 01803 832337.

The company running Dart Marina and Noss Marina also operate a number of moorings opposite Noss above the town which may be available on the day. Call Noss Marina (see below).

Marinas

Darthaven Marina is on the Kingswear side just upstream of the railway station (prominent steam locomotives in season). Call them on VHF Ch 80. If you arrive after the berthing master has gone home, tie up in a vacant berth and check the dock office, where vacant berths are chalked on a board. Move directly to one of these.

Dart Marina, recently up-graded on all fronts, lies immediately above the upper ferry. The rafting-up which was a feature of its past is now history, and finger pontoons are promised for visitors as of 1998. Showers, bathrooms and a launderette, power, telephone, fax lines and even TV lines on the pontoons. Push-bikes for hire, pump-out facilities and diesel on site.

Dartmouth. Not so easy to spot from the offing down at sea level

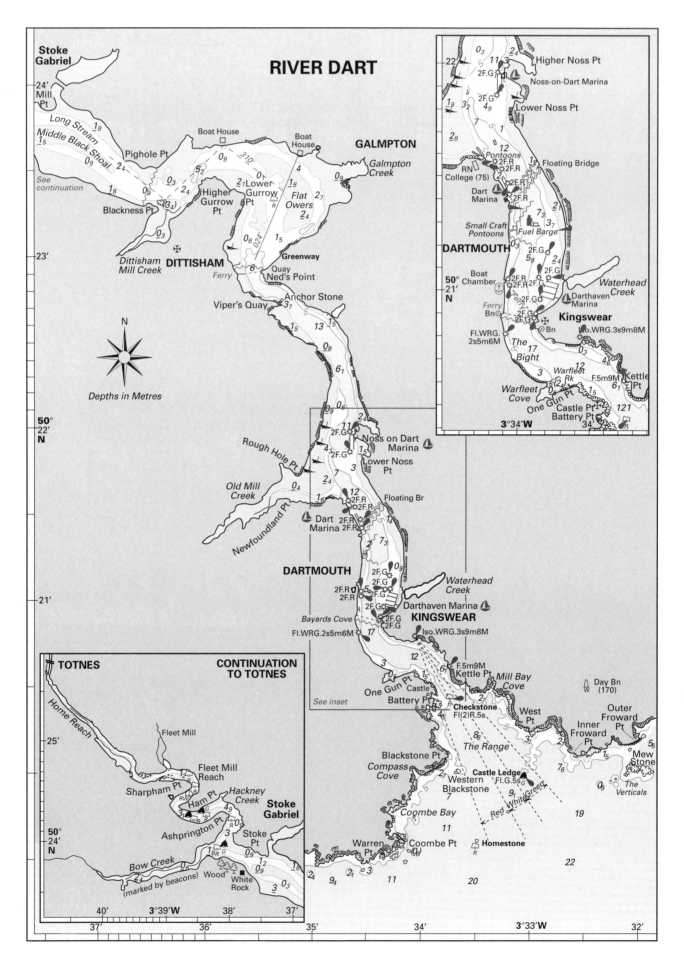

RIVER DART

GALMPTON

Stoke
Gabriel
Mill
Pt

Long Stream
Middle Black Shoal

Pighole Pt

Boat House

Boat House

Galmpton Creek

Blackness Pt

Higher
Gurrow
Pt

Lower
Gurrow
Pt

Flat Owers

Dittisham Mill Creek **DITTISHAM**

Greenway

Quay Ned's Point

Ferry

Viper's Quay

Anchor Stone

Higher Noss Pt

Noss-on-Dart Marina

Lower Noss Pt

2F.G
2F.G

Pontoons
2F.R
2F.R

RN College (75)

Dart Marina

Small Craft Pontoons

Floating Bridge

2F.R

2F.R

Fuel Barge

DARTMOUTH

2F.G
2F.G

Boat Chamber
2F.R 2F.R 2F.G

2F.G

Ferry Bn

Bn

2F.G

Fl.WRG. 2s5m6M

Iso.WRG.3s9m8M

Waterhead Creek

Darthaven Marina

Kingswear

The Bight

Warfleet Rk

F.5m9M

Warfleet Cove

One Gun Pt

Castle Pt
Battery Pt

Kettle Pt

N

Depths in Metres

**50°
22'
N**

Rough Hole Pt

Old Mill Creek

Noss on Dart Marina

2F.G
2F.G

Lower Noss Pt

Newfoundland Pt

2F.R
2F.R

Dart Marina
2F.R

Floating Br

DARTMOUTH

2F.G
2F.G

2F.R
2F.R

2F.G

Bayards Cove

Fl.WRG.2s5m6M

2F.G
2F.G

Waterhead Creek

Darthaven Marina

KINGSWEAR

Iso.WRG.3s9m8M

F.5m9M

Kettle Pt

Mill Bay Cove

Day Bn (170)

One Gun Pt

Castle
Battery Pt

See inset

Checkstone
Fl(2)R.5s

West Pt

Inner Froward Pt

Outer Froward Pt

Blackstone Pt

Compass Cove

The Range

Mew Stone

The Verticals

Castle Ledge
Fl.G.5s

Western Blackstone

White

Red

Green

TOTNES

CONTINUATION TO TOTNES

Home Reach

Fleet Mill

Fleet Mill Reach

Sharpham Pt

Ham Pt

Hackney Creek

Stoke Gabriel

Ashprington Pt

Stoke Pt

Bow Creek

(marked by beacons) Wood

White Rock

Coombe Bay

Warren Pt

Coombe Pt

Homestone

**50°
21'
N**

**50°
24'
N**

3°39'W

3°34'W

3°33'W

Mewstone from the southwest *Teignmouth approach*

Dartmouth day beacon from 1 mile offshore

Castle Ledge buoy, 6 cables SSE of entrance

Call VHF Ch 80 or ☎ 01803 835570 Ext 241.

Noss Marina, run by the Dart Marina people, this small, secluded marina lies opposite the upstream boundary of Old Mill Creek. Visitors' berths are available, and you can ride into town on the 'tripper boats' which call regularly bound down (or up) the Dart. There is also a water taxi. Facilities are what you would expect, and seem fine.

Call VHF Ch 80 or ☎ 01803 835570 Ext 248.

Embankment

Yachts can tie up to the Dartmouth embankment in front of the town, tide permitting, for short stays. There is a good scrubbing grid here, bookable through DHNA.

Up-river

Continue in mid-stream about two miles up-river as far as Dittisham, leaving the Anchor Stone with its ■

topmark firmly to port. 2½ cables above the stone you come to the village on the west bank with its waterfront pub and passenger ferry running to the impossibly picturesque Greenway Quay. On the Dittisham side there are a number of DHNA visitors' moorings. You will probably have to raft up in the season, but ask the harbour launch if in doubt, or call on VHF Ch 11. The buoys are an easy dinghy trip to a pontoon on the village jetty.

Upper reaches

Proceeding up-river from Dittisham to the east of Flat Owers Bank, keep the mooring buoys close to starboard to avoid the mudbank. Drying heights in Galmpton Creek, where many fine Brixham sailing trawlers, including *Provident*, were built, vary from 0·8m to 1·5m. Galmpton is not set up for visitors.

When there is sufficient water to work to the west of Flat Owers Bank, steer 024° for the boathouse at Waddeton until the red buoy is abeam to port, then swing round steadily to port and steer for the upper Sandridge boathouse on a heading of around 310°. When the upper Sandridge boathouse is half a cable in front of you, alter smartly towards Blackness Point, with its red beacon, keeping it just open on your starboard bow until High Gurrow Point is fairly close to port then steer for Blackness Point. When the beacon is half a cable or so ahead, swing steadily to starboard to head up for Pighole Point. You will see moorings away to port, but do not be tempted to follow their line. They are in a blind alley at some states of tide. After passing Pighole Point, the moorings come close on your starboard hand. Enter Stoke Gabriel creek, if desired, by rounding the green beacon, then follow the short channel marked by port-hand beacons with orange topmarks up to the landing pontoon, where there is also a tiny quay. Above here is a tidal weir submerged at HW, so any attempt to go higher up the creek will result in disaster.

If proceeding beyond Stoke Gabriel, bring Mill Point abeam, then come to port for the middle of the wood on the south bank of the river. Off the entrance to Bow Creek there are red and green channel buoys. Good anchorage can be found close to the west bank approximately half-way between White Rock and the red can. This is a lovely quiet spot, but you are close to the mud at LW, so place your hook with due care. Row up Bow Creek to take your choice of pubs for lunch if your visit coincides with a brewer's tide.

REVERSED

REVERSED

Above Dartmouth and, on right, Kingswear
Opposite Dittisham. (A) Greenway Quay. (B) Landing jetty and
dinghy pontoon. (C) Galmpton Creek. (D) Flat Owers

After passing between the red and green buoys off
Bow Creek, come round to starboard for the red
buoy off Duncannon. The following bend should be
taken wide, after which the river is marked with
buoys and beacons to the end of the Fleet Mill
Reach. Above here, the best water is in mid-stream
up to Totnes.

Obtain advice on limited drying berths at Totnes
from River Officer or Dartmouth Harbour Office
prior to arrival there.

Facilities
Totnes
An extremely attractive historic town with a castle,
shops, hotels, a quaint High Street and numerous
interesting pubs and restaurants. Boatyard.
Chandlery.

Dartmouth, Kingswear and Dittisham
A water taxi is on watch on VHF Ch 69, who also
advertises 'Meals on Keels'. These have not been
sampled by a frugal pilot compiler, but
recommendations would be welcome.

Chandlery in Dartmouth from two shops down
town, but the best working chandler is at the marina
at Kingswear. Fresh water on north and south
embankment and town pontoons. Also at any

marina. At Dittisham, from a tap in front of The
Ferry Boat Inn. Floating rubbish skip. Simple
provisions up the hill. Diesel only, no petrol, at both
marinas and from a barge moored in the middle of
the river between the upper and lower ferries. Hotels
and restaurants, good shopping centre. Yacht yards,
chandlers and all facilities. Travel-hoist at
Darthaven Marina. Yacht clubs: Royal Dart Yacht
Club (Kingswear), Dartmouth Yacht Club,
Dittisham Sailing Club. Launching sites: public

slipway at Kingswear next to Royal Dart Yacht Club, except near LW. Slipway at Dartmouth dinghy basin two hours each side HW, or slipway alongside upper ferry slipway at any tide, provided ferry is not obstructed.

Communications

The nearest rail connection is at Paignton, seven miles away. You can reach this by steam train in season from Kingswear, and a jolly fine trip it is too. If your luck is in, you could be hauled by none other than the *Flying Scotsman* herself. For the older at heart, there are buses to all parts.

Salcombe

Tides

HW approx −0523 Dover

MHWS	MLWS	MHWN	MLWN
5·3m	0·7m	4·1m	2·1m

Depths

The bar has a minimum depth of 1·3m on the transit, with 0·7m immediately to the east. These depths may vary. Inside the bar, a deep-water channel leads as far as Tosnos Point in the Bag. Above here to a point northwest of the Salt Stone there is 2m to be found with care. Thereafter depths shoal steadily, but craft drawing 2m can navigate as far as Kingsbridge from ¾ flood. For depths in the creeks, see plan.

General

Despite its appearance on the chart, Salcombe is not technically an estuary. No river debouches through its arms to the sea. It is, however, an excellent harbour, with minimal fishing activity and no commercial traffic. The village is extremely crowded in high season, but it is always a joy to lie on a mooring and watch the lovely Salcombe yawls racing around one's yacht. The entrance is spectacular and there are secluded anchorages available well away from the sea. The bar can be very dangerous in strong onshore weather, particularly on the ebb tide. Indeed, a lifeboat has been lost here. No attempt should be made to enter in these conditions, especially with the wind in the southeast.

Approach and entrance

With sufficient tide on the bar and in settled weather Salcombe presents few problems to the visitor.

The entrance lies just to the east of Bolt Head, an unmistakable promontory with a spiky silhouette. The Mewstone (19m) and Little Mewstone (5m) lie conspicuously southeast of the point.

The sea is often disturbed in the stretch from Prawle Point towards Bolt Tail. Mariners approaching Salcombe must bear this stoically in the knowledge that things will improve once they have gained the harbour. Strong southerly winds meeting the ebb by Bolt Head can set up overfalls, but these may be avoided by approaching from further east.

The only sunken dangers on the west side of the approach are rocks near the Mewstones, Cadmus Rocks, off the northeast corner of Starehole Bay and, much further in, Bass Rock, off Splat Point, about 100m to the west of the transit. To the east side, do not turn in too soon after passing Prawle Point. Rickham Rock, 4 cables short of the bar, has 2·7m over it.

The simplest answer is to alter course northward about a quarter of a mile east of the Bolt, then sail past Starehole Bay where lie the remains of the wreck of the barque *Herzogin Cecilie* under the high cliffs. Continue past the submerged Cadmus Rocks and the Great Eelstone, leaving this about a cable to port. The bar is now 2 cables to the north.

The front leading mark stands on Pound Stone Rock (dries 4m). The rear one is a red and white beacon with a ♦ topmark on Sandhill Point (DirFl.WRG.2s27m10/7M). This is not always easy to spot, but can be discerned by virtue of its situation in front of the left-hand edge of an unmistakable red-roofed house with two gables. If you still cannot make out the marks, a compass bearing on the left-hand edge of the house should suffice. By night, remain within the 5° white sector of the light. The dangerous nature of the bar in the wrong conditions of strong onshore winds against an ebbing tide cannot be over-stressed.

North of the bar, continue on the leading line, leaving to starboard the Wolf Rock (dries 0·6m), marked by a green conical buoy (Q.G.3s). As the *Blackstone* beacon light (Q(2)G.8s) comes abeam to starboard, swing to starboard, leaving to port the Pound Stone and two red and white beacons off Sandhill Point, then proceed on 042° up the middle of the wide fairway.

By night, there are leading lights to indicate this change of course and your subsequent heading. The front light is a quick flash, as is the rear one, which is sited on a stone column at 45m elevation. Both stand near Scoble Point on the east side of the Bag, and lead as far as the port-hand ferry landing light (F.R). You can continue on the transit to the Bag by bringing the rear light just open to the right of the front one when passing Snapes Point, provided there is sufficient moonlight to be sure of avoiding moored vessels. Note that the *Blackstone* beacon and *Wolf Rock* buoy keep the departing mariner off shoaling water on the eastern bank.

If you are proposing to sail up to Kingsbridge, leave the Salt Stone well to starboard, then look out for a series of red and white poles to be left to port which will lead you the 2 miles or so up to the quay. The first of these is about 1 cable northeast of Heath Point. Do not be tempted by a line of unlit red buoys beginning to the northwest of Charleton Point. These lead up to Balcombe Lake, where you do not want to go. Leave them well to starboard and concentrate on the red and white posts instead.

Anchorage and moorings

If the weather is settled, *Starehole Bay*, immediately north of Bolt Head, is a pleasant stop,

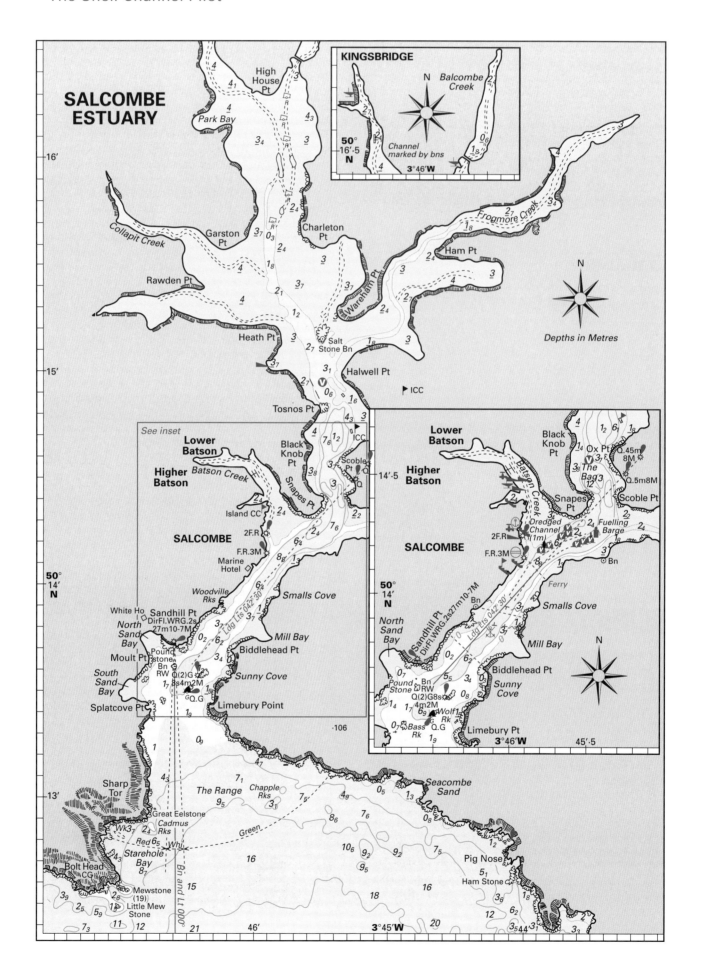

SALCOMBE
ESTUARY

KINGSBRIDGE

*Balcombe
Creek*

50°
16'·5
N

*Channel
marked by bns*

3°46'W

High
House
Pt

Park Bay

16'

Collapit Creek

Garston
Pt

Charleton
Pt

Frogmore Creek

Rawden Pt

Ham Pt

Wareham Pt

Heath Pt

Salt
Stone Bn

Depths in Metres

15'

Halwell Pt

ICC

Tosnos Pt

See inset

ICC

Lower
Batson

Higher
Batson

Batson Creek

Black
Knob
Pt

Scoble
Pt

Lower
Batson

Black
Knob
Pt

Ox Pt Q.45m
8M

*The
Bag*

Q.5m8M

Higher
Batson

Batson Creek

Snapes
Pt

Scoble Pt

14'·5

Island CC

Snapes Pt

*Dredged
Channel
(1m)*

Fuelling
Barge

2F.R

SALCOMBE

F.R.3M

Marine
Hotel

2F.R

SALCOMBE

F.R.3M

Bn

50°
14'
N

Woodville
Rks

Smalls Cove

Ferry

North
Sand
Bay

Ldg Lts 042·30

Smalls Cove

50°
14'
N

White Ho
North
Sand
Bay

Sandhill Pt
DirFl.WRG.2s
27m10·7M

Mill Bay

Sandhill Pt
DirFl.WRG.2s27m10·7M

Mill Bay

Moult Pt

Pound
Stone
Bn
RW Q(2)G
8s4m2M

Biddlehead Pt

Sunny Cove

Biddlehead Pt

Pound
Stone

Bn
RW
Q(2)G8s
4m2M

Sunny
Cove

South
Sand
Bay

G.Q.G

Wolf1
Rk

Splatcove Pt

Limebury Point

Q.G

Limebury Pt

·106

Bass
Rk

3°46'W

45'·5

Sharp
Tor

The Range

Chapple
Rks

Seacombe
Sand

13'

Green

Great Eelstone
Cadmus
Rks

Wk3

Red

Whi

Starehole
Bay

Pig Nose

Bolt Head
CG

Bn and Lt 000°

Ham Stone

Mewstone
(19)

Little Mew
Stone

46'

3°45'W

134

Salcombe entrance. The leading beacons nearly in transit with left-hand side of conspicuous red-roofed house with twin gables on the left of the picture. At this point you should come to starboard on to 042° transit for going up-harbour

but beware of the wreck of the barque *Herzogin Cecilie*, marked by a red and black isolated danger buoy, in the northwest corner.

Sunny Cove, on the east side of the entrance inside the Blackstone, gives access to a clean sandy beach and has 2m at LW. Settled weather only.

No anchoring immediately northeast or southwest of Mill Bay because of undersea cables. **Smalls**

Cove, however, is a popular anchorage when the sea is calm. Otherwise you may still feel the scend here. You can find about 2m at LW opposite the Marine Hotel. You can also anchor off the beach west of Ditch End on the edge of the shallow water which deepens rapidly into the channel.

If you are in search of peace, you will find it, subject to sailing schools and racing activities, in the last of the deep water in the vicinity of the Salt Stone. A good all-weather anchorage is to be had off Halwell Point with the Salt Stone beacon bearing north magnetic. Here there is water a-plenty.

The creeks offer seclusion and perfect shelter to those whose draught and sometimes readiness to take the ground permits them.

There are visitors' moorings on the **Salcombe** side of the channel off the Marine Hotel just below the town. Thereafter, a number of such buoys will be seen. The harbour staff will direct you from their launches, or call them on VHF Ch 14, *Salcombe Harbour* between 0600 and 2200 in summer. Three moorings between Ditch End and Scoble Point can accommodate craft of up to 100 tons by arrangement.

In **The Bag** there is a visitors' pontoon opposite Ox Point.

Salcombe Harbour. Leading beacons in view at left-hand edge of picture, together with the twin-gabled house. Central in the entrance is the Blackstone with its beacon

At *Kingsbridge*, do not try to berth at New Quay or on the private pontoon off the Quay on your port hand. Continue right up to the end, where there is a visitors' pontoon for bilgekeelers to starboard and a good wall for deep keels of up to 12m LOA to lean against on the west side. Both are well marked.

Facilities

Salcombe is supplied with most marine requirements. Fuel from barge VHF Ch 6 and ☎ 01836 775644. Fresh water on short-stay visitors' pontoon off Whitestrand Quay called Normandy Pontoon. One hour only from 0700–1900. Useful for shopping trips. Most facilities are grouped around here. Showers and toilets at Salcombe Yacht Club, or by arrangement at the Island Cruising Club in Island Street. Garbage skip on a barge off the town. There is a launderette in town, but it is overcrowded in summer. All normal provision requirements in town and at Kingsbridge (no fuel at Kingsbridge except by portage). Various chandlers, repairers and engineers, both mechanical and electronic. You can even have your liferaft serviced here. For a water-taxi service, call the Harbour Patrol launches on Ch 12 (if no response try 14). Salcombe Yacht Club and the Island Cruising Club both welcome visitors and can supply ice.

Scrubbing alongside the town by arrangement with the harbourmaster.

Salcombe town. Snapes Point is central in the picture with the Bag running away to the left behind it. Visitors are tied up to pontoons in the Bag, or at buoys off the town

Communications

Salcombe is not the easiest place to approach by public transport. However, regular buses run to Kingsbridge, with ferries an attractive alternative when tide permits. Thence to main-line trains, via a connection at Totnes.

River Yealm

Tides approx −0522 Dover

MHWS	MLWS	MHWN	MLWN
5·4m	0·7m	4·3m	2·1m

Depths

0·3m on the leading line south of the bar, but up to 3m immediately south of the transit, between the red buoy and the starboard-hand beacon on the foreshore. Sands are liable to change. Variable depths in the region of 1·5m at MLWS on the second leading mark as far as Misery Point. Thereafter, 2·5m or more to Yealm Pool. Newton Ferrers Arm dries – see plan – while the Yealm itself carries variable depth for a further mile or so.

General

The Yealm is an extremely beautiful river with good shelter in all but strong onshore winds. Visitors should take note, however, that it is crowded with moorings and that at peak times the Harbour Authority has reluctantly had to limit visitors' numbers to 90 boats per night. Problems of space sometimes arise in settled weather at holiday weekends, so these times should be avoided if

possible. The Authority stresses that notwithstanding this provision, no boat will be refused shelter from hard weather.

Approach and entrance

The entrance can be rough in strong onshore winds from the southwest, but otherwise presents no difficulties. Approach across Wembury Bay, noting that from Wembury Point rocks and ledges extend towards the conspicuous Great Mewstone Island (59m). The little Mewstone Rock (15m) lies on the southwest side of the Mewstone. If you are cutting close around this you must give a good clearance to the rock 50m off it, which is awash at low water. Further rocks or shoals extend 2 cables southwest of the Mewstone, and there are tide rips when the wind is across the stream. The Inner (dry 3m) and Outer Slimmers (dry 1·5m) lurk a quarter of a mile eastward of the Mewstone, and while these are unlikely to bother the rhumb-line navigator, an inbound yacht beating to windward should take care to be well clear of the Mewstone on her starboard tack.

Once the entrance to the river is opened up, look for a white cottage between trees near the summit of Misery Point on the south side of the river, and below it, above Cellar Bay, for a pair of leading beacons at 089°. These are topped by white triangles with a vertical black line. Bring these into line and, after leaving Mouthstone Point to starboard, move across to about 40m south of the transit, steering near the rocky shore on the starboard hand. In season a red buoy (Fl.R.5s) is placed to mark the outer end of the bar. A green beacon with triangular topmark on the south foreshore delimits the starboard edge of the channel, which is around 40m wide. By moonlight, the line of the hedge immediately south of the transit is readily identifiable and runs parallel to the line of the boards.

Approaching from the south or east, give Gara Point at least 3 cables' clearance to stay outside the Eastern and Western Ebb rocks (awash). Keep St Werburgh's Church (about a mile east of Wembury Point) bearing 010° and the Ebb Rocks will be left safely to starboard. Hold on until the black and white leading marks in Cellar Bay have been identified, then alter onto their transit.

When you have brought the green beacon abeam, alter to port to 047°, onto the next leading beacon. This will be seen to the northeast on the hillside to the right of a clump of trees about 3 cables east of Season Point. It is a white board with a red vertical line which leads up the first bend in the channel. Keep on the correct bearing, because an arm of the bar with only 0·6m at MLWS is close to port.

River Yealm entrance, with sand bar showing clearly

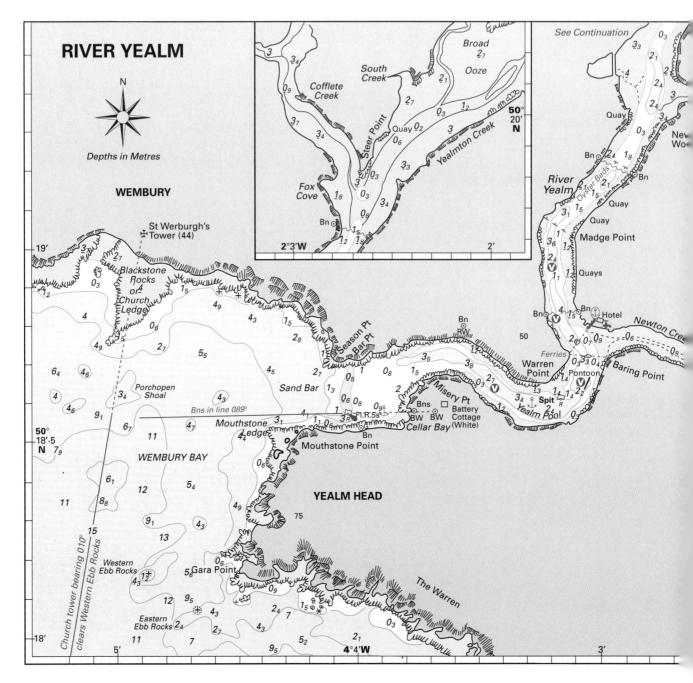

Hereafter, the river is clearly defined. Keep near mid-channel, leaving to port the red can buoy on the north side of the Pool. The deep channel is very narrow (50m) off the eastern extremity of Warren Point, with only 0·3m on its western side and 0·4m on the eastern (see plan).

The Newton Ferrers Arm opens out up the east side above Warren Point. Although wide, it dries out at low water. Above Warren Point, the Yealm itself continues first in a north-northwesterly direction before bearing through north to northeast. Depths vary from 3·4m to 1·8m for over half a mile, but with shallower patches as far as Shortaflete Creek. Note that anchoring is forbidden north of Madge Point.

Anchorage and moorings

The first visitors' moorings are encountered shortly after Misery Point comes abeam. These are for large craft, with the outer one being able to accommodate up to LOA 25m. Two cables further in on your starboard hand is a 46m (150ft) visitors' pontoon. Rounding Warren Point brings you to a series of fore-and-aft trots on the west side of the river which are also reserved for visitors. You may raft up on these. You may also pick up any vacant buoy that does not have a dinghy or a note on it. If it is inappropriate for you to remain there, the harbourmaster will advise when he visits you in his launch. Should you fail to make contact, report to the harbour office, in the driveway of the Yealm Hotel (convenient dinghy pontoon).

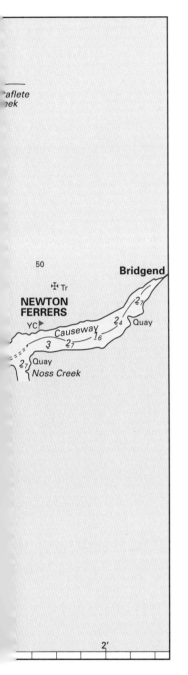

The Mewstone from the southeast with Rame in the distance to the left

Approaching the river Yealm entrance from SSW, keeping Wembury church open on starboard bow

Cellar Bay leading marks on 089° pass south of the bar. Note very conspicuous line of hedge to the right

You will be charged dues if you anchor, so little will be saved and much anxiety may be caused, as space is so limited outside the fairway.

Shoal-draught craft able to take the ground can dry out by arrangement on reasonably firm foreshore off Newton Ferrers or Noss Mayo. Above Noss Mayo is a public quay at Bridgend with 2m at high water springs. There are drying berths alongside here (by arrangement with harbourmaster).

Facilities

Fresh water from hose at Yealm steps pontoon (Yealm Hotel). No fuel. *Calor Gas/Camping Gaz* refills from Village Fayre, Newton Hill. No cashpoint. Toilets and showers at the Yealm Yacht Club. Good hotels and pubs. Meals at yacht club (weekend only). Six buses per day to Plymouth (fewer at weekends), where all services are available, as well as onward transport.

Plymouth

Tides

HW −0540 Dover

Devonport

	MHWS	MLWS	MHWN	MLWN
	5·5m	0·8m	4·4m	2·2m

Depths

Deep-water big-ship harbour. River Tamar fairway carries 2·4m as far as Neal Point, 1¼ miles above Tamar Bridge. Thereafter the river is navigable on the tide up to Gunnislake, 16 miles above the breakwater. Note, however, that there are some height restrictions: the Tavy Bridge is 7·6m, pylons cross the Tamar at Weir Point (19m), and 1½ miles further up is a 16m power line. The spectacular Calstock viaduct has 24m.

General

Plymouth, with its associated creeks and rivers, forms one of the Channel's greatest natural harbours. For centuries its fame has rested with the Royal Navy. From the days of Hawkins and Drake to nuclear submarines, the city has found a large part of its prosperity in the business of war. Great fishing fleets have sailed from here, as have voyages of discovery and colonisation.

Only in recent years has the haven become of any general use to the casual yachting visitor. Now, in addition to the possibilities of pushing up-river, or roughing it out with the fishing boats, there are three modern marinas. The city, rebuilt after the Blitz, is still fascinating to all seafaring people, and the rivers and creeks have much to offer the explorer.

Approach and entrance

Plymouth Sound lies with Penlee Point to the west, and Wembury Point and the Mewstone on the east. The north part of the Sound is protected by a long low breakwater built in the centre, with channels each side of it. Yachts may pass through either.

From the west a vessel will first round the unlit but unmistakable Rame Head, an almost conical promontory with the ruins of a chapel at its summit. Penlee Point, also unlit, a mile and a quarter further in, is a low headland with a turreted beacon. Note the Draystone rocks (over most of which there is 1·8m), extending ¼ mile to the southeast of Penlee Point, marked by a red can buoy (Fl(2)R.5s).

A conspicuous 23m white tower (Fl.WR.10s15M) marks the western end of the breakwater, now 1½ miles ahead. The lighthouse also has a Iso.4s10M light shining 4° either side of 035°, which is a safe course for big ships from *Draystone* buoy to the western entrance.

Drake's Island now lies conspicuously to the north. The main fairway leads northeast towards Plymouth Hoe, marked on the port hand by the red *New Grounds* (Fl.R.2s) and *Melampus* (Fl.R.4s) buoys, and thence through the Asia Pass (see plan). Yachts need not keep to this, and can pass any side of the buoys by reference to the chart.

There is a short cut to the Hamoaze, between Drake's Island and the Mount Edgcumbe shore, known as the Bridge. This channel has a least depth of 2·1m and is marked by two red and two green posts. Continue for a cable or so past the beacons, after which you are back in deep water. The Bridge beacons are lit, and in most tidal conditions and reasonable weather the channel is the logical route for small vessels.

Approaching Plymouth Sound from the east, it is important to note the firing range at Wembury Point. Firing may occur from 0930 to 1630 local time on Tuesdays to Fridays. Two large red flags are flown on the point when firing is in progress. Call *Wembury Range* on VHF Ch 16 (they work on Ch 10 and 11) or telephone the range officer on ☎ 01752 862799 (☎ 553740 extension 77406 out of office hours). If you are entering the sound during firing, you should pass to the west of the Eddystone Lighthouse, which lies 10 miles from the breakwater on a heading of 204°. There is talk of this firing range being discontinued (1999), so . . . hope for the best.

From the east, the Mewstone (57m) and the rocks extending 2 cables southwest of it will be left to starboard. Next the Shagstone, off Renney Point (a nearly square rock 1·2m high, marked by a black and orange beacon surmounted by a cone), should be given a good berth, as the tide may be setting across the rocks between it and the shore. Continue northward, passing between the eastern end of the Breakwater (LFl.WR.10s) and Staddon Point, and passing either side of Duke Rock lit west cardinal buoy. Now steer for the wide channel between Drake's Island and Mount Batten. From here, if proceeding towards the Hamoaze, you may leave Drake's Island well to port by day, or take the well lit Asia Pass by night. If bound for Queen Anne's Battery, Sutton Harbour or the Cattewater, hold on to Mount Batten breakwater end (Fl(3)G.10s),

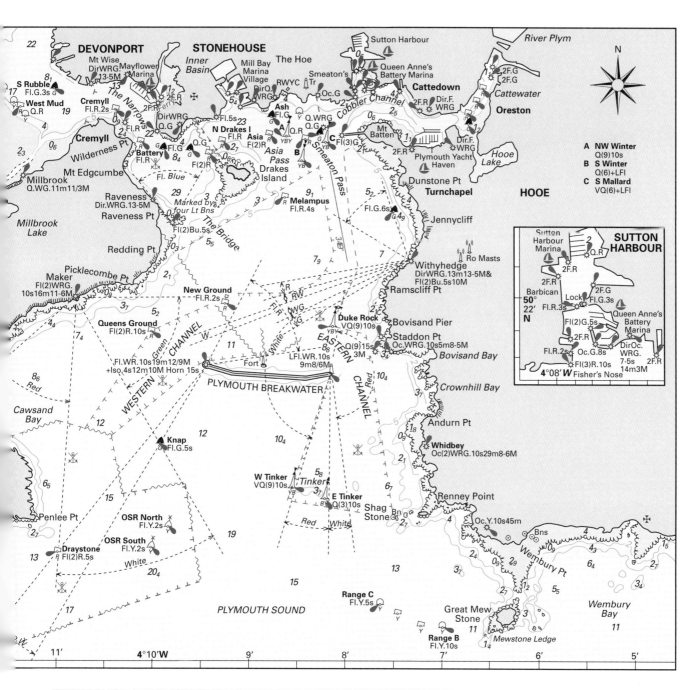

Plymouth Sound. *Panther* north cardinal buoy and the west
entrance to Plymouth Sound

Plymouth Sound. *Melampus* buoy with Drake's Island beyond

The Hoe showing from right Smeaton tower, the Naval War
Memorial and the Royal Western Yacht Club with flagstaff

Approach to Sutton Harbour with *South Mallard* buoy off
Mountbatten close to port

leaving it to starboard, and the lit south cardinal
South Mallard. If, as will usually be the case, the
3·6m Mallard shoal is of no consequence, you may
pass either side of the cardinal buoy and ignore the
green *West Mallard* (Q.G) a cable or so to its north-
northwest. Should you be concerned about the
depth, leave both to starboard before swinging up
the Cobbler Channel. By night, there is a white
sector to the Oc.WRG light on the wall of Queen
Anne's Battery which indicates the position of the
Mallard. The red sector clears it on your starboard
side.

Anchorage and moorings

Cawsand Bay in the Sound has good holding
ground and its gently shelving floor makes an
excellent anchorage in weather from southwest
through northwest.

Northeast of the pier on the north side of ***Drake's
Island*** is historically exciting, as legend has it that
here Drake lay in 1580 after his circumnavigation in
the *Golden Hind* while he sniffed the political wind.
Despite this, it can be an uneasy berth; the holding
is good, but it may be exposed in poor weather.

Anchor well in towards the shore in ***Barn Pool,***
south of Wilderness Point and due west of Drake's
Island. Sound in with care to the northern end of the
bay, inside a large mooring buoy. Buoy your anchor,

as the bottom may be foul. Expect tidal eddies. You
will be well sheltered from the west, and may walk
from here to Cremyll, whence a ferry runs to
Stonehouse. Cremyll has Mashford's famous yard
and a pub.

The Sir Francis Drake pub at the west end of the
Hoe maintains a few visitors' buoys. Land at the
small boat harbour nearby and 'sign on' in the bar.

The Royal Western Yacht Club, the Royal
Plymouth Corinthian Yacht Club and Queen
Anne's Battery run a few moorings in the
Cattewater – available on application.

Marinas
Mayflower International Marina
Approached either up Drake Channel and through
the Narrows or, if conditions of tide and weather are
suitable, through the Bridge, passing west of
Drake's Island. Once through the Narrows, the
marina's location is obvious. Call them on VHF Ch
80 for a berth, or tie up to the outer pontoon's
reception berth between two striped flags, and
report to the marina office. There are 30 visitors'
berths, and this has proved a good place to leave
boats for a period. All facilities are here, including a
clubhouse with bar which welcomes visitors. There
is a courtesy bus to Plymouth centre in the season.
Security is first-class.

Plymouth Sound – Western Channel. Breakwater lower right, Drake's Island at left and Mount Batten to the right. The green Hoe is just left of centre. *Right* Lock gates into Sutton Harbour with outer gate open. Note chevrons to show you which lock to go to and handy pontoon on right

Queen Anne's Battery

Approach between the *South Mallard* buoy and the end of the Mount Batten breakwater (Fl(3)G.10s), then shape up on around 030° to leave *Fisher's Nose* (Fl(3)R.10s) with its notice 'Speed Limit 8 knots to the east' to port. Queen Anne's Battery Marina is protected by a wall of vertical piling. Keep to starboard and follow this in. At night, you will be interested in the Oc.G light on the corner of the piling which effectively forms the entrance to the channel. Shortly after it, a Q.G indicates the end of the marina breakwater, which you leave to starboard, swinging round to head for the visitors' berths on the southernmost pontoon. You can call ahead on VHF Ch 80. You may have to raft up, but do not enter a vacant finger jetty without permission. They are reserved.

The marina has all facilities, including launderette, clubhouse and café. The Royal Western Yacht Club of England has its clubhouse here, and from it many of the great long-distance races are organised. The club very generously makes its premises available to visitors.

The marina water taxi solves the otherwise messy problem of how to get to town, neatly circumventing a long, uninspiring walk. It drops you off at Mayflower Steps by the Barbican for a sensible fee.

Sadly, 'QAB' is not a comfortable berth in heavy weather from a southerly quadrant. The snubbing of lines and general crashing around of pontoons can disturb even the most exhausted reveller.

Sutton Marina

Sutton Marina lies immediately north of Queen Anne's Battery which is left on the starboard hand as you approach Sutton Lock. The approach is dredged to 2m, the marina is right in the heart of town and its helpful staff welcome visitors. The harbour is entered through its lock, which exhibits standard traffic signals. The lock will open at any time, day or night, 365 days a year. Free flow is established in the top half of the tide.

Always call them on Ch12 (*Sutton Lock*) before entry.

The Cattewater looking west. Sutton Harbour and Queen Anne's Battery centre picture. Plymouth Yacht Haven has now replaced the old Clovelly Bay Marina seen here (1998) lower left

Sutton Marina is a first-class option for visitors to Plymouth. No sea ever surges into here, no matter what the weather, which cannot always be said for the other marinas.

If you want a cheaper night locked in, you may be allowed to lie on a 'waiting pontoon' inside the lock which does not connect to the shore, but which still offers full protection. You can use your dinghy and save a worthwhile percentage of the full fee.

The marina has excellent facilities, including a laundry, a well-stocked chandlery and fuel. Shops and restaurants lie close at hand. It is also hard by the Barbican, whose once-famous fish dock is now reduced to an extensive tourist store. The night life of a world seaport remains, however, offering a remarkable evening out for connoisseurs of noisy pubs and the human form, male and female, which patrols the waterfront in search of action in full 'battle dress' on Friday and Saturday nights. Sights are to be seen here which southerners in Britain rarely enjoy, and only in Hull has the Shell Pilot observed so many fun-seekers of the gentle sex.

Plymouth Yacht Haven

This new marina is on the site of the old Clovelly Bay Marina in the Cattewater and is part of the Mount Batten development. Nevertheless, it retains its connections with the traditional pilot village of Turnchapel. Shelter is excellent in all but the worst northeasterlies so, together with Sutton Marina, this represents a further viable alternative to groaning the night away across the Cattewater in strong winds from points south.

Prices reflect the less fashionable situation, but the water taxi will take you to the city for an acceptable fee if that is what you want. All facilities, and first-class security with 24-hour surveillance. Pubs to suit all tastes are a moderate walk away.

☎ 01752 404231, or call on VHF Ch 80 during office hours (up to 1700). Thereafter, use VHF Ch 37.

Facilities at Plymouth

Plymouth offers everything any vessel could require, be she a dinghy or a man-of-war. There are many yacht yards. The marinas offer all services and there are a number of yacht clubs. The city council has a dinghy park with a launching site alongside the Mayflower Sailing Club, Barbican. *Calor Gas* and *Camping Gaz* exchange at all marinas.

Communications

Ferries to Roscoff, etc. Main line trains, buses, car hire. All you could ask for.

Beyond Plymouth

St Germans or Lynher River

Spring tidal range is 0·5m less than Plymouth, with all LWs about 20 minutes later.

This is the first major tributary to the Tamar, opening on the west side north of the old Devonport Dockyards, now privately run, and beyond the warship moorings. The river dries extensively, though there is good water in the channel for the first 1½ miles or so. Thereafter, shoal-draught yachts can comfortably work the tide up to St Germans.

Leave the first red buoy (*Lynher* Q.R) to port, or close to starboard, then leave the smaller (*Beggars*) definitely to port, before swinging to port to pass between small-craft moorings and the green *Sand Acre* buoy (Fl.G.5s) to starboard.

The next red is inshore off Antony Passage, where you can anchor, row ashore and find a pub. In the next half-mile a power cable and gas line cross the bed of the river, so do not anchor here. Work towards Shillingham Point, noting that the deep water is about a cable offshore, then proceed on a heading of around 220° until Ince Castle bears a few degrees west of north. Now alter for the diminutive green *Ince* buoy, hard by the shore at Black Rock Point. Anchoring with Ince Point bearing a touch north of west on the east side has much to recommend it to the seeker after solitude, but care must be taken over soundings and one's tidal height calculations.

After leaving *Ince* buoy close to starboard, pass on to the isolated red can in mid-stream, sounding with care. Leave this close to port and swing gently down onto 220°, sounding for the channel, to take you on into the steep, tree-lined narrows between Redshank and Warren Points. Here, on the south side, you will find Dandy Hole, with 4m and more at LAT. It is a wonderful anchorage, with absolutely no facilities except those provided by Mother Nature, who will always show her generosity given a chance.

Stay in the middle, slightly favouring the south side as the river turns northwesterly, then pick up the red and green posts which lead through the drying mud-flats to the private quay at St Germans. Speak to the club right at the quay if open, about an overnight drying berth, or be ready to return to Dandy Hole on the tide. There is a tap on the quay. A delightful walk on the path up the river under the mighty viaduct brings you to a lovely village with a truly unusual shop and PO. Here you can buy most of what you need after refreshing yourself at the adjacent pub. Walking up the road is less satisfactory, but does lead to the same place, so long

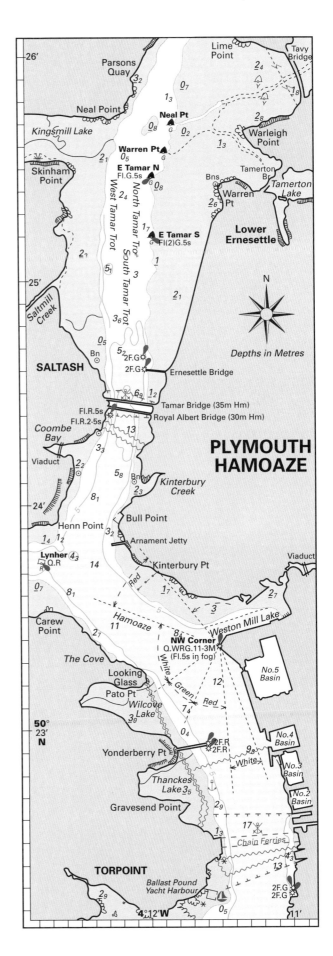

Sutton Harbour – Queen Anne's Battery on the right

Mayflower Marina.

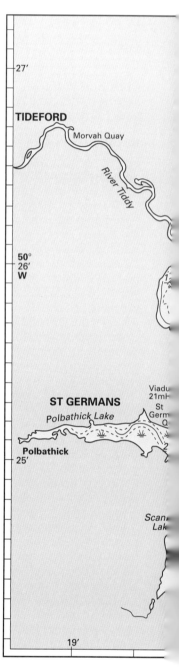

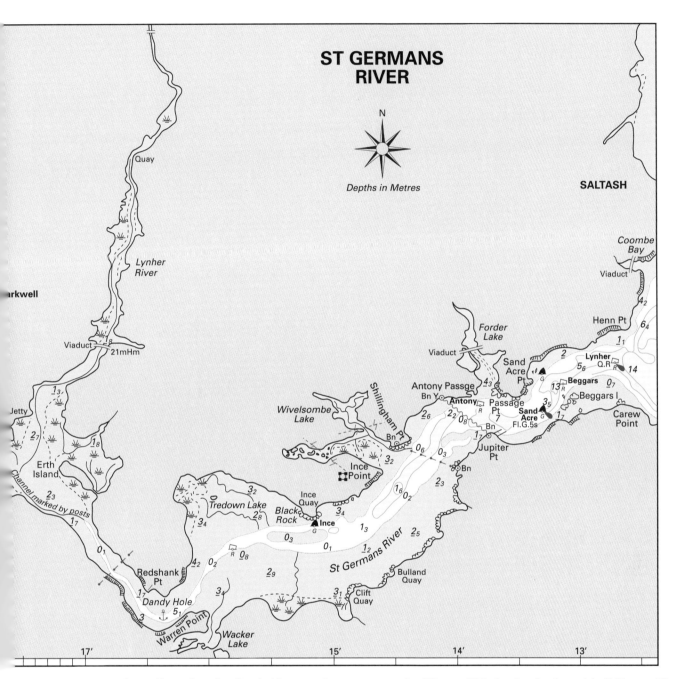

ST GERMANS RIVER

N

Depths in Metres

SALTASH

Coombe Bay

Viaduct

Henn Pt

Lynher Q.R

Sand Acre Pt

Beggars

Beggars I

Forder Lake

Viaduct

Antony Passge

Bn Y

Antony

Passage Pt

Sand Acre Fl.G.5s

Carew Point

Bn

Jupiter Pt

Bn

Shillingham Pt

Bn

Wivelsombe Lake

Ince Point

Quay

Lynher River

rkwell

Viaduct 21mHm

Jetty

Erth Island

Channel marked by posts

Tredown Lake

Ince Quay

Black Rock

Ince

St Germans River

Bulland Quay

Redshank Pt

Dandy Hole

Clift Quay

Warren Point

Wacker Lake

17' 15' 14' 13'

---

as you cross the railway by the footbridge at the station.

No recommendations are made in *The Shell Channel Pilot* concerning the other creeks off this river. They are there to be explored by those with big hearts and small draughts.

River Tamar

Above St Germans River the Tamar continues under the Royal Albert and Tamar Bridges, and thence northward by a gradually shoaling, but well marked channel past Weir Point and on to Cargreen.

If you intend to proceed more than half a mile above the bridges, you must consult the tide tables and the plan. There is a shoal which dries 0·6m east-southeast of Neal Point. This is best avoided by passing very close to the 3 conical green buoys opposite Kingsmill Lake, beginning with *E Tamar N* (Fl.G.5s). The next two are smaller and unlit. You should thus leave the shoal to port.

Above the red beacon (leave to port) and the yellow buoy (leave to starboard) off Weir Point, the best water is found on a line which leaves the chimney at Cargreen close to port. There is deep water at Cargreen and usually an empty mooring or two which you can pick up at your discretion. Ashore is the Spaniard Inn with easy landing at its car park immediately upstream. If you pick up one of its buoys, you'll be charged a fiver and recoup it from a free bottle of wine with your meal.

Across the street stands a charming village store which in 1999 was apparently unchanged in any respect since World War II, except that the lady proprietor could no longer supply Players Weights and powdered eggs.

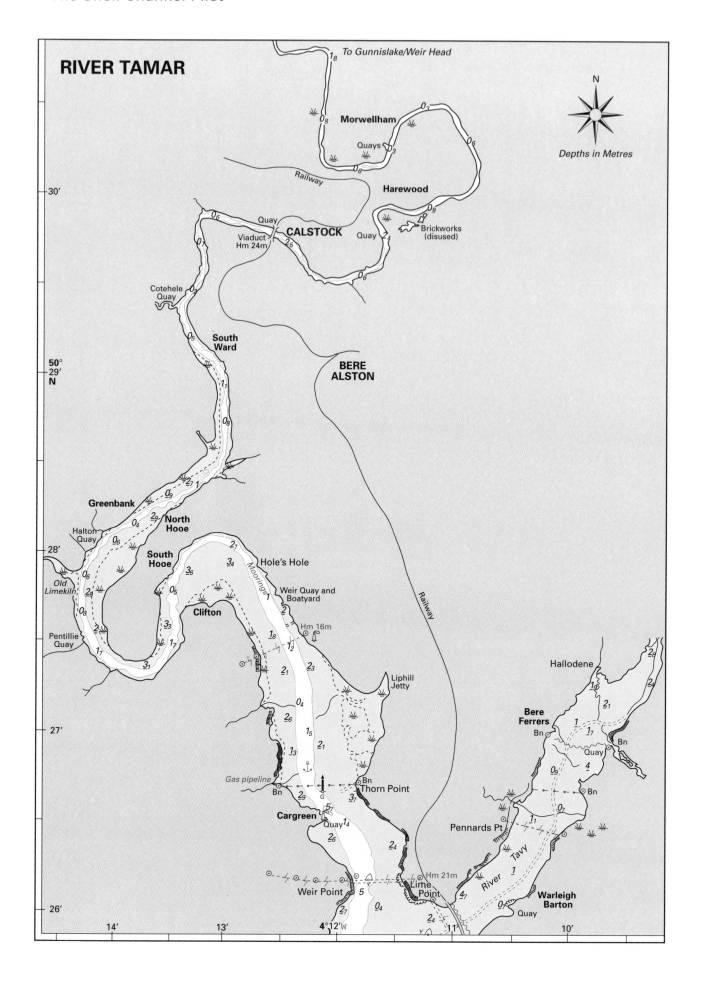

RIVER TAMAR

To Gunnislake/Weir Head

N

Depths in Metres

Morwellham

Quays

Railway

Harewood

Brickworks
(disused)

Quay

Quay

CALSTOCK

Viaduct
Hm 24m

Cotehele
Quay

South
Ward

BERE
ALSTON

Greenbank

North
Hooe

Halton
Quay

South
Hooe

Hole's Hole

Old
Limekiln

Weir Quay and
Boatyard

Clifton

Moorings

Pentillie
Quay

Hm 16m

Liphill
Jetty

Hallodene

Bere
Ferrers

Bn

Quay

Bn

Gas pipeline

Bn

Thorn Point

Pennards Pt

Cargreen

Quay

River Tavy

Weir Point

Lime
Point

Hm 21m

Warleigh
Barton

Quay

4°12'W

The Hamoaze and River Tamar

Below Cargreen, Tamerton Lake and the River Tavy are non-starters for yacht navigation because of their bridges.

The stalwart spirit can now work the tide upstream, but the channel is largely unmarked after the green pile a couple of cables above Cargreen. The deepest water is on the outside of the various bends, and sounding will reveal some pools deep enough for anchoring afloat throughout the tide for craft drawing 2m and more. Bear in mind, however, that this is a fairway and that excursion boats may not be amused by your presence in the middle of it.

Calstock has a line of moorings in just over 1m of water. There may be a spare one. Deep-draught vessels can dry against the quay. Fuel and water are available. Anchoring is not recommended below the viaduct, but a cable above it there is a 2·5m pool where yachts are reported to have lain.

Shoal-draught craft may manage to explore even further, and the river does not dry until a shoal patch just above Morwellham. Navigable water has been reported all the way up to Gunnislake, but you are advised to keep to the left-hand channel at Weir Head and use the redundant lock in order to avoid weirs (!) in the main channel.

Looe

Tides
HW −0538 Dover

MHWS	MLWS	MHWN	MLWN
5·4m	0·6m	4·2m	2·0m

Depths
Looe harbour and its entrance dry, with heights alongside of 2·4m (West Looe) and 1·8m (East Looe).

General
The important fishing port of Looe provides good shelter for craft able to take the ground. In offshore winds it is possible to anchor outside in depths of your choice, additional shelter being provided by Looe Island. The entrance is dangerous in strong onshore winds.

The town is picturesque, in a workaday sort of way, but crowded in summer. Historically, its luggers, which were famed for their speed and power, have provided an archetype for numerous transom-sterned yachts.

Approach, entrance and berthing
Looe is readily identified by the conspicuous Looe Island (St George's Island) off the entrance.

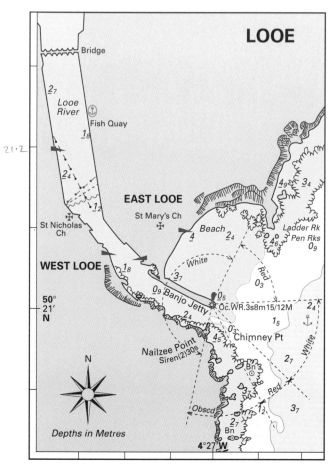

Approaching from the west the principal danger is the Ranneys rocks, which extend southeast and east from the island. These must be given a wide berth, but can be cleared in good visibility by keeping the beacon on Gribbin Head open of the cliffs at Nealand Point, west of Polperro, until the pier head (Oc.WR.3s) bears 305°. Steer straight for the pier head on 305°, staying in the white sector of the light after dark. A transit of the church spire in West Looe (don't confuse with St Margaret's in East Looe) 'on' with the pier head will keep you clear of trouble by day, and it must be said that for the stranger night entry is not recommended. It is better to anchor off and await the morning tide, but don't forget your riding light. Fishing boats may be moving whenever there is water to float them.

The overfalls south of Looe Island may be avoided in bad weather by keeping further to seaward. There is no passage suitable for strangers between Looe Island and the mainland.

Approaching from the east, keep Looe Island on the port bow until picking up the entrance. Then use the transit described above to keep clear of the rocks. Some of these are marked, but for a stranger the 'wide-berth' course is recommended.

Any safe approach must assume a sensible rise of tide to give a safe depth of water. Bear in mind that tides may run strongly in the entrance, so that entry under power is recommended.

Looe Harbour

Looe Harbour entrance dried out at low water between pier head (white band) and Chimney Rocks (left Mount Batten)

Berth

There is one berth for visitors among the fishing boats. It is at the south end of the quay in West Looe, and is marked with a 'Visitors' sign. The bottom is firm sand and gravel. Report to the harbourmaster on arrival.

Off East Quay there is a reverse eddy on the flood, but you are urged not to try to berth on the east side, which is reserved for fishing boats.

Facilities

Fuel, repairs, engineers. Gas from chandlers. Diesel from lorry (ask at harbour office). Petrol by portage from garage. Pubs, restaurants, and all small-town facilities. Toilets and one shower.

Polperro

Tides

HW −0554 Dover

MHWS	MLWS	MHWN	MLWN
5·4m	0·6m	4·3m	2·0m

Depths

Polperro harbour dries up to about 2·3m, giving rise to depths of 3·3m at MHWS and 1·5m at MHWN. The anchorage outside shoals from 4·6m up to the drying harbour entrance.

General

The classic Cornish village of Polperro saw its finest hours many years ago when smuggling was its principal occupation. It is still active as a fishing community, with tourism supplying an important income supplement.

The harbour lies at the head of an inlet open to the southeast, with the outer pier about 1½ cables in from the sea. The harbour entrance is less than 10m wide, and in hard weather it is closed by a hydraulically operated gate. The current harbour chart is based on an original survey by Captains Williams and Bell RN in 1857. Trawlermen confirmed 120 years later that little had changed. Shelter on the outer moorings is good in moderate airs from all but the south or southeast, or at times of heavy swell, when the berth can be exceedingly uncomfortable. The inner harbour offers an excellent berth with comfortable drying-out in all but the latter wind directions in heavy weather.

Approach and entrance

Approach is made from a southeasterly direction when the harbour piers open up. As is shown on the plan, the Raney (dries 0·8m) lies off the headland on the west side of the entrance, with further rocks at the foot of Spy House Point on the eastern side. There is deep water up to the entrance of the inlet except for a rocky patch named the East Polca which lies half a cable south-southwest, clear of Spy House Point. This is only 1m down, but causes no problems in good weather with sufficient rise of tide. Another rocky patch about 30m northeast of the Raney can also be disregarded by many vessels of a size to make Polperro a serious option, as it has 2·5m over it. Entry is dangerous in fresh southeasterly or southerly winds, or when a swell is running in, though the inlet is protected from southwest through west to northeast.

Keeping the west pier head 'on' with the end of the outer pier on 310° will maintain your position in mid-inlet, clear of all dangers, passing north of the shallowest part of the East Polca.

Leave the outer pier well to starboard and steer midway between the inner piers. The west pier head shows a black ball when the harbour is closed (F.R by night). When it is open, the light is white. Strangers should not attempt entry by night.

Anchorage and berthing

There is just room for a small yacht to anchor outside. The deep water is only 25m wide, so if this doesn't attract you, try to pick up one of the moorings laid outside the outer pier for boats to

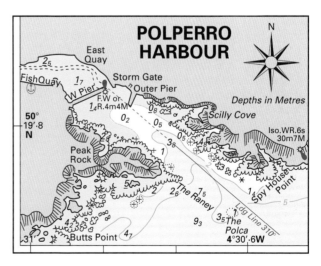

Polperro

await the tide. Moorings inside the harbour are for locals, but you may secure and dry out alongside the east quay wall just inside the entrance. It is a good idea to report to the harbour office, which is to be found in the fish market on the west side.

Facilities
Provisions, banks and pubs. Toilet opposite east quay. Fresh water on the quay. Petrol in cans from garage, and a smugglers' museum to explore while you wait for the tide to float you out. The Blue Peter 'one block back' from the west pier purveys real ales of global quality. These can be enjoyed while peering through low windows at the 'Pirates of Penzance' scene outside and listening to excellently canned blues music. Two or three hundred metres up the main street lies the Cottage Restaurant. Here, first-class local seafood is served by staff who understand about pleasing their customers.

Fowey

Tides
HW −0540 Dover

MHWS	MLWS	MHWN	MLWN
5·4m	0·6m	4·3m	2·0m

Depths
There is deep water throughout this harbour and up the River Fowey as far as 3 cables above Wiseman Point. There is less water on the Polruan side, but still plenty for most yachts. Pont Pill is dredged for the moorings to 2m, as is Mixtow Pill. Above Wiseman's Reach the river shoals, but with sufficient rise of tide dinghies and other small craft can navigate as far as Lostwithiel.

General
Fowey is a fine, active port featuring a powerful mix of serious commercial shipping and almost equally serious yachting. In the Middle Ages it was relied upon to supply more ships and armed men to support the monarch of the day than any other harbour in the West Channel. Later, it became famous for privateering, piracy and smuggling. It has inspired many great writers, among them Sir Arthur Quiller-Couch, Kenneth Grahame (*The Wind in the Willows*), and Daphne du Maurier, whose first novel, *The Loving Spirit*, is said to be styled around the old Slade's yard in Polruan, still successfully building heavy timber fishing boats under the ownership of Tom's. Transpose the name of Slade, and you will find many of du Maurier's characters still lying in Lanteglos churchyard above Polruan, as fine a walk as you will discover to enjoy on a long summer's afternoon.

Shelter is good, and Fowey is an all-weather entry, though this can be rough in an onshore gale on the ebb. In hard south or southwesterly weather a scend runs in, which can make lying in the lower harbour very uncomfortable, though quieter berths can often be found further up the harbour.

Approach and entrance
Fowey is easy to identify from seaward thanks to the unmistakable daymark on Gribbin Head 1¼ miles southwest of the entrance, a red and white tower 25·6m high standing on a base 71m above sea level.

Approaching from the east, the resident danger is the Udder Rock (dries 0·6m) 3 miles east of the entrance, marked by an unlit south cardinal bell buoy. By night, if you can see the red sector of Fowey lighthouse (LFl.WR.5s28m11/9M) you are south of the rock. The light cuts off to the north of the safe line.

The only dangers between this rock and the entrance are drying rocks immediately off Pencarrow Head.

The Cannis Rock (dries 4·3m) lies some 4 cables southeast of Gribbin Head. There are dangers south of the head as far as the rock, marked by a lit south cardinal bell buoy. To be safe, keep the cross on Dodman Point open southward of the 8m-high Gwineas Rock. If you have failed to see the *Cannis*

Fowey harbour. Polruan on right

Rock buoy after dark, the white sector of Fowey lighthouse (above) keeps you clear of it, with the western red sector opening immediately east of the buoy.

Arriving from the west, you can alter for the entrance once past the *Cannis*, but as there are rocky ledges off the west shore, give this side a good berth until close to the entrance. Within the narrows, the only dangers are the Punch Cross ledge on the east side, marked by a white beacon which should be given a berth of at least 60m, the Lamp Rock, marked with a white beacon nearly a cable beyond it, and the Mundy Rocks opposite on the west side.

At night, once clear of *Cannis* buoy, the white sector of Whitehouse Point leading light (Iso.WRG. 3s) will bring you safely through the entrance. Night entry is perfectly possible, but a stranger would need to be sure of where to go once inside. There are no further effective lights apart from two fixed reds (vertical) marking the end of a short jetty for the Polruan ferry east-northeast of Whitehouse Point.

Anchorage and moorings
The harbour and river come under the control of the Fowey harbourmaster. His office can be contacted on ☎ 01726 832471, but in any case call either *Fowey Harbour Radio* on VHF Ch 12 (office hours) or *Fowey Harbour Patrol* (0900–2000) on VHF Ch 12.

Short-term pontoon berthing is available at Berrill's Yard a cable or so upstream of Albert Quay, where the harbourmaster also maintains a pontoon. Here, you can stay for up to 2 hours free of charge. The harbourmaster encourages yatchsmen not to abuse these free facilities.

Upstream of Pont Pill on the east side there are a number of clearly marked yellow or white visitors' swinging moorings, as well as a 30m pontoon. A similar pontoon is established in Pont Pill, where there are also a number of fore-and-aft visitors' moorings where you may raft up.

Upstream of Pont Pill, opposite the first of the china clay berths below Upper Carne Point, is a further visitors' pontoon where rafting up is also permitted. This pontoon is almost always clear of the surge which can run a good way up the lower harbour, and so is sometimes to be preferred to the more seductive berths lower down. Yet another pontoon lies at the entrance to Mixtow Pill which, although primarily for locals, also often accommodates visitors at its southern end. If all this fails, 1999 saw the establishment of a rather awkward trot mooring opposite the main (east-west) china clay berth. This consists of a heavy hawser stretched between two big-ship moorings, to which visitors can secure fore and aft by means of rolling hitches. The berth is better than you might imagine,

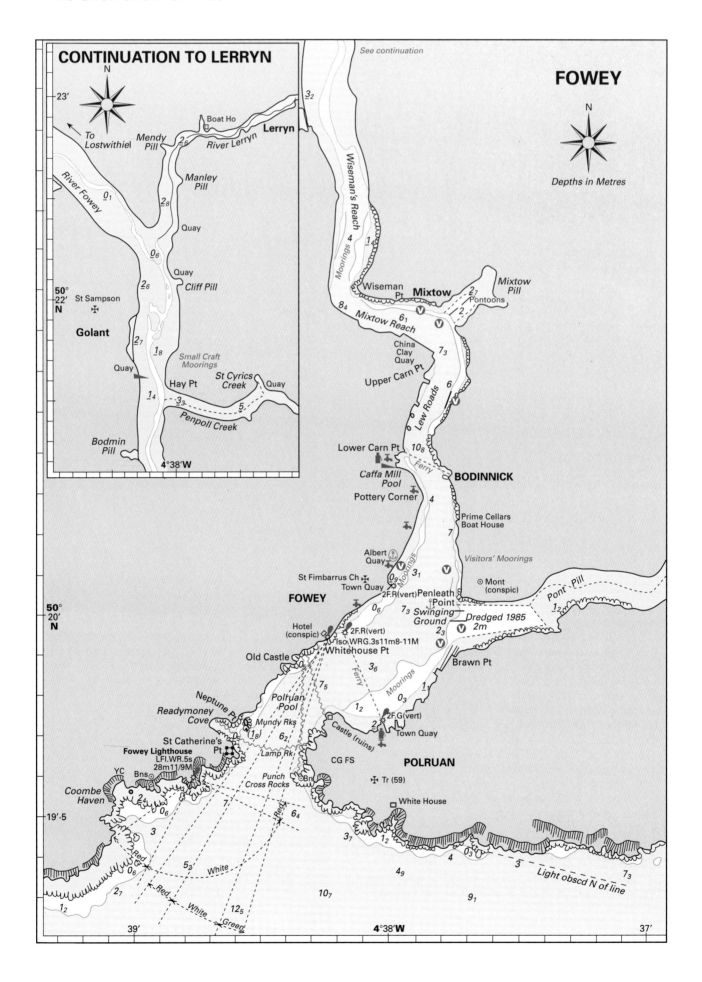

CONTINUATION TO LERRYN

N

23'

To
Lostwithiel

Boat Ho
Lerryn

Mendy
Pill
River Lerryn

River Fowey

Manley
Pill

0_1

Quay
2_8

0_6

Quay
2_6
Cliff Pill

50°
22'
N
St Sampson

Golant

2_7

1_8

Quay
1_4
3_3
Small Craft
Moorings

Hay Pt
St Cyrics
Creek
Quay

5

Penpoll Creek

Bodmin
Pill

4°38'W

FOWEY

N

Depths in Metres

See continuation

3_2

Wiseman's Reach

Moorings

4
1_4

Wiseman
Pt
Mixtow
2_7
Mixtow
Pill
Pontoons
2_7
2_7

Mixtow Reach
6_1
8_4

China
Clay
Quay
7_3

Upper Carn Pt
6

Lew Roads

Lower Carn Pt
10_8
BODINNICK

Caffa Mill
Pool
4
Pottery Corner

Prime Cellars
Boat House
7

Albert
Quay
Moorings
3_1
Visitors' Moorings

St Fimbarrus Ch
Town Quay
0_9
Mont
(conspic)
Pont Pill

2F.R(vert)
FOWEY
Penleath
Point
7_3
Swinging
Ground
1_2
0_6
Dredged 1985
2m

Hotel
(conspic)
2F.R(vert)
2_3
Iso.WRG.3s11m8-11M
Whitehouse Pt
Old Castle
0_5
3_6
Brawn Pt

Neptune Pt
7_5
Polruan
Pool
1_1
Moorings
Readymoney
Cove
Mundy Rks
1_2
0_3
1_8
2F.G(vert)
St Catherine's
Pt
0_5
6_2
Castle (ruins)
2
Town Quay
Fowey Lighthouse
LFl.WR.5s
28m11/9M
Lamp Rk
POLRUAN
YC
Bns
CG FS
Tr (59)
Coombe
Haven
2_4
0_6
Punch
Cross Rocks
Bn
White House
3
Red
6_4
3_1
1_2
5_2
White
0_6
4
0_3
3
Light obscd N of line
7_3
2_7
Red
4_9
1_2
White
Green
12_5
10_7
9_1

50°
20'
N

19'·5

39'
4°38'W
37'

154

Fowey approach. *Cannis Rock* south cardinal buoy ½ mile southwest of Gribbin Head with its red and white tower on skyline. Fowey lies 1½ miles to the northeast

but you'll need either an outboard or a good pair of oars to get to town, unless you are prepared to brass up for the excellent water taxi, who can usually hear your VHF even though you are behind a hill.

All vessels over 12·5m LOA should seek advice from the harbourmaster or the harbour patrol before berthing.

Anchoring is not encouraged but, subject to the need for large vessels to use the Swinging Ground off Pont Pill, it is sometimes possible to anchor here by permission on the edge of the moorings.

Wiseman's Reach, once a favourite funk-hole in bad weather, is now largely taken up with moorings, some administered by FHC (including one visitors' mooring), but bilgekeelers can still slink away to discover a secluded berth somewhere in the mud up-river.

Facilities

Water taxi (VHF Ch 6). Fresh water on the pontoon at Albert Quay, or tap at Polruan. Fuel from *Fowey Refueller* at the mouth of Pont Pill (VHF Ch 10, 16, ☎ 01726 833055), or in cans from the garage in

Upriver from Fowey. Golant Quay and slipway seen at low water after a prolonged lunch in the excellent pub. First-class walks on the gravel if you miss the tide back to the yacht, and plenty of water when it comes back

Lostwithiel Street, Fowey. Outboard fuel and diesel from Polruan Quay. Outboard repairs at J A Marine. *Calor Gas/Camping Gaz* from Upper Deck at Albert Quay in Fowey. *Camping Gaz* also from chandler on Polruan Quay. Banks in Fowey. Post office in Fowey or at Polruan. Heavy repairs or hauling at Tom's (☎ 870232), Polruan, who are also marine engineers. Otherwise Fowey Boatyard, Passage Street. Pump-out at Berrill's yard.

Simple provisions in Polruan. Most of what you need in Fowey. Good pubs and restaurants on both sides of the river, with Kittow's butcher's shop in central Fowey a 'must' for lovers of fine sausages, real bacon (ask for it specifically – no water, 100% happy pig!) and great pasties. Escape the mob at the pub at Bodinnick, just above the ferry.

Scrubbing by arrangement with harbourmaster at Brazen Island, Polruan. Royal Fowey Yacht Club welcomes members of affiliated clubs. Launching by arrangement at Tom's Yard, or at Caffa Mill. Rubbish skip in Pont Pill.

Trailer Jack reports a first-class slipway for trailer-sailers at Yeate Farm, Bodinnick (☎ 01726 870256). Camping with full facilities on site. From all accounts, a perfect set-up with pub to hand.

Communications
Buses to Par and main line railway.

Charlestown

Tides
HW approx −0555 Dover

MHWS	MLWS	MHWN	MLWN
5·1m	0·6m	4·0m	1·8m

These tidal heights are for the neighbouring china-clay port of Par. Charlestown is similar, but may not be identical.

Depths
Approaches dry 0·9m, with a drying height of 1·2m immediately outside the outer basin. Depths inside are adequate for small commercial vessels.

General
Charlestown is a privately owned artificial 19th-century harbour. It is the home of 'Square Sail', possibly Britain's premier company offering square rigged vessels and the skills of the traditional offshore seaman ☎ 01726 70241/67526. Visiting yachtsmen are welcome, and a number of heavyweight but useful facilities are available. A call here to see this visionary outfit could change your life.

The entrance and approach dry out, but a wet basin is maintained by a tidal lock. Shelter inside is total, but the entrance should not be attempted in any sort of onshore wind and sea, which will turn the outer basin into an untenable swirl of broken water.

Approach and entrance

On entering St Austell Bay from the southwest, Charlestown can be identified to the eastward of St Austell itself. Ideally, the entrance is approached on 287°, lining up a white patch on the west wall of the outer basin with the right-hand edge of a row of cottages which can be seen through the pier heads. This clears the rock shelves to both sides. Inside the outer basin, turn to starboard for the lock gate. If you wish to enter the inner basin you should either telephone the harbourmaster on ☎ 01726 67526 or call on VHF Ch 14. The lock will open on request from HW±2 hours approximately, but if more vessels are expected you may be asked to wait for a short while.

Do not attempt night entry, even though the south jetty carries a fixed red light and the north jetty a fixed green. The gates will normally open from 2 hours before HW when a vessel is expected. Note signals as follows:

Green light at night or red ensign by day – harbour open.

Red light at night or black shape by day – harbour closed.

There are a few alongside berths for visitors, but if you don't want to have the full experience, try anchoring off immediately east of the piers and come in by dinghy. There is a pub, and various other benefits, including lay-up and refit berths, shipwrights, shipwright joiners, spar makers, riggers, sailmakers, electronics and instrumentation. Traditional craft are particularly welcome, and can be hauled if required. Museum heritage centre and two good pubs.

Mevagissey

Tides

HW −0600 Dover

MHWS	MLWS	MHWN	MLWN
5·4m	0·7m	4·3m	2·0m

Depths

Alongside the outer end of the South Pier depths exceed 2m. Even at the inner end there is at least 1·5m. From an entry depth in the region of 2·5m, the outer harbour shelves to its rocky edges, and dries inshore of a line from the lifeboat slip to 25m from the outer end of the East Pier.

The inner harbour dries, but is not available to visitors.

General

Mevagissey is the perfect Cornish fishing village. As such, it is inevitably heavily populated with tourists in the summer months. The commercialism which goes with this has not, however, spoiled the picturesque nature of the place, which still operates a considerable fishing fleet. This is the harbour's main function. Depending on draught and tide, the outer harbour is also available to visiting yachts, but there is no particular encouragement in the way of copious visitors' berths. It is well sheltered by the land from winds from south-southwest to northwest. The North Pier offers some shelter from the north except in rough weather, but easterly winds bring in a surge. The harbour is poor in strong onshore conditions, and entry may well be dangerous.

The nearest ports of refuge are Fowey (7 miles) and Falmouth (14 miles).

Approach, entrance and berthing

There are no dangers in the offing, save Gwineas Rock to the south-southeast. While it is safe to pass inshore of this, strangers who are not expert pilots in possession of a large-scale chart are advised to pass to the east of the lit east cardinal buoy marking the group.

Charlestown. Lock can be seen at the right of the outer harbour

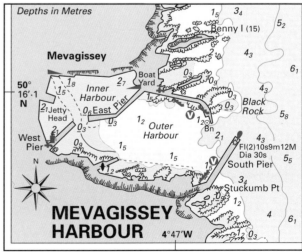

On arrival off the port, steer for the white lighthouse on the South Pier (Fl(2)10s9m12M). Do not come in from north of northeast on account of Black Rock Sand (dries 0·3m), which extends to the east from the North Pier. Enter between the piers and seek a berth, usually alongside the South Pier, sometimes rafted up to another yacht, or to a fishing boat by arrangement. Anchoring is not permitted within the harbour, but a spare mooring may occasionally be made available. Because space is so limited, the harbourmaster may direct visitors to anchor in the offing if the weather suits. If you do not raise the harbourmaster on the radio, report to his clearly marked white-painted office on the North Pier. The harbour office can be called on VHF Ch 16, or telephoned in advance on ☎ 01726 043303 (842406 out of hours).

Facilities

A fuel and water service is now available for yachts on the South Pier. There is an excellent traditional boatyard, shops, launderette, banks (with limited opening in summer months only), pubs, cafés, restaurants and a remarkable small fishing museum.

Communications

Buses to St Austell and its railway station.

Portmellon

Half a mile south of Mevagissey lies the small bay of Portmellon, which affords a good temporary anchorage between its headlands. Sound in to find your best berth. It should only be used in settled weather and offshore winds.

Mevagissey

Falmouth and Falmouth estuary (including Truro, St Mawes and Penryn)

Tides

HW −0558 Dover

MHWS	MLWS	MHWN	MLWN
5·4m	0·6m	4·3m	2·0m

General

Falmouth is one of the finest all-weather harbours in the British Isles. It can be entered in any conditions, and the inner harbour is sheltered in everything but hard easterlies. Even when these arrive, Falmouth Yacht Marina is still protected, and a good lee can be found in St Mawes. The River Fal itself is virtually a string of hurricane holes where all manner of ghastly gales can be ridden out in peace and tranquillity.

The town of Falmouth and its associated creeks and villages have a long history of seafaring. Foreign mail was dispatched from here for hundreds of years, and the local newspaper still enjoys the colourful title *The Falmouth Packet*. More recently, great sailing ships came from every corner of the world to anchor in Carrick Roads and await instructions from their agents as to where their cargo was to be landed. It could have been bought and sold two or three times while they were on passage, bound towards 'Falmouth for Orders'.

Falmouth maintains a flourishing commercial port. Amongst its other delights is a fleet of oyster dredgers which still work under sail. Indeed, any traditional boat enthusiast will be thrilled by a visit, for here he or she will be able to enjoy the sight of some of the best sailed gaffers in Britain racing several times a week in the summer months.

The harbour is a favourite jumping-off point for ocean voyagers, as well as those whose aims are less grand. A 100-mile reach to Ouessant is a joy to the Solent-based sailor, more usually faced with a 250-mile slog to windward.

Approach and entrance

Falmouth approaches are well sheltered in even the hardest westerly blow. Note, however, that after prolonged easterlies the sea lumps up very unpleasantly. It is safe enough to navigate, but there is little pleasure in it. The entrance lies between Pendennis Point, with its conspicuous castle, and St Anthony Head (19m white tower, Oc.WR.15s22/20M). From the south and west there are no dangers in the offing once the *Manacles* buoy (east cardinal) has been left to port. Should the buoy prove difficult to spot, the Manacles are also covered by the red sector of St Anthony Head lighthouse. From the east, overfalls may be found up to 1½ miles off the Dodman, breaking over the 6 or 7m-deep ledges of the Field and the Bellows. Up to 3 cables south-southwest of Gull Rock (38m high, just east of Nare Head) lie the Whelps. These dry 4·6m. 2½ miles northeast of St Anthony Head, the

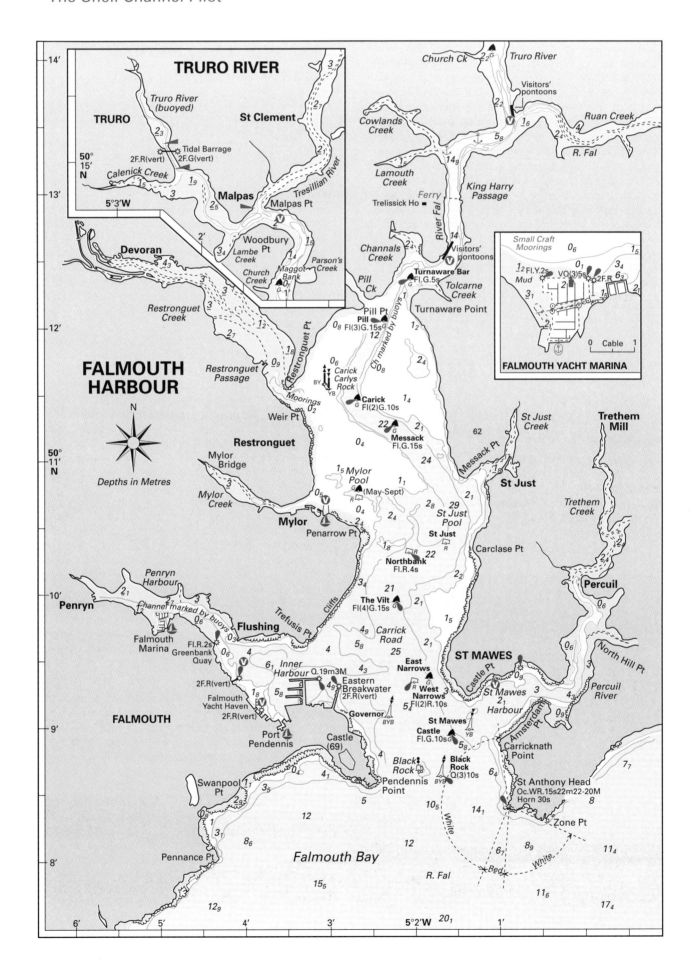

TRURO RIVER

TRURO

Truro River (buoyed)

St Clement

2_3

2_7

3

Tidal Barrage
2F.R(vert)   2F.G(vert)

50°
15'
N

Calenick Creek

5°3'W

Malpas

Malpas Pt

1_9

3

2_5

1_5

Devoran

$2'$

3_4

Woodbury
Pt

Lambe
Creek

1_4

Parson's
Creek

4_3

3

Church
Creek

Maggot
Bank

0_7
G

**FALMOUTH
HARBOUR**

N

Depths in Metres

50°
11'
N

Restronguet
Creek

2_7

1_2

1_2

1_8

0_9

Restronguet Pt

Restronguet
Passage

Moorings

Weir Pt

0_2

Restronguet

Mylor
Bridge

Mylor
Creek

0_5

0_4

Mylor

Penarrow Pt

2_4

Penryn
Harbour

2_1

2

0_6

Penryn

Channel marked by buoys

1_2

Falmouth
Marina

Fl.R.2s
Greenbank
Quay

0_6

0_3

4

Flushing

Trefusis Pt

Cliffs

6_1

Inner
Harbour

1_8

5_8

Q.19m3M

Eastern
Breakwater
2F.R(vert)

4_9

5_8

V

2F.R(vert)

Falmouth
Yacht Haven
2F.R(vert)

V

FALMOUTH

Port
Pendennis

Governor
BYB

Castle
(69)

Swanpool
Pt

7_1

3_5

2_3

0

1

3_1

Pennance Pt

8_6

12_9

4

Falmouth Bay

15_5

5

0_4

4_1

12

Pendennis
Point

Black
Rock

5

**Black
Rock**
Q(3)10s
BYB

R. Fal

10_5

White

6_7

14_1

Turnaware Bar
Fl.G.5s
G

Tolcarne
Creek

Turnaware Point

Cowlands
Creek

Church Ck

2_2
G

Truro River

Visitors'
pontoons

2_2

V

1_6

Ruan Creek

2_4

R. Fal

5_8

Lamouth
Creek

1_5

14_9

King Harry
Passage

River Fal

14

Ferry

Trelissick Ho

Channals
Creek

Visitors'
pontoons

V

Pill
Ck

Pill Pt
Pill
Fl(3)G.15s
G

0_8

12

1_2

2_4

1_2

Ch marked by buoys

0_8

0_6

Carick
Carlys
Rock
BY
YB

0_2

Carick
G Fl(2)G.10s

1_4

22
G

Messack
Fl.G.15s

0_4

62

24

Messack Pt

St Just
Creek

1_5 Mylor
Pool
G (May-Sept)
R

1_1

2_1

2_8

29
St Just
Pool

St Just

St Just

2_4

2_4

1_8

R

22

Northbank
Fl.R.4s

2_2

3_4

21

The Vilt
Fl(4)G.15s
G

2_1

4_9

Carrick
Road

5_8

4_3

25

2_1

1_5

**East
Narrows**
G
R

**West
Narrows**
Fl(2)R.10s

5_7

ST MAWES

Castle Pt

0_9

0_3

3

**St Mawes
Castle**
Fl.G.10s
G

St Mawes
Harbour

2_1

YB

5_8

Carricknath
Point

Amsterdam Pt

6_4

St Anthony Head
Oc.WR.15s22m22-20M
Horn 30s

8

Zone Pt

11_4

8_9

White

11_6

17_4

Percuil
River

4_3

0_9

North Hill Pt

Percuil

0_6

Trethem
Creek

2_4

**Trethem
Mill**

Carclase Pt

Small Craft
Moorings

0_6

1_5

1_2 Fl.Y.2s
Mud

VQ(3)5s

0_1

3_4

2F.R

6_3

3_1

2

1_5

2_1

2_3

0   Cable   1

FALMOUTH YACHT MARINA

5°2'W

20_1

Red

14'

13'

12'

11'

10'

9'

8'

6'   5'   4'   3'

Bizzies (3·7m and 4·6m) lie up to 1 mile east-southeast of Greeb Point.

The entrance is clear of dangers except for Black Rock, inconveniently sited just west of centre. This uncovers at LW and is marked by an unmistakable black beacon with two globe topmarks. Yachts can pass either side of this, giving it a respectable berth, but note that its shoal water extends for ½ cable north and south, and that 2·1m LAT extends almost a cable to the east. Those wishing to chance nothing to judgment can ensure success by leaving the associated lit east cardinal buoy to port. This is in any case prudent for strangers after dark, as Black Rock is unlit. Thereafter the deepest water is indicated by various main channel markers, shown on the plan.

If you are entering St Mawes, leave *Castle* green buoy (Fl.G.10s) well to port and look for the smaller *St Mawes* unlit south cardinal. This marks Lugo Rock (0·6m), and should be left to port according to your draught and the state of tide.

Most visitors enter the inner harbour of Falmouth by leaving the *Governor* east cardinal buoy to port,

though for any but the deepest draughts this is not strictly necessary.

Thereafter, round the East Breakwater (2F.R) and the North Arm of Queen's Jetty (Q). Now proceed on a westerly heading until the inner harbour opens up around the west end of the Queen's Jetty. From here, steer southwest towards your chosen berth.

If you are headed for the Penryn River (for the Falmouth Yacht Marina), round the East Breakwater and North Arm as before, then continue west-northwest, keeping the bulk of the town moorings on your port hand, towards Greenbank Quay. This is rendered conspicuous by the Greenbank Hotel sign painted in large letters on the wall, as well as the Royal Cornwall Yacht Club immediately to the south. Stay in mid-channel between Greenbank and Flushing, and pick up the red and green channel markers which lead up-river.

Entry into the River Fal is easy for most yachts after half flood, for none of the large area of the upper harbour dries, outside of the creeks. Watch out for Carick Carlys Rock (dries 0·8m) 3 cables

Flushing. Landing pier on the left

Mylor Yacht Harbour and moorings on the west bank of the River Fal 2 miles from the entrance

Approaching St Mawes from the southwest. *Castle* buoy on left *St Mawes* south cardinal buoy to the right of village

159

Above Falmouth, looking up-river to Penryn. Inner harbour on
extreme left. Greenbank Quay just right of centre
Below St Mawes

east of Restronguet Point. It is marked with unlit north and south cardinal beacons which are not always easy to see. The buoyed fairway has deep water at all states of tide, so deeper-draught vessels can follow it up from Carrick Road, confident that they can proceed all the way up-river as far as Maggoty Bank. Whether using the channel or not, all yachts should be sure to leave the small green buoy northwest of Turnaware Point to starboard in order to avoid the drying shoal between it and the Point. Above Turnaware Point, stay in mid-stream as far as Ruan Creek. Thereafter, favour the east side until *Maggoty Bank* buoy is identified. Leave this to starboard, then swing back to the centre of the river once more. Just south of the buoy is the minimum depth thus far at 2·1m (LAT).

Above Maggoty Bank, depths vary as far as Malpas. Between Malpas and Truro depths are very slender, but shoal-draught craft can work the last of the flood as far as the city by following the buoys. Truro is accessible two hours either side of HW. For those desirous of the city's benefits (including a large supermarket hard by the waterfront) but unwilling to chance their keels, a dinghy trip on the tide to Truro from an anchorage below Maggoty Bank is entirely feasible and can offer a welcome diversion for a gale-bound crew.

Anchorage and moorings

In Falmouth, anchor off Custom House Quay, keeping at least a cable clear of the commercial docks. You may be asked to clear out temporarily for shipping movements, but this is otherwise a secure and comfortable berth in all but strong east or southeast winds, though northerlies can sometimes funnel down the harbour. Depths vary from 1·5 to 2·5m LAT. It is deeper closer to the docks. If in doubt, call the harbourmaster (*Falmouth Harbour Radio*) on VHF Ch 16, working 12, or ask his launch. There is a small town marina here (Falmouth Yacht Haven) for 40 visiting yachts of up to 12m LOA, with a maximum depth of 1·8m. Call the harbourmaster to check availability. Raft up.

Dinghies may be left on the inside of the yacht haven.

There are a number of visitors' moorings between Greenbank and Prince of Wales Pier. *K1* to *K6* and *T3* to *T5* are marked *FHC*. A further 7 or 8 are marked *RCYC Visitor* and are administered by the club, which has a good slipway for landing and a launch (1000–1900) which listens on VHF Ch 37.

There is also a pontoon island for visitors' use, situated beyond the moorings approximately east of the Royal Cornwall YC. In the right conditions this can be a quiet berth for vessels of up to 12m LOA.

Pendennis Marina

Tucked in to the south right behind the shelter of the commercial docks is the modern marina development of Port Pendennis. Here, a small lock-in marina of mostly private berths has been added to on the outside with an all-tide section offering 73 berths in 3m depth. This new marina will certainly provide a number of visitors' berths, as well as housing some of the National Maritime Museum's collection, and promises to be an interesting stopover. All the usual facilities, and not too long a treck to town. Call on VHF Ch 80 or 37, or ☎ 01326 311113.

Falmouth Marina

70 visitors' berths. Approach up the Penryn River, taking care to stay in the buoyed channel, and identify a black and yellow pole with ♦ topmark (VQ(3)5s). Leave this to starboard, and two fixed red lights beyond the north end of a private pontoon to port, then proceed to the reception berth beside the conspicuous fuel berth for instructions. Alternatively, call on VHF Ch 80, particularly if over 13m LOA. Note the black and yellow pole with diagonal cross topmark (Fl.Y.2s) beyond the fuel berth. This indicates the northwestern extremity of the dredged water. Keep it open to port of the east cardinal for your final approach after dark.

There is enough water on the outer berths for craft with draught of 2·4m or more.

St Mawes

Anchor on the north side off the beach (covers at HW), keeping clear of the moorings and the ferry fairway. St Mawes Sailing Club maintains three visitors' moorings up the Percuil River, but depths are uneven, so without local knowledge apply to the club (☎ 01326 270686). St Mawes harbourmaster (☎ 01326 270553) may also be able to help out with a mooring. Generally speaking, Percuil River holds considerable attraction for the shoal-draught boat prepared to anchor and take the ground, though care should be taken about oyster beds.

Mylor

Mylor yacht harbour is due to expand by the beginning of 2001. 139 pontoon berths will be dredged to 2m with all-tide access. Visitors welcome. The marina is to be protected from the east by a floating breakwater. Deepwater swinging moorings are also available, served by a water taxi (VHF Ch 37 *Mylor Water Taxi*). Full facilities ashore, including showers, a restaurant and all repair services. Mylor and Flushing villages are a pleasant walk away, and the local grocers will deliver orders of reasonable size to your yacht. Call *Mylor Yacht Harbour* on VHF Ch 37 or 80. ☎ 01326 372121 372120. *E-mail* enquiries@mylor.com, or visit the wesbite at www.mylor.com.

Restronguet

Deep-draught yachts anchor west of Restronguet Point in about 3m, but you must work the tidal height to approach safely. Whether you pass north or south of Carick Carlys Rock you will find less than a metre of water at LAT. Shoal-draught craft can work the tide up to the pontoon off the fascinating Pandora Inn on the south shore (dries about 1m). Here, they will find showers, fresh water and a launderette for their added convenience as they take their sustenance. The upper creek dries, and the deep pool in the entrance is full of local moorings.

St Just

In easterly weather, anchor immediately south of the entrance to the creek or south of Messack Point, clear of the moorings. Land at the head of the inlet on the starboard hand. There is a shingle beach near Pascoe's Yard. The place is extraordinarily beautiful in summer.

River Fal

Once past Turnaware Point, with its small green buoy well to the north (which *must* be left to starboard), craft of any reasonable draught may anchor at the mouth of Channal's Creek, with a spectacular view up the lawns to Trelissick House. Shallower vessels may find a drying berth in the entrance to Tolcarne Creek, and a deep-water visitors' pontoon is located off Turnaware Bar.

A mile or so beyond Tolcarne, above King Harry Ferry, amongst a series of apparently permanently mothballed merchant vessels, the river swings 90° to the eastward at the entrance to Cowlands and Lamouth Creeks. Both offer delight to the dinghy explorer, and the yacht can anchor on the northwest bank clear of moorings in sensible depths by sounding in. Buoy your anchor. The ground chains from the merchant ships are serious tackle, and run close to the shore.

A quarter-mile further up, on the south bank, is the Smugglers Cottage Restaurant and Tea Shop. Here, visitors' moorings are maintained immediately upstream of a pontoon used by tripper boats. Secure to one, then settle up at the Cottage.

Ruan Creek is undeveloped, and a shoal-draught yacht could lie sweetly in the mud, undisturbed by much except the waterbirds.

The next reach runs northward to Maggoty Bank. Anchor at will in this stretch, or tie up to one of the midstream visitors' pontoons at its lower end, sounding towards the shoaling west bank.

Maggoty Bank buoy must be left to starboard. Above it is ample water for most boats to anchor until ½ mile short of Malpas, where depths begin to reduce considerably. There is a conspicuous pontoon below the yard at Malpas where shoal-draught craft can sometimes find a berth.

Malpas Visitors' moorings can be found here, marked *V1, V2, V3*, etc. Charge for dinghy.

If you choose to go on up to Truro, the channel is fully buoyed. The Authority are keen to encourage visitors and would be pleased to assist a larger vessel in making the passage from lower down the river. The harbour office listens on VHF Ch 12 (*Carrick One*). At the top of the river, you will find three branches – all navigational dead ends. Berth on the quay where the harbour office is located. The harbour office is in the western arm, and you should report there before drying out in soft mud. A boat of modest draught may float for a couple of hours either side of HW.

Facilities

Falmouth and Penryn have all the facilities any yachtsman could conceivably require.

Fresh water is available at both marinas, and at Mylor Yacht Harbour, Town Quay, Truro, St Mawes and Malpas. *Calor Gas* and *Camping Gaz* exchange at Falmouth Marina and Falmouth Chandlers, in Commercial Road, Penryn. Also at Mylor Chandlery. Fuel from the Falmouth Yacht Haven, summer only. Also from *Ulster Industry* barge moored opposite Trefusis Point, Falmouth Marina (24hrs) and Mylor Yacht Harbour in season. Falmouth Marina has refurbished showers and toilets, which are also available at the Royal Cornwall Yacht Club and St Mawes Sailing Club. Showers, laundry, chemical toilet disposal etc. in the 'amenity centre' at the top of the catwalk to Falmouth Yacht Haven. Launderettes also in Falmouth town centre, Falmouth Marina, Truro and Mylor Yacht Harbour.

There are a number of excellent chandleries and numerous fine boatyards. All town facilities.

Facilities at Truro include fresh water, garbage disposal, shower, toilets, chemical toilet disposal, mail delivery, an excellent restaurant, cinemas and all shopping.

Communications

Trains to Truro, thence connections to everywhere. Coach services.

The main road from Exeter to Falmouth is now first-class. The car journey can be executed rapidly with fine moorland scenery to enjoy for much of the way.

Helford River

Tides
HW −0613 Dover
Entrance

MHWS	MLWS	MHWN	MLWN
5·3m	0·6m	4·2m	1·9m

Depths

Deep water in the approach, shoaling inside to 3·4m half a mile west of Mawnan Shear, then variable depths, with a deep pool off Helford Point. Between here and Frenchman's Creek the plan or chart should be read carefully for depths. Above Frenchman's Creek the bottom shoals steadily into the drying mode within a mile, but it is possible for craft drawing 2m to work the spring tide up to Gweek Quay.

General

Helford River is as beautiful a stretch of water as the South of England has to offer. Despite being developed in its lower reaches, the river is still itself, with woods and enchanted creeks to explore by dinghy, if your draught does not permit your yacht to venture so far. To visit Helford without first reading Daphne du Maurier's *Frenchman's Creek* is to sell yourself short. Romantic it may be, but so is the place. She has caught it to a nicety.

Shelter in westerly weather is complete, but do

not expect too quiet a night in a strong easterly unless you are well upstream.

Approach and entrance

When coming from Falmouth, be sure to clear the dangerous Gedges Rocks, marked by a green conical buoy (Fl.G.5s), which lie south of Rosemullion Head on the northeast of the entrance. This buoy must be left to starboard. The buoy may be taken up out of season. If so a transit of Mawnan Shear and the wooded point immediately W of the pool just clears the danger.

Approaching from the east, stay in the middle of the entrance and be sure to leave Voose rocks to port. They are marked by an unlit north cardinal beacon some 4 cables east of Bosahan Point. Proceed through the narrows, avoiding the shoal marked by a green buoy on the north side opposite Helford Creek.

When coming from the west and south keep well clear of Nare Point and Dennis Head. If you are tempted by Gillan Harbour, note that the rock in the entrance lies further inshore of the east cardinal beacon which guards it than you might expect. Note also the large rock shelf (dries 2·6m) which extends in all directions to seaward of Men-aver Point. Unfortunately the best water is taken up with moorings, so only shoal-draught craft able to pass on into the drying water will benefit from the harbour's not inconsiderable delights.

Pressing on up Helford River above Frenchman's Creek, just over a mile beyond Polwheveral Creek the water divides. The south fork goes to Mawgan. You want the northern branch, which is marked by red posts with can topmarks to port, and by green posts with triangular topmarks to starboard. From here up to Gweek the channel dries completely at MLWS.

Anchorage and moorings

Anchorage can be obtained in calm weather in the bight on the north side of the entrance, off Porth Saxon.

In the pool off Helford village there are a number of visitors' moorings with green pick-up buoys. Do not try to anchor. Either pick up a spare buoy, call the mooring officer on VHF Ch 80 or 37, or, better still, look out for him in his launch.

If you prefer to anchor, the only feasible deep-water site is further upstream, approximately opposite Porthnavas Creek. Immediately west of its entrance on the south side of the main river are some deep pools with over 3m, and sometimes as much as 6m in small areas. This is a beautiful place, and you are well sited to *row* round the corner into Frenchman's Creek. Truly a magic place in fair weather and foul.

Shoal-draught yachts may just find room to anchor around the edge of Abraham's Bosom, the 2m pool at the entrance to Porthnavas Creek. The pool itself is full of moorings. In a small creek on the west shore is Porthnavas Yacht Club, where you may lie alongside and even dry out by arrangement. The club welcomes visitors, and has a bar and restaurant. Further up-river, Polwheveral Creek has more water, or rather less drying height, than Frenchman's Creek, and can produce some wonderfully secluded spots for the bilgekeeler ready to avail herself of her full potential.

Up at Gweek you will find a quay and a boatyard where you can dry out alongside for a modest fee.

Facilities

Helford River Sailing Club welcomes visitors and has excellent facilities. There is a landing-point on the west side of the creek at Helford Point, where the boatyard has a shop, restaurant, fuel and boats for hire. Helford village has a post office, shops, provisions and the thatched Shipwright's Arms. It

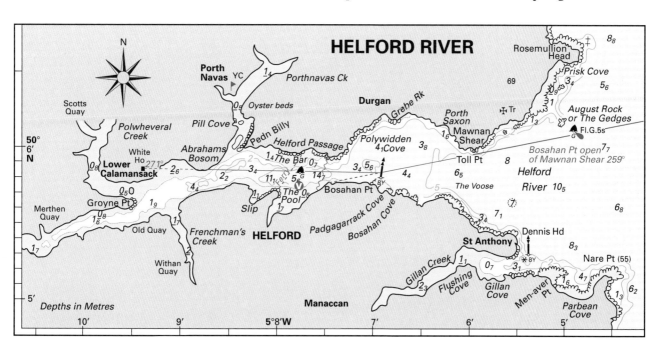

also has a gourmet restaurant. A ferry runs from Helford Point to The Ferry Boat Inn at Helford Passage, which is a hotel and restaurant.

There are boatyards at Helford, Porthnavas and Gweek. Launching site by the inn, which owns the car park.

The club at Porthnavas welcomes visitors. It has a bar, restaurant, dinghy landing and limited cranage. It can supply diesel and has the only petrol pump on the Helford River with the exception of Gweek. Minor repairs can be arranged. Provisions can be bought, and local oysters are available from the warehouse at the jetty.

Communications

Buses to Falmouth from the top of the hill at Trebah, behind the inn.

Right Helford River. Helford Passage and the Pool. Visitors' moorings centre. Anchorage extreme left.
Below Helford River from seaward. Mawnan Shear on the right

Coverack

Tides

HW approx +0607 Dover

MHWS	MLWS	MHWN	MLWN
5·3m	0·6m	4·2m	1·9m

Depths

The harbour dries completely, but has a minimum depth at the pier of 2·4m MHWN, or 3·5m at MHWS.

General

Coverack lies a little over 1 mile north of Black Head and the same distance south of Lowland Point southwest of the infamous Manacles rocks.

The tiny harbour with its small, colourful fishing village, is formed by a picturesque 18th-century wall, built out and then extending westward from the north side of Dolor Point.

Approach and entrance

Coming from the north, round the Manacles east cardinal buoy, then give Lowland Point with its offlying rocks (½M to seaward) a wide berth before shaping up into the Cove. From southward, beware of the Guthers, 2 cables off Chynhalls Point, halfway between Black Head and Coverack.

If rounding the end of the wall at a 'touch-and-go' state of tide, the best water will be found by hand-railing about 10m off. In any event, keep fairly close to the wall, because rocks on the west side of the entrance extend well out.

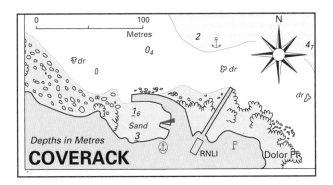

Coverack

Berthing

Yachts can dry out inside the wall in suitable conditions, and shelter in settled weather or moderate offshore winds is surprisingly good.

If no berth is available, or you do not fancy taking the ground, there are a number of moorings in the offing. These are laid for local craft, but there should be no complaint if you take a free one. There is no guarantee as to the state of the tackle and you should rely on your own judgement. Charges are modest. Alternatively, anchor in a clear space.

Landing from the dinghy is easy. There are ladders on the pier and a slipway.

Harbourmaster is Mr Carey, ☎ 01326 280583.

Facilities

Lovely cliff walks.

The Paris Hotel pub standing above the quay sells beer, meals and rooms. Toilets close by. Basic provisions and a memorable ice cream shop whose rum and raisin special rejoices in the name of 'Yo-ho-ho'. No water and no fuel, unless you enjoy lugging your cans 2 miles from the nearest garage.

Porthleven

Tides

High water +0551 Dover

MHWS	MLWS	MHWN	MLWN
5·5m	0·8m	4·3m	2·0m

General

The harbour at Porthleven was built originally in 1811. It maintains a few fishing craft and has a famous history of boatbuilding, with pilots coming from as far away as Wales to commission sailing craft of 50ft and more, noted for their speed, seaworthiness and beauty. The harbour, which lies about 8½ miles northwest of the Lizard, dries and is wide open to the southwest. As a result, it is rarely visited by yachts, but it is not crowded, and suffers little from tourism.

Approach and entrance

Porthleven is entered between the Little Trigg rocks off the south pier head and the Deazle Rocks on the northwest side. It is a difficult entrance because it is only 60m wide, and the Deazle Rocks are not marked by buoys or beacons, nor are there clear leading marks to the centre of the entrance. It would be unwise to attempt the entrance without local advice except by day under particularly favourable conditions in offshore winds. For a visitor to attempt entry by night would be madness.

Approach should be made on a course parallel with the long inner side of the pier, but about 20m northwest of it. This course crosses a bar formation (which is liable to change). At the entrance there are ledges of rock extending about 75m or more off the pier. The entrance lies between these rocks on the east side and the Deazle Rocks on the west. There is 2·4m at the entrance, followed by 4·1m, after which shoaling begins rapidly.

The outer harbour dries 0·9m to 1·8m, and there are rocks fringing the foot of the pier. The inner harbour also dries out completely, and can be closed with baulks of timber in bad weather and in winter. When shut, a red ball is displayed from the mast to the left of the clock tower looking in from seaward.

By arrangement with the harbourmaster (☎ 01326 574270) yachts may berth alongside the quay with about 3m at MHWS in the deepest berth. The bottom appears firm for drying out purposes. In the absence of a prior arrangement, tie up to the wall in the inner harbour as convenient, then try to contact the harbourmaster, whose office is on the east side of the inner harbour.

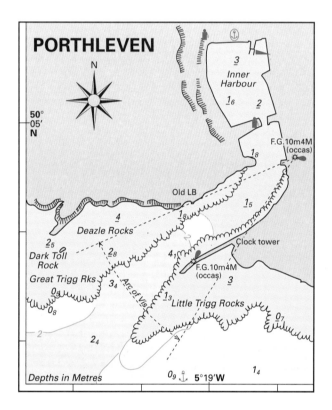

Porthleven harbour

A F.G light is shown about 30m from the pier head when traffic can move. A second light of similar characteristics shows when required over an arc 033°–067° for craft entering. This is sited on the east side of the harbour near the entrance to the inner harbour.

Facilities

Fresh water, fuel and basic stores. Two small hotels. Good bus service to Penzance and Falmouth.

Launching sites: trailed boats of any size from ramp, slipway at the head of the inner harbour near HW for smaller craft only.

Porthleven. Dried out in the inner harbour with the gate closed for the winter. Note the clock tower visible from seaward

St Michael's Mount

Tides
HW +0550 Dover

MHWS	MLWS	MHWN	MLWN
5·6m	0·8m	4·4m	2·0m

Depths
Harbour dries from 1·5m to 3m, but the anchorage has at least 2·5m LAT.

General
The tidal island of St Michael's Mount makes a remarkable landmark, with its romantic, turreted skyline. It was of great importance as a commercial port from Roman times, when it was a base for tin trading, through the long centuries until the civil war. It then provided a perfect centre for Royalist gun-running. The harbour was rebuilt in 1727, and its prosperity continued until Penzance finally eclipsed it with its better facilities. The isle has been the home of the St Aubyn family for over 300 years.

Approach and entrance
Do not approach the east or north sides of the Mount. They are foul with shoals. Instead, come in from Penzance Bay with Gear Rock astern (black beacon with cage topmark) and the north end of the harbour wall on 074°. This will clear the unmarked Outer Penzeath Rock (awash at LAT) about ½ mile east of the harbour entrance, and the Great Hogus Rock, an extensive shoal area which dries 4·9m.

If you prefer to round the isle to starboard, beware

St Michael's Mount

of Maltman Rock (dries 0·9m) nearly a cable south-southwest of the south point. To the east of this, a shoal drying 2·4m extends from the island. These dangers are unmarked, and so the point should be given a wide berth.

The approach shelves gradually to 2·7m a cable west of the entrance, after which depths reduce to the drying heights of the harbour itself. Hogus Rocks lie 1 cable north of the pier head, so do not pass far off this.

If approaching from the south, after giving the south point a good berth (see above) follow the west shore at a distance of about a cable. You may cross a rock (2·1m) and an obstruction (2·4m), but if you are intending to enter the harbour itself you will have sufficient tide for these to pose no problem. Be careful if coming to anchor around LW. Alter for the anchorage when the pier head bears 060°, or ideally when the right-hand side of Chapel Rock comes into transit on 053° with a grey truncated clock tower about 100 yards east of the root of the causeway.

Night entry is a non-starter for the stranger.

Harbour and Anchorage
There is a pleasant anchorage a cable or so west of the west pier, in depths of around 2·7m. This is usable in settled weather with breezes from north to southeast through east. Anchor to seaward of lobster pots. Entering the drying harbour, berth on the west wall (firm sand bottom) and report to the

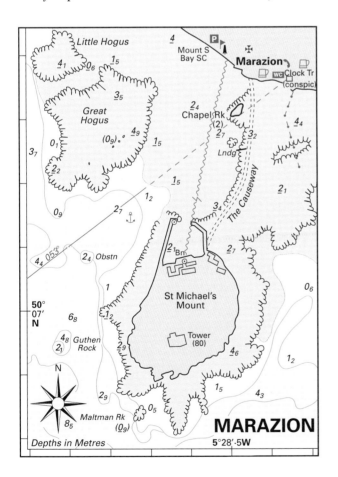

harbourmaster, whose office is on the opposite side. The East Quay is used by ferries and launches.

Facilities

Little on the Mount itself, but most requirements can be met in Marazion, half a mile northward across the causeway at LW or by dinghy at HW. Fresh water can be found; there is also no shortage of shops. Launching site on beach at west end of Marazion, with car park adjacent.

Buses run to Penzance, 3 miles distant.

Penzance

Tides

HW −0635 Dover

MHWS	MLWS	MHWN	MLWN
5·6m	0·8m	4·4m	2·0m

Depths

1·8m to seaward of South Pier. The outer harbour dries from 1·6m to 2·1m, except for a channel 0·6m deep leading up to the lock gates close along the South Pier. The gates open HW−2 to HW+1; the depth inside is 1·5m below datum, giving a depth at neaps of 5·8m.

General

Although its commercial importance has diminished since its early 19th-century heyday, Penzance remains an attractive option for the visiting yacht. The tidal basin, open 3 hours out of 12, gives complete shelter. Yachts can be left here safely for a period at sensible rates, so during prolonged bad weather Penzance has much to recommend it. Be careful of approaching in strong southerlies or southeasterlies, however. The shoaling water and lee shore of Mount's Bay can render it dangerous.

Approach and entrance

If approaching from around the Lizard, give the point 2 to 3 miles clearance in rough weather, then pass outside the Boa, 3 miles further west. Now pass southward of the unlit south cardinal *Mountamopus* buoy to clear all the shoals off Cudden Point. Thereafter, shape up for the harbour entrance, clearing Gear Rock with its isolated danger colouring (black and red with ⁑ topmark). By night, the white sector of the light on South Pier

(Fl.WR.5s11m17/12M) clears all inshore dangers, including Gear Rock and the rocky ledges between Penzance and St Michael's Mount.

From the westward, leave the *Runnelstone* south cardinal buoy to port and continue a mile or so offshore past St Clement's Island. *Low Lee* lit east cardinal buoy is situated just under a mile north-northwest of St Clement's Island and marks shoals of 1·5m and 1·8m. If in doubt, leave the buoy to port, but a suitable tide rise may well allow you to ignore it. A heading of 345° for the head of the South Pier will clear Gear Rock (see above) and Battery Rocks, which lie just east of south from the entrance. 4 cables east-northeast of the entrance lie the Cressar Rocks, marked by a south cardinal beacon.

Anchorage and berthing

If waiting for the lock to open in settled or offshore weather, you can anchor safely enough in modest depths a cable or more east-northeast of the end of Albert Pier (2F.G). The inside of South Pier is used by the Scilly Isles ferry, but the berth is usually clear from 0930 to 1830 on weekdays. It is used on Saturday lunchtimes and all day on Sunday, when the ferry does not sail. If using this berth, lie by the ladder, not the steps near the lock, as these are in constant use. Contact the harbourmaster either personally or on VHF, call Ch 16, working Ch 12, or ☎ 01736 66113. Sometimes the harbourmaster will allow you to dry out alongside Albert Pier, but the generally preferred option is to enter the wet dock through the locks, which open from HW−2 to HW+1. The berthing master will direct you, and will also issue a key to the showers and toilets beneath the berthing office by the lock gate.

Lock signals

Shown from the harbourmaster's office, wet dock, north arm and indicated by a mast. The port entry lights are as follows:

3F.R(vert) – Dock gates closed
3F.G(vert) – Dock gates open

Facilities

Fresh water and diesel by arrangement with berthing master. Petrol from garage. *Calor Gas* and *Camping Gas* exchange through berthing master on the harbour side. A launderette will be discovered

Penzance Harbour entrance from the east. Lock gates and dock are under church tower

Penzance

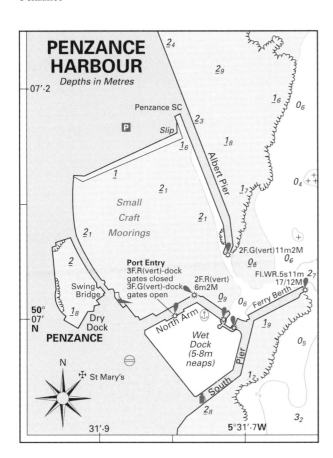

near railway station. Engineers, electronics and sailmakers all in town. 8-ton crane, but repair facilities limited. All the usual town facilities, with a wide selection of pubs. Also fish and chips. Various restaurants, some very reasonably priced, including the Bosun's Locker and the Waterside, both of which are on the harbour side.

Communications
Ferry to Scilly Isles. Bus and rail to all mainland destinations.

Newlyn

Tides
IIW +0600 Dover

MHWS	MLWS	MHWN	MLWN
5·6m	0·8m	4·4m	2·0m

Depths
A minimum of 2·1m in the entrance and alongside the west side of Mary Williams Pier, where visiting yachts generally lie. Greater depths (see plan) in Gwavas Lake, and south-southeast of the South Pier, either of which may be used to anchor.

General
Newlyn is approachable in nearly all weathers, subject to the same provisos as Penzance concerning hard onshore blows. If it is blowing stiffly from south or southeast, then the nearer to HW you can time your arrival the better. Inside shelter is good

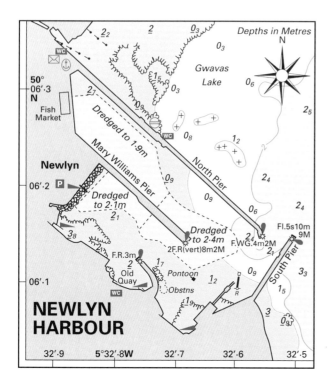

Newlyn. Mary Williams Pier in the centre of harbour. If in doubt, raft to a fishing boat well in on the west side

except in strong southeasterlies, when a swell rolls in, but the harbour is not set up for yachts. It is commercial, with fishing its overriding concern. However, short-stay visitors and overnight shelter can usually be arranged with a good grace.

Approach and entrance

Follow the instructions given for Penzance; alter for Newlyn when the South Pier head (Fl.5s9M) bears due west. Swing in between it and the North Pier (F.WG) and shape up to leave the head of the Mary Williams Pier (2F.R) to starboard. On your port bow is an unlit red spar buoy marking the end of a slipway. Note that the western part of the harbour dries out, but that there is a dredged channel (2·1m or more) alongside the pier.

Anchorage and berthing

Yachts can lie to anchor in moderate offshore weather in Gwavas Lake, or south-southeast of the South Pier head. Show a riding light. Depths to suit most tastes.

Inside, tie up to a fishing vessel towards the northwest end of the Mary Williams Pier, on the southwest side of the pier. In this vicinity the boats may well be laid up for repairs. Report to the harbourmaster, who will do his best to accommodate your vessel. He can be telephoned on ☎ 01736 62523, or called on VHF Ch 16, working on Ch 12 or 9.

Facilities

Fresh water from quay. Diesel in quantity by arrangement with harbourmaster. Petrol from garage. Showers and toilets for both sexes at the Royal National Mission to Deep Sea Fishermen, on the North Pier, plus a noble breakfast in the refectory. Repair yards are largely fishing boat orientated, but may help in an emergency. There is

no yacht club, but there are plenty of pubs and eating places. A launderette can be found on the Penzance road. All town facilities.

Communications

Bus to Penzance, thence onward by bus or rail.

Mousehole

Tides

HW +0550 Dover

MHWS	MLWS	MHWN	MLWN
5·6m	0·8m	4·4m	2·0m

Depths

Shoal in the north passage round St Clement's Isle, though with care 2·1m can be found at low water halfway between the mainland and the island. Ample depths on the south side of the island, drying out progressively to 1·3m in the immediate offing from the entrance, and 1·9m inside the outer ends of the piers.

General

Mousehole (pronounced Mowzle) is a classic Cornish fishing harbour with massive, well maintained, granite walls, a narrow entrance and water to float in from around half-tide onwards. Though long past its great days as a mackerel and pilchard centre when a man could walk across the harbour on moored boats, it has not lost its independent spirit and still retains great charm. In settled weather, a night at anchor between St Clement's Island and the south pier can repay your trouble, while for those prepared to dry out on its clean sandy bottom, the harbour offers good shelter in all but east or southeast blows. Winds from the east have so evil a reputation in these parts that back in the days when fishermen had no weather forecasts, it was well known that if slugs and snails in the garden became inactive, the wind would soon blow up from the east. This meant that the fish in the sea would also lose interest in life. As a result, easterly weather was a good time for gardening.

Speed boats are not allowed in Mousehole by the harbourmaster, but sailors should beware of children who still swim in the harbour as in days long gone by.

Approach and entrance

Mousehole is distinguished from seaward by St Clement's Isle with its obelisk daymark. Note, however, that the height of this, given as 7m above MHWS, includes the island itself. The 'obelisk' is really more of a modest cairn. Approaches round the north side of the island should only be made with the greatest care, eyeballing to keep halfway between the land and the isle. This will ensure a minimum of 2·1m at LAT. Both sides of this passage are rocky.

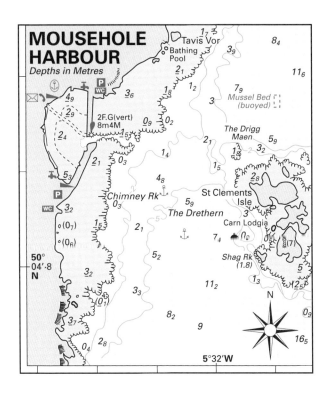

Leaving the island to starboard presents no difficulty so long as you keep more or less halfway between it and the mainland. When Shag Rock (divided from the island at all states of tide) is in line with the end of the southern pier head, turn in and keep the rock astern. There are now no dangers at all, save the rocks close in around the piers themselves (see plan). Enter round the south pier head. There are 2 F.G vertical lights on the north pier, but night entry is not a good idea for strangers.

Anchorage and berthing

The anchorage mentioned above has good holding ground. It is open to south and southeast winds, and even westerlies can hook a swell. Settled weather is therefore desirable if a quiet night is what you are after.

Inside the entrance, berth on the south pier as tide, draught and space allow. There is a reasonable depth in the harbour from half-flood onwards.

The harbourmaster may well make himself known in due course.

Note that from November to April the harbour entrance is closed with baulks of timber. A F.R light indicates 'Harbour Closed'.

Facilities

All good town facilities. Fresh water. Toilets on the quay. Garage. Good pubs, cream teas and various restaurants including the Lobster Pot. Buses to Newlyn and Penzance.

Mousehole

Isles of Scilly

Tides
HW approx +0607 Dover

St Mary's Roads

MHWS	MLWS	MHWN	MLWN
5·7m	0·7m	4·3m	2·0m

Depths
2·1m in St Mary's Pool, with increasing depths further from the shore. 3m if required in Porth Cressa. 0·8m at Crow Bar on the northern passage round St Mary's, but deep water if approaching south-about via St Mary's Sound. Depths in New Grimsby Sound between Tresco and Bryher vary from 11m outside Hangman's Island to 3·6m inside, diminishing to drying heights further into the passage. Tresco Flats from New Grimsby Sound towards St Mary's and points south can safely be taken as drying 1·4m on the recommended route.

General
The 48 Isles of Scilly are a marine wonderland. Half-sea, half-land, they lie out in the ocean, a paradise for sailors in fair weather, an interesting stop-over when the breezes are moderate, but a place for the stranger to avoid vigorously when the spume rises over the rocks and the gales blow hard.

The inhabitants of the islands are true sea people, taking to boats as naturally as mainlanders do to their cars, so that it seems most families have some nautical connection. Historically the sea was all, and outside the usual fishing, trading and smuggling of other West Country folk, Scillonians were able to make a substantial contribution to their annual budgets by profiting from the steady parade of ships piling up on their outlying rocks. Of these, some of the most distinguished belonged to the Royal Navy battle fleet under the command of Sir Cloudesley Shovell, which ran ashore under sail in a grand spectacular with colossal loss of life and property.

Only five islands are inhabited, all very different from their neighbours: St Mary's, St Martin's, Tresco, Bryher and St Agnes. St Mary's is the biggest and most populous, with Hugh Town serving as the 'capital'.

It is possible to spend a considerable time exploring this fascinating archipelago. A shoal-draught boat able to take the ground and in no hurry could spend a summer here. However, the detailed information required for this lies beyond the scope of *The Shell Channel Pilot*. There are a number of specialist books available, including The RCC Pilotage Foundation's *Isles of Scilly* and *A Yachtsman's Guide to Scilly* by Norm which, if not available 'from all good bookshops' on the mainland, is conspicuously for sale in Hugh Town. Buy a copy and read it. Not only does it keep you off the rocks, Norm's asides about local customs and characters leave you in no doubt about where you stand socially as well. . .

The Shell Channel Pilot will therefore confine its interest to Hugh Town, Porth Cressa (its backyard in certain conditions) and New Grimsby Sound at Tresco/Bryher. Between them, these anchorages can

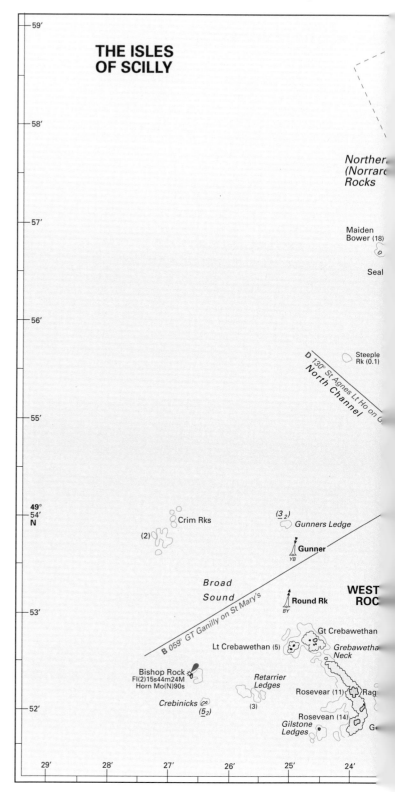

offer shelter to most vessels in all reasonable conditions. You may be safe, but you will not always be comfortable, because the swell of the ocean is never far away. Scilly is for sailors, and for them its rewards can be great, provided they come equipped with proper ground tackle. If you want a guaranteed quiet night, stay on the mainland.

Off-lying dangers
These are all well charted and tend to rise steeply from deep water. Because of their isolation in the extreme west, the Crim Rocks (2m) and others near them lying about 1½ miles north of the Bishop Rock are worthy of special mention. The others are too numerous to note, and mariners are warned to carry a detailed chart of the area and to study it assiduously.

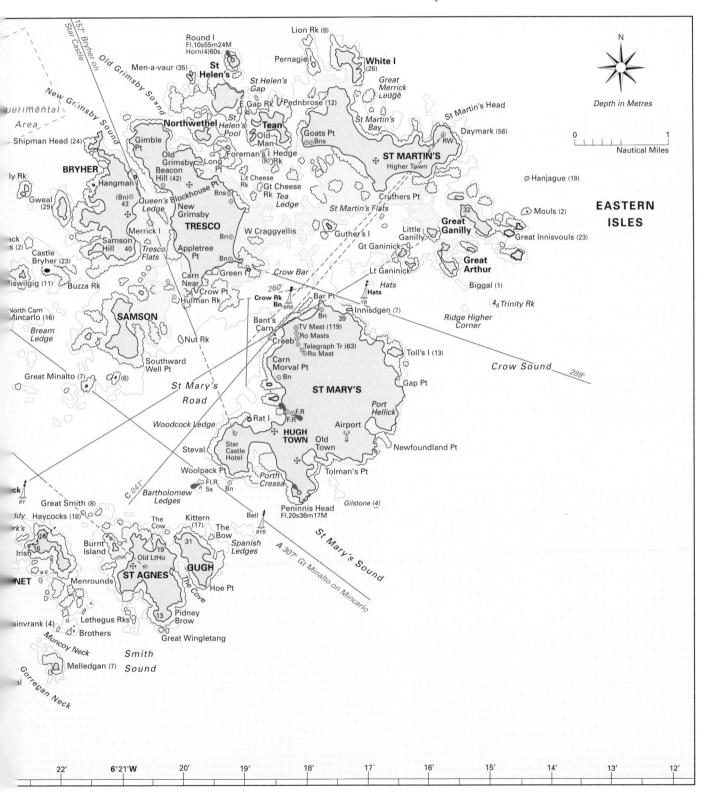

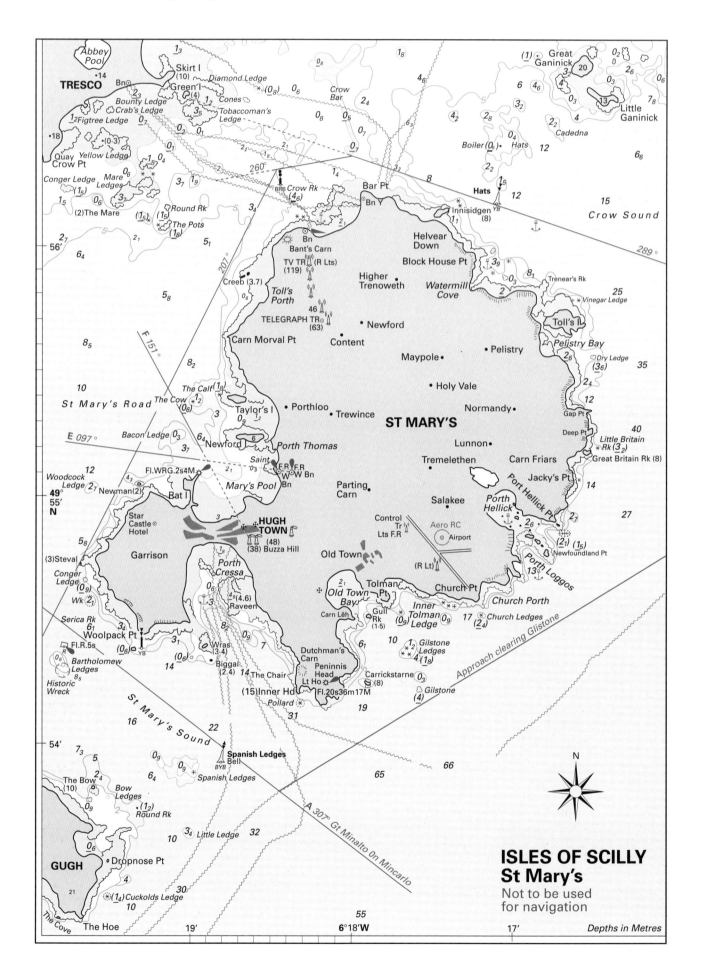

TRESCO

Abbey Pool

Skirt I
Diamond Ledge
Green I
Cones
Bounty Ledge
Crab's Ledge
Figtree Ledge
Tobaccoman's Ledge
Quay
Yellow Ledge
Crow Pt
Conger Ledge
Mare Ledges
(2)The Mare
Round Rk
The Pots

Crow Bar

Crow Rk

Bar Pt
Bn Y

Hats
Innisidgen
(8)

Crow Sound

Great Ganinick
Little Ganinick
Cadedna
Boiler
Hats

BRB

Helvear Down
Block House Pt
Watermill Cove
Trenear's Rk
Vinegar Ledge

Bant's Carn
TV TR (R Lts) (119)
Higher Trenoweth
Toll's I
Pelistry Bay
Dry Ledge

Creeb (3.7)
Toll's Porth
46
TELEGRAPH TR (63)
Newford
Content
Maypole
Pelistry

Carn Morval Pt

Holy Vale
Normandy
Gap Pt

St Mary's Road
The Calf
The Cow
Taylor's I
Porthloo
Trewince
ST MARY'S
Deep Pt
Little Britain Rk (3₂)

Bacon Ledge
Newford
Porth Thomas
Lunnon
Carn Friars
Great Britain Rk (8)

Saint
Mary's Pool
Tremelethen
Jacky's Pt

Fl.WRG.2s4M
F.R F.R
W W Bn
Bn
Parting Carn
Salakee
Porth Hellick

Woodcock Ledge
Newman(2)
Bat I

Star Castle Hotel
HUGH TOWN
(48)
(38) Buzza Hill
Old Town
Control Tr Lts F.R
Aero RC
Airport
Newfoundland Pt

(3)Steval
Garrison
Porth Cressa
Old Town Bay
Tolman Pt
Church Pt
Church Porth

Conger Ledge
Raveen
Gull Rk
Inner Tolman Ledge
Church Ledges

Serica Rk
Wk
Woolpack Pt
Wras
Carn Lêh
Gilstone Ledges

Fl.R.5s
Bartholomew Ledges
Biggal
The Chair
Dutchman's Carn
Peninnis Head Lt Ho
Carrickstarne
Gilstone

Historic Wreck
Inner Hd
Pollard
Fl.20s36m17M

St Mary's Sound

Spanish Ledges
Bell
Spanish Ledges

The Bow
Bow Ledges
Round Rk
Little Ledge

Approach clearing Glistone

GUGH
Dropnose Pt
Cuckolds Ledge

A 307° Gt Minalto On Mincarlo

The Hoe
The Cove

N

**ISLES OF SCILLY
St Mary's**
Not to be used
for navigation

Depths in Metres

6°18'W

Sailing into these islands in thick weather is extremely dangerous, and the greatest caution is needed when the distant leading marks cannot be positively identified. Choose your weather carefully for a first visit, and if in doubt, lie off.

Approaches to St Mary's from the east

The generally recommended approach to St Mary's Road from the east is by way of St Mary's Sound which is deep and adequately marked, though approach can be made, given suitable weather and state of tide, via Crow Sound. At night it may be helpful to note that Peninnis light (Fl.20s36m17M) becomes obscured on a bearing of about 231°, but island navigation after dark is not recommended in the absence of local knowledge.

Crow Sound

The flood tide tends to set onshore in this vicinity, so, having given the Eastern Isles and their associated rocks a berth of at least half a mile, one should leave the unlit south cardinal *Hats* buoy close to starboard to put the rock off Innisidgen Island (7m high), which dries 1·6m, clear to port. From the *Hats* buoy steer 289° with Green Island, a 4m-high rock off the nearest corner of Tresco, ahead. When Bar Point (the northernmost point of St Mary's Island) comes abeam, alter to 260° and leave the red and black beacon (⁙ topmark) marking Crow Rock well to port. Charted soundings on the Crow Bar Sands, formerly 0·9m, are likely to be unreliable, so allow plenty of clearance. Entry should not be atttempted without ample tide. The best water will often be found where sand and weed meet; this can be eyeballed in the clear water. Once round Crow Rock, it is safe to alter to the southwest and the deep waters of St Mary's Road.

St Mary's Sound

The greatest danger approaching St Mary's Sound is the Gilstone (dries 4m), which lies a touch under 4 cables from Peninnis Light on a bearing of 095°. So long as you keep south of this clearing line on your approach, the rock will not trouble you. The recommended leading marks for Transit A (see plan) may prove difficult for the stranger to identify, but there is plenty of water close to the south of Peninnis Head, with its white pepper-pot lighthouse on a black trellised base (Fl.20s36m17M). Leave the unlit *Spanish Ledges* east cardinal bell buoy to port, also the unlit red can buoy on Bartholomew Ledges. Do not get too close to the south cardinal *Woolpack* beacon south of Garrison Hill, as there is a 0·6m patch half a cable west of it.

After leaving the *Bartholomew* buoy to port, swing steadily round to the north-northeast. Deep-draught yachts arriving around LW may want to take Transit C (Creeb Rocks with St Martin's daymark on 041°), widely clearing Woodcock Ledge, with 2·7m over it.

Approaches to St Mary's from the west
Broad Sound

Transit B on 059°, leaving Bishop Rock Lighthouse to starboard, will bring you in all the way to St Mary's Road, but the leading marks are over 7 miles

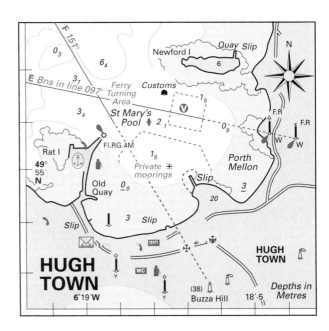

away and may not be identifiable. Fortunately, the channel is buoyed with unlit cardinal marks. Leave the Bishop half a mile to starboard, followed by the *Round Rock* north cardinal buoy north of Great Crebawethan. The *Gunner* south cardinal is left well to port, after which a heading of around 060° will clear the ledges northwest of Annet, and the Old Wreck Rock. The *Old Wreck* north cardinal buoy should be left fairly close to starboard in order to keep clear to the southeast of the Jeffrey Rock (0·9m). The leading marks should now be picked up, but if they are still invisible, steer 059° towards the left-hand edge of St Mary's. It is important to remember the danger of cross-sets at all times.

North Channel

Transit D 130°. Once again, be on your guard for cross-tide. Here, however, the leading marks are readily spotted in reasonable visibility. The most significant danger is Steeple Rock (0·1m). Lying a touch over 6 cables southwest of Mincarlo, it is also less than 2 cables to port on the transit. Maintain your heading on the transit until you come onto the Broad Sound Transit B, which you will see easily at this range in reasonable visibility. Now alter course to 059° into St Mary's Road, in deep water all the way.

Entrance to St Mary's Pool and Harbour

There are two main dangers between St Mary's Road and the pool: Bacon Ledge (0·3m) and the Cow (dries 0·6m). The most commonly used entry is Transit E on 097°, which lines up two white beacons north of Porth Mellon. There is a triangular topmark on the front one and a cross on the higher rear one. Each has a F.R light. Transit F leads you in from the northwest on course 151°, between the Cow and Bacon Ledge, bringing the squat Buzza Mill tower on the high ground behind Hugh Town into line with a small shelter on the esplanade, with a white roof and white vertical stripes on either end of its front elevation.

St Mary's. Hugh Town from the south. Anchored yacht in Porth Cressa in the foreground. Tresco and Round Island in the background

38 strong visitors' moorings have been laid in St Mary's. They will be found inshore of the moored lifeboat. The outer two lines are for larger yachts up to 18m (60ft) LOA. If the buoys are full, anchorage is still available outside the trots, but beware of anchoring amongst the moorings themselves. They are laid on long ground chains and you may well foul your tackle.

Drying berths are often available well inshore on the harbour wall.

Whatever your intentions, you will be better received if you first call the harbourmaster on VHF Ch 16, working Ch 14.

Always leave plenty of room for the *Scillonian* ferry and remain aware that the quay and harbour are much used by large, powerful launches carrying on the islands' business.

Porth Cressa

St Mary's Pool is extremely uncomfortable in winds from north of west, and may become untenable. Porth Cressa, immediately south of the Hugh Town isthmus, then offers good shelter as well as easy access to the town. If coming from St Mary's, leave the *Woolpack* unlit south cardinal beacon well to port and *Bartholomew Ledges* red can buoy to starboard, then steer to give Biggal Rock (2·4m high MHWS) a sensible berth to port. After rounding Biggal, swing onto a heading a touch west of north and work into the anchorage leaving the 3·4m-high Wras Rock on your port side, paying due heed to the large rock shelf (dries 4·9m) which clutters the eastern half of the bay. The Raveen rock (4·6m high) is conveniently sited just inside the southwestern extremity of this reef. Porth Cressa offers depths to suit most vessels and is sheltered from west-northwest through north to east. The bottom is sound and the holding is adequate, given a good scope of cable. No problems reported or experienced from the submarine cables (see plan) but, if in doubt, buoy your anchor. Facilities are the same as for Hugh Town. Land on the clean sand beach at the head of the bay.

Alternative anchorage

If a blow from the southwest is imminent, large yachts are said to be able to anchor in Crow Sound southeast of the *Hats* buoy off Watermill Cove in the northeast of St Mary's Island. This will not be at all comfortable, but may be safe.

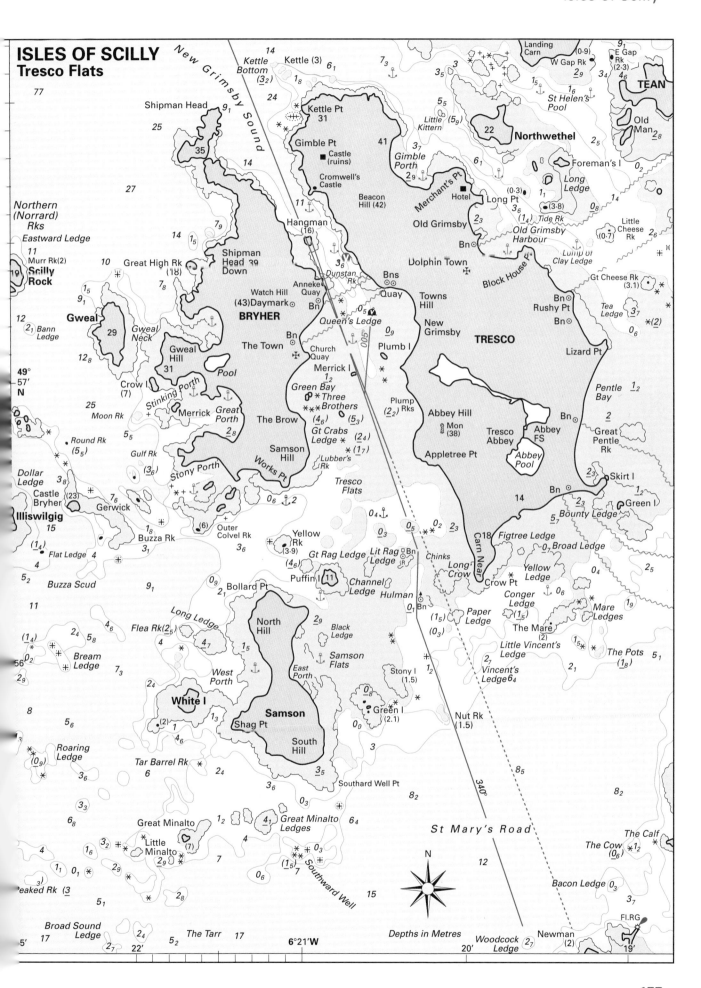

ISLES OF SCILLY
Tresco Flats

77

New Grimsby Sound

Shipman Head

Kettle Bottom (3₂)   Kettle (3)   14

Kettle Pt 31

Gimble Pt

Castle (ruins)

Cromwell's Castle

Beacon Hill (42)

Little Kittern (5₉)

22   **Northwethel**

Landing Carn (0·9)   E Gap Rk (2·3)

W Gap Rk   **TEAN**

St Helen's Pool

Old Man 2₈

Foreman's I

Long Ledge

Hangman (16)

Gimble Porth 2₉

Merchant's Pt   Hotel

Old Grimsby 2₃

Long Pt 3₆   (0·3) 1₁   (3·8)

(1₄) Tide Rk

Old Grimsby Harbour

Little Cheese Rk 2₆

Northern (Norrard) Rks

Eastward Ledge

11   Murr Rk(2)

Scilly Rock

10   Great High Rk (18)   Shipman Head Down 39

14   1₅   7₉

Watch Hill (43)Daymark⊙

BRYHER

Anneket Quay   Bn

Queen's Ledge

Dunstan Rk   3₆   Bns

Quay   0₅

Dolphin Town

Bn⊙

Block House Pt

Lump of Clay Ledge

Gt Cheese Rk (3.1)

Tea Ledge 3₇   (2)

0₆

12   Bann Ledge (2₁)

Gweal   29   Gweal Neck

7₈

12₈   Gweal Hill 31

Crow I (7)

Pool

Stinking Porth

Moon Rk 25

The Town   Bn

Church Quay

Merrick I 1₂

Green Bay

Three Brothers (4₆) (5₃)

Towns Hill

New Grimsby

TRESCO

Plumb I

0₉

Rushy Pt   Bn⊙

Bn⊙

Lizard Pt

Pentle Bay 1₂

5₅   Merrick   Great Porth 2₈

The Brow

Gt Crabs Ledge

Samson Hill   Lubber's Rk

Plump Rks (2₂)

Abbey Hill   Mon (38)

(2₄) (1₇)

Works Pt

Stony Porth

Gulf Rk (3₆)

Dollar Ledge 3₈

Castle Bryher (23)

Gerwick 7₆

Illiswilgig 15   1₈   Buzza Rk 3₁

(1₄)   Flat Ledge 4   4

(6)   Outer Colvel Rk

3₆

Tresco Flats

0₆   2

0₄

0₃   0₅   0₂   2₃

Appletree Pt

Tresco Abbey

Abbey FS   Abbey Pool

Abbey 2₃

Bn⊙

14

Skirt I 1₂

Green I

Bn⊙   2₃   Bounty Ledge 5₇

Figtree Ledge

18   Carn Near

Broad Ledge 0₇

5₂   Buzza Scud

11   2₄   5₈

(1₄)   0₂

56   Bream Ledge

2₉   7₃

9₁   Bollard Pt 2₁

Long Ledge

Flea Rk(2₅)   4₇

2₄   1₅

0₉

Yellow Rk (3·9) (4₆)

Puffin I   11

Gt Rag Ledge

Lit Rag Ledge   Bn JR

Channel Ledge

Hulman   0₁   Bn

Chinks

Long Crow

Crow Pt

Yellow Ledge

Conger Ledge (1₅)

0₄

Mare Ledges

The Mare (2)   Little Vincent's Ledge

2₇   Vincent's Ledge 6₄

1₅   The Pots (1₈)

5₁

North Hill 2₉

Black Ledge

Samson Flats

West Porth

East Porth

Stony I (1.5)

1₂

(1₅)

0₂

2₄   **White I**   1   1₃

(2)   4₆

8   5₆

4₃

Samson

Shag Pt

South Hill

Green I (2.1)

0₈   0₀

Nut Rk (1.5)

(0₃)   (1₅)

8₅

340°

Paper Ledge

3   3

Roaring Ledge (0₉)   3₆

Tar Barrel Rk   6   2₄

3₃

6₈

Great Minalto

3₂   Little Minalto (7)   2₉

4   7

1₁   0₁

3₁   2₈

1₂   4₁   Great Minalto Ledges   6₄

0₃

(1₅)   7

0₆

Southard Well Pt

0₃

8₂

St Mary's Road

15

N

12

8₂

The Cow (0₆)   The Calf 1₂

Bacon Ledge 0₃

5₁   Broad Sound Ledge

17   2₄

22'   5₂   The Tarr   17

6°21'W

Depths in Metres   20'

Woodcock Ledge (2) 2₇

Newman (2)

Fl.RG

19'

Facilities

Hugh Town on St Mary's offers most facilities, including post office, chemist, hospital, provision stores, banks, hotels and bistros, with the Mermaid a notable mecca for seafaring men and women. Water and fuel on the quay. Good showers in the Quay Building hard by the harbourmaster's office. There are chandlers, boat repairers, a sailmaker and an active customs service. Also daily helicopters to Penzance, with connecting bus services. Ferries leave every afternoon in the summer for Penzance. The harbourmaster is on ☎ 01720 422768. Yacht club: Isles of Scilly Yacht Club.

New Grimsby Sound – Tresco/Bryher

In spite of its appearance of being open to the north-northwest, New Grimsby Sound is probably the best all-weather harbour in the islands. Except in strong northerly weather it is a perfectly viable first port of call, approached from seaward. Its other entrance is entirely dependent upon rise of tide. The anchorage is beautiful and atmospheric.

Approach and entrance

From the northwest or west, simply leave Shipman Head to starboard and shape up towards Hangman Island, an unmistakable pile of rocks 16m high. It is surmounted by a well maintained gibbet, now patronised only by visiting yachtsmen whose patience with their crew has expired. Leave the island to starboard and stand on into the anchorage.

From the east, leave White Island and Lion Rock (8m high) with their associated dangers well to port. Now head past Round Island, the same shape as its name, surmounted by a classic white lighthouse (Fl.10s55m24M Horn(4)60s). Tide Rock (dries 2·3m) and Black Rock (6m high) lie halfway between Lion Rock and Round Island. Deep Ledges, with only 0·6m and 2·7m over them, lie up to a cable to seaward, so the stranger should aim to stand at least half a mile north of Lion Rock to be sure of safety.

Pass round the mighty Men-a-vaur rock, then steer about west-southwest, keeping on or north of the transit of the north edge of the rock and the north edge of Round Island. This clears all further dangers. The transit recommended on the Admiralty chart for entering New Grimsby is difficult for the stranger to identify. It is therefore preferable to stay on the Men-a-vaur/Round Island transit until Cromwell's Castle (18m round tower, not to be mistaken for the ruined King Charles' Castle on the hilltop behind it) is well open of Gimble Point, then swing in to your final approach, favouring the Shipman Head side so as to clear a group of rocks immediately north-northwest of Gimble Point. Once the Point is abeam, stay in the middle, leaving Hangman Island to starboard. Tides in the channel run at up to 2 knots. Their direction is controlled by the uncovering of Tresco Flats.

Tresco Flats

The passage from St Mary's to Tresco is not nearly so difficult as the chart makes it appear. The sands dry approximately 1m along the route, but if you allow for 1·4m instead you will have more confidence.

Leave St Mary's, avoiding Bacon Ledge (see St Mary's), and shape a course towards Nut Rock. At 1·5m high at MHWS, this is easier to identify than you might imagine. Leave the rock about 50m to port, then steer 340°, bringing *The Hulman* (a platform with a balustrade topmark) onto your starboard bow. (Distance about 4 cables.) Leave *The Hulman* at least 10m to starboard, and swing around to starboard so as to leave Little Rag Ledge with its red topmarked beacon 15m to 20m to port. Steer 340° with Merrick Island 'on' with the Hangman until, approaching Merrick Island, the root of Tresco Quay (gable end of Quay Shop conspicuous) lines up with the left-hand edge of Plumb Island. At this point you should steer halfway between Merrick and Plumb Islands on about 005°. As Plumb Island comes abeam, shape up towards the visitors' moorings on the east side of the 'fairway'. This will clear Queen's Ledge, which dries 2·5m.

Anchorage and moorings

In settled weather, deep-draught yachts can lie to seaward of Hangman Island and south-southwest of Cromwell's Castle. Better shelter is available south-southeast of the island, sounding in to find a suitable depth (see plan) in good, sandy holding. A series of visitors' moorings is established on the Tresco side of the channel, administered from Tresco. A boatman will call for your dues.

Land on the quay (do not leave your dinghy near the end) at Tresco, or on the wooden jetty on Bryher. Launches use both, so ideally you should take advice before leaving your dinghy unattended.

Fresh water is available on the quay at Tresco, which also has a useful village store, up the hill from the New Inn, and a direct helicopter service. Diesel by can, from Tresco estate workshop (ask at the estate office). There is a slipway with easy HW dinghy landing only 50 metres from the pump. Bryher has no pub, but a shop of surprising excellence is hidden away just north of the landing place. Local produce is for sale by the laneside. Buy some bulbs for your garden and keep your holiday for years.

This is a fine place for dinghy voyages. If you run short of outboard fuel, it can be purchased by arrangement on Tresco from the estate workshop. In the same complex is an efficient laundry.

One of the best nights out on offer in the English Channel is to take the local support boat from Tresco Quay for the evening gig racing in St Mary's. Enquire locally about which evenings and what time. The cost is modest, and seeing a fleet of six-oared gigs, some over a century old, striding out into a serious seaway makes coming to Scilly worth the trip by itself.

II. The French coast
Dunkerque to L'Aber-Wrac'h

Principal headlands

With two notable exceptions, the headlands of northern France are of less importance than their English counterparts. The reasons for this are twofold. East of the Cherbourg peninsula, the coast runs in general without salient promontories. West of the root of the peninsula, the shoreline is often beset with off-lying dangers and islands. These make coast-hugging a proposition which, while feasible in parts, does not fall within the scope of *The Shell Channel Pilot*. Nonetheless, the two great headlands at the northeast and northwest corners of this crucial landmass are of great significance to navigators. They also produce some of the most spectacular tidal effects in the Channel.

To avoid inaccuracies, tidal stream data are given with relation to the times of high water at Cherbourg or St Malo. For reference:

HW Cherbourg is −0308 HW Dover
HW ST Malo is −0506 HW Dover

POINTE DE BARFLEUR

Tidal streams in the offing
Northwest-going stream commences 3 hours after HW Cherbourg and runs until 3 hours before HW.

Spring rates can approach 5 knots in either direction. Inshore, there is an early turn of up to two hours on both east-going and west-going streams. This is particularly noticeable on the end of the west-going, with an easterly eddy creeping further and further offshore as the main Channel tide comes up to the turn.

Pointe de Barfleur can throw up a very nasty race indeed, particularly on the northwest-going tide, when dangerous seas may be encountered in strong westerly or northwesterly winds. These are caused not only by the seabed, but also by the north-going stream running up from the direction of St Vaast meeting the more general westerly stream in the main Channel. You will be well advised to give the whole place a wide berth under such conditions.

The headland is low-lying, and the grey, black-topped light tower (Fl(2)10s29M), at 75 metres high, is the most prominent feature. It stands close to the shore, to which it is joined by a causeway.

Close north of the lighthouse stands the flat-topped grey tower of the signal station, surmounted by a mast. There is a fog signal (Horn(2)60s), and the light is obscured when bearing less than 088°.

CAP DE LA HAGUE

Tidal streams
These must always be considered in relation to the neighbouring Race of Alderney, where streams can achieve over 8 knots.

Close inshore, streams run at an almost unbelievable speed, with 10 knots and more being recorded. The northeast-going stream begins an hour before HW St Malo, the southwest-going 5 hours after, with a strong eddy to the west up to two hours earlier along the north shore.

Cap de la Hague is possibly the most stream-lashed headland in the Channel. Portland Bill comes close, but its dangers lie more offshore in the Race. Cap de la Hague is beset with rocky inshore dangers, over which streams set with a strength that may render useless any attempt to escape by a small yacht, even under power in flat-calm conditions. The area must therefore be given a wide berth when the streams are in full spate or in hard weather, and treated with the utmost respect at all other times.

The lighthouse stands immediately offshore on a rock called Gros du Raz. The French pilot book records a passage inside the rock which can avoid the worst of the tide, but offers no details concerning its access. *The Shell Channel Pilot* therefore makes mention of it and no more. We have no information as to how it may be passed, and the compiler, whose yacht is very dear to him and draws 2m (6ft 6ins) of water, makes no apology for not having ventured in to take a look.

The light is exhibited from a grey, white-topped tower, 51m high (Fl.5s48m23M Horn 30s).

Making landfall on Cap de la Hague from the north in good visibility, you will probably first see the huge square building and associated chimney etc. of the nuclear power station. This stands on high ground southeast of the light tower not far from a radio mast. By night, these exhibit F.R lights at 3·8M and 4·5M to the southeast of the light.

Harbour pilotage

Dunkerque

Tides

HW +0050 Dover

MHWS	MLWS	MHWN	MLWN
5·8m	0·7m	4·9m	1·4m

Streams

Streams run hard in the offing, up to 3½ knots at springs.

ENE-going begins −0140 Dover

WNW set starts +0415 Dover

Depths

Dunkerque is a deep-water harbour with locked basins to float ships. There is plenty of water in the channels up to the marinas. The Yacht Club de la Mer de Nord has 3m on its waiting pontoon and 2m+ generally inside. The Port de Plaisance au Grand Large is also deep, with 3m or more.

General

Dunkerque will always be famous for the evacuation of the British Expeditionary Force from its beaches in 1940. Without this miracle, it is said that there would have been no British Army, no Battle of Britain, and no survival. Today, a visit to Dunkerque's beaches and breakwaters can do a little to recapture in the mind the heroic deeds that were performed more than 50 years ago in weather that the gods kept fair. Particularly remembered are the Little Ships which, together with their low-profile crews, have passed justifiably into legend.

Dunkerque is a major industrial town and a port capable of handling all but the largest ships. It is a bustling centre of population which still maintains

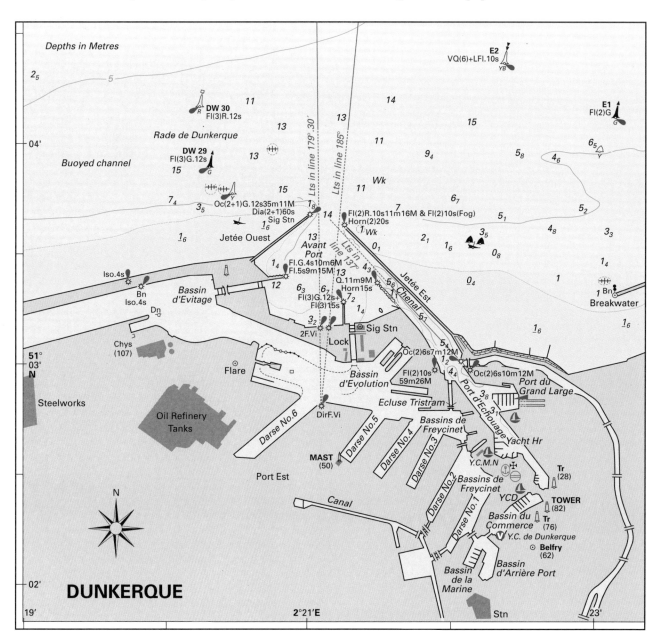

Above Dunkerque. Enter following Jetée Est seen here on the left-hand side.

Looking across the harbour

some residual charm, and boasts the unusual benefit on this coast of an all-tide entrance which is approachable in any reasonable weather.

Approach

From the east, clear Nieuwpoort Bank and take departure from *Nieuwpoortbank* lit west cardinal buoy. A track of 235° leads 4 miles further on to *E12* and *E11* buoys. *E12* is a lit south cardinal and *E11* is a tall green buoy (Fl.G) which the channel leaves to port. (Note that the red/green channel orientation runs from west to east, NOT towards the Dunkerque entrance.)

From here, steer approximately south-southwest past the unlit red can buoy *E10* on your starboard hand, down to the next pair of lit buoys: *E8* (red pillar Fl(3)R whistle, leave to starboard) and *E7* (green pillar, Fl(3)G, leave to port). A mile or so further on is *E6* (Q.R), to be left to starboard, after which a course along the coast leads to *E4* (Fl.R), and thence to the green *E1* buoy (Fl(2)G, leave to port). Off on your starboard bow is the lit south cardinal *E2* (VQ(6)+LFl.10s), from which the entrance is 1¼ miles on a southwesterly heading.

From the west, shape a course to the red and white Dunkerque fairway buoy (*DKA*, LFl.10s); proceed thence on an easterly heading to *DW6* (red pillar buoy, Q.R) and *DW5* (green pillar buoy, Q.G). After passing between these, follow the buoyed channel (reds to port, greens to starboard) as far as *DW30* (Fl(3)R) and *DW29* (Fl(3)G), then carry on to the harbour entrance on a southeasterly heading.

Entrance

Note that the really big lighthouse, 59m high (Fl(2)10s26M), stands *inside* the harbour, 8 cables southeast of the entrance. The west jetty, to be left to starboard, has a 35m lighthouse (Oc(2+1)G). It is conspicuous from a distance by virtue of the 3 unmistakable flanges which protrude beneath the lantern. It sounds a fog signal Dia(2+1)60s, and exhibits standard light traffic signals.

The eastern jetty has a white lattice tower, painted red on the top (Fl(2)R.10s16M Horn(2)20s), only 11m high.

Note the violet leading lights with intensified sectors (see plan), established to assist pilots bringing in big ships on a heading of 179° to 185°. These can be useful to check your set and drift, as can two occulting white leading lights on 137°, sited at the entrance to the Wateringuet canal immediately opposite the big lighthouse. Unless you are proposing to lock in, these give your course inbound from the harbour mouth towards the marinas.

Berthing

Port du Grand Large ☎ 03 28 63 23 00, or VHF Ch 9 is found on your port hand beyond the inner end of the Jetée Est, shortly after passing the lock gates on either side. Turn in sharp to port and leave the wave breaker to starboard. In 1999 there was a 'visitors' sign here. The visitors' pontoon runs all the way up to the dock at the north side of the marina. It is very long, so if a surge is running, the further in you moor, the better. You will also have a shorter walk to the showers, bar and telephone. Report to the dockmaster in a portacabin at the top of the ramp.

Fuel berth at the inner end of the visitors pontoon. 35-ton travel lift. No water on visitors' berths, but plenty on the adjacent pontoons. Bring your own hose.

This is a modern, commercial marina with all you need for a trouble-free stay. Unfortunately, unless you are a jogger, you may also need a private taxi, because you are 0·6M to the nearest shops which include the baker. A hot dreary mile brings you to the wonderful fish shop 'La Halle', and you must hack on a further ¼M to the real town centre with pavement cafes and proper shops. On the other hand, the war museum is only half a mile away on the rhumb line for town.

Yacht Club de la Mer de Nord is situated a couple of cables further in, immediately before you would arrive at a new lifting bridge ☎ 03 28 66 79 90 or VHF Ch 9. You will be welcome at this friendly, 'clubby' facility. Secure to the waiting berth near an unmissable yellow 'visitors' sign, then make yourself known to the harbourmaster (open 0800–1200 and 1600–2000) who may well direct you to an inner berth.

There arc theoretically 35 visitors' berths here, but note that the outer ones can be somewhat bouncy in a north/northwesterly wind.

Showers (old fashioned) on dock. Also washing machine and tumble drier. Engineer. The clubhouse with bar, etc, is open to visitors. Turn left outside the gates for the town. A sub-industrial stroll of only 2 cables brings you to 'La Halle' fish shop, where you will not believe your eyes at the wonders of the sea. The rest of the shops are rather further, but by no means a 'killer'. Restaurants and the town generally are reasonably handy.

Other berthing

In the past, yachts have been known to enter the Dunkerque dock system through Tristram Lock and put up at the Yacht Club de Dunkerque in the Bassin de Commerce. While this may still be possible, it is not recommended for casual callers. The pontoons at the club are locked and if you arrived during untended hours (most of the day and night) you would be stuck on board. Furthermore, there is the aggravation of locking in. All in all, the YCMN is a better bet.

Facilities

Boatyard and scrubbing berths. There is a crane for masts at the Bassin du Commerce, where there is also a 24-ton fixed crane. Slipway in the Port de Pêche. Power, fresh water, showers and toilets at marinas. The town offers bars, restaurants, banks, and all the amenities you would expect from a community of 200,000. Communications other than by road are surprisingly awkward.

Port Ouest

This tempting-looking harbour 7 miles to the west is for commercial vessels only. It may only be used by yachts in dire emergency.

Gravelines

Tides
HW +0045 Dover

MHWS	MLWS	MHWN	MLWN
5·9m	0·4m	4·8m	1·7m

Streams

Streams run hard in the offing. See Dunkerque for details, which are similar.

Depths

The entrance channel dries. To what extent is unclear, but if you reckon on 1·5m, you will be on the safe side. Inside the lock sill, craft of up to 2m can lie afloat, although in some areas this may fall to 1·5m when the sill closes. The bottom is said to be very soft mud so if your keel pokes in, it won't be too serious. The lock opens HW±3 hours, although this may be a shorter period on some tides.

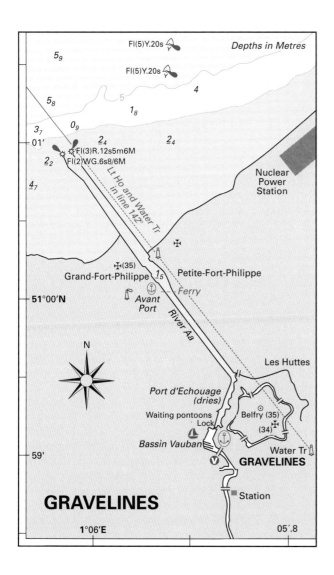

Gravelines. Conspicuous old lighthouse at Petite Fort Philippe on east bank at harbour mouth. Its light is extinguished

General

Gravelines, onto whose off-lying shoals Drake once chased the Spanish Armada with fireships, is now a suburb of Dunkerque. While the place had little to offer the Flower of Spain, it holds a touch more to tempt the yachtsman, with its small but ancient, moated town and excellently preserved Vauban fort. A massive nuclear power station has risen on the featureless shoreline to the immediate northeast, but despite having declined in the last hundred years, the port still operates a useful fishing fleet said by the late Captain Coote RN to take its catches from the shoals feeding around the rotting timbers of the Armada.

Gravelines itself is an attractive community of 20,000 set in and around a remarkably preserved moated fort. How this survived the bombardments of the Second World War is a mystery, but survive it certainly did, and the town is well worth a visit. The harbour entrance, however, can be dangerous in strong weather with any north in it. To be safe, you would be unwise to consider it for the first time in any onshore wind above a moderate breeze.

Approach

By day, starting from a safe position well in the offing, align the redundant lighthouse in Petit Fort Philippe on the east side of the harbour with a conspicuous blue and white water tower to the left of the church steeple on 142°. The lighthouse is painted in black and white spirals and cannot be missed. By night, steer in on a sensible heading in the white sector of the light on the west breakwater,

Above Gravelines
Below Gravelines - 'round the corner' - Bassin Vauban

the outer end of which may submerge at high water. If coming from the west, stay well clear of the green sector (078°–085°), which covers inshore shoals. The light is set on a white steel tubular structure 9m high, with a red drum on top surmounted by the light (Fl(2)WG.6s), wind instruments, etc. The eastern breakwater, which also covers at its outer end, has a less ambitious pedestal for its light (Fl(3)R.12s). Note that half a cable or so to seaward of this, a beacon has been established carrying a VQ.6m4M light

Entry and berthing

Enter down the long channel between the breakwaters when height of tide permits, favouring the west side. The entrance actually is wider than it appears on the chart. Once inside the shoreline, the less shoal water is well marked by clearly numbered red and green dolphins. Following these, the cut appears to be a dead end with a light structure on a white lattice tower with a red topmark and a white bullnose underneath. As you get nearer to this, it becomes obvious that this is where you turn to starboard, leaving the structure to port. Four cables ahead of you now are the lock gates of the Bassin Vauban with their fine digital depth gauge. There are various drying pontoons in the channel, of which 40 berths are for visitors. The bottom is believed to be mud. The pontoon on the east side of the Port d'Echouage outside the lock is a waiting pontoon for visitors wishing to lock in. It is often recognisable by the green and yellow lifeboat, labelled *SNSM*, moored alongside.

The locks open as stated above (see 'Depths'). They can be called on VHF Ch 9 around the time of high water, but note that the associated lifting bridge has been known to refuse duty in heavy weather. It is, however, generally open in July and August and at weekends. If shut, contact the lock-keeper or the Post Office (close at hand).

Beware of sluicing water in and around lock gates. Secure to the well-marked, clean 'Visitors' pontoon on your starboard hand – fresh water and power. Raft up if necessary.

Facilities
Two chandlers on the quay by the visitors' berth, mechanic, electricians. Fuel by can from the petrol station at the lock gate. Supermarket by the lock gate. Old-fashioned showers (1999) with the key from the harbourmaster near the visitors' berth. 3-ton crane and a larger one on request from the port office.

Communications
Sally Line ferries from Dunkerque West to Ramsgate. Entry to the French Canal system is possible from the Bassin Vauban, but you will need to divest yourself of your mast.

Calais

Tides
HW +0048 Dover

MHWS	MLWS	MHWN	MLWN
7·1m	1·0m	6·0m	2·0m

West-going stream of up to 3 knots begins at HW Dover +3 hours. East-going starts at HW Dover −3½ hours.

Depths
The Ridens de la Rade shoal, running parallel to the shore half a mile north of the entrance, varies in depth and may, in parts, dry up to 0·5m. The Avant Port is dredged to 9m, but depths decrease to 0·5m in the approach to the lock for the Bassin de l'Ouest, where the Port de Plaisance is situated. The basin itself is dredged largely to 7·8m, with berths for craft drawing from 2·5m to 5·0m.

General
Until what the generous-minded might call an error of judgement in 1558 by Queen Mary (married at the time to King Philip II of Spain, no less), Calais was a part of England. Mary died with the town's name engraved on her heart for having lost the place, and there British military interest ended until the First World War, when Calais came uncomfortably close to the front line but was never taken, while in 1940 a sacrificial rearguard action in the area by the Green Jackets kept the Panzers from

Calais. Enter keeping the ferry berths to port

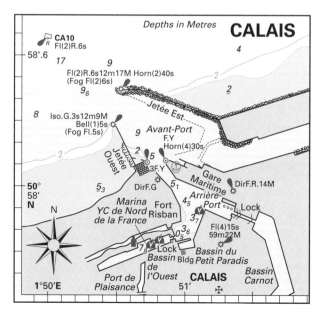

outflanking Dunkerque to the west until most of the British Expeditionary Force had been evacuated. Now, up to 140 shipping movements per day maintain the close links Calais has always had with England, just 21 miles away across the Dover Strait.

Given sufficient rise of tide to enter the lock of the Bassin de l'Ouest, Calais would be an all-weather harbour, except that it must be clearly understood that in gales from any northerly direction the entrance can be very uncomfortable indeed, with a 1·5m swell running into the Avant Port. Under such circumstances, entry in a small vessel must be considered imprudent.

Calais. Bassin de l'Ouest. Ship in centre is just leaving from the wall opposite yachts

Approach and entrance

In reasonable weather the Ridens de la Rade sand can safely be crossed in the top half of the tide, to the west of *CA 10* red buoy (Fl(2)R). To be absolutely safe, leave *CA 8* buoy, a mile west of the entrance, to port, or if you really don't like the look of the seas, go right down west to *CA 6* (VQ.R) buoy, which lies in deeper water a further 2 miles to the west.

In the centre of town is a mighty Fl(4)15s light 59m high with a white octagonal tower. This can just be seen from the English coast, and a steady bearing of 114° brings you straight in to *CA 8* from Dover west entrance. Peel off the entrance channel by day when the west breakwater comes 'on' with the big lighthouse mentioned above, on 138°. By night, shape up towards *CA 10* from *CA 8* until the intensified sector of the F.R.14M light at the Gare Maritime lines up with the west breakwater (Iso.G.3s12m9M). By day, the west breakwater is marked by a white tower with a green top. It has a bell fog signal. The east breakwater has a green tower with a red top, 12m high (Fl(2)R.6s12m17M). In fog, the west breakwater light shines Fl.5s white and the east breakwater Fl(2)6s white.

Enter between the pier heads, giving a good berth to the west wall which has a knuckle at its root, and head for the Arrière Port with the big lighthouse now dead ahead. The ferry terminals are in serried ranks away on your port bow. Until you swing round towards the lock, you may not see the yachts in the marina as they are often tucked up on the north side by the clubhouse. If the lock is not open, pick up a buoy in front of it and wait for the lock and the traffic lights. The waiting moorings are in depths varying from 0·5 to 3m and in all but calm conditions can be far from comfortable. The ineptly named Bassin du Petit Paradis dries completely and is foul with diverse creatively placed obstructions. It is therefore best to try to coincide with lock opening times which are, HW−1½ hours to HW+½ hour, except on weekends, public holidays, and generally during the summer months. At these times the lock opens from HW−2 to HW+1. By night, call *Calais Port* on Channel 12 to let them know you are there and waiting.

Berthing

On entry to the basin, tie up as near to the club house as you can – flags on top to starboard – and report to the *capitainerie* inside, where the harbourmaster speaks first-class English. There is plenty of room, plenty of depth, and yachts of up to 20m LOA can be accommodated without prior arrangement. Depending on the size of your boat and available space, you may end up on the wall opposite with a short ladder to climb. The marina is on ☎ 03 21 46 00 00 or VHF Ch 12.

By arrangement, yachts can tie up in the Bassin Carnot and remove their masts prior to entering the canal system.

Traffic signals

Full code International Port Traffic Signals are shown from the *capitainerie*, on the Quai de Marée near the Gare Maritime. In addition, white over red over green lights indicate absolute priority to harbour traffic.

Lock gates for Bassin de l'Ouest:
F.Y – 10 minutes before opening
F.R – All movements prohibited
F.G – Movement authorised
4 blasts – 'I request permission to enter'

When leaving, it is useful to tell the bridge operator of your intentions.

Facilities

Handy telephone, excellent clean showers in cubicle, plus a good deep basin for washing clothes and dishes. *Gasoil* on an easy tie-up pontoon. Fresh water. Spent sump-oil dump. Three-ton crane and scrubbing grid for large craft which dries 3·2m (enquire at *capitainerie*).

Two launderettes reasonably close by near the town square and three excellent restaurants recommended by the harbourmaster a five-minute walk away. A floating restaurant is berthed just inside the lock on a three master with no yards crossed.

Calais market square was bombed in the Second World War, but is once again a buzzing centre, with fashionable girls, pavement cafés, shops and casino. The stores in town are ready to deliver booze etc. to your boat if you are loading up in earnest.

Communications

Fast and moderate-speed ferries to Dover and Folkestone. SNCF to Paris, etc.

Boulogne

Tides

HW is the same as Dover (UT), but do not forget you are in Zone −1, so the 'clock time' will differ.

MHWS	MLWS	MHWN	MLWN
8·9m	2·25m	7·2m	2·75m

Depths

Entrance channel inside the harbour dredged to 5m minimum. Visiting yachts berth in Port de Marée where there is also a minimum of 5m.

General

Boulogne is France's most active fishing port. Historically it has been the site of various preparations for the invasion of England – under Napoléon Bonaparte and G. Julius Caesar, to name two of the better candidates. A 13th-century walled town dominates the city, and the prominent dome of the 19th-century cathedral of Notre Dame is a feature of the skyline. The building was erected to replace a predecessor laid waste by the revolutionaries. Napoléon's legacy to the town's silhouette is a 143m-high column dedicated to his Grande Armée.

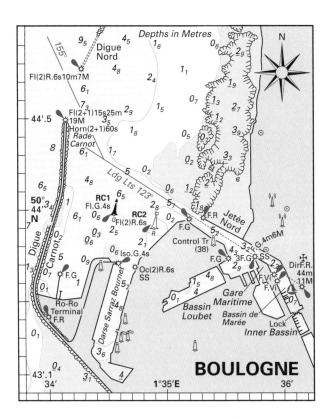

The harbour can be entered regardless of tide in nearly all weather and is thus important on a coast where such benefits are not liberally bestowed. The outer harbour (Rade Carnot) is over 4 square miles in area. The north part is largely shoal and the south is given over to commercial traffic. Visiting yachts head for the Port de Marée where shelter is good and the water deep.

Approach and entrance

The offing is free of significant dangers to small craft and yachts. From the north, the breakwaters stand out well. Coming along the coast from the south, you will not see them until you bring Cap d'Alprech abeam. Eight miles to the north is the mighty light of Cap Gris Nez (Fl.5s72m29M), and Cap d'Alprech at Fl(3)15s62m23M is no slouch either in the 'illumination stakes'. Note that Cap d'Alprech still has a radiobeacon; call sign *PH* on 294kHz. If still in doubt about the whereabouts of the entrance, watch for ferries.

Do not be confused by the fact that the outer part of the north mole is submerged. You cannot miss the rectangular 'box' structure on its extreme end carrying the small light structure (Fl(2)R.6s7M). Received wisdom is that no matter what you may see locals doing, you are best advised to leave this light to port, turning your back on any temptation to cross the obstruction.

The south mole carries a conventional white light tower 25m above the water (Fl(2+1)15s19M). This is obviously left to starboard on entry, and in fog you will hear its 2+1 horn once every minute.

As soon as you are through the pier heads, steer 155° or so for ½ mile to be sure of missing the shoal water on the north side of the Rade. Once the inner

Above Boulogne entrance. Digue Carnot on right. End of Digue Nord (largely submerged) left of centre. Harbour entrance in background
Below Inner entrance to Boulogne – Jetée Nord top left

Boulogne – Bassin de Marée. The marina is outside the lock (all-tide access) at left centre. Street fish market opposite

entrance is fully open (leading lights at night on 123° – DirF.R behind on Quai Gambetta, and F.G in a triangle in front on the end of the jetty north of the Gare Maritime) steer in through the inner pier heads. The southwestern one (F.G Horn 30s) carries a signal station. Its partner carries a F.R light. Continue down the jetty on your port hand to the yacht harbour in the Port de Marée. There is plenty of water as far as the last pontoon. Thereafter, rocks await. When the river Liane is in spate there can be some lively currents hereabouts.

Traffic signals

These must be observed. International Port Traffic Signals, plus:

Green over white over red – No entry or exit, with the following exceptions:

F.G – vessels with special permission to enter

F.R – vessels with special permission to leave inner or outer harbour

2F.R – vessels with special permission to leave inner harbour only

Berthing

The marina is not the most salubrious in the Channel, but it has the benefit of being in deep water and not locked in, so it has all-tide access. It carries 114 berths of which 17 are for visitors with moderate-sized yachts. If 15m or more, go alongside the customs cutters which are berthed immediately before you arrive at the visitors pontoons (first three) of the marina, then report to the harbourmaster who will find a berth for you. ☎ 03 21 31 70 01, or VHF Ch 9.

Facilities

Two scrubbing grids are either side of the lock above the marina. These are really set up for large fishing boats, but might be pressed into service. The east one is the better. Crane. An engineer can be called by the harbourmaster if necessary. Electricity and water down on the pontoons, where a diesel pump is also to be found.

The showers and loos are basic in the extreme but might serve in an emergency. They are open 0700–1900. The yacht club associated with the marina welcomes visitors and, while the general atmosphere is rough and ready, the whole set-up is just a hop from the centre of town across a handy bridge. There, restaurants, post office, launderettes and the rest await. You can buy telecartes from the harbourmaster.

Immediately opposite the marina is a lively street fish market. The stalls are 'manned' by fishermen's wives and each carries the boat's name. The produce is as fresh as can be. Dover Sole a speciality.

Communications

First class. Fast trains to Paris (2 hours). Ferries to Folkestone and Dover. Flights from Le Touquet.

Le Touquet/Etaples

Tides

HW −0010 Dover

MHWS	MLWS	MHWN	MLWN
9·6m	1·2m	7·7m	3·0m

The tide in the offing runs north from 2½ hours before HW Dover, turning south 3½ hours after. Rates can rise to 3 knots.

Depths

The river Canche dries to a trickle for up to 2 miles offshore, but within an hour of MHWS 3m has been reliably reported as far as the small marina at Etaples. More is claimed locally. This will reduce to 1·2m at neaps. Le Touquet dries completely, but there is likely to be 1·5m up to it at MHWN, with considerably more at springs.

General

The Canche looks an attractive proposition at high water, but at low it would curdle the blood of all but the most optimistic ditch-explorer. Le Touquet, with its reputation for high life and casinos, holds many attractions for some, but sadly its drying foreshore features patches of quicksand which can render the pleasure-seeking yachtsman's stroll to the esplanade more adventurous than he might have wished.

Etaples, with a drying pontoon marina in the centre of a pretty little town, is a better proposition for the visitor in a smallish yacht. Each *pêcheur* has his own fish stall on the waterfront, and across the street is a gourmet's delight of small seafood markets. *The Shell Channel Pilot* failed to sample the restaurants, but did extraordinarily well on a DIY

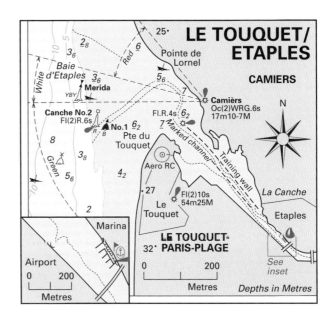

seafood bonanza meal. The Coquilles St Jacques, 'cleaned while you wait', were Olympian.

There is talk locally of a dredged, locked marina downstream of the current one, which will accommodate some visitors. This project has been rumoured for some years (1999). The money is now in place but, as so often happens with such schemes in France, it is currently stymied by political resistance. We look forward to better news, as Etaples is a really nice place.

La Canche River. Pte du Touquet at right. Etaples bridge in the distance

Etaples. Looking seaward from bridge. Fish markets
immediately ashore from tiny marina

Approach

Try to time a first visit before the top of springs, just
in case you fail to find the channel near HW.

Look out for the 54m orange octagonal lighthouse
with the brown band and green and white top
(Fl(2)10s25M) situated about a mile south of the
Pointe du Touquet. You may also be able to discern
the red pylon of Camiers light on the east side of the
river. By night this has a white sector which will
place you north of the most recent position of the
channel, but strangers are emphatically advised to
give the place a resounding miss after dark.

The outermost buoys of the channel are found 4
cables south-southeast of an unlit west cardinal
buoy which marks a wreck on the edge of the drying
line. The buoys are a lit red pillar, *Canche No.2*, and
an unlit green cone, *No.1*. Thereafter, the buoyed
channel meanders northeast towards the shore.
Observe the buoys with great care. After a mile or so
the channel swings to starboard, towards a light
structure (Fl.R.4s) northeast of Pointe du Touquet.
Further up towards Etaples, buoys stop and red and
green beacons begin. Upstream of the yacht club the
channel runs straight. Do not stray from it because
it is bounded by training walls which will be
submerged if you are afloat. The outer part of this
channel is liable to major changes at any time. The
important thing is to locate *Canche No.2* buoy and
then follow the others slavishly.

Berthing

As you come up to Etaples you will pass the
shipyard with its slipway on the left bank and the
long town quay reserved for fishing boats.
Immediately downstream of the bridge are the five
pontoons of the simple drying marina. The current
runs very hard towards the bridge before HW, so be
ready to take appropriate action. There is little space
to turn, but once alongside you should 'wind ship'
so as to breast the young flood when it arrives after
low water, sometimes with bore-like ferocity. You
are also then ready to depart. The bottom is soft
mud.

Facilities

The smart modern *capitainerie* and clubhouse are
immediately beside the pontoons, and there you will
find toilets and showers. The shipyard can handle
yacht repairs and there is an 8-ton crane. Fuel may
be brought to you by arrangement (☎ 043 21 94 66
96). The town has good provision shops and, as
noted above, seafood is a speciality. Small boats can
be launched near HW from a concrete slipway. The
capitainerie listens on VHF Ch 9 from 2 hours before
to 2 hours after HW, ☎ 03 21 84 54 33.

Le Crotoy

Tides

Tidal heights and times are similar to those at St Valéry-sur-Somme, across the estuary (see page 192).

Depths

Approaches similar to those at St Valéry-sur-Somme, but the berths all dry.

General

Le Crotoy is a charming fishing village (population 2,500) which boasts a casino, a beautiful bathing beach, a number of useful restaurants and a well sheltered dock where craft of modest draught can dry out alongside in softish ground.

Approach and entrance

The immediate approach begins at the left-hand fork in the general channel into the Somme which divides, as described in the St Valéry-sur-Somme notes, at a west cardinal buoy. The channel up to Le Crotoy shifts dramatically, so you must be on your guard over the buoys, whose numbers are prefixed *C*. Nevertheless, you should find 2m on a mean tide an hour or so before HW. Try to come here for the first time a few days before the top of springs to avoid any possibility of being neaped.

When the buoys run out you are nearly there, so steer for the quay (where there may well be a fishing boat or two) and thence along the wall and around the corner up to the yacht harbour, where access is limited to HW±1½ to 2 hours on a mean tide ('Coefficient 90'). There are 130 berths, all technically filled by yachts owned by members of the local sailing club. However, at any given time at least ten boats are usually away, so these berths become available to visitors. Do not come at all unless you are prepared to take the ground. The mud is not very soft and a deep-keeled yacht would certainly lie over. Shelter is excellent, however, with electricity and water on the pontoons.

Drying out amongst the fishing boats alongside the wall on your port hand approaching the yacht harbour could prove chancy because of the uneven bottom.

Facilities

Fresh water on the pontoons. No fuel. A repair yard and a 3½-ton crane. The town features pretty waterfront pavement restaurants, bistros, minimal foreign tourism and the cheapest mussels in northern France for the galley gourmet.

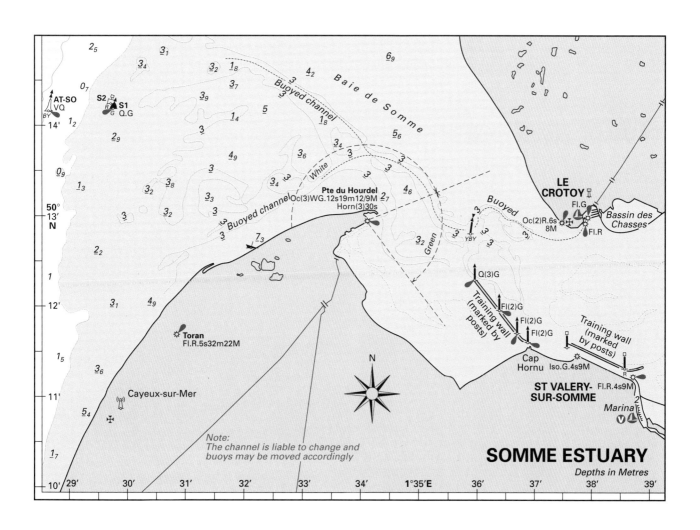

Le Crotoy. Keep near to the wall on your port hand to avoid
the shoal

St Valéry-sur-Somme

Tides
HW −0020 Dover

MHWS	MLWS	MHWN	MLWN
10·0m	No data	8·0m	No data

Depths
2m at HW neaps in the approaches. There is a
minimum of 2m in the marina.

General
The 20th-century history of the Somme is too well
known to be mentioned here. It is not common
knowledge, however, that Duke William embarked
at St Valéry for his adventure to 'put the breeze up
the Saxons', or that St Joan of Arc was brought there
from Le Crotoy by her English captors. From the
visiting sailor's viewpoint, St Valéry is, quite simply,
the nicest place on the coast.

Le Hourdel, immediately inside the south point of
entry to the river, has a tortuous channel, no room
for visitors and little to recommend it. Le Crotoy
(see page 191) is an interesting little town, while St
Valéry itself is positively attractive as well as being
good value both historically and topographically,
with its steep slopes and fine views.

St Valéry-sur-Somme. Looking seaward down the long entrance
channel

The channels in the Somme dry in a big way, but nevertheless are deeper and less fraught than the neighbouring Canche river.

If you are bent on exploring this coast, you are advised not to tackle the Authie, 9 miles north of the Somme. The drying bottom is notoriously uneven in consistency and there have been unpleasant instances of bilgekeelers coming seriously to grief on drying out.

Approach to the Somme

There are no dangers in the offing, save the generally shoal nature of the shoreline. The critical mark is the north cardinal buoy very approximately 4 miles west of Pointe du Hourdel, marked *AT S0*. Local information stresses that to find this mark is imperative. The buoy is lit and lies within the red sector of Ault lighthouse, Oc(3)WR.12s95m 18/14M, though as with the Canche, night entry is not a realistic possibility for strangers.

Give not a thought to entering the Somme in strong onshore winds. To do so would be an enterprise of dire folly for the stranger. In fair weather, however, matters are simple enough for those with good eyes and an understanding of the tide tables. An hour or two before HW is the ticket to peace of mind.

From *AT S0* buoy, try to identify the entrance channel. If the buoys are not visible, steer east until you are in 5 or 6m of water, by which time all should become clear. The first buoys are *S1* lit green and *S2* unlit red can. The channel now works its way inshore past Pointe du Hourdel until it divides at a conspicuous though small west cardinal buoy.

From the west cardinal buoy, the channel to St Valéry-sur-Somme is the right-hand option. It is also the deeper of the two, with over 2m at HW neaps. Follow it carefully to the lit green beacon (Fl(3)G) marking the beginning of the starboard-hand training wall. This ends at Cap Hornu. From here there are more green beacons, plus the occasional buoy, followed by small-craft moorings. A second training wall is set up to port in the last ¾ mile to the entrance. It is marked with red posts and, like the other one further out, is often submerged. The tide positively roars up and down this channel. At the end of the eastern harbour wall is a red light (Fl.R.4s) on a slender white structure. Looking up-river as you come along past the east training wall, the entrance does not appear obvious, but as you get nearer you can see the river bears right. Leave the light structure with steps going up to it to port and follow on down the middle to the marina, where berth depths are 2m at LW and boats of 15m can be accommodated. There are 30 visitors' berths. The Club Nautique Valéricain runs the marina (☎ 03 22 26 91 64 or VHF Ch 9). The passage from the outer approach buoy will take a little under 2 hours at 5 knots through the water.

Facilities

Fresh water on pontoons. Fuel by portage. Noble toilets and free showers open 24 hours per day in the club. Entry to Canal de la Somme (lock ☎ 03 22 60 80 23). 6-ton crane, boatyard with engineer, chandler, etc. Bars and restaurants. The town is very interesting and there are a number of riverside walks, both up into the medieval town and along the esplanade to view the Somme.

Le Tréport

Tides

HW −0025 Dover

MHWS	MLWS	MHWN	MLWN
9·4m	0·7m	7·4m	2·4m

Depths

The entrance channel is dredged to a drying height of 2m. The Port de Plaisance is situated inside the locked Bassin de Pêche, with up to 3·7m depths. There are a number of berths for larger craft of up to 4m draught. The lock opens at HW±3 hours.

General

Le Tréport is a fishing town halfway between Dieppe and the Somme, at the mouth of the Bresle river. Local industry is supplied by coastal vessels drawing up to 4·5m, in spite of the outer harbour's drying out to over a cable to seaward of the breakwaters. The scene used to be discouraging to visiting yachtsmen, especially as they were obliged to berth nearly ½ mile away from the civilised part of the town. Now, however, with the Bassin de Pêche open to visitors, the place does have a certain gutsy appeal.

About 4km inland is the ancient town of Eu, with its 12th-century abbey curiously dedicated jointly to Notre Dame and St Laurent O'Toole, sometime primate of Ireland, while within comfortable walking distance to the eastwards is Mer-Les-Bains,

Le Tréport

well worth a visit for its bizarre seaside architecture and safe bathing beach.

Approach

The approaches to Le Tréport are free of dangers. The entrance appears as a gap in high white cliffs 4 miles southeast of Ault Light (Oc(3)WR.12s95m 18/14M). Immediately south of the entrance is a prominent crucifix at an elevation of 91m, while the square church tower in the town centre also stands out well.

By night, the 20M light on the western breakwater (Fl(2)G.10s15m20M) is conspicuous. It is a white tower with a green top; its foghorn is Morse code N every 30 seconds. The eastern jetty light (Oc.R.4s6M) is mounted on a 7m white column, beside which stand the traffic signals. Watch out for cross-sets.

Shape up for the lock, (decorated with jolly flags at its southernmost end) with traffic lights on the north corner (seaward side). The lock is actually 150m or so inside a 'false' entrance which helps to break the sea. It opens ±3hrs HW. Try to arrive during these times. If you do not, you may have a sticky time in the drying approaches. In strong onshore winds the water in the Avant Port becomes agitated, and approach in these conditions should not be attempted by strangers.

Berthing

Upon entry into the Avant Port, shape up for the southernmost lock, which may be obscured from you initially. Do not try to enter the northern lock to the Bassin à Flot, which is reserved for commercial traffic. As you approach the lock gates (call on VHF Ch 12, ☎ 02 35 50 63 06), watch out for a sluice immediately to the south, which sometimes debouches at considerable velocity.

The yacht berths are at the far end of the dock on your starboard hand, with 20 reserved for visitors. If nobody comes to help, secure to a spare berth and make yourself known at the 'information' kiosk by the lock. Here, they will take your money and put you straight.

Facilities

Fresh water on the pontoons; toilets, showers. There is no fuel on the dock, but petrol by portage is at 200m. Diesel in quantity comes by lorry, ☎ 02 35 86 15 33 – 'SHIPP'. Launderette nearby in the town. Chandler, engineer. Ice from the fish market. There is a 6-ton crane at the Yacht Club de Bresles on the Avant Port, and various mobiles are available on request.

Launching of small craft (up to 6m) is possible from the stony beach.

The *capitainerie* can be reached on ☎ 02 35 86 17 91.

Dieppe

Tides

HW −0011 Dover

MHWS	MLWS	MHWN	MLWN
9·35m	0·85m	7·35m	2·65m

Depths

Entrance and Avant Port dredged to 5m. Up to 4·2m on berths in the marina, known as the *Port Jehan Ango*.

General

Over the centuries the English have maintained considerable interest in Dieppe. It was occupied by them from 1420 to 1435, Henry II started the building of the church of St Jacques, Oscar Wilde, Aubrey Beardsley, Sickert and Whistler came here to write and paint, and many others ended their days in the war-graves plot during World War II.

The port has a fine marina in the Port Jehan Ango, named after a 16th-century Norman privateer. The entrance is far easier than it once was, and if you like mooring right in the centre of a lively French city, the scene is better set than ever before for an enjoyable stay in perfect shelter.

Approach

Before you enter the outer harbour, you are obliged to call *Dieppe Port* on VHF Ch 12. If your French is not up to the job, English is fine, but speak slowly to help out. Watch for the dredger and its cable which

Dieppe, with new ferry terminal (centre)

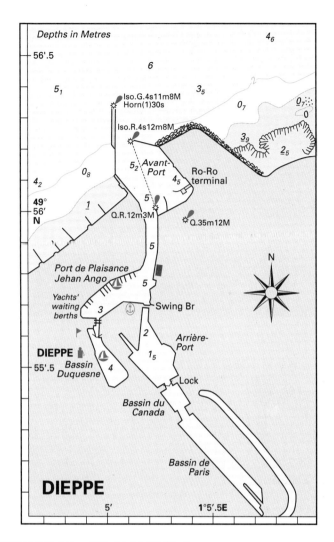

Dieppe. Port Jehan Ango tucked safely inside

often works here showing a yellow light. Obey the traffic signals, which are complimentary for people without VHF, and never contravene them, on pain of a stiff fine. The approach is free of dangers except for a wreck with 1 metre over it. This is marked by a lit north cardinal buoy, 1½ miles off the prominent Point d'Ailly with its white square tower lighthouse (Fl(3)20s95m31M). Point d'Ailly light also has a 50M-range radiobeacon (*AL*) on 305·5kHz.

Dieppe's gap in the 30m-high white cliffs is fairly wide. The church of Notre Dame de Bon-Secours, with its blunt spire, stands on the cliff top on the east side of the entrance. Close to it is a signal station. Call the port on VHF Ch 12 if you feel the need, but in any case obey the traffic signals as follows:

3 reds flashing – serious emergency, all vessels stop
2 greens over white – free passage
3 reds – vessels may not proceed
3 greens – one-way traffic from the direction lights can be seen
green/white/green – only proceed when authorised specifically

Leave the west breakwater to starboard (Iso.G.4s 8M) and steer in to the south. Pass the east jetty (Iso.R.4s8M) and the end of the old west jetty, now extended by the breakwater mentioned above. As you enter the narrows, leave a Q.R light to port and follow the wall round to starboard until you arrive at the marina. Call *Port Jehan Ango* on VHF Ch 9 as you come in. The harbour office is open 24 hours in summer, but only 0900–1900 in winter. If you arrive after hours in winter, you will be locked in on your berth until morning, so don't expect to arrive at 2200 on Christmas Eve and be able to nip ashore for a swift Pastis. The port takes visitors up to 20m and while it charges a little more than the rest of the

coast, the management say with some justification that this reflects the 24-hour access.

Facilities

Water and power on pontoons. Diesel and super (4-star) from a pontoon behind the marina wave breaker as you enter harbour. Lifting facilities and excellent security, with magnetic key access to pontoons and showers. CCTV helps this along. New launderette 100yds from berths.

Really, all you are likely to need. The marina is even blessed by an almost adjacent Indian takeaway and eat-in. Just in case this fails to tempt you, the place is literally surrounded by restaurants, boutiques and food shops. A fish market is just round the corner.

Fast ferries to England and very fast trains to Paris – 170km.

St Valéry-en-Caux

Tides
HW −0044 Dover

MHWS	MLWS	MHWN	MLWN
8·8m	1·0m	7·1m	2·4m

Depths
The entrance and the approaches dry out (2·5m) up to a cable to seaward of the breakwater ends. The Bassin à Flot carries over 3m in the visitors' berth, with a controlling overall depth of 2m.

General
St Valéry is a very attractive little town of 5,300 inhabitants. Its buildings are largely modern, the centre having been flattened in the early days of World War II when the 2nd French Cavalry and the 51st Highland Division made a heroic last stand against the Wehrmacht. Nevertheless, the place has great character and a warm atmosphere as it nestles between its cliffs. A former fishing port, the harbour is now almost totally given over to yachting. There are 580 berths in the long, narrow locked basin.

Approach and entrance
There are no dangers in the approach, but the entry should not be attempted in strong northerly winds, with northeast the worst. The tide sets at up to 2·8 knots across the approaches. To aid recognition of the narrow gap in the cliffs from seaward, note the power station 3 miles to the west and a conspicuous brown and blue building on a hill which bears 180° with the harbour ahead of you. By night the Fl(2)G.6s14M light on the western breakwater head should be visible, followed later by its Fl(2)R.6s counterpart on the eastern jetty.

Proceed up the entrance according to the plan, favouring the east side to avoid the bank of shingle which has built up on the west harbour wall. This is cleared by leaving the 3 red posts marking a ramp at the outer end of the eastern jetty close to port.

Having negotiated the entrance, you can now steer up the middle to the lock. If you should arrive

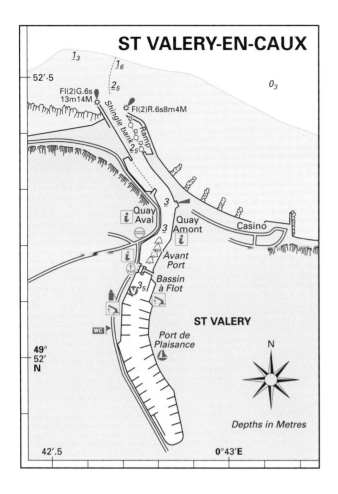

early, there are a number of waiting-buoys outside. There is 2m of water in the channel at half-tide, so if you are in any doubt about conditions, enter nearer to HW. The waiting-buoys are untenable in strong onshore winds.

Berthing

The entrance is available to most yachts from half-tide onwards, and the lock opens ±2½ hours HW during the daytime. By night it is available from ±½ hour HW. The bridge inside the lock opens every half-hour by day. By night it opens on demand.

The Port de Plaisance can be telephoned on ☎ 02 35 97 01 30, or called on VHF Ch 9 from 0800–1800 or at 'tide times'. Instructions to visitors are displayed in English on a board on the lock-keeper's house, which is also the *capitainerie*. Your berth is initially immediately to starboard inside the lock. If you want to stay more than 24 hours you may be invited to move further up the basin, in which case watch out for the clearly marked remains of an old bridge halfway up. Depths reduce, so if in doubt advise the harbourmaster of your draught. The amount of water in the basin may fall while the gates are closed. There is a tide gauge at the lock gates.

Facilities

All fuel available, but only from the local service station, though consignments of above 500 litres of diesel can be arranged by lorry. Toilets and showers at the new yacht club building. Launderette situated very conveniently. Mobile cranes up to 6 and 10 tons. Chandler, engineer, ice, and *Camping Gaz* exchange. All small-town facilities, including provisions, bars, restaurants and bank.

Fécamp

Tides

HW −0044 Dover

MHWS	MLWS	MHWN	MLWN
8·4m	1·2m	6·85m	2·95m

Depths

Minimum 1·5m dredged in entrance. 2m on outer port berths, 5m in Bassin Bérigny.

General

Fécamp made its name as the home of a major fleet of deep-sea trawlers. Today this is in some decline, but the town is still famous for being the fountainhead of Bénédictine liqueur. A visit to the museum in the ex-monastery is well worth the time.

Fécamp has a tradition of friendship to English yachtsmen. It can be entered at most states of tide, but note that onshore weather can make the entrance awkward or even dangerous. If in doubt, arrive near high water; in a whole gale, go somewhere else.

Approach and entrance

Apart from a rocky shelf extending up to 1½ cables from Pointe Fagnet there are no off-lying dangers.

St-Valéry-en-Caux. Note build-up of shingle in right side of entrance

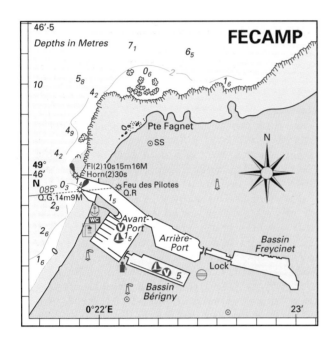

The town can be recognised from seaward by the prominent water tower on rising ground southwest of the entrance, in proximity to the churches of St Etienne and La Trinité. On high ground to the east stands the church of Notre Dame du Salut, surmounted by a fine gilded statue.

Approach from the west (the leading lights shown on the plan give a line of 085°), keeping to starboard on entry between the pier heads. If you are well before high water, be ready for a northerly set.

The north breakwater has a grey tower with red top (Fl(2)10s16M). The south wall shows a green tower with a Q.G.9M light. This light lines up on 085° with the Q.R *Feu des Pilotes* on the north side of the entrance immediately inside the harbour. The north breakwater has a reed fog signal, 2 blasts every 60 seconds.

Note the traffic signals shown on the south jetty as follows:

Green over white over green – passage with permission

White – harbour open

Red over red over red – no passage

The harbour may be called on VHF Ch 9.

Whether you intend to berth in the Avant Port at the main marina or lock into the Bassin Bérigny, you must turn hard to starboard as the Avant Port opens up.

Berthing

Reception for outer marina is on 'V' pontoon. To enter the Bassin Bérigny with its locked pontoon berths, call *Ecluse Bérigny* on VHF Ch 12 or ☎ 02 35 28 23 76. Access is from HW−2 to HW.

The Avant Port is subject to surge in strong onshore weather. The Bassin Bérigny is not only perfectly sheltered, it is also cheaper.

Facilities

Fuel. Fresh water on quays and pontoons. A palatial new shower block has been established within 50m of one of the few surviving Clochemerle-style street urinals on the Channel coast. A must for the

Fécamp

connoisseur of ethnic plumbing, as well as those who feel that in this respect France may have lost her way.

Launderette in town. Mobile cranes to cope with anything up to 35 tons, chandlers, engineers, *Camping Gaz* exchange, ice and general repairs. Restaurants, bars and the rest up to normal French standards. Slipway in the Avant Port.

Communications

SNCF to Le Havre, Rouen and Paris.

Le Havre

Tides

HW −0103 Dover

MHWS	MLWS	MHWN	MLWN
7·9m	1·2m	6·6m	3·0m

Depths

Deep water in approaches. Port de Plaisance is dredged to 3m (LAT) on visitors' pontoon.

General

Built as the 'Havre de Grace' on the orders of King Francois I in 1517, Le Havre is still the third most important port in Europe, serving major commercial interests with container ships of up to 260,000 tons, and handling 500,000-ton tankers at the neighbouring terminal of Antifer. The city was almost totally destroyed with 4,000 civilian deaths in 1944, and is now largely a modern urban development. It carries ferry traffic, and has an all-weather, all-tide entrance to its deep-water marina.

Le Havre also provides entry to the Tancarville canal, 25km along the 115km to Rouen, with Paris a further 235km. This entrance avoids the passage up the somewhat exposed Seine estuary.

Approach and entrance

Cap de la Hève light structure (Fl.5s24M) is a white octagonal tower with a red top, 32m high and 123m above the sea. Nearby is a prominent communications pylon with a dish aerial. Inside the port near the head of the entrance channel (107°) are tall chimneys 247m high.

Yachts of less than 19·8m LOA are specifically forbidden to use the 10M-long entrance channel. Cross it if you must, under power if necessary, at right angles. This instruction is important if approaching from the southwest. From anywhere north of west it makes sense to home in on Cap de la Hève, then slide southwards to the vicinity of *LH14* (Q.R) or *LH16* (VQ.R) red buoys. From here you can round the Digue Nord with its 15m white tower (Fl.R.5s21M Horn 15s). Next, leave the short breakwater attached to the Digue Nord to port (Fl(2)R.6s) and make a turn to the north to leave the end of the south breakwater of the yacht harbour to starboard. This has a weak light (Fl(2)G.6s) on a metal pole.

After rounding this breakwater, steer to starboard and berth on the outside of the first pontoon you come to. This is O pontoon. If there is no free berth, either call the *capitainerie* on VHF Ch 9 (☎ 02 35 21 23 95) or find a vacant berth and then report. Protection is excellent.

If you are making a first approach by night, French authorities recommend that you study your charts carefully. There is a multitude of lights which must be carefully dealt with. This apart, no problems should be experienced.

Le Havre. Yacht harbours in foreground to the left and conspicuous chimneys (centre)

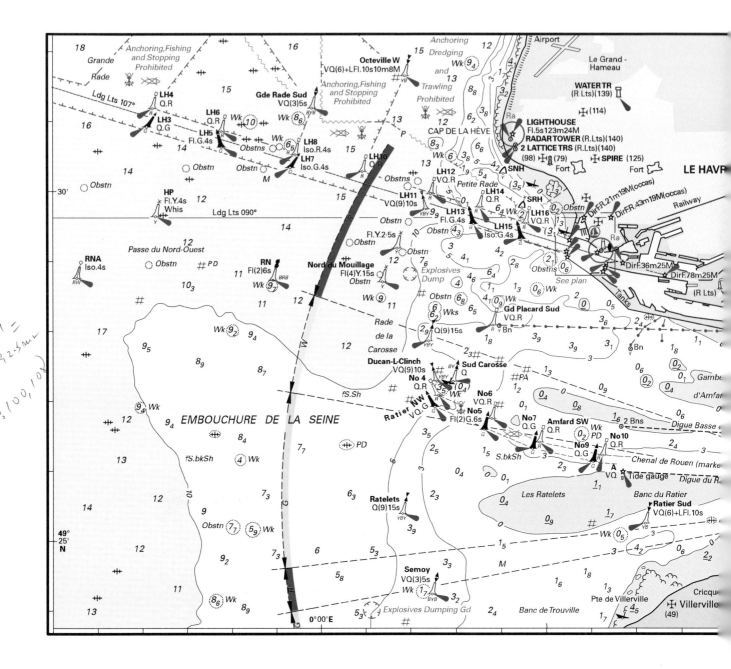

Facilities

Le Havre is less convenient for shopping than you might imagine. The shops are there, all right, but you need to take your hiking boots. Some other facilities are more proximate. Fresh water and fuel in the yacht harbour. Showers and toilets in office hours. Launderette, chandlery, engineers, repairs and a 4-ton crane on site. There is a scrubbing grid in front of the clubs which dries up to 3m at mean springs, and a launching ramp in the Anse des Régates. There is also a 30-ton slipway. Ice can be obtained. *Camping Gaz* exchange.

The Sport Nautique de Havre is a friendly club with a bar open each evening except Mondays (all day weekends). The Société des Régates du Havre (the westernmost club building) is more formal, and visitors must dress accordingly. Its restaurant is first-class, so it is reasonable for the members to expect you to wear a tie around your neck.

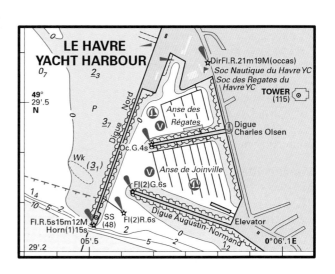

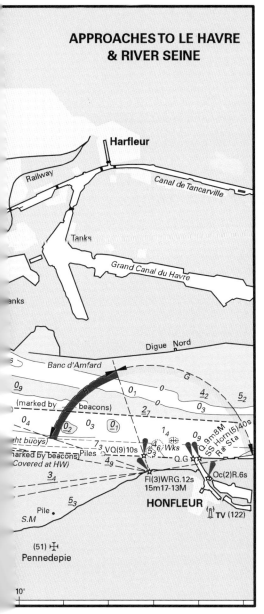

APPROACHES TO LE HAVRE & RIVER SEINE

Conspicuous St Joseph's Church overlooks Anse de Joinville yacht harbour

Harbour Control at north entrance of Bassin de la Manche leading to Tancarville Canal for those bound for Rouen or Paris

Two blocks inland from the esplanade is the Rue Augustin Normand. Here, from Nos 114 to 120, are a sailmaker (☎ 02 35 43 16 70), an engineer (☎ 02 35 42 00 41) and a chandlery.

Communications

Ferries to Portsmouth. Trains etc. to all continental destinations – Paris 2 hours. Le Havre/Octeville Airport has flights to London and Brussels as well as domestic ones.

Tancarville Canal

As noted above, this can allow you to avoid bad weather in the Seine estuary. Nonetheless, it has problems of its own. You must lower your mast, but you'll need to do this anyway if proceeding up the Seine as far as Paris. There are also a number of bridges and locks which will need to be opened.

Ask at the Société des Régates or at the *capitainerie* for more details.

Seine estuary traffic control tower

Honfleur

Tides

HW −0135 Dover

MHWS	MLWS	MHWN	MLWN
7·9m	1·2m	6·6m	3·0m

Currents can run at up to 5 knots outside Honfleur, up-river or down-river in accordance with HW and LW, but there is a 2-hour stand at HW, which is the favoured time to arrive. The lock does not open until LW ±2.

Depths

At least 2m in the Vieux Port, and more in the Avant Port. Least depth in approach to the lock is approximately 1m at MLWS. Depths have been reported as varying in the final approach to the lock, so it is safest to assume some degree of silting takes place from time to time. Allow an appropriate extra clearance when working out your entry depth.

General

Honfleur is perhaps the most picturesque of all Norman ports. You lock in to lie, if there is room, in

Honfleur – Vieux Bassin lower right. Note Lieutenance building, centre, and the fine schooner secured in front of it, just where the harbourmaster likes to put such picturesque craft. The Bassin de l'Est is at the extreme right, upper centre, and the tiny striped toilet block can be seen between the water and the roadside on the town side of the lock

the middle of the medieval town. The town has known many famous days, with both Champlain and Jacques Cartier sailing west from within its walls. The 16th-century Lieutenance building, which now harbours the port office and was once the governor's seat, is immediately by the old lock into the Vieux Bassin. The church of St Catherine, also 16th century, was built by shipwrights and is composed entirely of wood. At the top of the town are excellent views over the Seine estuary.

Approach and entrance

Honfleur lies on the south bank of the Seine estuary. To approach it, the main channel to Rouen is used. This is defined on the north side by the buoyed Digue Basse du Nord, with which you should take no chances. Three quarters of a mile west of the entrance stands the white square tower of the Falaise des Fonds lighthouse (Fl(3)WRG.12s). Its white sector leads loosely into the outer end of the channel, while the green covers the Banc du Ratier to the south.

Pick up *No.4* red buoy (Oc(2)R.6s) about half a cable southeast of the colourfully named lit west cardinal buoy *Duncan Clinch*. From here, the channel is clearly buoyed (plenty of them lit) as it runs east-southeast, then a degree or two south of east, for the 7½ miles or so total to the entrance. This is found on your starboard hand immediately upstream of the lit *No.19* green buoy. The west

corner of the entrance is lit by a Q.G light, the east side by a quick white with a Horn(5)40s fog signal.

The lock is visible as soon as the entrance is rounded. The keeper listens on VHF Ch 73, *Honfleur Radio*, switching to Ch 9 to pass messages. Enter the lock, then proceed, ideally to the Vieux Bassin. The bridge into the Vieux Port opens to coincide with the lock at 0730, 0830, 0930 and 1030. It does not open again until 1730, 1830, 1930 and 2030. Tie up outside the bridge on or near the waiting jetty if necessary.

Berthing

Owners of Old Gaffers will be delighted to learn that they may well be offered free berthing for a reasonable period in the Vieux Bassin. This is a decent quid-pro-quo from the harbour authorities, who recognise that tourism is cranked up by a few traditional craft on the scene. If you get such a deal, play the game and leave your main up and scandalised if it's not blowing a gale. The artists will love you.

Visitors' pontoons are maintained on the eastern part of the northern wall of the Vieux Bassin (see plan). Boats of significance which appeal to the harbourmaster's aesthetic sense may be invited to lie immediately to starboard on entry, against the eastern end beneath the Lieutenance. This plum berth is more likely to be available in August when the fishing fleet is away at sea.

Yachts too large for the joys of the Vieux Bassin may be berthed on the northwest wall of the Avant Port, or they may lie in the Bassin de l'Est. See the harbourmaster for details. There is also a waiting berth on the east side of the jetty immediately outside the Vieux Bassin.

A new clubhouse and Port de Plaisance are to be built in the Bassin Carnot at the south end of the Bassin de l'Est. This will be a poor substitute for those arriving too late for the guinea seats in the Vieux Bassin, but the place will still be worth a visit. The walk to the action is not long. The only real sufferer will be the photographer, who will no longer be able to take shots of his yacht under the most colourful buildings in Normandy. Harbourmaster's ☎ 02 31 89 20 02.

If nobody calls on you for dues, payment for berthing is taken at an office down a street on the east side of the basin. This is not easy to find at the first time of looking, but it does exist.

Facilities

Fresh water on the quays. Limited shower and toilet arrangements are provided in the single-storey vertically-striped building handy to the lock for the Bassin de l'Est. Further such facilities may still be discovered beneath the Lieutenance building. A better deal in this respect is promised, but was not in evidence in 1999.

Diesel in quantity can be trucked in by Taupin ☎ 02 31 88 09 43. There is a chandlery and engineers, and a good boatyard by the eastern basin.

The old town is charming in the extreme, with shops, restaurants and the rest to match. Tourists love the place, so do artists and so does every yachtsman who visits it.

Communications

Railway station and buses to Le Havre and Deauville.

Deauville/Trouville

Tides

HW −0130 Dover

MHWS	MLWS	MHWN	MLWN
7·75m	1·1m	6·4m	2·8m

Depths

The entrance channel crosses shifting sands and generally dries up to 1·8m. Once you have locked in, depths in excess of 3m are promised in all the yacht harbours.

General

Deauville and Trouville are a long-standing pleasure resort for people of quality, which definitive has at times been stretched to include British yachtsmen. The twin towns are separated by the Touques river, which virtually dries. The Trouville foreshore is reserved for fishermen and consists of a long fish market with a fine selection of restaurants and shops to back it up. The river entrance is dominated by the baroque casino, featuring both thalassotherapy and cult movies.

On the west side of the river, Deauville is a favourite watering hole of the jet set. Here you can escape the horrors of yacht cruising or racing and lose your shirt among the rich and infamous at either the tables or the race track. Walk *les planches* on the edge of the beach and elbow your way into Ciro's Beach Bar for a swift bottle of Dom Perignon. Captain Coote advised shrewdly that sailors should

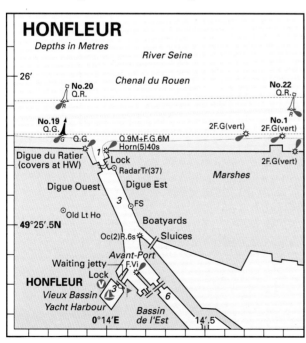

HONFLEUR
Depths in Metres

Above Deauville at low water. Above, approach showing half-tide wall. Port Deauville on the right
Below Port Deauville

take care not to be trampled by 'Tory landowners, inside traders accoutred by Gucci, or dishevelled pop stars with their expensive doxies'.

Berths may be available in Port Deauville or the old port of Deauville/Trouville. The former is a typical modern marina development with designer flats. It is a half-mile hike from the action, but has the advantage of being open from two hours either side of low water. Since no boat of stature could traverse the shoaling entrance any closer than this to the bottom of the tide, this effectively means it is open whenever you can get there. The older harbour is much handier, but lock openings have been reported to be unreliable. Charges and depths are the same in either basin, but even on a good day the old lock is unlikely to open more than 2½ hours before or after HW.

Approach and entrance
The entry can be dangerous in strong onshore winds. It is perfectly feasible at night in good weather, but all entries should have a good rise of tide.

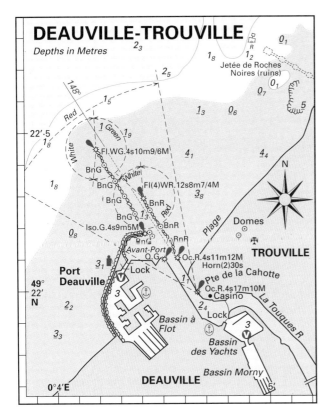

DEAUVILLE-TROUVILLE
Depths in Metres

that it is a full, 2-gate affair with no free flow except near HW. Visitors' berths are on the long pontoon on your starboard hand. Larger yachts may berth on the wall before this is reached. The lock listens on VHF Ch 9. There are red and green traffic lights.

Bassin des Yachts and Bassin Morny (Le Vieux Port)

Go straight on past Port Deauville between the east and west inner breakwaters (Oc.R and Q.G). Once you are past the casino, the lock for these basins is in front of you. This opens and shuts automatically when the height of tide reaches 5·5m which, on exceptional neaps, may mean it does not open at all. Traffic lights on the mast on the southwest side of the lock indicate what you should do. The favoured berth is on the pontoons in the southeast corner of the Bassin des Yachts. By arrangement with the warmly hospitable Deauville Yacht Club you may be able to pass through into the Bassin Morny.

Facilities

Water on pontoons. Diesel by pump at Port Deauville, otherwise by portage. There is an 8-ton crane near the yacht club. Showers and toilets at Port Deauville and the Bassin des Yachts, also at the club. There is a launching ramp in the Avant Port, a 100-ton slipway. All repair facilities, including sails. Chandlers, *Camping Gaz* exchange and ice. Two good restaurants are reported close to the footbridge by the yacht club. These are L'Ocean, opposite the Bureau du Port, and L'Esperance, in the Rue Victor Hugo, 1½ blocks westward.

Communications

Very fast train (2 hours) to Paris. 1¾ hour bus ride to Le Havre. Thence ferry to Portsmouth. Alternatively, Ouistreham is not far, also with regular ferries to Portsmouth. St Gatien airport (7km; ☎ 92 31 88 31 28) has flights to Nice, London and Jersey in season.

Dives/Port Guillaume

Tides

HW −0135 Dover

MHWS	MLWS	MHWN	MLWN
7·45m	0·85m	6·1m	2·4m

Depths

Entrance channel dries up to 2·6m and deep water disappears a mile to seaward of the entrance. Port Guillaume itself has at least 2·5m.

General

This port, now gaining a modest significance as a yacht harbour after many years as a drying river mouth, was of great importance to Duke William. He not only established his independence of the King of France here in 1059 during a notably nasty battle, but is also said to have massed his ships and troops here to invade England seven years later. Whilst such ports in Normandy are almost as common as 'King Charles slept here' signs in

The casino is readily spotted from seaward, and the rear leading light (Oc.R.4s10M) is situated immediately to its right-hand edge on a white metal tower. The front leading light (Oc.R.4s12M) stands on the inner end of the east breakwater where extreme seaward extension shows (Fl(4)WR.12s7/4M) on a white red-topped tower. The west breakwater extends almost 2 cables to seaward of its eastern partner and terminates in a black pylon on a dolphin 16m high (Fl.WG.4s9/6M). Both breakwaters cover before half-tide and are marked with red or green piles. Try to come in on a heading of around 148° as indicated at night by the leading lights. The eastern breakwater is showing its white sector for some distance either side of the transit.

If you are coming down from the north or east, you must keep well clear of the shoal water – Banc du Ratier and Les Ratelets – which extends well offshore.

Wherever you are sailing from, pay particular attention to the lit east cardinal buoy 2 miles north-northwest of the entrance and within 3° of the leading transit. It must be left to starboard, as it marks wrecks somewhat to seaward of its position which are virtually awash at LAT.

Berthing

Port Deauville

This lies on your starboard hand, inside the western breakwater 'proper' with its Iso.G.4s light on a green pole. Be sure to leave to starboard the green posts off this breakwater. Further in are unlit buoys – reds to port, greens to starboard. The lock will open when the rise of tide is at least 4m, but note

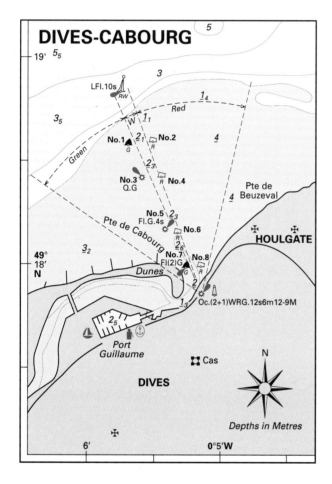

English pubs, it does seem that Dives may have a genuine claim.

During the 19th century Dives developed as a resort around its casino, and much of the bizarre architecture of that period survived the last war. Now, property developers are having their wicked way and Dives' character is being watered down. The new harbour of Port Guillaume has realistically opened the place up to visiting yachts for the first time.

It will be apparent to sensible observers that this entrance is emphatically not an all-weather pushover, though from half-tide on shoal-draught craft can enter in fair conditions, with deeper-draught craft coming safely to haven nearer the top of the tide. The entrance is reported to be dangerous in winds from northwest to northeast of force 5 or more.

Approach and entrance

By day, look out for the gap between Houlgate (wooded and hilly, with a conspicuous church standing on the seafront) and Cabourg, where high-rise apartments terminate a half-mile or so of sand dunes to the west. By night, enter the 5° white sector of the lighthouse (Oc(2+1)WRG.12s) on a heading of around 160° while still well to seaward.

About a mile offshore in the white sector you will find the red and white (LFl.10s) safe water buoy *DI*. Halfway in from this is the pair of unlit green and red buoys *No.1* and *No.2*. Thereafter, the green beacon *No.3* (Q.G) and the unlit red buoy *No.4* are followed by green beacon *No.5* (Fl.G.4s) and *No.6* unlit red buoy. Finally, you will find *No.7* green buoy (Fl(2)G) and a last unlit red, *No.8*. By day, the lighthouse structure itself is a reddish-brown hut with a prominent white stripe. By night, from *No.3* beacon onwards you must leave the white sector and follow the green lit markers, though night entry is not recommended for a first time.

Approach the shore close to the 'light hut', then swing round parallel with the land and quite close to it, running beside the railway and the road, which is brightly lit with a row of street lamps. Now steer to leave the fish quay close to port, ignoring the two green posts indicating a channel to the north. This is the river Dives, with its drying moorings. You should watch for the small green buoy, to be left to starboard, followed by a red post (leave to port). There are two further green posts (leave to starboard on a west-southwesterly heading) leading to the lock gates. On the south side of the lock is the prominent eight-sided *capitainerie* building with its conical grey roof. To starboard is a red and white windsock.

Berthing

The lock opens with a rise of tide of 4·5m, giving 2m on the sill. This is generally around half-tide. Boats drawing in excess of 1·5m can often enter from HW±2½ hours, but attention is emphatically drawn to the requirement for careful calculation of an individual tide. Berth inside the locks on either side. Call VHF Ch 9 or ☎ 02 31 24 48 00.

River Dives. Channel at half-tide swinging clockwise from seaward. (A) Houlgate Church and (B) Starboard-hand beacon

Approach to the River Dives, showing all buoys and beacons
Below Port Guillaume

Facilities

All good marina facilities, including repairs, fuel, chandler, etc. Showers, toilets 24 hours, and all-night launderette on site. Launching ramp by the fish quay and 30-ton slipway. 1·5-ton mobile crane on quay accommodating 2·5m draught.

Shoreside facilities are not exciting, but there may be further scope for exploration of the town.

It is reported that there is 3m of water at springs in the river channel up to Cabourg. There they will find a firm bottom to dry out on and a welcoming yacht club.

Ouistreham/Caen

Tides

HW −0118 Dover

MHWS	MLWS	MHWN	MLWN
7·6m	0·95m	6·35m	2·75m

Depths

Entrance channel dredged to 6m as far as ferry terminal. Thereafter 3m as far as yacht lock and waiting pontoon. Depths inside marina are 3·5m. There is 8m in the Caen canal, and 4m in the visitors' berths in the city.

General

Ouistreham is best known today as a major ferry port, though often under the name of Caen, the cathedral city lying at the end of the 8-mile canal running parallel to the river Orne.

The area was the scene of bitter fighting after the D-Day landings in 1944. The British airborne drop secured Pegasus Bridge, 4km up the canal, and it carries the name to this day. There is a museum next to the pub on the west side of the bridge itself.

The port of Ouistreham has little to offer the pleasure-seeker unwilling to walk 1½ miles to civilisation, but it is approachable as far as the waiting pontoon at all states of the tide and in most weather except strong northwest to northeast winds.

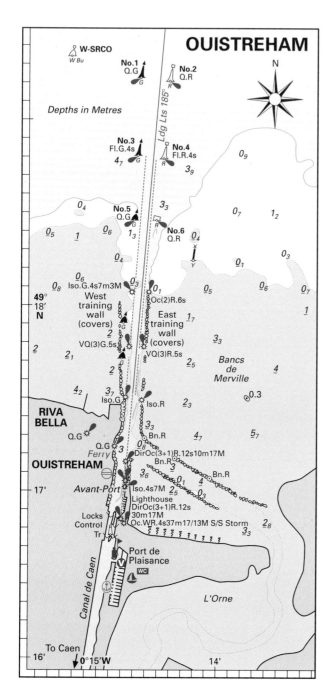

OUISTREHAM

W-SRCO
W Bu

No.1
Q.G
G

No.2
Q.R

Depths in Metres

Ldg Lts 185°

No.3
Fl.G.4s
4₇   G

No.4
Fl.R.4s

0₉

No.5
Q.G
G

3₃

0₄

No.4
Fl.R.4s

3₉

0₅   1   0₆   1₃

No.6
Q.R   0₄

0₇   1₂

0₄

X   0₃

Y

0₁   0₅   0₆   0₇

0₆   Iso.G.4s7m3M   0₃

49°
18'
N

West
training
wall
(covers)   0G

0₈   0₁
Oc(2)R.6s

East
training
wall
(covers)

1₇

1

2

VQ(3)G.5s

2

VQ(3)R.5s

2₅

Bancs
de
Merville

4

2   2₁

2

3₃

4₂   3₇
Iso.G.

2   Iso.R   2₃

0.3

RIVA
BELLA

3₃

Q.G   Bn.R   4₇   5₇

Q.G   3   DirOc(3+1)R.12s10m17M

Ferry

OUISTREHAM   Bn.R   3

Bn.R

Avant-Port   3₆
Iso.4s7M   0₁   4
2₅   0₅

2₈

17'

Lighthouse
DirOc(3+1)R.12s
30m17M
Oc.WR.4s37m17/13M S/S Storm   3₃

Locks
Control
Tr

Port de
Plaisance
wc

Canal de Caen

L'Orne

To Caen
16'   0°15'W   14'

The first house to be liberated in France (June 1944). Airborne
Forces' Museum is next door to the pub

Caen. La Fonderie swing bridge leading into Bassin St Pierre.
Turn to starboard for yacht pontoons

Approach and entrance

Approaching from the west, it is important to
maintain a good offing of at least 3 miles to keep
clear of the Plateau du Calvados, watching for the
two unlit spar buoys, *Roseberry* (E cardinal) and
Essarts de Lagrune (N cardinal). In the northwestern
approaches to the *Ouistreham* (E cardinal) buoy
there are a further 2 spars (*Luc* and *Lion*, E
cardinals), which must be left to starboard as they
mark wrecks with little clear water.

The only distinguishable feature on the foreshore
is a line of beach huts at Riva-Bella, to the west of
the entrance. These end abruptly near the west bank

Pegasus Bridge at Bénouville, 2½ miles upstream. Wait
alongside wall on east bank, just out of picture (left)

Canal de Caen, Ouistreham. Note waiting pontoon on left-hand side of entrance, then the Port de Pêche and the lock

of the canal. There is also a white 37m-high lighthouse (Oc.WR.4s) hard by the lock itself.

From the *Ouistreham* (E cardinal) buoy it is just over a mile on a southerly heading to the first pair of buoys in the entry channel. These are *No.1* (Q.G) and *No.2* (Q.R). From these you should come onto the leading lights on 185°. These are Oc(3+1)R.12s and are visible well to seaward from their lattice red towers.

The channel is also well buoyed (see plan). Note that the breakwater ends are both submerged. The port-hand one (St Medard) is marked by a red tower beacon 16m tall (Oc(2)R.6s). Its opposite number is *Barnabe No.5* (Iso.G.4s). Note the white-painted tower at the *visible* end of the west breakwater (Iso.G.4s7M). This sounds a 10s horn when required. Keep well clear of all ferries, especially when they are berthing or unberthing on the west side.

If you are early or late for the eastern lock (the only one available to yachts), there is a waiting pontoon with deep water something over a cable beyond the ferry terminal on the east side. It is not salubrious, and can be crowded with craft whose line discipline may be poor, so stand by for squalls. Beyond this are the drying Port de Pêche and the locks.

Depending on tide range, the lock opens ±3 hours HW, but do not try to force a passage too near to the end of the period as the lock fills slowly, particularly in times of drought. The lock listens on VHF Ch 68 at tide times. The *capitainerie* is also on VHF Ch 68, or ☎ 02 31 85 85 85.

Note the lock traffic signals: entry is permitted by green over white over green with a further white alongside the group.

The yacht harbour entrance lies a cable above the lock on the port side. Visitors' berths are well marked, to port of you or straight ahead. You may have to raft up if the harbour is busy.

Facilities

Fresh water on pontoons. Fuel at marina, open 30 minutes before locks. Toilets and showers at yacht club; also public facilities with combination locks. There is no launderette. All chandlery and repair facilities you could wish for. There are various cranes and a slipway near the Port de Pêche. About 2 miles up the canal towards Caen is another boatyard with many facilities, including a serious slipway.

Caen

The 15km canal to Caen is free of difficulty, except for the various bridges. Reasonably enough, the authorities are unwilling to open these for individual yachts, so convoys are arranged, free of charge. These normally leave Ouistreham in the afternoon and return from Caen in the morning. Times for ascent to Caen are posted at the yacht club by the Port de Plaisance. If in doubt ask at the lock. In Caen, times are posted at the *capitainerie* for return to the sea. Ask at the lock for times of ascent, and at the *capitainerie* in Caen for coming back to the sea.

After the last bridge you will find yourself in a cul-de-sac which forms the arm of a 'T' across your passage. Turn to starboard and berth on the marina. There are good toilets and showers in the *capitainerie*, water on berths, and a convenient launderette.

Caen was largely flattened in World War II, but a number of ancient buildings survived. Fuel is available, as are most back-up facilities. As you would expect, there are restaurants and other city attractions to suit everybody.

The harbourmaster can be contacted on ☎ 02 31 95 24 47 or VHF Ch 12 and 68.

Caen yacht club (S.N. de Caen et du Calvados) is at 132 Rue Basse.

Communications

From Caen there is a regular train service to Bayeux, a remarkably lovely town where the famous tapestry can be viewed. It is stunning. The station is only 500m from the marina. Ouistreham has ferries to Portsmouth.

Courseulles-sur-Mer

Tides

HW −0300 Dover

MHWS	MLWS	MHWN	MLWN
7·4m	1·1m	6·15m	2·85m

Depths

The entrance channel dries up to 2·6m as far as 0·8M offshore. There is 3m in the Bassin Joinville, and berths for yachts of 1·5m (not visitors) in the Bassin de l'Ile de Plaisance. This is reached via a sill which dries 3m. The short-approach river up to it beyond the swing bridge dries 2·8m.

General

Courseulles is built around the river Seulles as it reaches the sea. The adjacent beaches were 'Juno Beach' during the 1944 Allied landings. The town is now a quiet holiday resort still taking advantage of its sandy foreshore. It has a remarkable *château* whose history already dated back more than half a millennium when it was stormed by Henry V. There are berths for 750 vessels, including at least 30 for visitors. The entrance is dangerous in strong north or northeast winds.

Approach, entrance and berthing

By night you will see the mighty Pointe de Ver light (Fl(3)15s42m26M), but its low tower is not conspicuous by day. Instead there are 3 unmistakable churches, which perspective causes to appear equidistant from one another. The entrance seems to lie to the west of the westernmost church, about as far from it as the next place of worship.

The landfall buoy (red and white, Iso.4s) lies 9 cables at about 346° from the west jetty. By night, the white sector of the Iso.WG.4s light on the end of the west jetty clears the worst of the rocky ledges adjacent to the shore. Lined up with the Oc(2)R.6s light on the eastern jetty well inshore, it gives a good lead in. Leave the western jetty light to starboard and steer for the Oc.R, keeping it on your port hand as you come to starboard into the Avant Port.

By day, note that, as is so often the case in Normandy, the outer breakwaters cover. In this instance the outer light on the west jetty therefore appears as an isolated dolphin surmounted by an open tower. This must be left to starboard. Beyond it, both walls are marked by red or green perches with topmarks. From the approaches, the inner lighthouse on the east jetty mentioned above appears as a white tower that can be lined up with the western dolphin to find acceptable water in the offing. The deepest approach is with the Oc.R lighthouse 'on' with the red beacon at 198°, but it cannot be over-stressed that the vicinity of Courseulles is strewn with off-lying dangers which just dry or are awash at MLWS, so adequate rise of tide and a good clearance are vital if you are to remain afloat.

Once inside, proceed up the Avant Port to the lock for the Bassin Joinville. This opens two hours either side of HW, together with its attendant bridge. Call port control on VHF Ch 9 for

Courseulles-sur-Mer at low water, showing half-tide training wall

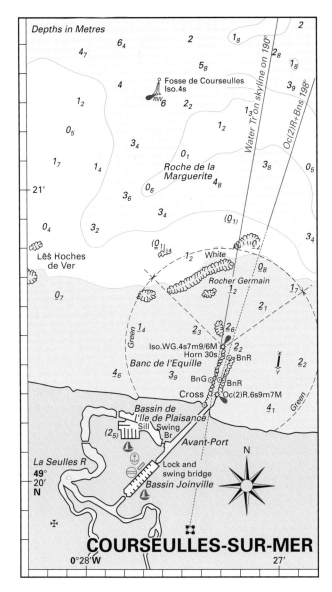

Depths in Metres

Fosse de Courseulles
Iso.4s
RW 6

Roche de la
Marguerite

21'

Les Roches
de Ver

White

Rocher Germain

Water Tr on skyline on 190°

Oc(2)R+Bns 198°

Green

Iso.WG.4s7m9/6M
Horn 30s

Banc de l'Equille

BnR

BnG

BnR

Cross

Oc(2)R.6s9m7M

Bassin de
l'Ile de Plaisance

Sill Swing
Br

Avant-Port

La Seulles R
49°
20'
N

Lock and
swing bridge
Bassin Joinville

N

COURSEULLES-SUR-MER

0°28'W   27'

instructions. If you do not make contact and nobody indicates where you should secure, make for pontoon 'X' on the east quay.

The newer harbour of the Bassin de l'Ile de Plaisance has no visitors' berths.

For obvious reasons, you should time your approach to coincide with lock openings.

Facilities
Fresh water on pontoons. Fuel by portage from Citroën garage. Launderette in town square. Good showers and toilets at the *capitainerie*.

There is a useful yacht yard (Chantier de la Seulles, ☎ 02 31 37 42 34) close by which can tackle most repairs. It also sells chandlery. The yacht club welcomes visitors.

All the facilities in town that you would expect from a rather upmarket resort, including a fine fish restaurant and various hotels.

Transport is by taxi (☎ 02 31 96 54 07, or 02 31 37 15 15) to Caen railway station, etc.

Arromanches
Tides approximately as Courseulles.

General
Arromanches lies 6½ miles west of Courseulles and represents a remarkable piece of modern history. There is no harbour in this crowded village, but artificial protection of the foreshore was created in 1944 by the sinking of a large number of 60m concrete barges, or caissons, in a ring offshore. This bold Allied enterprise permitted stores of war to be landed, thus keeping supply lines open for the invasion troops who had landed on the beaches, but had not thus far secured a major port for supply ships to enter.

Approach
Paying full heed to various off-lying spar buoys and giving the Rochers du Calvados a respectful berth, it is perfectly feasible to enter the harbour between a pair of small, unlit red and green buoys. The green lies almost due north of the red, despite the basically east-west disposition of the 'harbour wall', so you will have to enter on a southwesterly heading.

Anchorage
The 'official' anchorage is in 6m or so immediately inside the caissons west of the entrance, but you may find more shelter closer in. Pay the greatest heed to the plan, and buoy your anchor, because there is still considerable debris on the seabed.

Arromanches can make an atmospheric overnight stop in calm weather, but winds must be light and settled. As a lunch break en route from Courseulles to Port-en-Bessin it would be a 'must' for the student of history, or for anyone else with an interest in why we are all here and still free to go yachting.

Facilities
Few. Only those of a small village dedicated to informed tourism. The museum is fascinating.

Port-en-Bessin

Tides
HW −0215 Dover

MHWS	MLWS	MHWN	MLWN
7·2m	1·1m	5·9m	2·6m

Depths
The outer harbour dries up to 2m. There is up to 3·5m in the first locked basin and 2·5m in the second.

General
Port-en-Bessin is one of the few harbours in Normandy to have escaped the flood of yachts. It is purely a fishing harbour, but it is well protected and can accommodate a few visitors who do not outstay their welcome. There is an active market on Sunday mornings; there are also good restaurants, and the *pêche à pied* at LW springs is great fun. Here visitors can vie with canny locals as they scour the rock

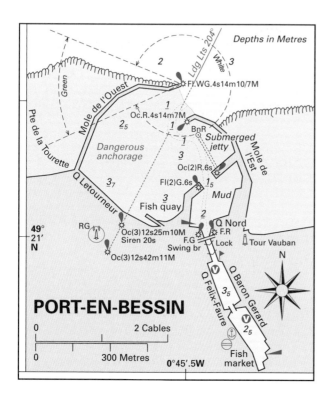

PORT-EN-BESSIN

pools for any fruits of the sea unwise enough to have stayed around.

Approach and entrance

In gales from north or northeast, do not attempt the harbour. In lesser but still strong conditions, strangers are recommended to stick to an hour either side of HW.

There are no dangers in the offing. The leading marks are a white house, 42m up, behind a white pylon with a green top immediately behind the quay on 204°. Both are Oc(3)12s, and the tower boasts a siren (20s) when required.

The western breakwater has a sectored Fl.WG.4s light whose green sector covers the rocks west of the western mole. The eastern mole has a red tower (Oc.R.4s14m7M) on its outer end. Pass between these and shape up between the pier heads of the inner harbour. These are Fl(2)G.6s to starboard and Oc(2)R.6s to port. Note that the western half of the outer harbour is foul with dangerous rocks. Outside the eastern inner breakwater is a submerged jetty whose northern extremity carries a red beacon with a ■ topmark.

If the lock is closed, wait at the northern end of the inner western quay on the side nearer to the

Port-en-Bessin. Note half-tide jetty left of centre

lock. The southern end is obstructed by a slipway whose outer limit is denoted by a painted strip on top of the masonry.

Traffic signals

Red over green (lights or flags) – basins closed.

There is also a F.R light in the middle of the lock gate when shut. The fixed reds on *either* side are not traffic signals.

Berthing

Taking the ground in the outer harbour on smooth mud is possible, but not recommended in any but the fairest weather, as a scend runs in.

The lock and bridge keeper listens on VHF Ch 18 at HW±2 hours to advise on lock and bridge opening. He may also put you straight on where to berth. If you do not receive advice, berth as seems sensible – even alongside a fishing boat by arrangement – then report to the harbourmaster's office halfway up the second basin on the west side. Have nothing to do with the small section marked 'Plaisance', as this is used by diminutive local yachts. The harbourmaster is on ☎ 02 31 21 70 49, and the lock-keeper is on ☎ 02 31 21 71 77.

Facilities

Fresh water on the east quay. There are two boatyards capable of timber or fibreglass repairs, and there are at least two engineers at the dock. Electronic repairs can be arranged at L K Electronique on the inner basin. Rudimentary chandlery at Hutrel, 5 Rue le Fournier, one block west of the inner basin.

Real town facilities, little sullied by tourism. Some visitors in recent years have not been charged for a few days' stop-over.

Grandcamp Maisy

Tides

HW −0220 Dover

MHWS	MLWS	MHWN	MLWN
7·2m	1·3m	5·9m	2·7m

These heights are approximate, as Grandcamp is the site of some tidal anomaly.

Depths

The approach dries 2m from up to 2 cables to seaward of the lock. Inside is up to 2·5m, with at

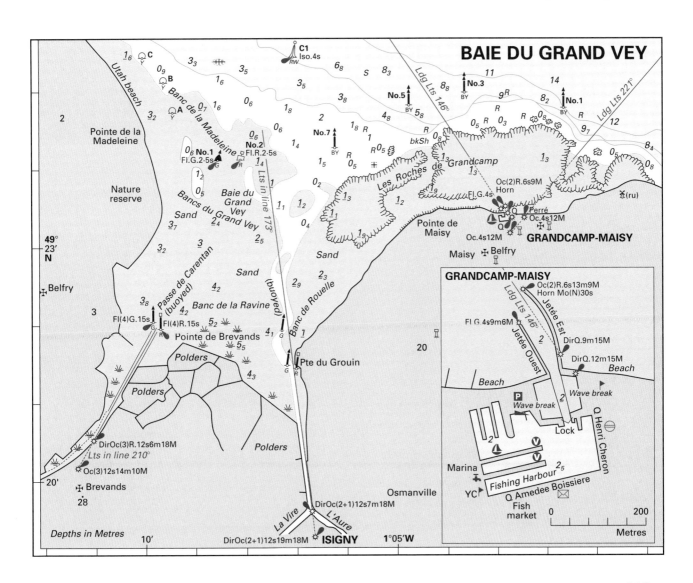

Grandcamp-Maisy

least 2m on the visitors' berths at HW, falling to 1·5m at LW.

General
Grandcamp Maisy is an undistinguished resort town with a considerable fishing fleet. The lock-in harbour is approachable in most conditions given a good rise of tide, but may be dangerous in strong onshore weather, notably from the northeast.

Approach and entrance
For some obscure reason, the rhythm of tides at Grandcamp follows the same hours as Dunkerque. The locks officially open about 3 hours either side of local HW, but this coincides almost exactly with the full period of the flood at Dunkerque. Thus, you will probably get in any time between LW Dunkerque (lock opens) and HW Dunkerque (when it closes).

Immediately south of the harbour is La Maresquerle light tower on its 12m-high white mast (Oc.4s28m12M). This transits on 221° with Perré light (Oc.4s8m13M), on a 7m green pylon set on a white hut on the foreshore. The transit is of no use close in, but may give you a good start if you are coming from the northeast. The best approach is from a point between *No.5* and *No.3* north cardinal spar buoys (unlit) which will place you on the transit of two quick flashing leading lights. These bring you in past the east and west jetties with their white light structures (see plan) to the inner jetty heads, where you must alter onto a heading of south by east for the lock gate. If you can't spot the leading marks by day, do not worry. Any approach heading between southeast and southwest is safe because Grandcamp rock ledge is as smooth as a billiard table. Note that the outer ends of both jetties cover, leaving only their light structures as salient features.

There is no satisfactory waiting place in the outer harbour, so you should be sure to arrive when the gates are open. The harbour authorities listen on VHF Ch 9 (☎ 02 31 22 63 16).

Berthing
Tie up in the outer twelve berths on either side of the northern long pontoon on your starboard hand inside the entrance. Lie alongside if you end up on the hammerhead, otherwise bows-to with your stern secured to the relevant mooring.

Facilities
The harbour office in the southwest corner of the port has toilets and showers. Fresh water is available

on the pontoons and fuel at the eastern fish quay (Henri Chéson). Restaurants etc. are undistinguished, though La Marée on the east side of the basin, is reported to serve excellent fresh fish.

Some chandlery and repair facilities. There is a small yacht club open only at weekends. The large launching hard on the north side of the basin where local boats often lie is not available for visitors to dry out, which may discourage larger yachts.

Isigny-sur-Mer

Tides
HW −0225 Dover

MHWS	MLWS	MHWN	MLWN
7·3m	dries	6m	dries

Depths
Craft drawing 1·8m can creep up at HW±1½ hours at neaps. More water at springs. All berths dry.

General
Isigny is an undeveloped small Norman town. Its total unsuitability for all forms of *plaisance* have kept its rather rude waterfront free of the sort of aids to convenience without which some seem unable to live. For the intrepid explorer of creeks who is on the hunt for a chunk of 'real France', Isigny may therefore prove a satisfying port of call. It must be stressed, however, that the berths all dry and that the bottom, while fairly soft, is uneven. In an ideal world, it would be prudent to eyeball the bottom at LW before committing your yacht to it.

Approach and entrance
From the north, make for the red and white buoy *C1*, with its Iso.4s light. This is not always notably easy to spot, so be ready with your binoculars. If

Isigny – easiest berths bottom left

arriving from St Vaast, you must press on. It is too easy to take a cavalier attitude and find yourself arriving after HW. Now steer on to buoy *IS*, an unlit north cardinal. Here you will join up with any mariners arriving from the east, who will either have crossed the Grandcamp rocks (dry 2m) if bound from Grandcamp Maisy, or skirted the other north cardinals stretching away to the east, north of the shoal.

From *IS* buoy, steer south-southwest and look for a pair of unlit channel buoys, followed by more of the same. These lead in a fairly straight line with a green perch halfway up coinciding with a gap in the series, arriving ultimately at a green-topped beacon to starboard followed by a red to port, marking the outer ends of a pair of training walls. The channel now runs straight between these on 173° and is defined, for those locals prepared to give the channel a go in the dark, by intensified leading lights set up at the junction in the river, both of which are DirOc(2+1)12s18M.

The front light is on a conspicuous white beacon which is left to starboard at the divide. From here, stay in the middle up to the town.

Berthing
The advised berth is on pontoons at, or just past, the yard on your starboard hand. These dry out at LW, so leave some slack in your lines so as not to strain your cleats. The bottom is soft but uneven.

If you are lucky you may secure a berth in the small 'dock' inset from the stream on your port hand, further up towards the town. Here you may dry out with some confidence on a shelving, hard bottom. There are walls on either side to lean on, and as depth diminishes away from the river, a bilgekeeler could dry out comfortably in the middle so long as she lay at right angles to the stream with her bows to the bank.

Further up near the bridge is not recommended, as the bottom may be foul and where it is not there are holes left by fishing boats. Drying out can be safely if uncomfortably achieved, but not without prior inspection at LW.

Facilities
Good local shops and restaurants. The yard can handle some repairs. Fresh water at the yard.

Carentan

Tides
HW −0225 Dover

MHWS	MLWS	MHWN	MLWN
7·2m	1·3m	5·9m	2·7m

Depths
The approach channel dries completely, but craft drawing 1·5m can use it at HW neaps ±2 hours. An hour before or after a moderate spring can accommodate the needs of a boat drawing 2·4m, but in order to be sure, consult the tidal graph below. The lock sill has about 1·8m at HW neaps. Inside

Carentan. *Capitainerie* is on the left in the branch of the 'T'

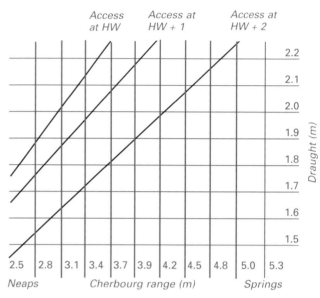

	Access at HW	Access at HW + 1	Access at HW + 2	Draught (m)
				2.2
				2.1
				2.0
				1.9
				1.8
				1.7
				1.6
				1.5

2.5 2.8 3.1 3.4 3.7 3.9 4.2 4.5 4.8 5.0 5.3

Neaps   *Cherbourg range (m)*   *Springs*

Carentan tidal graph

the marina basin there is plenty of water.

Note, if you are creeping up, heart in mouth and eyes on echo sounder, that the shallowest water is at the kink in the buoyed channel immediately before the canal. If you float through there, you've made it!

General

Carentan is a fascinating county town, seriously beaten up in the battles following D-Day, which now presents a delightful prospect for the cruising yachtsman. Shelter is perfect, facilities in the quiet marina are good, and the town has good shops and restaurants in addition to considerable recent historic interest.

Approach

Do not attempt either Carentan or Isigny for the first time by night. You are extremely unlikely to succeed if you do, because of the winding nature of the largely unlit channel. Such lights as there are are shown on the plan.

First, find the red and white safe water buoy *C1*. You are now abeam of Utah Beach. From here, steer approximately 215° for something in the region of 1¼ miles, until you come to the first pair of channel buoys, labelled *1* (green, Fl.G.2·5s) and *2* (red, Fl.R.2·5s). The water is now shoaling, and if the wind is powerful and blowing in, it may be prudent to abort. Otherwise, carry on up the well-buoyed channel, which will not be described in detail because of its shifting nature. About 2½ miles in from *Nos 1* and *2* buoys you will arrive at a red and a green beacon to be left to port and starboard respectively. The course is now 210°, and you will in due course see the structures carrying the leading lights. As you pass the first of these, you will swing round to starboard and proceed up-river between gentle reedy banks in deep water marked by withies until the lock appears ahead.

The lock will open from HW−2hr to HW+3hr and can be called on VHF Ch 9 (☎ 02 33 71 10 85). Once inside, proceed up the long, narrow basin. There are at least 50 visitors' berths in the marina at the top of the basin, and room for plenty more. Either tie up in a vacant spot and report, or call the *capitainerie* on VHF Ch 9 (☎ 02 33 42 24 44).

It is all too easy to dawdle on your way to Carentan, resulting in having to tackle the river and the channel as the tide is beginning to ebb. Since this can run strongly, you are then in a no-win situation. Try to arrive at *C1* at least an hour before HW, and preferably 1½ or 2 hours.

Facilities

The church is 15th century, and some of the shops have medieval stone arcades which survived the serious bombardment following the landings. Middle-aged people still living in the town remember hiding in cellars while the battle raged in the streets above.

Fresh water, fuel and good chandlery at the head of the basin. Showers etc. in the *capitainerie*. Launderette in town.

All provisions, restaurants, postal services, etc. from the town centre, which is 10-minutes' walk through the streets. There is a reasonable bar on the waterfront for a late night *café et Calvados*.

If it could be arranged with the harbour authorities, who are friendly and helpful, Carentan would be an excellent, secluded place to leave a yacht for a few weeks.

St Vaast-la-Hougue

Tides

HW −0240 Dover

MHWS	MLWS	MHWN	MLWN
6·65m	0·9m	5·4m	2·3m

Depths

Approach dries up to a height of 1·8m north of the Grande Jetée. However, there is well over 2·5m inside at HW. At LW, depths inside the lock drain off to 2·5m on the official visitors' berth, where the bottom is hard, or 2·3m in the marina, where you may well be berthed.

General

St Vaast is a fine harbour, even if it is bound by tidal constraints (see 'Approach' and 'Entrance'). It is perfectly sheltered and, given a good rise of tide, can be entered in most weathers. The town is a fishing community and the influx of yachts since it was locked and dredged in 1982 has not spoiled it. A walk across the causeway to Ile de Tatihou at LW springs reveals the oyster industry in full cry, the Saturday morning market is one of the best in northern France, and the waterfront bars and bistros are well up to standard.

The locals are extremely friendly, and St Vaast has become one of those ports where, if you loll on a bollard for long enough, you will meet every sailor you ever knew.

Approach

From the north, round Pointe de Barfleur with a 1½ mile clearance, being aware that if the wind is blowing hard against a spring tide this is one of the nastiest corners in the Channel. With the light abeam on a south-southeasterly heading, carry on for 6 miles until Pointe de Saire (white 10m tower, Oc(2+1)12s10M) is bearing 295° and in transit with Reville church. Now alter to 200° until Ile de Tatihou with its characteristic fort is well abaft the beam and *Le Gavendest* unlit south cardinal whistle buoy is on the starboard bow. Leave this to starboard and steer about 260° to round *La Dent*, a second unlit south cardinal.

By night, pick up the transit of Fort de la Hougue

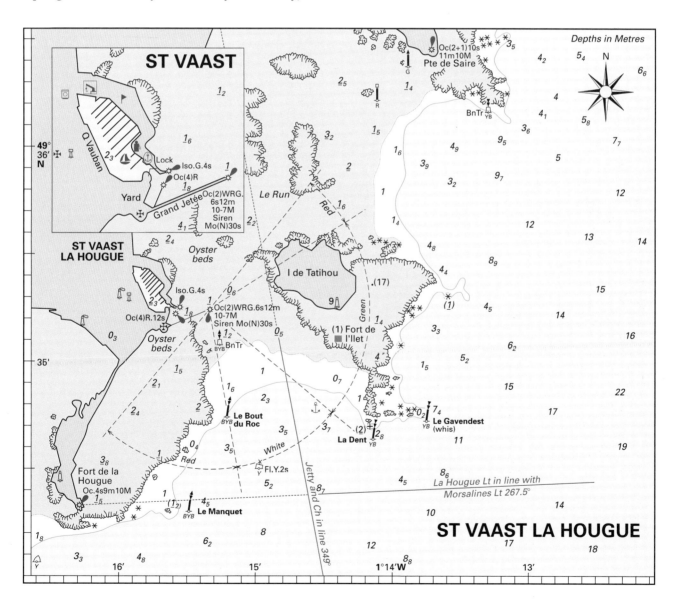

(A) Fort de la Hougue. (B) Morsalines lighthouse 1·7 miles inshore

Rounding east end of St Vaast Grande Jetée to enter open gates. Note Chapelle des Marins at the landward end of the mole

(Oc.4s9m10M) and Morsalines (Oc(4)WRG.12s 11-8M) on 267°. This will take you well clear of the dangers south of Tatihou. It should also be used when outward bound after dark. Once you are well into the white sector of the Grande Jetée light (see plan) you are safe to steer so as to leave it close to port. By day, you can turn in, given enough water, when a cable or so past *La Dent*, though the best water is said to be found by approaching the jetty end on about 335°.

From the south, by day, spot the Ile de Tatihou and the small, fairy-tale Fort de la Hougue. Keep the latter to port, the former to starboard until you are close enough to spot *La Dent* (see above) and *Le Manquet* east cardinal buoy. This should be left to port, as must *Le Bout du Roc*, just under half a mile north-northeast. From *Le Bout du Roc* you can steer for the pier head, giving *Le Creux de Bas* east cardinal daymark a healthy berth to port. By night, the white sector of the light on the breakwater clears all these dangers, as it does their opposite numbers around Tatihou.

Strangers are not advised to pass north-about round Ile de Tatihou, though at the right state of tide this is perfectly feasible with local knowledge.

Entrance
Round the Grande Jetée, then steer for the single lock gate, inside the two inner breakwaters. Priority is given to inbound vessels, but watch out for eddies and strong currents which can set you on alarmingly, both inward and outward bound. The harbourmaster listens on VHF Ch 9, but he also displays a board at the *capitainerie* on the right inside the gates which indicates which pontoon you should head for.

Berthing
Large craft berth on the big pontoon immediately inside on the starboard hand. Others as described above. When the gates shut there is about 2·5m depth on the big pontoon. As the last of the fishing boats charge in or out a deep-draught yacht may bump, but it isn't for long. Once the gates shut, all is peace. You can even take a short cut to town across the gates.

It is possible to dry out on the north side of the Grande Jetée, which dries 1·4–1·8m. The bottom is muddy.

Whilst waiting for the lock, or even simply for a quiet, economical night in settled weather, there is good anchorage on clean sand east or south of the *Bout du Roc* buoy. A riding light is essential because you are effectively in the fairway. You may find more peace on the line between *Bout du Roc* and *Le Manquet*.

Facilities
As already noted, St Vaast has nearly everything a sailor could ask for. Fresh water on the docks, showers and toilets in the yacht club and the *capitainerie*, and a launderette *face au port*. There is a good shipyard where yacht repairs can be

St Vaast-la-Hougue

undertaken, *Camping Gaz* exchange and some chandlery. There are also engineers, diesel on the quay, a 15-ton mobile crane and a launching ramp beside the *capitainerie* on the seaward side.

For the shopper after provisions the town is akin to heaven, with many small stores selling all the delights, plus the noble emporium of the famous M. Gosselin a block back from the Quai Vauban. Here you can buy anything in the delicatessen line, with one of Normandy's best wine stocks as a bonus. The fine wines are in the dark room at the back and if your French is less than perfect you can browse through the vintages without fear of embarrassment. Should your tastes be less sophisticated, M. Gosselin also bottles his own at popular prices.

On no account miss the Saturday morning market.

There are a number of waterfront bistros and bars of acceptable quality for a quick *moules et frites* lunch, but the serious diner has traditionally been well advised to visit the Hotel des Fuchsias. Catastrophically, on a recent visit with chums, the compiler noted that this famous establishment appeared to have suffered a set-back. It is to be hoped that all is now put to rights, but in the meantime the recommendation should be treated with caution.

Communications

St Vaast is not far from Cherbourg and its ferries and trains.

Fishing boats use old town quay to port inside gates at St Vaast

Barfleur

Tides

HW −0208 Dover

MHWS	MLWS	MHWN	MLWN
6·5m	1·2m	5·3m	2·6m

Depths

Deep water in the approaches, rapidly shoaling to an entrance which dries 0·6m and quayside berths which dry in the region of 2m.

General

Except for deep water berths, Barfleur offers most of what the discerning cruising sailor could ask for. The town is quiet and little patronised by yachts because of its awkward berthing. As a result, one is something of a curiosity in the local fishermen's bars, but this need be no impediment to having a good time. The town is a classic grey-stone Norman fishing village, and seems little changed by time, except that the Renault Clio has almost completely ousted the ox-cart with solid wheels.

The bottom on the northwest quay is clean for taking the ground and shelter is good in all but east or northeast winds, in which case you should not enter at all. If you are caught inside, you must clear out as soon as you float.

Approach and entrance

It is unwise for the stranger to enter Barfleur until about 2 hours before HW.

Note that tidal streams reach up to 3 knots in the offing (and far more off the notorious Pointe de Barfleur, a couple of miles north). North-going stream starts at HW Cherbourg +2¼; south-going at HW Cherbourg −4½.

Always consult the tidal stream atlas, and be sure you make no mistake at Pointe de Barfleur, where a wicked race develops east of the light.

Even in good weather, keep at least a mile offshore until you see the unlit green conical buoy with topmark, *La Grotte*. Round this, then steer south-southwesterly to pass between the green unlit buoy, depressingly named *Roche des Anglais*, and its red partner, *Le Hintar*. A course of 219° should make the transit of two square white towers which bear leading lights synchronised to Oc(3)12s. The front tower is in a roughshod car park on the down-market side of town, while its rear counterpart sits on the roof of a prominent house at the top of the harbour.

This transit actually passes inshore of the end of the south jetty, but once you have passed *La Vimberge* (green buoy), *La Filleule* (ditto), *La Raie* (red daymark) and *La Grosse Haie* (ditto) you can shape up safely for the harbour mouth. The southern breakwater has an Oc.R.4s light, and the inner end of the north breakwater shows a Fl.G.4s; the outer end is very close to a small green beacon.

Berthing

In suitable wind conditions it is possible to anchor immediately outside the entrance to await sufficient tide to work up to a berth. The best berths are on

Barfleur

Barfleur. Approach on 219°. The church's square tower is conspicuous by day

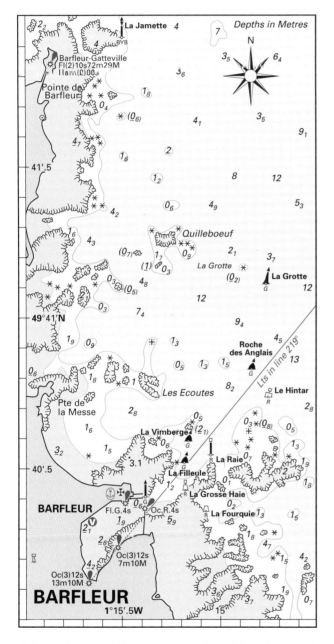

Barfleur. Front leading light next to caravan park

Facilities

Water, good shops and bars, and a marine mechanic (☎ 02 33 54 02 66). Toilets are basic. Fuel by portage. There is a workaday bistro by the waterfront and a good hotel with restaurant up the obscurely titled Rue de St Thomas à Becket (Archevèque de Canterbury). There is a further excellent restaurant (the Moderne) in the Place Charles de Gaulle, down the back streets towards the rear leading mark for the harbour entrance.

Like St Vaast, Barfleur is fairly handy for Cherbourg with all its onward travel possibilities.

Cherbourg

Tides

HW −0308 Dover

MHWS	MLWS	MHWN	MLWN
6·35m	1·15m	5·05m	2·55m

Depths

Cherbourg is a deep-water harbour where any yacht but a total giant can lie at any state of tide. The approaches are also deep.

General

From the average British yachtsman's point of view Cherbourg is the most important port on this stretch of coast. It is strategically sited in the central Channel and, because of the northern-thrusting aspect of the peninsula, it is the closest of all harbours to the ports of central southern England. With its well marked, broad entrances and sheltered inner harbour, it is approachable in absolutely any weather and at any state of tide. Shelter in the Chantereyne yacht harbour is perfect, and for those unwilling to pay 'le price' and prepared to dinghy

the northwest wall, on your starboard hand beyond the fishing boats, where you will dry out on clean sand or shingle. The wall is appropriately equipped with ladders.

The southwest wall is used by locals and partly encumbered with 'haul-offs'. The southeast wall is foul with rocks.

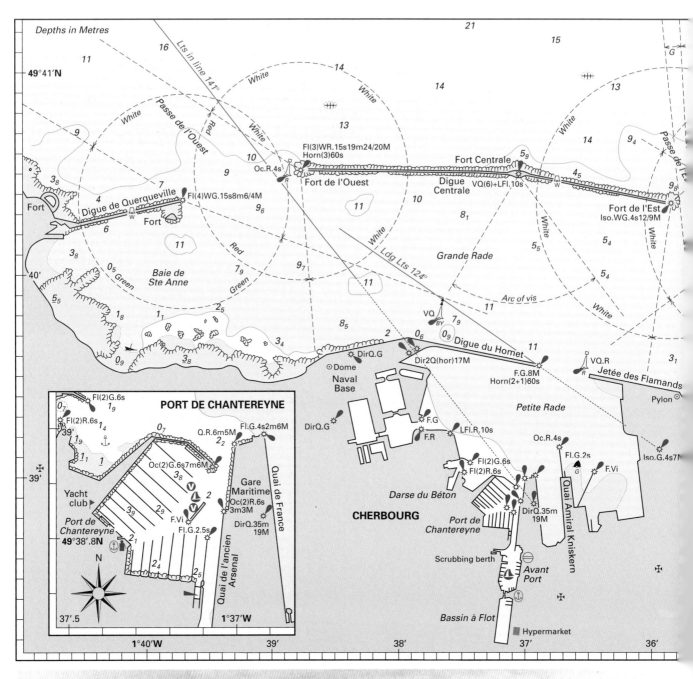

Depths in Metres

49°41'N

16 Lts in line 141°

Passe de l'Ouest

White White

White

White

White

21

15

14

14

White

White

13

Passe de l'E

9 White

9₄

9

7 Fort

Digue de Querqueville Fort

10

Fl(3)WR.15s19m24/20M
Horn(3)60s

Oc.R.4s

Fort de l'Ouest

Fort Centrale

Digue Centrale

5₉

VQ(6)+LFl.10s

4₅

9₈

3₈ 4

Fl(4)WG.15s8m6/4M

9₆

10

8₁

White

Fort de l'Est
Iso.WG.4s12/9M

6

3₈

11

Baie de
Ste Anne

Red

White

Ldg Lts 124°

Grande Rade

5₅

5₄

White

40'

0₅ Green
Green

7₉

9₇

Green

11

5₄

1₈ 1₁

2₅

8₅

11

Arc of vis

White

5₅

0₉

3₄

2

0₆

VQ
BY

7₉

0₉ Digue du Homet

11

3₁

3₈

DirQ.G

Dir2Q(hor)17M

F.G.8M
Horn(2+1)60s

VQ.R

Jetée des Flamands

39'

⊙ Dome
Naval
Base

DirQ.G

F.G

F.R

LFl.R.10s

Petite Rade

Pylon ⊙

PORT DE CHANTEREYNE

Fl(2)G.6s

1₉

Fl(2)R.6s 1₄

39' 1₉

0₇

Q.R.6m5M

Fl.G.4s2m6M

2₂

Oc.R.4s

Fl.G.2s

G

F.Vi

Oc.R.4s

Iso.G.4s7M

Oc(2)G.6s7m6M

3₈

Gare
Maritime

Oc(2)R.6s
3m3M

DirQ.35m
19M

Fl(2)G.6s
Fl(2)R.6s

Darse du Béton

CHERBOURG

DirQ.35m
19M

Yacht
club ▶

Port de
Chantereyne

3₉

2₉

V

2

Port de
Chantereyne

F.Vi

Fl.G.2.5s

49°38'.8N

2₁

2₄

2₅

Quai de France

Quai de l'ancien Arsenal

Scrubbing berth

Avant
Port

37'.5

N

1°37'W

Bassin à Flot

■ Hypermarket

1°40'W

39'

38'

37'

36'

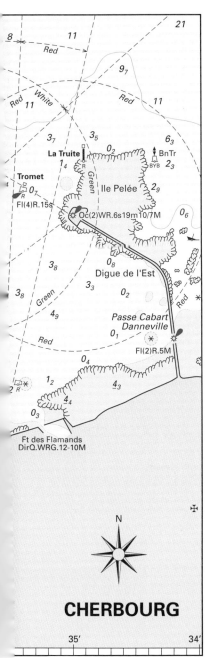

CHERBOURG

half a mile or so, the Petite Rade offers an excellent anchorage where space, for once, is not an issue.

Cherbourg's massive fortifications were conceived in Louis XVI's time, but not finally completed until 1853. There is now a military port on the west side of the Petite Rade and ferries at the eastern end, making use of the old transatlantic terminal from which the first scheduled service to New York began in 1869. Inside a further breakwater lies the Chantereyne marina and, further in still, the Avant Port where yachts used to lie in the heart of the city. Beyond this is the lock-in Bassin à Flot where, by arrangement, quite large craft can be left.

It is fashionable amongst old lags of the central Channel to be blasé about Cherbourg and its attractions. Why this should be, *The Shell Channel Pilot* cannot imagine. In foul weather the town has all anyone could wish for except pastoral scenes and nature in the raw. There is, it must be said, a half-mile walk from the marina to the action, but this is not unpleasant. If it is raining, as often seems to be the case, there is no law against taking a cab to the supermarket.

Finally, there is one overriding benefit if the weather never does get better and you run out of time: you could not be better placed for the ferry home. The yacht will be perfectly safe until next weekend, and by this expedient you can offset your costs by importing a double consignment of wines at sensible French prices.

Approach and entrance

The tide positively gallops past the Cherbourg peninsula, so wherever you are coming from, you must have its movements uppermost in your mind. Approaching from the north, continue making tidal offsets to your course (or lock onto your 'cross-track error') until you reach the entrance; otherwise you will wish you had. Always shape a course towards a point a mile or two up-tide of the entrance. Simply to steer for it is the road to frustration.

In good visibility, Cherbourg is first seen as a dip in the land to the left of the high ground behind Cap de la Hague, whose massive nuclear power station is extremely prominent, particularly at night. Ferries from Poole or the Solent making a beeline for the harbour are also a reassuring confirmation of your whereabouts. There are no particular dangers in the offing except the various rocks off the coast (notably in the vicinities of Barfleur and Omonville), all of which are well marked with buoys or beacons. The Ile Pelée off the eastern entrance should be treated with respect.

Top opposite Eastern entrance to Cherbourg. Light on the end of Digue Centrale, with Fort Centrale at right-hand edge. The west entrance is 3·7m distant at the far end

Bottom opposite Cherbourg. The eastern end of Digue du Homet. Everywhere immediately to the right of the beacon is forbidden. White building to the right are part of naval dockyard

Cherbourg. Looking in past Fort de l'Ouest, across the Grande Rade to the Digue du Homet. The area immediately fronting the Naval Base (see plan) is forbidden

The major lighthouse is on Fort de l'Ouest (Fl(3)WR.15s24/20M), but if you are approaching from the north your first light will be Cap de la Hague or Barfleur. Staying out of the red sector of Fort de l'Ouest gives a very safe clearance of the Pointe de Querqueville. There is plenty of water to within 60m of the fort and the breakwater, but be sure to leave the red buoy (Oc.R.4s), just inside it, to port.

If you are favouring the eastern entrance, the green sector of the Fort de l'Est light (Iso.WG.4s12/9M) indicates the position of the Ile Pelée, as does the red buoy (Fl(4)15s) in the entrance, which you must leave to port. The Oc(2)WR.6s Ile Pelée light, which shows red in any but the most westerly of approaches, will turn to white as you pass the buoy. Favour the western side of this entrance, but note that debris from the fort fouls the water for 100m or so around it. By day, give a wide berth to the unlit red beacon (La Truite) on the northwest extremity of the Ile Pelée rock shelf.

The southern edge of the Ile Pelée white sector now guides you to the entrance of the Petite Rade, though you may be better served by shaping up for the F.G.10m8M on the end of the Digue du Homet and the red buoy (VQ.R) immediately off the unlit Jetée des Flamands on a heading of around 220°.

There are a number of directional leading lights and transits set up to assist ships making for both eastern and western entrances. These can be useful in checking set and drift. They are shown clearly on the plan and may well prove to be of value. However, Cherbourg is lit like the proverbial Christmas tree, and the stranger would be well advised to decide which lights are important to him and stick with them. The ones described above will serve well.

From Fort de l'Ouest, the track to the Petite Rade is beautifully clear. Simply line up the F.G on Digue du Homet with the DirIso.G behind it on 124°. This will take you past La Tenarde lit north cardinal buoy and clear up to the entrance.

In daylight, the whole entrance procedure is entirely unambiguous and can be negotiated by a beginner, provided always that current is borne in mind.

Once inside the Petite Rade, steer approximately 200° for 6 cables towards the unmistakable old transatlantic terminal, with, very likely, a ferry alongside. By night, you want the Q.R light, not the green flash to its left, which is for the ferry terminal. As you leave to port the red light on the big jetty end, you will see the breakwater for the marina, with its Oc(2)G light on a white pillar. Swing to starboard inside and make for the marina, which is well lit up at night.

If it is blowing hard, there is room for all but the largest yachts to round up inside the last breakwater to drop sails.

Berthing

Visitors' berths are officially on G pontoon, the second from the north end. Larger yachts may sometimes berth stern or bow-to on the north side of the northern pontoon, held off by moorings. The outer berths on pontoons J through Q running north from the south wall also sometimes accommodate visitors. There is a waiting pontoon island in the middle from which you may conveniently dinghy ashore. There are 300 berths here for visitors, including specials for multihulls and big yachts.

There is anchorage in the Petite Rade on the north side of the marina wall, with adequate depth and fair shelter. No charge is made. The marina is no longer as reasonably priced as it once was. No anchoring is permitted under any circumstances inside the marina breakwater.

Facilities

Absolutely everything you need. Toilets and showers are best in the marina *capitainerie* building. To reach the town, set course for the statue of Napoléon on his horse (conspic). Thence, carry on up the wide street running away from the water. At the top of this, take a left and follow your best instincts. Good luck.

The hypermarket is found by following the water down to the old Bassin de Commerce. Cross the bridge at its northern end. The hypermarket is on its eastern shore. It is conspicuous by the hordes of Brits staggering out behind trolleys piled high with booze and other benefits. You can take your dinghy up here to avoid the inevitable cab-full of bottles, but only at HW±2 hours or so. *The Shell Channel Pilot* compilers failed to note this and were left with the embarrassing portage of a loaded punt across the zebra crossing. Fortunately, it was raining as usual (cf. *Les Parapluies de Cherbourg* – classic accordion music) and the boat slid sweetly across the greasy cobbles before the little green man on the traffic lights turned red.

Communications

Ferries to UK, and trains to the Continent.

Omonville-la-Rogue

Tides

HW −0330 Dover

MHWS	MLWS	MHWN	MLWN
6·2m	1·1m	5·0m	2·6m

Depths

Omonville dries alongside, but it has a number of moorings in over 3·5m (LAT).

General and facilities

The port of Omonville-la-Rogue is little more than a roadstead with a small stone breakwater. In fair weather, with no east in the wind (and little north) it can provide a strategic stop-over for the Race of Alderney. The village is very pretty, with small restaurants and shops. It is about 1 mile distant. There is a bar/bistro at the root of the pier, much frequented by locals, who enjoy the mussels. Close at hand is a first-class fish restaurant of no great appearance. Do not be put off by its workaday looks.

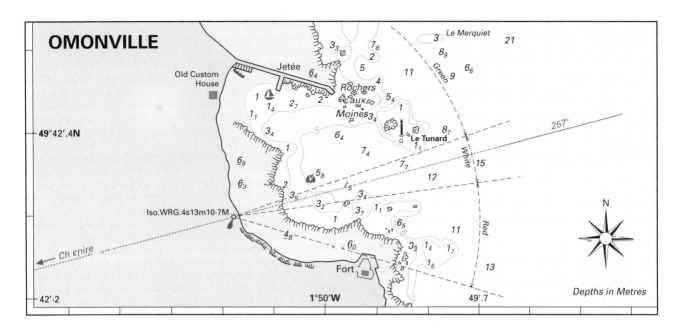

OMONVILLE

Old Custom House

Jetée

Rochers aux Moines

Le Tunard

Iso.WRG.4s13m10-7M

Ch spire

Fort

Le Merquiet

Green

White

257°

Red

N

Depths in Metres

49°42'.4N

42'.2

1°50'W

49'.7

There are basic *sanitaires* and not much else, barring the freshwater tap. No fuel, even by portage. Beaumont-Hague is 5km inland, with all town facilities and buses to Cherbourg.

Approach and berthing

By night, keep well clear of the shore until you are firmly in the white sector of the Iso.WRG.4s light at the root of the bay. This will bear about 255° and will bring you in past *Le Tunard* green unlit beacon. When you have discerned this abeam to starboard, swing 40° or so to starboard and make up towards the moorings. This night approach is not recommended to strangers.

By day, from the east, keep a mile or so offshore, leaving the *Raz de Bannes* unlit north cardinal beacon well to port. You will see the 13th-century chapel of Omonville with its little steeple on rising ground above waterfront cottages. Line this up with a white lattice beacon (the light structure) with a red top in the southeast corner of the port on 257° until *Le Tunard* beacon is abeam to starboard. Now turn in to the moorings or the inner quay.

From the west or north, the safe transit is *Le Tunard* 'on' with an old fort at the south point of the bay, on 195°. The fort has a small block of flats on it. Jink to port around *Le Tunard*, then swing to starboard up to the moorings.

The inshore end of the breakwater has a clean bottom and dries about 1m. If there are no fishing boats you could dry out here, but this is emphatically not advised unless you are sure of the weather. A yacht could take a wicked pounding in an easterly scend.

The visitors' moorings are a safer option, because if conditions took a turn for the worse you could escape to seaward even after dark by using the white sector of the light. This has been done by a number of yachtsmen even after eating and drinking their fill in the fine restaurant mentioned above.

Omonville-la-Rogue

Diélette

Tides
HW −0440 Dover

MHWS	MLWS	MHWN	MLWN
12·2m	1·6m	9·2m	4·3m

Depths
Channel dredged to LAT. Sill dries 5·5m, threshold of open swing gate 4m. 2m in commercial harbour. Up to 2·5m in locked harbour

General
Diélette is a well established small port which was never of practical use to yachts until the new marina opened in 1997. Like Carteret to the south, the port is now of strategic value to yachts cruising the Channel Islands and the St Malo area. Its tidal accessibility is greater than Carteret, with the offing providing the same sort of straightforward approach, given reasonable weather and height of tide.

The town has undergone a series of historical changes governed by its commercial purpose, altering from a granite quarry to an iron mine and now to nuclear electricity. Its buildings reflect this but the latest phase of its life is attracting new investment and restaurants etc. are now appearing.

You cannot see the nuclear power station when you are in the harbour.

Approach and entrance
Having ascertained that the height of tide is suitable, and that onshore winds and seas are not rendering the approach too difficult, shape up for the pier heads on a heading of around 125° to clear all dangers. Be aware of the prohibited area extending 5 cables offshore from Diélette to Cap de Flamanville.

The Jetée Ouest has a white tower with a green top (Iso.4s22m7M), while a red light structure (Fl.R.4s5M) appears on the end of the Digue Nord.

Once inside, either tie up on the waiting berths in the commercial harbour on your port hand or, if the tide serves, proceed to the entrance of the wet dock.

Access to the outer, or 'commercial' dock for vessels drawing 1·5m should be permanent at mean

Diélette

tides or less and 10 hours or so at mean springs.

Access over the lip of the sill gate to marina for 2m draught should be HW±2½hr, depending a little upon the tide, while for 1·5m draught, access is promised from HW±3hr, regardless of tidal coefficient.

Facilities
Usual marina facilities. The small village has some shops and an hotel with restaurant. What cannot be obtained there in the way of provisions is available a mile up the hill at Flamanville.

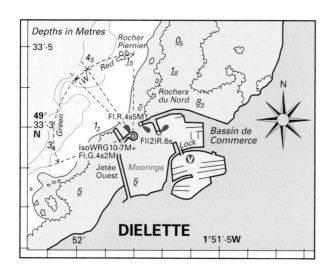

Carteret

Tides

HW −0440 Dover

MHWS	MLWS	MHWN	MLWN
11·2m	1·4m	7·9m	4·0m

Depths

Approach dries up to 3·7m at the pier head. Berths alongside the harbour wall dry at around 5·5m. The channel up to the yacht harbour dries 5m. There is 2·3m dredged depth inside the locked marina. The sill dries 5·5m and there is 1·3m over the threshold when the gate opens at around HW±2½hr.

General

With its massive drying heights, Carteret might appear a dubious proposition for most visitors. Nothing could be further from the truth. So long as you can time your arrival to a couple of hours either side of HW, entry to the locked marina is extremely simple unless it is blowing hard from south or southwest, in which case, forget it. The town is delightful (see Facilities) with a number of facets which make it worth more than a one-night stop-over. It is much visited by Channel Islands yachtsmen, who have not been slow to discover its benefits and strategic potential when cruising between Cherbourg and St Malo. In the old days

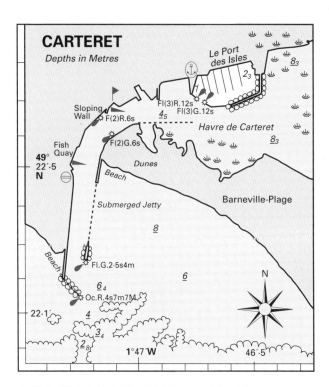

Carteret. Inside the entrance looking upstream with the fish quay in the foreground. The white hotel is conspicuous left of centre. Note the red beacon marking foul ground immediately left of the fishing boat and the lit red and green beacons left and right of the hotel. The marina is visible far right of centre

Carteret. The new marina now lies immediately to the right of the old drying 'marina' to the right of centre at the top of the picture.

before the marina was opened, yachts were known to have enjoyed a peaceful tide dried out in a fisherman's berth, to leave when their host returned on the evening flood. This option still remains.

Approach and entrance

Carteret is easy to identify because of the prominent 15m square grey tower of Pointe Carteret lighthouse on the cliff immediately west of the breakwater, and the even more conspicuous lattice communications tower (F.R) which now stands immediately behind it. The lighthouse lantern is 81m above sea level and shows a Fl(2+1)15s, Horn(3)60s.

Apart from the generally shoal waters and the well charted offlying dangers, there are no special

227

Carteret. Entrance to Port des Isles showing the sill on thre right-hand side and the traffic lights on the left

problems close in. The extended western breakwater with its hooked, 'semi-submersible' outer end stands north/south and is lit at the extremity by a white beacon with a red top (Oc.R.4s). A hundred metres or so inshore at the elbow of the jetty stands the small truncated tower of the now redundant lighthouse. About halfway along this jetty on the eastern side of the entrance is a training wall submerged at MHWS. This has a white beacon with a green top at its outer end (Fl(2)G.5s). Both red and green beacons submerge their white lower sections at MHWS. On the best approach line, these beacons can be lined up as a useful transit to combat the strong cross-set which develops. Before you are close enough in to use this, it pays to find a natural transit of your own in order to avoid being set unduly. The current runs north from an hour or so before HW for the rest of the time that the sill will let you in, and at times flows particularly hard across the entrance. If you are sailing in and the wind is at all fluky, it would make sense to have your engine turning over.

Entry is not recommended to the stranger in strong onshore winds, particularly on the ebb. It is also worth noting that in a hard sou'wester rough seas have been noted on the 'red' side of the entrance, with easier water on the starboard hand when entering.

Once inside, continue straight along the wall to the pair of lit red and green beacons 900m inside the pier head. At the inner end of the quay is a beacon with a port-hand topmark indicating the beginning of foul ground extending up to 20m from the landward side of the harbour. Before the beacon, the wall is steep-to. After, it is footed with rubble as far as the conspicuous white hotel at the bend of the river. From the lit pair of beacons, swing steadily to starboard until you see the traffic lights for the marina ahead. The sill lies to the right of these and is marked by a flashing red and flashing green beacon. Do not be confused by the berthed yachts on your port hand just before you reach the traffic lights. These are on drying trots and are nothing to do with the marina.

Berthing

Drying berths may be had alongside the quay opposite the green beacon at the outer end of the training wall. These are somewhat exposed in all but the most settled weather. Make sure that you do not secure in the ferry's berth.

Enter the marina and continue to the farthest (easternmost) pontoon. There are alongside berths for 20 or so visitors on its easter side. Raft up if need be. Immediately to port on entry, detached from the main body of marina pontoons, is a 'ponton d'acceuil' which accommodates the lifeboat. Larger vessels or classics may well be invited to lie on this prime berth.

Facilities

Carteret Marina, or the Port des Iles as it is known, is a lovely place. It is spotlessly clean and has excellent toilet and shower facilities underneath the diminutive modern yacht club, to which visitors are cordially invited. Fuel is available inside the locked basin. There is no launderette, but a selection of fine sinks are dedicated for this purpose and one can, after all, hang out the washing from the rigging like mother used to.

Village facilities are close by and are more than adequate, with a selection of restaurants, a modest supermarket and a carefully stocked *cave* used by locals whose young manager is more than happy to deliver wine consignments of reasonable size to your yacht. The Bar du Port beside the diminutive drying dock called the Port des Americains (worth exploring as a possible scrubbing berth at spring tides only) has a sunny terrace in the morning which becomes a shady one in the afternoon heat. It serves draught Guinness.

If you chance to be in town on a Saturday morning, walk up the hill (1½M) to the small town of Barneville, where you will find a major country street market in full swing. The community also has a large supermarket, *poissonerie* and every other victualling facility.

Across the drying stream bed opposite the marina is a series of sand dunes. Scramble over these to find one of the best and least-used sandy beaches in Normandy. Wonderful bathing with views of the sun setting over Jersey.

Passenger ferries to the Channel Islands.

Portbail

Tides

HW −0440 Dover

MHWS	MLWS	MHWN	MLWN
10·9m	1·1m	7·9m	3·9m

Depths

As at neighbouring Carteret, depths are non-existent, with the whole port and its approaches drying to a great height. The entrance is reported to dry about 5m along the best approach. The river outside the 'marina' dries 6m, so there is a respectable amount of water for shoal-draught craft even at neaps. *The Shell Channel Pilot* has seen deep sailing craft of at least 1·8m draught lying against the inside of the harbour wall, but it is generally recommended that only vessels which dry out upright should attempt this because of the possibility of rafting up.

General

Portbail (pronounced 'Por bye') is definitely 'different'. Inside, shelter is fair, but it should not be attempted in strong onshore winds, when wall-to-wall breakers could well be your portion. The village, which is reached by walking across a causeway from the harbour, is unspoilt, and the possibilities for anchoring on the drying sands with the birds for company will appeal to more than a few yachtsmen equipped with suitable vessels. The harbour area has an 'outpost' feel which has a certain attraction.

Approach and entrance

The waters to seaward of Portbail are shoal, but entirely navigable when there is enough tide to contemplate entry. This should be within an hour either side of HW, not only to ensure that you stay afloat, but also to avoid the excesses of flood and ebb, which can readily notch up to 5 knots at springs.

There is a prominent water tower immediately to the north of the entrance which bears very approximately 030° from the fairway buoy, *Portbail*

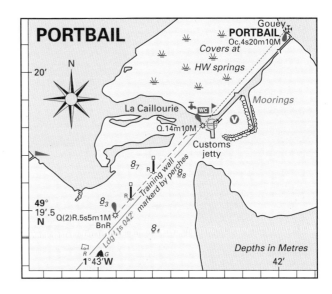

(red and white, unlit). From the buoy, shape for the beacon (Q(2)R.5s5m1M) on the end of the training wall (see plan). Soon you will see the unlit red and green entrance buoys, between which you should steer. The training wall itself covers so that you will probably not see it, but it is marked with a line of poles. Come in a couple of boats' lengths from these, after favouring the green side of the channel for the first cable or so by steering straight for the white leading mark on the foreshore (see below)

Portbail, showing training wall to be left to port

from the green buoy. From the next-to-last pole, steer for the end of the short pier, rounding it to enter. Be careful of the slipway on the end of the jetty, and the ferry pontoon (regular passages to Jersey as tide allows) immediately round the corner.

There are leading lights on 042°, consisting of a front light (Q) on a white pylon with a red top, and a prominent belfry in the town (Oc.4s). If you can discern this transit in the daytime it may prove useful.

Berthing

There is a visitors' pontoon on the inside of the quay wall beyond the ferry pontoon. The bottom here is smooth. The drying 'marina' has 200 berths, 15 of which are for visitors. Moorings here are on buoys. When you pick one up, you will find two forward 'risers' and two aft, one for each bow and quarter; each pair is seized together, leaving just two lines to come aboard, one forward, one aft. Secure accordingly. Maximum LOA is realistically around 9m (30ft). To enter the marina, steer straight for the end of the mole from the jetty head, thus avoiding a muddy bar which forms parallel to the jetty.

There is every possibility of finding a fine place to dry out in privacy up-river, but this is not recommended without prior low water survey, on account of a few isolated rock patches. If you fancy this, stay with the crowd to start with, take a stroll at low water, then move at the next high.

Facilities

Lovely village, after a short, unusual walk, with the regular shops, restaurant, etc. There is fresh water on the jetty, showers, toilets, and a payphone. There is also a bar/bistro within half a cable of the jetty.

The Channel Islands

Alderney - Braye

Tides
HW −0400 Dover

MHWS	MLWS	MHWN	MLWN
6·3m	0·8m	4·7m	2·6m

Depths
Deep water in the approaches. Small-craft moorings are generally laid in 4m or much more. Anchorage in Braye Bay can be anything from 7m if you need it, down to drying berths on the sandy beach.

General
For most yachts, Alderney lies within a 12-hour passage from the Isle of Wight and is no more than an 'overnighter' from the West Country. The island is less than 6 miles square, and has a winter population of around 2,000. Like most islanders, the residents of Alderney are friendly to visiting sailors.

Alderney arrived under British rule as part of the Anglo-Norman package arranged by Duke William. It now exercises a moderate degree of independence on questions of tax on booze and other necessities of life. Licensing hours are dangerously flexible; there is no VAT, and, as the late Captain Coote was swift to point out, no hurry.

There are excellent visitors' moorings and a fine, stable water-taxi service that seems to work all civilised hours, so the 'closing-time shuffle' at the dinghy berth may be avoided by those bent on serious enjoyment of the island's varied facilities.

Braye Harbour is safe in all weathers except strong northeasterlies, but it can become uncomfortable with winds from northwest through northeast. With

Cap de la Hague from the north, a 51m grey tower well clear of the land. It marks the eastern side of the Alderney Race

Alderney lighthouse at the western end of the Race, seen from the north

this proviso borne strongly in mind, it is otherwise an all-weather, all-tide refuge.

It is worrying to report that during the last decade of the second millennium, the future of the great Braye breakwater has fallen into doubt. One option proposed by the board in Guernsey that is responsible involves the construction of a new breakwater inside the big old one, allowing the outer part of the original works to decay. This would reduce the real harbour size by two thirds, with obvious knock-ons for visitors. The residents are resisting the move robustly. The rest of us must hope for the best.

Landfall approach

Alderney is all about the tidal stream. It sits off one of the most tide-swept of all headlands, and the race between this and the island is of international notoriety, achieving streams of over 5 knots on the tidal diamonds, but up to 9 knots in real life. *The Shell Channel Pilot* compiler recalls running 14 miles between accurately fixed positions in one memorable hour in a 32ft yacht whose log read 6½ miles for the hour's run. Nor was the spinner foul.

We checked.

Slack water is half an hour before HW Dover. The tide then runs southwest for 5½ hours. It switches northeast 6 hours before the next HW Dover and doesn't slacken a lot until 5 hours later.

This intelligence is crucial to anyone coming from Cherbourg because if they are not careful they will end up in Guernsey. Arriving from the south, the most careful planning is also needed. Nor is the Swinge between Burhou and the north coast of Alderney, to be taken lightly. It is full of overfalls and beset with rocks, but can still be managed. Check the tidal stream atlas for the full story.

Making landfall from the northwest, you should arrive at an early decision – before reaching the Casquets ('whiter than white' lighthouse and associated buildings Fl(5)30s37m24M) – about whether to go for the direct approach north of Burhou or, if the tide is being awkward, to leave Alderney to port and approach south-about. It is only 3 miles more and can save a great deal of time, due to the west-running eddy along the top of the island on much of the east-going stream.

From the southwest (Guernsey way) in the last hour before the Race turns foul, you may be served

Braye Harbour

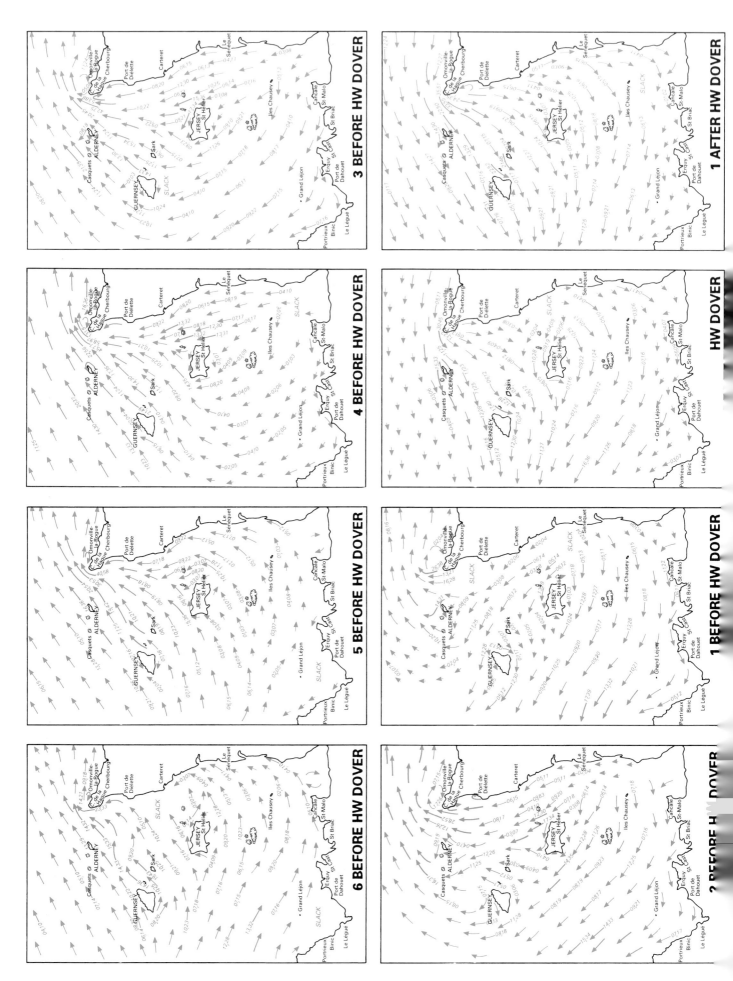

3 BEFORE HW DOVER

1 AFTER HW DOVER

4 BEFORE HW DOVER

HW DOVER

5 BEFORE HW DOVER

1 BEFORE HW DOVER

6 BEFORE HW DOVER

2 BEFORE HW DOVER

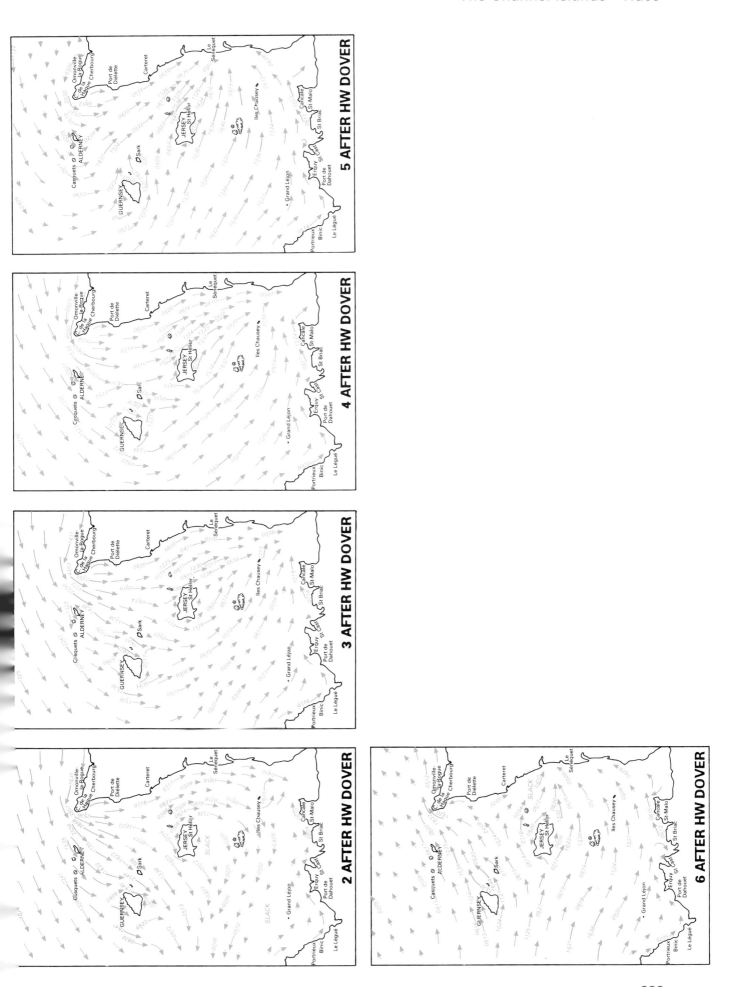

5 AFTER HW DOVER

4 AFTER HW DOVER

3 AFTER HW DOVER

2 AFTER HW DOVER

6 AFTER HW DOVER

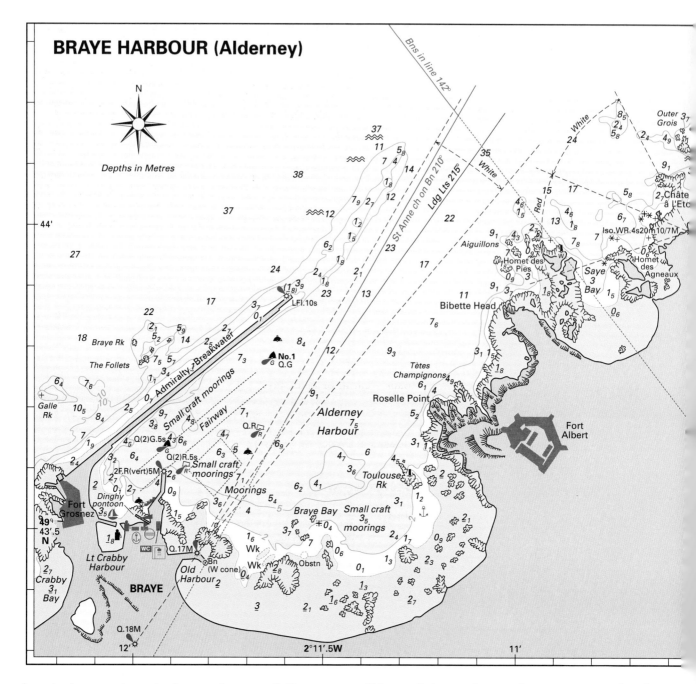

BRAYE HARBOUR (Alderney)

by nipping up through the rough seas of Ortac Channel between Burhou and the Casquets to arrive from the north. Even if you end up having a hard time, it will be better than the alternative.

It is worth noting that the Alderney radiobeacon (*ALD* 383kHz 30M) is still in operation (1999). If you are using Decca or GPS and are disinclined to believe the excesses of your cross-track error, think again.

Lights

Before you see the grey tower of Cap de la Hague lighthouse (Fl.5s48m23M), you will raise the square buildings of the nuclear power station on the high ground behind it. Coming from the Solent at night, the loom of this monster may be your first indication that there is life to the south.

Alderney light stands near the eastern extremity of the island. It is a round white tower with a black band, 37m high in all (Fl(4)15s28M).

Half a mile west of this big light is Château à l'Etoc light, a white column showing Iso.WR.4s. The white sector (111° to 151°) clears the outer edge of the submerged Braye breakwater; this clearance is underlined by lining the light up with the main lighthouse, also on 111°.

Alderney main lighthouse has a fog signal (Horn 30s), as does Casquets (Horn(2)60s).

The breakwater end now has a LFl.10s light.

Approach to Braye Harbour

In the daylight, line up St Anne's Church (squat steeple, not to be confused with a water tower to its right) with a white pyramid on the end of the old

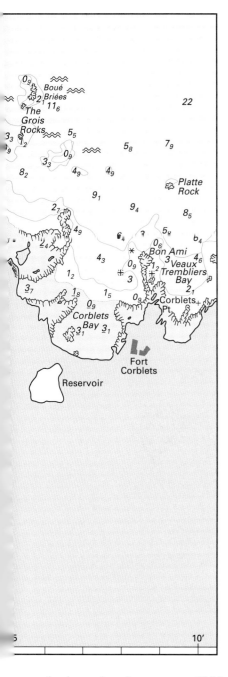

of the big breakwater. Note the green buoy (Q.G) – leave to starboard – inside the breakwater head, and the Q.R red buoy well up the harbour. Leave this well to port. Pick up a vacant mooring, or raft up in fair weather. Fly a yellow 'Q' flag wherever you have come from. The harbourmaster will visit you shortly. The formalities are simple, but must be observed. The harbourmaster's representative will do the whole job for you in a very pleasant manner indeed.

Do not attempt to tie up on the jetties, which are commercial. You may anchor anywhere out of the fairway and clear of the moorings, but this is getting more difficult as moorings proliferate. To the east of the fairway is the favourite place for large craft (16m is the largest possible craft for the moorings, and this could be pushing your luck). Shoal-draught cruisers have been seen happily dried out on the beach, but if you are a stranger you should survey your site first. There are a number of isolated rocks.

Facilities

Fresh water, showers and toilets near the harbour office and the yacht club. Diesel and chandlery from Mainbrayce in Crabby Harbour (see plan). Draught 2m ±3 hours HW. Call on VHF Ch 80 first). *Calor Gas* reported in Braye Street. There is a dinghy pontoon near the entrance to Crabby Harbour, and a small supermarket nearby; also the famous Diver's pub, where you can meet your mates, and The First and Last Restaurant, justly well known in Channel waters. Also at Braye are excellent fish and chips, round the back – eat in or takeaway.

St Anne is a charming community with all small-town facilities. It is well worth the modest climb. The island is great for walks, full of reminders of the Nazi occupation almost 60 years ago, some of which housed activities that may be best forgotten.

Guernsey

Tides

HW −0449 Dover

MHWS	MLWS	MHWN	MLWN
9·0m	1·0m	6·7m	3·5m

Depths

Various – see below, and see plans.

General

Guernsey is the seat of government of the Bailiwick of Guernsey, which includes Alderney, Jethou, Herm and Sark. 55,000 make up its permanent population, which number is added to by almost half a million visitors annually, attracted by the romance of island life, the beaches, the hotels and the duty-free shopping.

There is usually room in St Peter Port, where you berth in the town centre, either on moorings or in a marina. The harbour is well sheltered, though it may become lively in an easterly. It is deep, well lit and approachable at all states of tide, day or night. By catching the Race of Alderney, it seems surprisingly close to the Needles, and it is actually only 65 miles from Weymouth.

The moorings are quiet in most weather conditions. Overspill is into Havelet Bay, where one can anchor in the absence of anywhere better. Safe you may be in westerlies, but life can be rough in here, with rolling as your reward 3 hours either side of high water in any but the calmest of conditions, and a poor time of it getting ashore. It is clearly a non-starter with winds from the east, so you should then go elsewhere – the Grande Grève or Havre Gosselin, in Sark, offer joyous diversion if things are not too boisterous. Beaucette Marina at the north end of Guernsey is a further possibility.

Above all, St Peter Port is a fun place to be.

harbour breakwater on 210°. This clears all the rocks, also the wretched unmarked hazard of the outer breakwater debris. If you can't make out the marks, steer for the middle of the entrance, but be aware that the shoal off the breakwater extends 3 cables, has only 1·2m of water in places, and causes overfalls.

After dark, the leading transit is the Q.17M light on the old harbour breakwater with the Q.18M light behind it, on 215°. The lights show in a fairly narrow sector.

Berthing

There are well organised visitors' moorings all the way along the inside

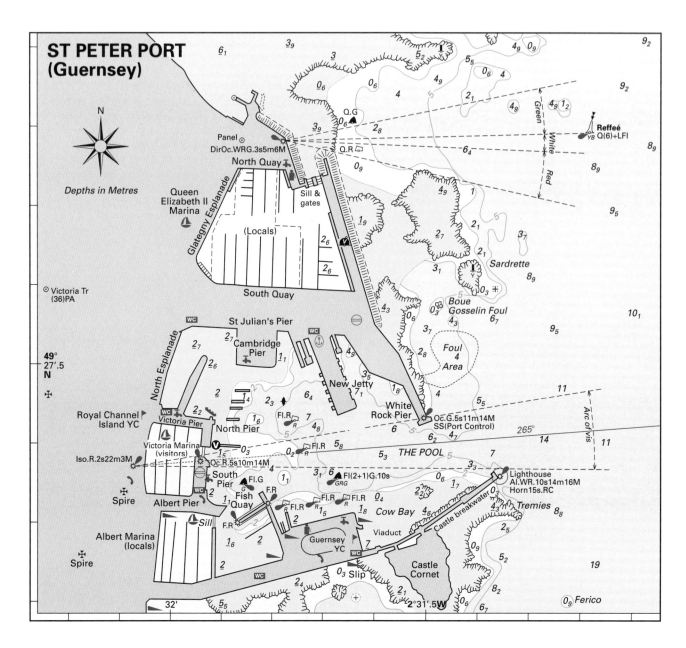

Approach

The island has the appearance of a flat plateau. With the sun in the right direction you may well see its light flashing off the 'Guernsey Tom' greenhouses before you ever see the beaches. There is a radiobeacon (*GRB* on 361kHz) of 30M range situated 1 mile northeast of the southwest corner of the island. There is also an interesting radio device on St Peter Port breakwater. This radiobeacon (*GY* 304·5kHz 10M) works conventionally, but the long dash for homing in starts at exactly the same moment as the St Peter Port fog signal sounds (every 15s). Count the time in seconds between them, multiply by 0·18, and you have your distance off in miles. There is truly no end to the wonderful works of man.

From the Race of Alderney, the Little Russel Channel is the obvious and favourite route in. Avoid the Banc de la Schôle en route; it is very shoal indeed and can kick up a wicked sea. Tidal streams in the channel

itself run largely 'fore and aft', but cross-sets can be expected to the north. The tide starts ebbing to the southwest 1½ hours before HW Dover. 6 hours later it reverses.

In the dark, your first mark will be Platte Fougère (Fl.WR.10s16M). This is a 15m black and white horizontally striped tower. Its red sector covers rocks to the northwest, and it features a racon call sign *P*. On your port bow you should see Tautenay beacon tower, a vertically striped black and white varde (Q(3)WR.6s) whose red sector (215°–050°) covers various nasties to the northeast. In daylight, if you are approaching from the northwest, keep the south point of Sark open eastwards of the north end of Herm. This clears everything.

The steel lattice tower of Roustel, 8m high (Q.7M), stands in mid-channel and can safely be left to either side. If you line it up with the 19m-high flat fort on Brehon (Iso.4s9M) on 198° you have an

Above St Peter Port viewed from seaward. Castle Cornet sheltering Havelet Bay on the left. Victoria Marina centre right

Below St Peter Port from north. Queen Elizabeth II Marina is in the foreground. Havelet Bay beyond the long wall

Left Platte Fougère 25m-high white octagonal light-tower with black band to be left to starboard entering Little Russel, 1½ miles northeast of Beaucette. It has a WR.10s light and horn every 45s in fog. Red sector guards rocks to NW

Middle Brehon Fort one mile SW of *Roustel* beacon, due west of Herm
Right Les Hanois lighthouse at SW corner of island, 36m grey tower with helipad. View from WSW with Fort Saumerez beyond (left). Many off-lying dangers lurk to seaward of the lighthouse

excellent safe line in through the dangers as far as Roustel.

Alternatively, line Brehon up with the lighthouse on St Martin's Point, south of St Peter Port, on 208°.

Brehon is left to port, and if on the latter transit you must do this in plenty of time, because rocks lurk nearly 2 cables to the west of it. Just before you reach Roustel (leave to starboard on this line) you will see the prominent Belvedere House, at 57m elevation south of the town, line up with a white patch on the east end of Castle Cornet, at the harbour entrance. Go for the transit on 223°, and follow it until the entrance opens. If you are coming in leaving Roustel to port, simply head for Castle Cornet, having lined a part of it up with some prominent background feature of your own choosing. The home-made transit will serve you well.

All routes leave La Platte (NOT to be confused with Platte Fougère) to starboard. It is a 6-metre green varde (Fl.WR.3s7/5M) standing 8 cables east-northeast of St Sampson.

By night, in decent visibility, you simply cannot miss the leading lights. These excellent illuminations are on 220°, clear all dangers, and are: rear – Oc.10s61m14M – small tower with orange stripes, close by Belvedere House, and front – Al.WR.10s14m16M. By coincidence, these lights, whose structures can be plainly seen in daylight, are almost in transit with two radio masts displaying red lights.

The north breakwater head shows an Oc.G.5s light visible for 14 miles, and the south breakwater is, of course, the front leading light (see above).

Do not be alarmed by looking at the chart of the Little Russel. It is wider than you might imagine, and in decent visibility is easy enough to follow.

The Big Russel channel, between Herm and Sark, is a safer option if visibility is in doubt. If the weather is or seems likely to become foggy, do not go to Guernsey until things improve. It is not an easy place to enter in fog. Should you opt for the Big Russel, head in towards the big light on Sark (Fl(4)WR.15s6M) until you can safely shape across to the lit south cardinal *Lower Heads*, or St Martin's Point. Round *Lower Heads* and shape across to the harbour.

From the south there is no problem. Leave St Martin's Point to port and shape up for the Castle Cornet.

From the northwest, if the tide serves, there is much to be said for leaving the awesome Les Hanois light (Fl(2)13s33m20M) to port and approaching south-about. Les Hanois needs a wide berth, not only because of the rocks to seaward of it, but also because it is one of the good old Channel's rougher corners. The lighthouse has a conspicuous heli-pad on top.

Note that the tide along the south coast shows a strong preference for running east-west.

Berthing in St Peter Port

You will probably be met by a harbour patrol launch and told where to moor. The choice is mooring to a buoy or a pontoon, with rafting up, or the pleasant and reasonably priced Victoria Marina, which has a busy waiting pontoon. You may well have to wait for the marina. The sill dries 4·18m, giving about a metre over it at half-tide. The entrance shows a tide gauge. Visits are limited to 14 days.

If you are not met in St Peter Port, move slowly in via the clearly buoyed channel, swinging round to starboard to where you see visiting yachts moored. If you cut the corner, you may well hit the mud.

Alternatively, for stays of more than 4 days or so, you can ask to be admitted to Queen Elizabeth II Marina (see plan), once called the North Beach Marina. This is a snug berth, though a slightly longer walk to town, but this is little hardship for a thirsty sailor. Depths are 4·5m just inside the sill and no less than 2m anywhere else. Approach on 270° from close to the south cardinal lit *Reffée* buoy, in the white sector of the DirOc.WRG.3s5m6M light. If the light goes green, nudge to port. If red, vice versa.

By day, line up a yellow triangular board in front with an orange rectangular board to the rear.

Facilities in St Peter Port

Simply everything you could want, except possibly major repairs. These are undertaken at St Sampson 'next door'. Central Guernsey is equally good news for the family yacht or the 'rugby club trip', as either will be superbly catered for in civilised but relaxed surroundings. The only sadness is that whereas in the bad old days *The Shell Channel Pilot* used to call in at Guernsey to stock up with the best pullovers in the world at knockdown prices on the market, visitors must now pay the same as mainland customers. Never mind. You can save the difference by replenishing your essential rations at the best prices in the English-speaking world, and if your crew are too lazy to launch the dinghy to get ashore from the pontoons, call the water taxi on Ch 10.

Diesel and petrol on the south wall of the pool. You won't need to rouse out your long lines as there is a pontoon to hang onto and super-long fuel hoses.

Showers and loos are better on the south side of the marina. Big chandlery at the fuel dock and on the quay.

Food is excellent in the market – fresh fish, meats, with lovely veg and cheese. No handy full-scale

Beaucette Yacht Marina

supermarket, but Marks and Spencer on the front has a food store.

Beaucette Marina

This flooded quarry at the northeast end of the island is now run by Premier Marinas, who handle Falmouth Marina and Port Solent. The dynamited cut into the old workings gives good shelter for 200 boats. Be wary of the entrance in strong onshore winds however, when it is not recommended to strangers. Some surge can run inside the harbour with stiff weather blowing in.

Join the approach channel about halfway between Platte Fougère and Roustel (see above, under 'Little Russel'). The entrance is not easy for the first-timer to identify, but it lies about 2 cables south of the more conspicuous Fort Doyle. Call in from here on Ch 80 or 37.

The channel starts to the south of the south cardinal beacon *Petite Canupe*. This can be hard to spot in daylight with its tiny topmarks and legend 'PC'. Look instead for the *Beaucette Channel* fairway buoy (vert RW stripes), then four pairs of substantial red and green channel markers. Leading marks are set up to assist. By day, these are: front mark – red arrow on white ground just to the north side of the entrance; rear mark – white arrow on red ground set up on the white club house on a small hill immediately behind the marina. If in doubt about identification, this building also sports a fine windsock. By night, both marks are vertical red lights made up from screened neon strips.

The rocks on either side of the entrance are painted white. A jink to port is recommended here to keep clear of rocks marked by a south cardinal beacon. Immediately inside is a breakwater of old tractor tyres which is left to starboard, after which you are well and truly 'in'. Don't even ask about the depth. There is at least 18m! At night, the entrance is floodlit, which does much to defuse what might otherwise be a stressful arrival for strangers in lively weather, as the gap you must negotiate is exceedingly narrow, though readily passable for all but the largest yachts. Check in with the harbour office if you have not been met on arrival.

The sill dries 2·4m, and a tide gauge reads out the present depth over it. Recommended entry is ±3hrs HW, but there will be 1·9m on the sill at ±2hrs LW neaps. On springs you will have to wait a little longer. Consult the tide gauge if in any doubt and make allowance for any surge which may be running.

Eight yellow waiting moorings have been laid just north of the entrance, and in some conditions these can be very useful.

There are at least 50 visitors' berths and harbour staff who are keen to fit you in.

The harbour listens on VHF Ch 80. The harbourmaster is on ☎ 01481 45000.

Facilities include fresh water and power on the pontoons, diesel, showers, toilets, provisions, *Gas* and *Gaz*, some chandlery and a floating launderette.

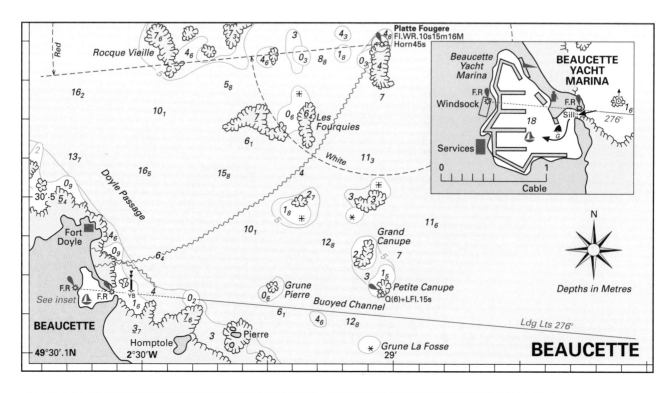

Beaucette Yacht Harbour. Entrance only 8m wide. Leading marks: orange board above tide gauge in line with flagpole and windsock at right-hand end of clubhouse

Petite Canoupe south cardinal beacon outside Beaucette Yacht Harbour

Custom clearance can be arranged from here, as can car or bicycle hire (ask at office). There is a 16-ton boat hoist and a 12-ton crane. The harbour also has one of the most famous restaurants in an island celebrated for its cuisine. St Peter Port and the airport are a long taxi ride, but the marina has a community of its own, and neighbouring L'Ancresse Bay is generally agreed to be the finest beach on the island – perfect for family bathing.

St Sampson

A commercial harbour which dries out beyond its entrance. Major repairs can be undertaken here. From a point equidistant between Platte and Brehon, steer 286° on the leading marks of the post on the south pier head (F.R.5M) and the 12m-high clock tower (F.G) on the south side, near the inner harbour entrance.

Communications

By air or sea to other Channel Islands or French destinations. Fast ferry to Weymouth, Poole, Jersey and St Malo.

Jersey

Tides

HW −0455 Dover

MHWS	MLWS	MHWN	MLWN
11·1m	1·3m	8·1m	4·1m

Depths (St Helier)

Deep-water approaches, then 2·7m on the leading line in the small road and 2·2m in the New Harbour. The marina sill dries 3·5m and there is 2·1–2·4m inside. La Collette basin is dredged to 1·8m.

General

Jersey is the largest Channel Island, at 10 miles by 5½. Its population of 80,000 copes with 800,000 visitors per annum. Money is the island's other industry, with *The Financial Times* a bestseller, but the island is also filled with history, from William of Normandy's time to the Nazi occupation of 1940–45.

Jersey is a mere 12 miles west of the Cherbourg peninsula, and 36 from St Malo, but until the deep-water marina was opened in the heart of St Helier it was little favoured by visiting yachts – hardly surprising, with a 10m range of tide and no deep-water harbour available in those days.

Approach to St Helier

Access to the main marina is usually around half-tide for most yachts, and there is a waiting pontoon in 2·2m for those who would cross the sill. La Collette Yacht Basin has 3·1m at MLWS.

From the north, round Point Corbière (Iso.WR.10s36m18/16M), noting that the tide runs south from 3 hours after HW Dover (−4½ hours HW St Helier) and runs strongly eastward along the south coast until 5 hours before HW Dover, which is HW St Helier. This benefit enables the determined mariner to make St Helier in one tide from the Race of Alderney.

Corbière is a nasty corner, like its equivalent in Guernsey, Les Hanois. Give its 19m white stone tower (36m up) a wide berth. Its foghorn sounds Morse C every 60 seconds and it has a 20M radiobeacon *CB* on 295·5kHz with a distance-finding device (see your almanac for details). Its red sector slips you the wink if you are cutting too close to Grosnez Point by night, or are taking a flier with the buoyed channel past St Brelade's Bay.

The Pierres de Lecq are cleared at night by staying out of the red sector of Grosnez light (Fl(2)WR.15s50m19/17M). By day, if you keep Point Corbière open of Grosnez you are well to the west of danger. *Desormes*, a lit west cardinal buoy 4M north-northwest of Grosnez Point, will also be helpful.

After rounding Corbière, run parallel to the shore, about half a mile off, for 3 miles, passing close to seaward of the black and white hooped tower on Noirmont Point at 18m elevation (Fl(4)12s13M). To starboard you will see the lit north cardinal buoy,

La Corbière lighthouse off the southwest corner of Jersey seen from the north. Note the causeway linking the shore Noirmont Point from the west

Les Fours, off the Grand Four shoal. Do not confuse this with the lit north cardinal *Passage Rock* buoy marking the entrance to the western passage you are now joining. You will leave this buoy well to starboard. You can now alter onto 082°, leaving an unlit red, then a lit red buoy (Fl(2)R.6s) to port, and a green buoy (Fl.G.3s) to starboard. You are now on the first leading line in, lit by front Oc.G.5s11M

Coming off the 'red-and-green transit', rounding into the inner harbour. Port Control Tower centre right. Entrance to La Collette obscured by round 'buffer' behind the dory. Yacht club centre left.

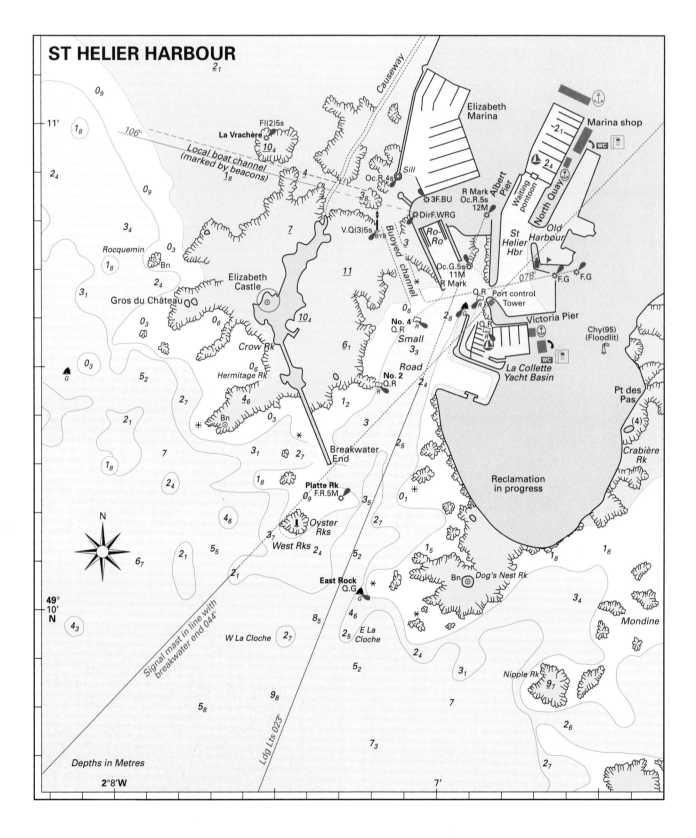

ST HELIER HARBOUR

and rear Oc.R.5s12M. By day, you should see the white pillar and globe on Dogs Nest Rocks; line it up with the red vertical board on a white tower 20m high a mile or more beyond it. This back marker is notoriously difficult to identify, Don't worry if you fail to do so, just plug on for the very conspicuous Dog's Nest. You'll soon spot the lit green buoy

(Q.G.) marking East Rock 2 cables your side of it. This is also on the transit and can conveniently be used to check your drift.

Just before this buoy, alter to port onto 023°, which is the so-called 'red+green' transit up the final 7 cables to the entrance. The rear leading light is Oc.R.5s12M on a red structure and the front one is

St Helier Harbour

Entrance to Old Harbour at high water

Left Le Grève d'Azette light on the waterfront one mile southeast of St Helier. Vertical orange board on pylon. By day it is the rear mark for 082° transit with *Dogs Nest* beacon. By night it is the front light on the same transit with Mt Ube light one mile ENE

Jersey. St Helier Harbour. Approaching the open lock of St Helier Marina. Note traffic lights and depth gauge on the starboard hand at entrance.

Oc.G.5s11M on a white daymark. You will pass the *Platte Rock* (F.R.5M) red lattice beacon on your port hand after first leaving the *Oyster Rocks* red and white beacon also well to port. Swing to starboard off the transit when two F.G leading lights (or the harbour entrance in daylight) come on, bearing 078°. Then either come to starboard again for La Collette or enter the New Harbour on your port side and make up for the sill or the waiting pontoon.

From southwest-about the Minquiers, head for *Passage Rock* lit north cardinal buoy off St Brelade's Bay. The mark is 2 miles from Corbière light on a bearing of 125°. Leave it to starboard and continue as for the western passage described above. Alternatively, steer for the Demie de Pas yellow and black light tower (Mo(D)WR.12s14/10M Horn(3)60s).

Keep watching for the 'red+green' transit described above. You will come onto it 1½ miles short of Demie de Pas. When the lights or the daymarks come on, turn up them and you are in the guinea seats. Don't wander though; there are rocks to starboard. Note that this entry crosses a 1·2m patch (LAT).

From the east, or east-about the Minquiers, steer to leave Demie de Pas (above) two or three cables to starboard and make a track of 314° towards a black and white mark in St Aubin Bay. Leave the red can buoy *Hinguette* (Fl(4)R) to port, and keep going on 314° until you come onto the 'red+green' transit mentioned above.

Whichever pass you are using, remember the tide – up to 3½ knots at springs, 1½ knots at neaps. The harbour listens on VHF Ch 14, and appreciates a call. Also, keep an eye open for the fast, wave-piercing ferries which can appear as if from nowhere, particularly astern. If one passes close by you, the wash can be seriously uncomfortable, so hang onto your tea.

Berthing in St Helier
On arrival in St Helier, you have a choice of either La Collette yacht basin with all-tide access, or locking into the St Helier Marina over a half-tide sill. It may be that one will be full and you will be sent to the other, but generally, it is up to you. Don't assume that because La Collette is always available it is necessarily the best option. It may suit you, but many prefer St Helier Marina in the middle of town.

La Collette Yacht Basin Leave the dolphin to starboard and both red buoys to port, then make for either the waiting pontoon on your starboard bow or the permanent berths to port.

Traffic lights
Green – enter
Red – leave
Red and green – don't do either
Q.Y – craft under power of <25m may proceed against the signals

Find a berth, usually on F or G pontoons, the furthest ones from the entrance. Larger yachts than 12·5m LOA or 2m draught may be accommodated nearer the entrance on A. Harbour office ☎ 01534 885588, *Fax* 885599 (harbourmaster) or 885509 (marina). La Collette ☎ 885529. Most users of La Collette are waiting for a place/water to enter the new marina.

Facilities include toilets and fresh water. Diesel is near the yacht club by the South Pier elbow, as is *Calor Gas* exchange. La Collette is a hike from town.

St Helier Marina has a gate over the sill which closes with the tide, leaving only 0·8m of water. A Fl.R light means it is about to close. A F.R means it is closed. Take no chances with the flashing red unless you have no option, for reasons of manoeuvring commitment. There is a comfortable waiting pontoon if you don't make it.

The visitors' berths in this first-class establishment are clearly marked, but in any case you will probably be directed to a suitable spot by one of the friendly staff. This fine marina has every facility, including laundry. Visit the yacht club and don't miss the Maritime Museum right on the dock. It is well worth a call for adults, but if you have children and it's raining, you'll never have better value than to let them loose on the interactive exhibits inside. All facilities you could want are here.

The new Elizabeth Marina with its buoyed channel east of Elizabeth Castle is not available to visitors unless you want to stay for several weeks, in which case you may be sent there by the harbourmaster. If so, it is a good, safe option for leaving your boat. From the casual caller's point of view, the best thing about the Elizabeth Marina is that many local boats have left the St Helier Marina to go there. As a result, the overcrowding that was once a feature of St Helier is a thing of the past. The

Gorey Harbour

harbourmaster says he will get you in somehow, no matter what.

St Catherine This rather open deep-water harbour lies at the northeast corner of the island. It is wide open between east and south-southeast, and you must anchor off. Ashore, facilities are thin on the ground. Approach from due east or a little north of it. Note that the only light in the vicinity is the Fl.1·5s18m13M on the end of the breakwater. Tuck in round this and anchor in 3·5m about a cable offshore. Be aware of Pillon Rock (0·9m), just under 2 cables east-northeast of the light.

Gorey lies 1½ miles south of St Catherine. It dries 4·9m, and has little room, but is very pretty as it sits under the floodlit castle of Mont Orgueil. There is plenty in the way of hostelries to entertain you ashore as your yacht dries out alongside the pier, if room, otherwise on visitor's moorings in the harbour entrance (dry an hour or so either side of LW). There are further visitors' moorings near the beach at the head of the harbour accessible at HW±1 or so.

Whichever your direction of approach, keep half a mile to seaward until you find the leading marks on 298°. These are the light tower on the end of the pier (Oc.RG.5s) 'on' with Gorey church steeple (Oc.R.5s). Don't even think of entering at night as a stranger. Passage from St Helier is via Violet Channel, which could well be a test for 'extra-yachtmasters'. Find *Canger Rock* lit west cardinal buoy 2¾ miles south-southwest of the Martello tower on La Rocque Point (and 'rock' is the word for it!), leave the buoy close to starboard and make good 075° to the red and white safe water mark (LFl.10s) two miles further on. Now alter to 010°, and be sure you pick up the 332° leading line of Verclut Point at the inshore end of St Catherine's breakwater 'on' with the turret on Coupe Point, the right-hand edge of the land half a mile beyond it. Stay on this 332° transit with the turret just open of Verclut Point for about 3 miles made good until you pick up the entry transit mentioned above.

On the way, you will leave to port *Le Giffard* unlit buoy.

St Aubin is the very attractive home of the Royal Channel Islands Yacht Club, and it also dries out – to half a mile from the entrance. The harbour is packed out, so do not just pitch up. If you feel you must go for it, wait for half-tide plus, then make good a course of north-northwest from *Diamond Rock* red buoy (Fl(2)R.6s) for something in the order of 1 mile. You should now pick up small channel buoys marking the way in. Dry out alongside the North Quay. The yacht club is very friendly.

Iles Chausey

Tides

HW −0500 Dover

MHWS	MLWS	MHWN	MLWN
12·9m	1·9m	9·8m	4·9m

Depths

Drying approaches from the north, and shoal water (0·3m) in the south part of the approach. It is, however, possible to lie afloat in the anchorage at all states of the tide in 2m or more (LAT). In fact, the phenomenal tidal ranges mean that it is possible to enter and leave the anchorage by the southern route an hour or two either side of LW on all but the biggest tides. This makes the islands even more attractive when planning a trip to one of the many lock-in harbours which surround them.

General

Chausey is an impressive pile of rocks and reefs covering 12 square miles. Largely covered at HW, they poke out of the sea at LW springs in a sort of moonscape that really must be seen by any mariner with an adventurous spirit. Spectacularly beautiful at LW in fair weather, the anchorage can be uncomfortable and sometimes alarming in heavy going, particularly if the wind hooks round into the southeast and blows in against the south-going spring tide. Should this happen, you may have no option but to clear out, so watch the sky and the barometer.

Grand Ile is inhabited by around 100 souls who 'do a spot of fishing' and milk the tourist trade from Granville. As a result, the islands and the anchorage can be crowded at weekends in season. Otherwise they are a pure delight.

Cows once did well here, and were said to graze placidly around the keels of grounded yachts at LW. Sadly, this colourful diversion was no longer present at the compiler's most recent visit, but the house of Marin Marie, sailor, artist, dreamer and author of the classic *Wind aloft, Wind alow* still exists by the pool, now augmented by a simple memorial to another Breton hero, 'Eric Tabarly, lost at sea'.

All the business of the island is transacted at its southeast end, which is also proximate to the moorings and anchorage. The charts make the place look horrendous, but with care and modest adherence to the tide tables the two main roads to the anchorage are simple enough.

Approach

If coming from the north for the first time, leave the lit east cardinal *Northeast Minquiers* to starboard and shape a course across the strong streams to pass well clear of the western rocks of the Iles Chausey. The *Cancalaise* south cardinal beacon near the southwest corner is your only mark. When this bears 110° it is safe to alter to leave it to port by at least a cable to be sure of clearing a rock (dries 1m) west-southwest of it. A track of 095° until the square 19m Pointe de la Tour lighthouse bears 035° will clear all further dangers, after which you can track in towards the

Iles Chausey. Pointe de la Tour lighthouse as seen from the south. Note east cardinal beacons and *vedette* moorings.

Iles Chausey. Looking south from the moorings with La Crabière on the left opposite the north cardinal. Note *vedette* moorings.

three east cardinal perches, all to be left to port, at the corner of the island. The first of these is 1½ cables south-southwest of the light. Bear in mind that you will cross a 2·3m shoal. If this is a problem, first open *La Crabière*, a lit tripod beacon in south cardinal livery but lacking a topmark (Oc.WRG). If you bring it 'on' with the black and white tower on *L'Enseigne* at 332°, you have a transit good for all states of tide, except that just past the green buoy in the entrance a shoal approaches its line from west. Stay a touch to the 'right' of the transit, therefore, until you pass the *Crabière* beacon to starboard and enter the deep-water pool, with depths from 3–5m.

If approaching from south or southwest, join this approach plan in the vicinity of a point south of Pointe de la Tour.

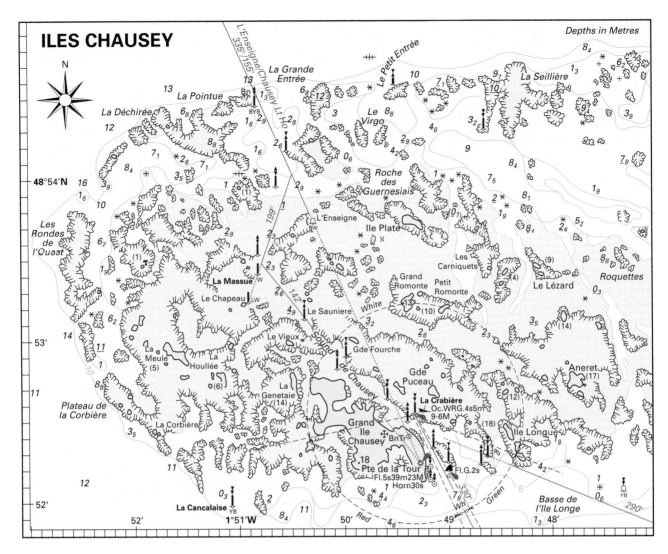

ILES CHAUSEY

Depths in Metres

The tide runs southwest at up to 3½ knots past the west end of Chausey from HW Dover −2½ hours, turning northwest 5 hours later. Close north or south of the islands the tide runs east from 2½ hours after HW Dover for 7 hours, then it turns west for 5. Within the anchorage the stream flows northwest at under 3 knots for 9 hours, then southerly for 3½ hours at most.

The Northwest Channel

This is best found for the first time starting from the moorings, and is therefore given here 'outward bound': note that the channel dries over 4m, and make the necessary calculations.

Leave the anchorage on 310° and proceed between the pair of east and west cardinal beacons a cable or so northeast of the north end of Grand Ile. From here, head 325° for 9 cables, with the east cardinal *Grunes de la Massue* beacon fine on your starboard bow and its white chimney beacon on your port bow, passing a west cardinal beacon 50m to starboard on the way. You will also notice another white chimney beacon, *Le Chapeau*, about 2½ cables to port.

Approaching *Grunes de la Massue*, swing to starboard onto 018° to bring the white beacon into

transit with its fellow on *Le Chapeau*. This will leave the east cardinal beacon to port. 3 or 4 cables after the course change you will have the black and white daymark of *L'Enseigne* abeam to starboard. Keep on your transit until this lines up with the lighthouse tower on Pointe de la Tour. Now swing to port and sail clear out on this transit, heading 335°. You will pass a west cardinal beacon to starboard and an east to port. Thereafter, you are in deep water and can break open the drinks locker.

Berthing and facilities

Yacht Club Granville has some moorings in the pool. Tie up fore-and-aft on trots. Raft up if need be, but *note the depth*. The vedettes do not usually stay overnight, so their buoy may be free. Half a cable to seaward of the S cardinal beacon immediately NW of *La Crabière* is a customs mooring which is clean, tidy and often unused. This represents a good option, and French yachts certainly lie to it overnight, although they are doubtless ready to leave should the cutter arrive unexpectedly. Use a mooring if possible but do not be afraid to anchor. The available water can be challengingly tight at springs, but at mean tides there is enough room for a 40-footer to lie to a well-dug-in hook on a shortish scope between the south cardinal beacon mentioned above and the rocks on the island side of the channel. At neaps this would be an easy berth. There is room elsewhere, so sound around and make a choice north of the jetties. Be careful if you arrive at HW, as the vedette jetty NE of the lighthouse may well be under water. It is marked by two east cardinal beacons whose message is to be taken seriously. Do not attempt to lie alongside the jetty or the slipway, where you will not be welcome, and don't forget an extra-long dinghy painter. The spring range is 11·3m (37ft)!

Limited provisions from a small store, and a welcoming hotel with a decent restaurant.

Granville

Tides
HW −0510 Dover

MHWS	MLWS	MHWN	MLWN
13·0m	1·4m	9·8m	4·6m

Depths
Approaches dry up to 4·0m from *Le Loup* beacon onwards. The sill into the yacht harbour dries 5·25m and depths inside are maintained at 2·5m on the visitors' berths.

General
Granville is an ancient walled community built on a 50m-high promontory jutting westward from an otherwise straight stretch of coast. Some fishing craft remain, but the port is now noted for its yachting. The great days of the far-ranging 'Bisquine' three-masted luggers have been revived by the town's building of the full-sized replica, *Granvillaise*. Even a modern yacht has only to sail alongside this flying machine for a few minutes before being seen off. What hope can the poor British revenue men have had against smugglers of her calibre when they swept across the channel on moonless nights, loaded with contraband and sailed by characters straight out of *Frenchman's Creek*?

Approach and entrance
The first thing you will see on raising Granville is the 16m grey lighthouse on Pointe du Roc (Fl(4)15s 23M). 1½ cables northwest of it is *La Fourchie* red daymark. Give the point at least 3 cables' clearance, heading southeast to pick up *Le Loup* isolated danger daymark (black/red/black, ⁞ topmark, Fl(2)6s8m11M). This is kept about a cable to your south as you line up the white tower at the seaward end of the Hérel marina breakwater (Fl.R.4s) with a small *château* on the hill with a lawn in front of it on 057°. With sufficient rise of tide, this transit is not critical.

The marina is kept full of water by a sill with a 'gate' in it. The sill dries 6m and the gate dries 5·25m. It does not open, however, until it has 0·65m over it. Thus, at the time of opening a vessel of draught 1·4m can scrape in. Thereafter the tide rises considerably, admitting larger vessels.

The final approach can be a trifle unnerving as you are unsighted from the actual marina entrance until you have rounded the end of its breakwater, where you make a sharp turn in. The illuminated display can be hard to read with the sun wrong, so take care if you are in doubt regarding the sill. '00' means no entry. Its first reading on opening is likely to be in the region of 1·4m. It is strictly forbidden to

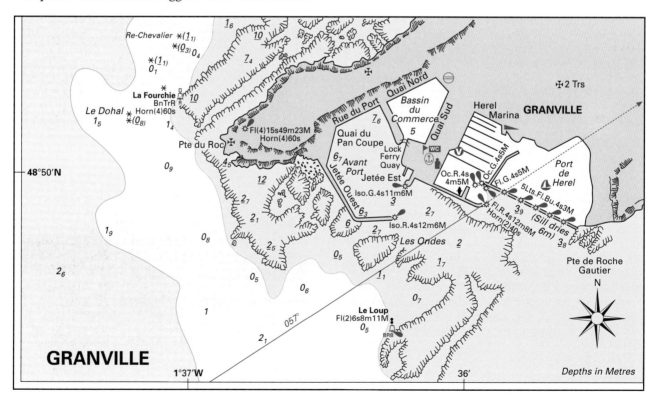

Granville. (A) Red and green poles on entrance to submerged sill

cross the gate with the tide gauge reading zero, no matter what the circumstances.

To arrive at the gate, round the breakwater mentioned above and turn sharply to port. On your starboard hand is a short breakwater (Fl.G.4s), and ahead you will see two poles, one red and one green (Oc.R and Oc.G). They are 4m high at HW springs. Pass between them and shape up for the visitors' berths on F or G pontoons – see plan. The marina has 1,000 berths, including 150 for visitors. If desired, the marina can be called on VHF Ch 9 during office hours (☎ 02 33 50 20 06).

By arrangement with the harbourmaster, very large yachts can lock into the Bassin à Flot, which has 5m depth. The lock opens from 1½ hours before to 1 hour after HW.

Facilities

There is a splendid yacht club which caters for most bodily needs. Fresh water is on the pontoons. Fuel and launderette also in the marina. There is a slipway (dries 7m) in the Avant Port, various mobile cranes, and a grid-iron. Excellent shops. Chandlery, mechanics and boatyard. For additional diversion you can always lighten your wallet in the casino, or take the kids to the aquarium. There are good restaurants in town and ferries to Jersey and the Iles Chausey.

Granville. *La Loup* beacon

Granville. Day transit for entry: 057° with beacon at end of Hérel breakwater in line with *château* between trees with conspicuous lawn

Cancale

Tides

HW −0500 Dover

MHWS	MLWS	MHWN	MLWN
13·3m	2·0m	10·3m	5·1m

Depths

Dries extensively.

General

Cancale is famous for its oysters and, amongst sailors, for its three-masted luggers. The *Cancalaise* berths here, drying out tide by tide, so afficionados of vessels of quality might feel inclined to make a pilgrimage to visit her, particularly if HW is around lunch time. They will then be able to anchor off, or tie up on the Môle (from HW±2 hours), run ashore, and enjoy the benefits of the lovely restaurants and oyster bars on the seafront. With luck, the great lugger herself will be dipping to her mooring, itching to set to sea and beat up a few British cutters.

Afloat moorings owned by the Hotel Continental (good meals reported) can be found north of the town, but the tide runs hard, so getting ashore may prove problematic. Better to approach the shelter of the conspicuous Môle de la Fenêtre, sound in, then either anchor or tie up. Once round the Ile des Rimains with its old fort, giving it a half-mile's clearance, you can swing steadily to starboard and stand in towards the pier head – distance about 1½ miles. There are no further notable obstructions to your timely arrival.

Overnight stays are not recommended except in the finest weather with no hint of east anywhere to be seen in the wind. In such circumstances, drying out would be perfectly possible, either on legs, perhaps on the wall, or on bilge keels.

There are no facilities aimed at the cruising yacht, but if you want to buy oysters this is the place. You will never find them fresher.

Cancale

St-Malo/St-Servan

Tides
HW −0506 Dover

MHWS	MLWS	MHWN	MLWN
12·25m	1·5m	9·25m	4·4m

Depths
Deep-water approaches in the main channel. Bas-Sablons has 3m minimum depth on visitors' berths inside a sill which dries 2m. Port Vauban (main town) locks in to 7m depths; this marina is approached via a channel dredged to 4m (LAT).

General
Dinard and St-Malo shelter behind a chain of rocky shoals and outcrops lying up to 3 miles offshore. The ports could not be more different. Dinard has all the opulence of a bygone age, when yachts used to roll their masts out at anchor as their owners played the tables.

St-Malo, with its walled city (Ville Intra Muros), was flattened in 1944, but it has been faithfully rebuilt in a manner suited to the trading and buccaneering traditions of the city. Real shopping is hard to come by, but there is ample opportunity to off-load cash in the many tourist shops. *Boulangeries* are readily available at breakfast time, but you must search diligently to find the fish shop and the other couple of proper outfits which serve the inner sailor. These all exist up a side alley above the site of the 'retired' vegetable market (half-left from the first town gate you come to). They are worth hunting out, for the crabs if nothing else. The supermarket is discretely hidden away in a basement one block to the right of straight ahead through the same first gate. It is hard to believe that 50 years ago it was a heap of ruins. Walking its alleys, it seems as though they have been there for ten times as long.

St-Malo and neighbouring St-Servan now furnish two excellent marinas. Dinard has sunk back to obscurity, at least as far as yachtsmen are concerned.

Approaches from the west
Chenal de la Petite Porte This is the main fairway. It holds no hidden nasties, except in fog, so even if you don't fancy the alternative approaches, this one should be no problem.

Navigate to the vicinity of the *St-Malo Fairway* buoy, or cut the corner to the next stage. Take note of *Le Bunel* lit west cardinal buoy, marking a 3·8m drying rock. Leave the green tower of Les Courtis to starboard (Fl(3)G.12s14m7M) and steer in towards Le Grand Jardin (Fl(2)R.10s15M) with its grey tower situated half a mile southwest of the prominent Ile de Cézembre. Leave this and its red beacon a cable or so to port and, if it is dark, pick up the leading lights as shown on the plan on 129°. Note that the rear F.G light is intensified on the transit.

There are now various buoys (see plan), and *Le Buron*, a stubby, green 14m tower, lit Fl(2)G.6s7M. This is left to starboard, as are the green buoys and

St-Malo. Anse des Bas Sablons on right. Lock for Bassin Vauban immediate 'above' end of pier

the north cardinal spar buoy marking the Plateau de la Rance, which you will pass 3 cables before reaching the main breakwater, the Môle des Noires. This is marked by its Fl.R.5s13M light, set on the top of an 11m white tower with red top. Whether by night or by day, be sure you are not set sideways towards the Plateau de la Rance, or its buoy.

Swing round the mole onto 070°, which takes you

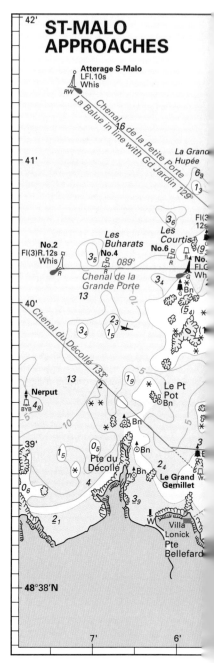

ST-MALO
APPROACHES

St-Malo. Le Grand Jardin with associated beacon.

Lock entrance to the Bassin Vauban

St-Malo. Approaching from NNW. Grand Jardin on the left and Le Courtis Green Beacon tower on the right.

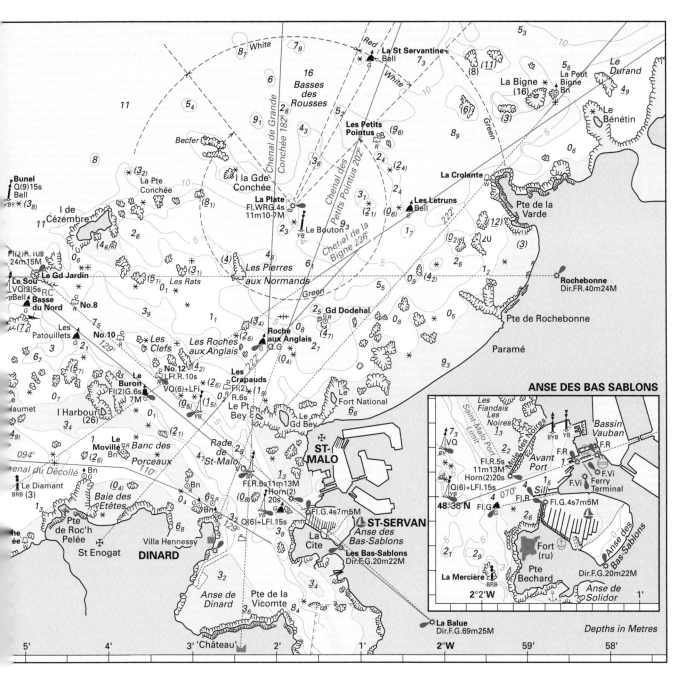

up to the lock for the Bassin Vauban. There are leading lights for the dark hours – see plan. Peel off to starboard for the Bas-Sablons marina – see 'Berthing' below.

Chenal de la Grande Porte Coming from the west, this saves a little time. Leave the red *No.2* pillar buoy (Fl(3)R.12s) to port, followed by reds *Nos 4* and *6*. *No.1* green pillar buoy (Fl.G.4s) is left to starboard. The whole while, you are steering 089° towards Le Grand Jardin (see above). By night, Le Grand Jardin lines up with Rochebonne light, away on the shore (DirF.R.40m24M). You will come onto the main leading lights for the Chenal de la Petite Porte as you swing to starboard onto 129° a cable before Le Grand Jardin.

Le Chenal du Décollé This is not easy for a stranger to eyeball, so it might be better starting outward bound the first time. Nevertheless, here it is; the channel is unlit.

From the vicinity of *No.2* red buoy (see above under 'Grande Porte'), pick up two white beacons on 134°. The front one is on Le Grand Gemillet, a heap of rocks, and the rear one is the Roche Pélée, on a promontory ashore. Continue on this line until the islet off Pointe du Décollé is abeam, then alter to 105° and follow the marked route to the Pointe de Dinard, 2½ miles east-southeast. This will leave the green beacon *Le Petit Genillet* to starboard and the red, *Le Petit Buzard*, to port. You now pass over a 0·8m patch and swing to port onto about 094° to leave the green *Le Rochardieu* to starboard. Away to port ¼ mile later is *Le Mouillé*, which is red and sits on an extensive rock which dries 12m. When this is abeam, alter to 110° to pass down the channel between a red beacon, followed by a green, a further red and a green immediately off Pointe de Dinard. You may pass over the edge of a 2m-drying patch right at the end.

Approaches from the east

All these channels end up crossing the shoal of 0·5m northwest of the Petit Bey fort. They are all unlit and are not always easy to spot on first meeting them. Better to try them outward bound, though they can save up to 3 miles.

Chenal de la Bigne Leave *Basse aux Chiens* east cardinal buoy to starboard and line up *La Crolante* white beacon tower, off Pointe de la Varde, with the right-hand edge of Le Grand Bey island, on 222°. You will see the fort on Le Petit Bey open to the right of this transit. This will take you past *La Petite Bigne*, a green beacon, left to starboard. Stay on the transit until the distant Villa Lonick, by the white-painted Pointe Bellefard, lines up with *Le Buron* (stubby green tower). In 1999 the white paint on the point was faded badly and the villa, while unambiguous, was never easy to spot. Care is needed here, therefore, and a good pair of binoculars. This transit leads down past Pointe de la Varde and a green buoy (leave to starboard) ¾ mile further on. It is now safe to steer in a southwesterly direction to leave the red beacon of the *Grand Dodehal* to port and the lit green buoy guarding the Roches aux Anglais to starboard. Thence proceed to the main channel, leaving the unlit red *Les Crapauds du Bey* to port. Round Le Petit Bey and you are in with the main stream.

Chenal des Petits Pointus Leave the *St Servantine* green buoy to starboard, then *Les Petits Pointus* (red daymark) to port. Now line up the right-hand edge of Le Petit Bey fort with Point du Dinard. Join the Chenal de la Bigne in the vicinity of the Roches aux Anglais.

Chenal de la Grande Conchée Leave the fortified islet La Grande Conchée 3 cables to starboard on course 182°. Shortly you will pass *La Platte* beacon and *Le Bouton* south cardinal buoy to port. Still on 182°, make sure you leave the green beacon on Les Pierres aux Normands and the Roches aux Anglais green buoy to starboard, then join the Chenal de la Bigne.

If in doubt, use the Chenal de la Petite Porte, but when bound out to the east the Chenal des Petits Pointus is easy enough, provided there is enough water in the first mile or so.

Berthing

Port Vauban (VHF Ch 9, ☎ 02 99 56 51 91). It is generally not necessary to call the lock. As the locals say, merely 'present yourself' in front of the gates at the appropriate time. The lock-keeper should see you and do the necessary. The lock is available from HW−2½ to HW+2. Inbound openings on the tidal half-hour, out-bound on the hour. This is a big-ship lock much used by commercial traffic, but do not let this be a source of anxiety. Common sense can generally prevail. Obey the conspicuous traffic lights and let large craft in before you, slipping in behind if there is room. The lock-keepers will soon tell you if you are wrong. The lock sides are high, but a couple of hands will be standing by with heaving lines to assist you. The water movement in the lock itself is gentle, so there is actually no cause for alarm. Opening times are posted on the side of the *capitainerie* at the head of the Bassin Vauban in case you are in any doubt about when to leave.

Although the berths are now very popular, there is usually room for a visitor of up to about 40ft to squeeze onto the pontoons at the head of the basin which are marked according to length. Yachts somewhat longer than this often berth on the other side of the dock, on the wall in the northeastern corner just past the entrance to the Bassin Duguay-Trouin with its traffic lights. This is no hardship at all, and 55-footers can lie here if there is space.

Larger yachts still, and long-stay boats can berth in the readily accessible Bassin Duguay-Trouin. Try to arrange this beforehand. If this proves impossible, raft up, find a berth and walk over to ask at the *capitainerie*. If all else fails out of hours, the gate may well be open, in which case you could probably slip through with the traffic lights and declare yourself in the morning. There is acres of space inside and a number of yachts are generally in there. The *capitainerie* works office hours with longer evenings in summer. There are three waiting-buoys outside the lock, marked 'Vauban'. Diesel in quantity by telephone and lorry (☎ 02 99 81 30 71). Toilets and showers. Fresh water on the quay and pontoons. Small crane for masts etc. All repairs, chandlery and back-up. More restaurants in the Intra Muros than you can count on a good evening walk.

Port Vauban is very handy for the town.

Port des Bas-Sablons (VHF Ch 9, ☎ 02 99 81 71 34). Leave the ferry pier close to port, keeping the marina breakwater open on your starboard hand, and the 40-metre wide entrance with its sill is right in front of you. The sill dries only 2m, so the marina can be entered at most states of the tide except for an hour or two either side of low water. Note the digital depth gauge on the marina breakwater visible only from seaward. Those inside wanting to get out must settle for an old-fashioned affair at the breakwater base. A couple of white waiting buoys have been established outside the sill.

Inside are all the facilities you would expect from a modern marina, including fuel. St-Servan itself is a pretty town with better food shops than St-Malo. It features a lovely waterfront opening onto La Rance and the famous Solidor Tower, as well as numerous waterfront bistros etc. Very agreeable indeed, except in stiff northwesterlies, when the visitors' pontoon, being nearest the sill, is somewhat bumpy. The marina is a cab-ride from the Intra Muros, but maybe you won't want to go there. Don't try to walk it unless you are desperate.

La Rance

Depths

At least 2m as far as St Suliac. The next 6 miles partially dries, up to the Chatelier lock, which opens usually at chart datum +8·5m. Port du Lyvet marina inside the Chatelier lock has 2m or a little more on visitors' berths. The Port Lyvet harbourmaster advises that from the Chatelier lock to Dinan there is a maximum of 1·4m in the canal, though up to 1·9m has been reported by other sources. In times of drought, there may be less than either. The suspension bridge at Port Hubert has 23m clearance, and the railway viaduct a mile above Mordreuc clears up to 19m. A power cable crossing the river just below Dinan has an draught of 16m.

It is worth noting that as a general rule, HW in the Rance will occur 2½–3hr after HW St Malo, but this is by no means reliable.

General

The hydroelectric barrage across La Rance 1½ miles south of St-Malo has a lock passable by yachts. This opens up an extensive cruising area inside and permits access to the ancient town of Dinan, 12 miles above the lock, at least for shoal-draught yachts. There is one further lock at Chatelier.

The walled town of Dinan was saved in 1395 during a difficulty with the English by the local champion, one Du Guesclin, who gained a 'points' verdict from the judges in a single combat contest against Canterbury, the Duke of Lancaster's man. The port is now a picture-book Breton stone spectacular set in a deep gorge with the main town up above it. There is a beautiful view from the 'English Gardens' inside the ramparts, and from this port suitably shallow vessels with masts lowered can complete a passage to the Bay of Biscay via a further 47 locks.

Main barrage and entry locks

Because of the need to maintain a head of water to do its business, the barrage's opening times appear eccentric to the uninitiated. Check hours with the harbour office at one of the St Malo marinas. The *capitaineries* at St Malo and St Servan issue tide tables from *Electricité de France*, but these may not be rigorously adhered to by the lock-keepers, whose

job is to maintain a head of water for the hydro-electric arrangements. There is also a recorded message on ☎ 02 99 16 37 37, and at times are published in *Ouest France*.

The above port authorities will advise as to Chatelier lock and its opening times, and they will issue you with the printed instructions you must have to be a legal operator inside the barrage. There is an English version available, but your attention is drawn to the excellent Carte Guide *Navigation Fluviale No.12*, which also gives The Word in English. The power company are on ☎ 02 99 46 21 81, or try VHF Ch 13.

In short, the lock can open when the level is 4m above datum, giving at least 2m in the lock. Normally it opens every hour when there is 4m in the Rance basin at St Suliac, 3 miles further on. The lifting bridge will open at any time during the first 15 minutes of the hour. The lock works from 0700–2100 local civil time.

There are waiting berths on dolphins useful only near high water, and it is recommended by the lock-keepers to arrive here 20 minutes or so before 'opening time'. On no account be tempted to pass between the dolphins. They are joined together by a wooden paling which may well be submerged when you arrive. If you don't fancy the dolphins, hang around in sight of the gates.

Approach

Leave St-Malo and push across to the west side of the river, picking up the red beacon on Bizeux, a rocky pile opposite Pointe de la Vicomté. Leave Bizeux islet to port, and continue to the south, leaving red buoys to port and *La Jument*, a lit green tower 6m high, to starboard. There are two unlit green beacons just before the lock, whose opening is signified by traffic lights.

Note that there are prohibited areas both upstream and downstream of the lock marked by round floats strung together on cables.

Once inside the barrage, observe the buoyage. There are many anchorages, but St Suliac is worthy of note for its waterside restaurant. Anchor or moor (caveat: see 'Berthing').

At Mordreuc, you can sometimes muscle in alongside in 1·5m. Here you can buy fuel and enjoy the view of the small *château* opposite. The river now narrows seriously.

The channel up to the lock at Chatelier is well marked with unlit red and green beacons, but the lock should only be approached with 8·5m of 'rise'. See your local instructions for times. Even the harbourmaster at Port Lyvet will not commit himself far in advance as to what these may be. The lock-keeper is on ☎ 02 96 39 55 66 and VHF Ch 14 – worth a call to be certain.

Berthing and facilities

Note that when anchoring in the Rance, depths may vary and you cannot refer to your tide tables in the usual way. The hand-out may prove helpful, but if in doubt, reduce to soundings and assume the

La Rance. Road bridge and lock gates at western end of barrage open for passage of yachts

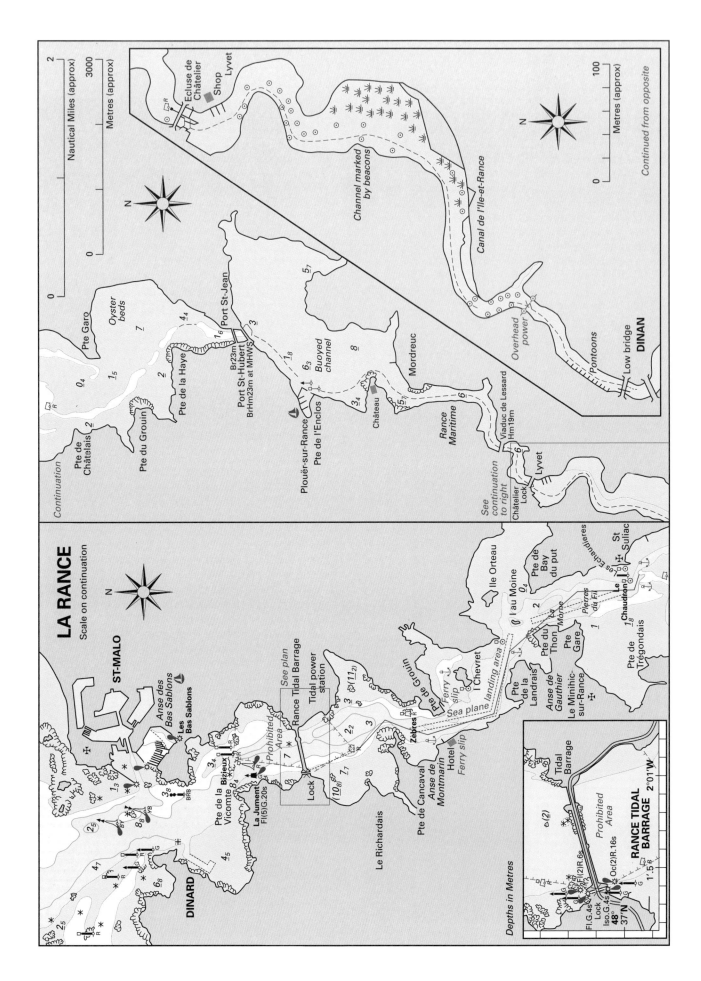

LA RANCE

Scale on continuation

ST-MALO

N

Anse des Bas Sablons

Les Bas Sablons

DINARD

Pte de la Vicomte   Bizieux

La Jument
Fl(5)G.20s

Rance Tidal Barrage

See plan

Tidal power station

Prohibited Area

Lock

Le Richardais

Pte de Cancaval
Anse de Montmarin

Hotel
Ferry slip

Zèbres

Pte de Grouin

Ferry slip

Sea plane landing area

I Chevret

Ile Orteau

l'au Moine

Pte de Bay du put

Pte de la Landrais

Anse de Gauthier

Le Minihic-sur-Rance

Pte du Thon

Pte Morne

Pte Gare

Pierres du Fil

Le Chaudron

Les Echaudpières

St Suliac

Pte de Trégondais

Depths in Metres

RANCE TIDAL BARRAGE   2°01'W

Tidal Barrage

Prohibited Area

Lock
Fl.G.4s
Iso.G.4s
Oc(2)R.16s
Fl(2)R.6s
48°37'N

Continuation

Pte de Châtelais

Pte du Grouin

Pte Garo

Oyster beds

Pte de la Haye

Port St-Jean

Port St-Hubert
Br23m
BrHm23m at MHWS

Plouër-sur-Rance
Pte de l'Enclos

Buoyed channel

Château

Mordreuc

Rance Maritime

Viaduc de Lessard
Hm19m

See continuation to right

Châtelier Lock   Lyvet

Ecluse de Châtelier
Shop   Lyvet

Channel marked by beacons

Canal de l'Ile-et-Rance

Overhead power

Pontoons

Low bridge

DINAN

Continued from opposite

Nautical Miles (approx)

Metres (approx)

Metres (approx)

N

Approach St Suliac, 3 miles from barrage. Note pagoda on headland

Approach to lock in the Rance barrage. The building in the centre is the lock office with the lock immediately right of it. Note La Jument just right of centre, also various red buoys, including the lit one opposite La Jument. The prohibited area marks can just be discerned left of centre immediately below the barrage

Bridge at Port St Hubert with 23m clearance

worst. Levels can drop alarmingly, particularly at night.

St Suliac is a delightful large village with limited facilities but the waterfront restaurant is reported to be good. Anchor outside the moorings, or pick one up if you can find a suitable one free. There is a long stone slipway for landing and a rough beach.

Port de Plouer has a sill accessible with 8·5m water level (depth gauge in entrance) and a number of alongside visitors' berths. Facilities are thin on the ground here, but there is at least a bar.

There is a 250-berth marina at Port Lyvet, immediately inside the Chatelier lock. Also moorings opposite. Here, there are showers, electricity, fresh water, a kiosk for basic provisions, and one or two bars and restaurants. 1km up the road is the pleasant small town of Viscomtes with all domestic facilities, though little for boats.

At Dinan, berth on the quay. there is adequate shopping. Fuel arranged via Bar des Vedettes. WC and showers on the quay. A selection of fine

De Lessard railway viaduct one mile upstream from Mordreuc with 19m clearance. Note fishing nets either side of well marked channel

Chatelier Lock, 3 miles from Dinan

waterfront restaurants, including the Relais Corsaires beloved of Captain Coote, awaits the enthusiastic diner, all at the bottom of the hill. Do not be dismayed by the English subtitles on the menus, or the numbers of Brits toddling around the wharves. The fare remains top class.

St-Briac-sur-Mer

Tides
HW −0515 Dover

MHWS	MLWS	MHWN	MLWN
11·2m	1·3m	8·5m	4·1m

Depths
Dries from 1·2m to something over 6m. No alongside berthing.

General
St-Briac makes a convenient day-sail with a lunch stop-over for yachts based in St-Malo. It is open to the northwest, but otherwise adequately sheltered. Its natural beauty and peace are somewhat disturbed by water-sports enthusiasts, but nonetheless it is a worthwhile picnic stop. If you want to stay overnight you'll have to be prepared to dry out in the middle on the sand bottom.

Approaches
From the east (St-Malo), either creep round the Pointe de Dinard and follow the rock-hopping Chenal du Décollé, ultimately popping out past Pointe du Décollé and its various beacons on the 314° transit, or head down the main channel as far as Le Grand Jardin. With this abaft the beam and not before, steer west, between green *No.1* and red *No.6* buoys. Then leave *Nos 4* and *2* red buoys to starboard and the east cardinal *Nerput* daymark to port. Thence, leave *Ile Agot* and *Les Herplux* red beacons to port (it is easier that way) and shape up for the entrance on 125°. Give *Les Herplux* a wide berth if the tide demands. A rock (dries 5·3m) lies 1¼ cables north of the beacon. Leave *La Moulière* north cardinal beacon to starboard, then leave red beacons to port and greens to starboard as per the plan.

From the west, leave the unlit east cardinal buoy *Les Bourdinots* to starboard and steer for the Ile Agot until you pick up the entrance beacons on 125°.

Anchorage
To suit the weather, drop anchor on either side of the small headland on the north side, just beyond the last red beacon. Do not cut inside the beacons or approach the headland, for it is rocky. Alternatively, pick up a spare mooring. There are lots.

St-Briac. Northwest entrance channel viewed from the dried-out anchorage

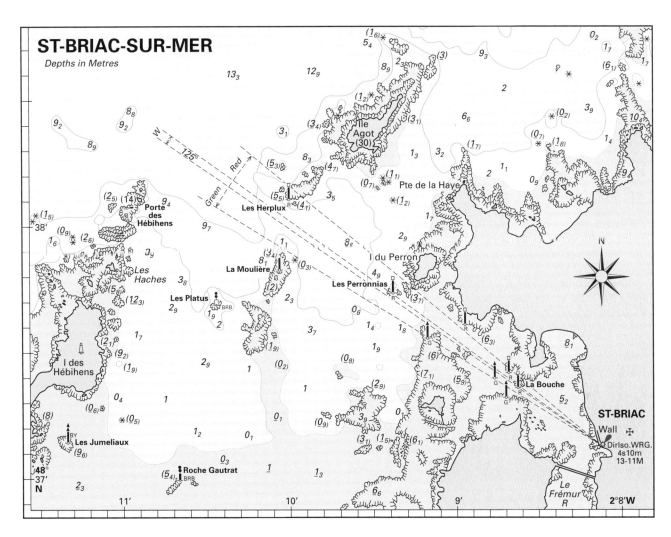

ST-BRIAC-SUR-MER
Depths in Metres

Cap Fréhel lighthouse, 33m grey square tower 85m above sea level, as seen from the ESE off St Cast. It is often the first landfall on passage to St Malo from outside the Minquiers.

Facilities
Beach café and local yacht club with shower and toilet. There is a Vietnamese restaurant, a few shops and some hotels.

Conspicuous semaphore station on Point de St Cast

St-Cast

Tides
HW −0515 Dover

MHWS	MLWS	MHWN	MLWN
11·2m	1·3m	8·5m	4·1m

Depths
1·5m on the buoys or alongside the mole.

General
St-Cast is a classy summer resort with a fine sweep of beach a mile long. There is little room to anchor, but the helpful harbourmaster seems always willing to assist with a mooring. Anchorage is possible either side of Point du Garde where the yacht club can be found, but take care not to foul oyster beds with your tackle.

The place has a claim to fame of ambiguous joy for the British visitor. In 1758, 2,400 British invaders were apparently slain here. A monument has been erected to celebrate this locally satisfactory event.

It is expected that in winds of north through southeast this will be an uneasy berth.

Approach
Watch out for Les Bourdinots rocks, marked by an unlit east cardinal spar buoy. Ideally this should be left to starboard, but there is plenty of water to pass between the buoy and the Pointe de St-Cast. Just stay in the middle to avoid the rocks on both sides of you. In the dark, use the white sector of the light to clear the rocks. To anchor off Pointe de la Garde, sound in from the northeast.

As you leave the breakwater end to starboard, leave the *Bec Ronde* red beacon to port. Note also *La Feuillade* red/black/red isolated danger mark. Check the plan very carefully if arriving when these dangers are covered.

Berthing
The first two lines of buoys from the mole are fore-and-aft fishing boat moorings. Find a vacant yacht mooring. Ten are marked 'visiteurs'. Then ask the harbourmaster. There are waiting-buoys outside the Bec Ronde if you prefer to pick one up and then enquire from your dinghy about where you should be. The maximum LOA that can be accommodated

is 13·5m. 2m draught presents no problems.

Facilities
Fresh water, petrol and diesel on the quay. Showers and toilets, small boatyard and chandlery. The town is about 1 mile distant, with the other facilities you would expect to find, including a launderette.

Dahouet

Tides
HW −0520 Dover

MHWS	MLWS	MHWN	MLWN
11·35m	1·25m	8·65m	4·05m

Depths
2·5m inside the basin. The entrance dries up to 5m. The sill dries 5·5m.

General
Dahouet is a quiet, unspoiled fishing village, made accessible by the wet dock with its marina and visitors' berths. The port can be entered 2 hours either side of HW by most yachts whose owners are on the lookout for a quiet stopover with simple food and pleasant cliff walks.

Approach
In strong onshore winds Dahouet is not recommended, on account of the breaking seas across its entrance. Otherwise, a boat drawing 1·5m can safely enter 2 hours either side of HW. Deeper yachts are readily accommodated towards the top of the tide.

Verdelet island is conspicuously conical and lies 1½ miles north-northeast from *Le Dahouet* unlit north cardinal buoy. Leave the buoy to starboard and steer about 115° towards *La Petite Muette*, a green-topped white varde bearing a sectored light (Fl.WRG.4s10m9-6M). *La Petite Muette* is notoriously difficult to spot from seawards, particularly on cloudy days, so do not be discouraged. By night, the white sector would see

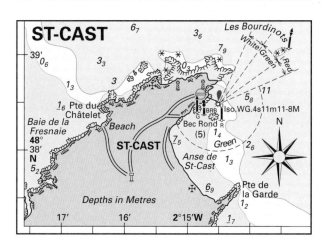

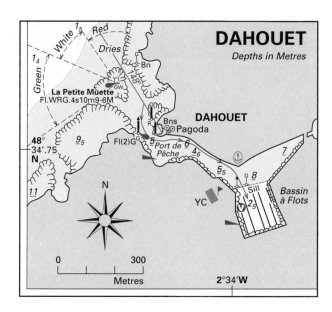

Dahouet. Beware of the sill across marina. Entry at its western end

you through this far, keeping you off the Plateau des Jaunes to the north (red sector) and Le Dahouet shoal and others (green sector).

Leave the sprawling rock of *La Petite Muette* to starboard and a red stake well to port. By night, the green beacon in the entrance (Fl(2)G) opens as you pass clear of the *Petite Muette* and can be taken as your next mark. By day, steer for the green beacon when you are halfway between the *Muette* and the pagoda-shaped shrine of Notre Dame de la Garde. You won't have seen much of the port yet, and may be wondering if it's really there, but by the time the light structure is abeam a boat's length or two to starboard, all should be revealed, or nearly so. Now swing to port and run along the quay until you see the entry to the sill at the western end of the marina, marked by a red and a green post. Enter with sufficient rise of tide.

Note that there are two transits in the entrance which are of no assistance. One is on the cliffs, a pair of white beacons now in disrepair, which probably defines the position of one of the offlying shoals. The other, which is made up of two small white posts right in the entrance, has been the source of some confusion in the past, not least to the compiler of *The Shell Pilot*. These appear to lead in through an entrance to the southwest of *La Petite Muette*. Such an approach is fraught with peril and you are warned against trying it by the locals as well as the *Pilot*.

Berthing

Berth in the marina on the westernmost pontoon ('O' pontoon – marked '*Visiteurs*') or, possibly, dry out against the Quai des Terre-Neuves east of the *capitainerie* (dries 7m). There are numerous drying moorings in this area. The *capitainerie* is on VHF Ch 9, or ☎ 02 96 72 82 85 during office hours.

Facilities

Two or three waterfront bistros and a useful chandlery. Marina has toilets and showers. All other requirements modestly available in the old village which is just round the harbour, the sort of short stroll a determined yachtsman could execute while portaging a case of *vin ordinaire*. Fuel on the Quai des Terre-Neuvas (dries 7m). There is a scrubbing grid immediately outside the wet basin. It dries 6·5m and is thus not a favourite at neaps. There are 4-ton and 6-ton cranes as well as engineers and some repair facilities. *Camping Gaz* exchange and ice are on hand. A walk over the hill from the town to Grande Plage gives access to many shops and restaurants.

Le Légué (St Brieuc)

Tides

HW −0520 Dover

MHWS	MLWS	MHWN	MLWN
11·45m	1·4m	8·7m	4·1m

Depths

Entrance dries up to 6m 2 miles to seaward and is highly dangerous in strong onshore winds. Local authorities put the absolute maximum as force 5 northeasterly for a small sailing yacht. Inside, however, there is at least 4m in the locked basin (sill dries 5m) and perfect shelter, though surroundings are not the most agreeable.

General

Le Légué is the port for the town of St Brieuc, across the river, which is the provincial capital. The quays give perfect shelter, but are noisy during the day, and in dry, windy conditions can cover your decks with a virulent grit. In the mid-1980s Captain Coote noted that the port was mainly for fishermen and coasters, but added that determined yachtsmen could penetrate its locks and find good shelter. There are now 20 visitors' berths in Bassin No. 2, and boats of up to 15m LOA are welcome. The sight of the entry channel at LW once you are safely inside can be a source of either satisfaction or ulcers, depending upon the balance of your humours.

Approach

The approaches to Le Légué can be dangerous in northeasterly winds of over force 5.

By day, come to the *Le Légué* red and white whistle buoy (Mo(A)10s). From close to this, steer about 200° for a couple of miles to *No.1* green unlit buoy. Note the prominent folly on the south side of the estuary. Now follow all the buoys, greens to starboard, reds to port, until the lock appears ahead. Point de l'Aigle (see plan) is an old-fashioned stone lighthouse with a green lantern built on the end of a very short, bullnosed pier. The beacon on Jetée de la Douane (Iso.G) is white with a green top. If you need to wait, tie up at the wall on the south side just before the lock. The lock is on VHF Ch 12, 16, and 9 towards tide times. It is also on ☎ 02 96 33 35 41. The lock opens HW−2 to HW±1½, depending on the tide coefficient.

Night entry is not recommended, but if you must, try to place yourself on the line joining Pointe de l'Aigle (VQ.G.13m8M) and the VQ(9) *Rohein* west cardinal beacon 7½ miles to the north-northeast of it. This sets Pointe de l'Aigle on about 208°. As you close the land you should try to spot the unlit channel markers, but note that the Jetée de la

La Légué

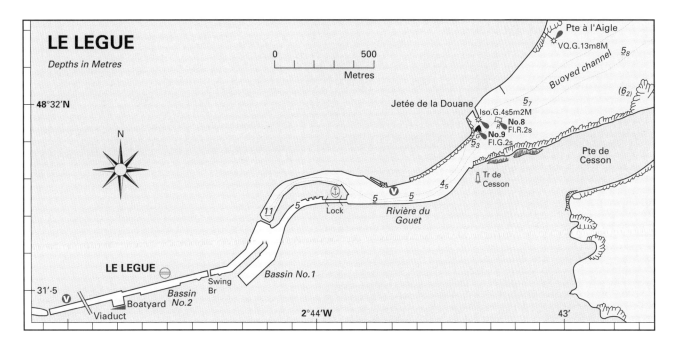

LE LEGUE

Depths in Metres

0   500

Metres

48°32'N

N

Pte à l'Aigle
VQ.G.13m8M
5₈

Buoyed channel

Jetée de la Douane
5₇

(6₂)

Iso.G.4s5m2M
No.8
Fl.R.2s

R   **No.9**
G   Fl.G.2s
5₃

Pte de Cesson

Tr de Cesson
4₅

5   5
Lock

5   5
Rivière du Gouet

11   5

Pte de Cesson

LE LEGUE

Swing Br
Bassin No.1

31'·5
V   Bassin No.2
Boatyard
Viaduct

2°44'W   43'

Douane carries an Iso.G.4s light and that the red buoy before it (*No. 8*) is lit Fl(2)R. *No. 9* green buoy, immediately past the jetty against the shore, is Fl.G.2s. Thereafter the channel heads southwesterly to the left bank, and thence west by south to the lock.

Berthing

Once inside the lock, proceed according to the plan to Bassin No. 2. This is really a 'canalised' part of the Gouet river. The swing bridge does not open often and not at all between 2100 and 0700. Once through, if no one tells you where to berth, tie up on your starboard side in the vicinity of the viaduct. Beware of blowing sand and grit. You may have to raft up.

Facilities

All manner of repair and back-up facilities. Fresh water by tap on the quay west of the viaduct, fuel from service station on the quay. Public toilets and showers reported. One or two bars and restaurants, but a 7-minute bus ride (about every hour – times posted at bus stop west of viaduct on north side of quay) to St Brieuc will offer the bon viveur a greater variety of watering holes. Those of a more frugal turn of mind may elect to cope with a mile or so along the road towards Pte de l'Aigle, where a totally real coastal village will be discovered. Bars/*jeux, ménus ouvriers* at lunch-time for a genuine 55Fr including *boisson*, good chandler, etc., plus views of the entrance to make your hair curl.

Binic

HW −0525 Dover

MHWS	MLWS	MHWN	MLWN
11·45m	1·4m	8·7m	4·1m

Depths

The approaches dry 4·5m to a distance of ¾ mile. There is, however, from 1·4m to 2m in the basin generally, with deeper water (up to 3·5m) near the north end of the visitors' pontoon.

General

A sometime fishing harbour; now mainly *plaisance*, since the installation of the locked basin. The entry is dubious in strong winds from east to southeast. The lock only officially opens when the tide height reaches 9·5m. As a result, dead neap openings are very short or not at all. On mean tides or above, the lock opens an hour or so either side of HW. The port can normally be approached by craft of modest draught at any time in the top half of the tide.

Approach

The offshore approach to Binic is clear of dangers at the sort of tide height that will enable the user to come close to the port. Care must be taken, however, about the Roches de Saint Quay. These can readily be passed on either side by reference to the clear navigation marks (see plan, page 264). Indeed, the inside passage is the best part of half a mile wide at its narrowest point.

The first sign of the harbour may well be the 12m white tower (Oc(3)12s12M) on the end of the northern breakwater of Binic. A transit of this tower and the church steeple on 275° clears absolutely everything, even when the approach is dry, but is not really necessary for safe navigation. It may, however, be a useful guide to set and drift in the later stages of your approach.

There is no reason why a prudently navigated yacht should not come to shelter in Binic by night,

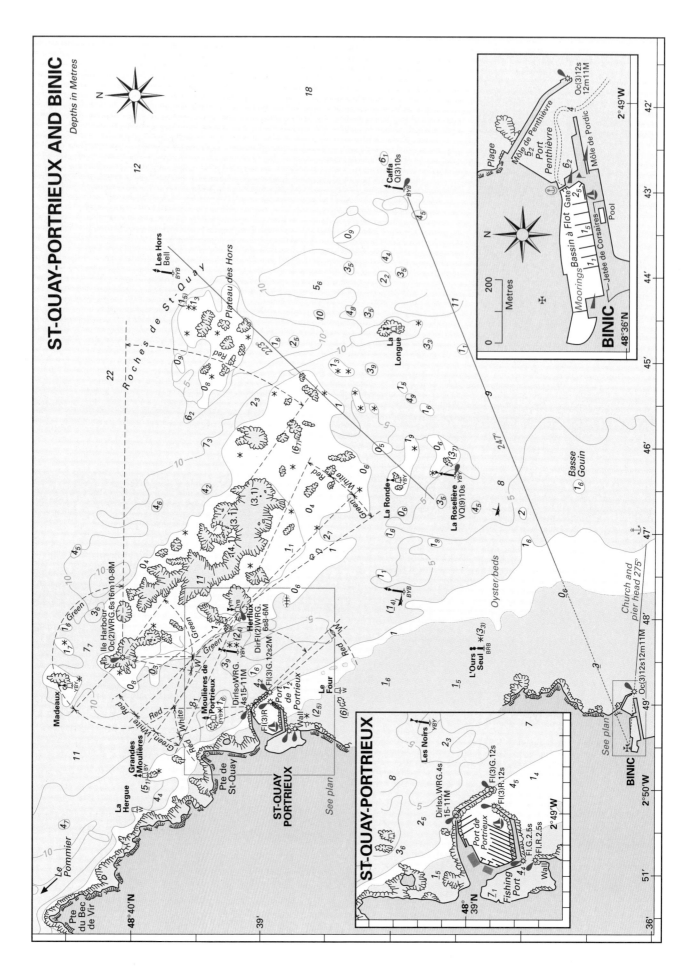

ST-QUAY-PORTRIEUX AND BINIC

Depths in Metres

BINIC

48°36'N

ST-QUAY-PORTRIEUX

2°49'W

48° 39'N

BINIC

2°50'W

48°40'N

Binic

using the easier (after dark) passage south-about round the Roches de Saint Quay. The white sector of *Roheim* west cardinal beacon (VQ(9)WRG.10s 13m11-18M) keeps you south of all the associated horrors, and you can keep this on a back bearing of around 060° until you pick up Binic light (see above).

Once past the breakwater, hang about for the lock, or tie up temporarily, watching your echo sounder. A green light means enter and a red means don't. There is no VHF at the lock, but the Port de Plaisance monitors VHF Ch 9 in office hours (☎ 02 96 73 61 86).

Berthing

The first pontoon you reach is officially designated 'visitors', though you may end up seizing the main chance of a berth. If over 10m LOA you may be directed to deeper water on the quay wall (still inside the gate) rather than a pontoon. You could be able to dry out on the inside of the breakwater (dries 4·5m – sand and mud).

Facilities

Showers and toilets reported. Fresh water on the pontoons, but fuel by portage only. Good chandlery; also repairs, *Gaz* exchange and ice. For the pleasure-seeker, particularly one with a young family, Binic has all the facilities of a moderate-sized summer resort, with a well-stocked, picturesque waterfront and glorious beaches to match. These are very convenient to the port, and when the tide is out, a sea-water swimming facility has been created right on the harbour wall. There is a handy supermarket.

All in all, Binic is one of the nicest of the North Brittany resort towns, and well worth a visit.

St-Quay-Portrieux

Tides

HW −0520 Dover

MHWS	MLWS	MHWN	MLWN
11·4m	1·4m	8·6m	4·1m

Depths

Deep-water approaches to a deep-water marina, with berths dredged to 3·5m at LAT.

General

This is one of the few all-weather, any-tide harbours along this stretch of coast, and as such it is important. The place has beaches, restaurants and shops, a casino, and a string of rocky reefs 2½ miles long outside the front door where lobsters can fatten themselves up for the pot. The harbour is accessible at day or night, which goes some way to making up for its rather bleak, brand-new atmosphere.

Approach from the north

By day, start by sorting out *Madeux* west cardinal beacon and leave it well to port. Now find *Moulières de Portrieux* east cardinal beacon and steer a southerly course to leave this well to starboard. If the visibility is good, you will pick up a distant water

tower. Line this up with the *Moulières* on 172° and you will have a useful transit to check your drift. When *Herflux* comes 'on' with the distant *La Longue* south cardinal beacon on 119°, steer down this transit for a third of a mile until the marina breakwater head bears south. Now peel off and go for it. Swing round hard to starboard to enter the marina. If you cannot discern *La Longue*, just make sure you leave the *Moulières* at least 2 cables to starboard if it is less than half-tide.

By night, come in on the white sector of Port de Pontrieux light (DirIso.WRG.4s15-11M). Keep an eye on the red sector of *Herflux* (DirFl(2)WRG.6s), and when it turns white steer towards it on about 120° until you enter the narrow white sector of Ile Harbour light (Oc(2)WRG.6s) behind you. You are now safe to alter for the Fl(3)G on the pier head. Round this to starboard, leave the Fl(3)R on the south breakwater to port, and you're in.

Approach from the south

By day, leave *Caffa* (lit east cardinal buoy), *La Longue* (south cardinal beacon) and *La Roselière* (west cardinal buoy) all well to starboard, then steer for the entrance on about 317°, making sure to leave a single east cardinal spar buoy to port. There are

St-Quay-Portrieux

shallow patches of possibly as little as 0·3m on this line, but the best water (1·1m) is on the transit (317°) of *La Hergue* white beacon beyond the harbour, and the distinctive white summit of an islet called Le Pommier nearly 3 miles northwest of it.

By night, entry is easy. Round the *Caffa* (lit east cardinal) and *La Roselière* (lit west cardinal) buoys, giving a fair clearance, then home in on the white sector of the Portrieux light (DirIso.WRG.4s15-11M). This leads to the pier heads, Fl(3)G and Fl(3)R. Enter between them.

Berthing
There are visitors' berths on pontoon '7' for craft drawing up to 3·5m and up to 18m LOA. The port office monitors VHF Ch 9 day and night and is on ☎ 02 96 70 49 51. Alternatively, you can sound in and anchor south of the southern jetty, tide permitting.

Facilities
Fuel and fresh water in the marina, as are large-scale toilet and shower facilities as well as a launderette. All back-up requirements for your yacht are taken care of, including chandlers, engineers, *Camping Gaz* and ice. There is a 25-ton crane and a slipway in the old harbour. There you can also dry out if you have a mind to, after consulting the port office. The town is a lively resort, though some say less attractive than neighbouring Binic.

Communications
By bus to St Brieux, thence by train to your interior destination, or by plane to Paris from St Brieux airfield.

Paimpol

Tides
HW −0525 Dover

MHWS	MLWS	MHWN	MLWN
10·95m	1·45m	8·35m	3·95m

Depths
Paimpol has silted up considerably in the late 1990s. Depths in the approach are as follows: Drying 5·22m south of *No.3* buoy, then drying 6m right on the line in to the tide gate after rounding the Jetty of Kernoa. Locks can accommodate 3m draught at neaps and 4m at springs.

General
Paimpol is a fishing town built around the deep-water Icelandic and Newfoundland cod industry. Until 1935, topsail schooners and ketches of the type known locally as 'Dundee' put out to sea from here in spring to spend the summer line-fishing in the sub-Arctic. They returned in autumn with holds full of salt fish and, as one may imagine, great was the revelry.

Today, the town offers an interesting visit for the cruising yacht. It is picturesque and maintains a strong interest in its past, having hosted in recent years one or two very successful festivals of the sea.

Approach and entrance
There are a number of secondary channels into Paimpol, none of which saves more than 4 miles overall, and most of which require delicate pilotage. Some are indicated on the plan. The main road in is straightforward and is called the Chenal de la Jument.

First, identify *Les Charpentiers*, an east cardinal daymark to seaward of the Roches du Roho. Half a mile northwest of it stands a white pyramid, *La Cormorandière*. If coming from the east, you may first discern the Lost Pic lighthouse a mile south-southwest of it. This is a distinctive 20m square white tower with a red top (Oc.WR.4s11/8M). By night, you can come in initially in its northeastern white sector, which will turn red as *Les Charpentiers* comes abeam.

There is a useful daytime transit to take you as far as the *Gueule* red buoy. Line up the isolated white house on Pointe Porz-Don with a column on the skyline on 269°. Porz-Don light (Oc(2)WR.6s13m 15/11M) has a 3° white sector from 269°–272°. The northern edge of this, just in the red, corresponds to the transit. If you cannot identify this daytime transit, a white building on top of Pointe Brividic 'on' with Paimpol church spire gives 260° and will take you down to the *Gueule* buoy and *La Jument*.

The final leading marks on 264° are a 4·3m truncated white tower with a red top labelled 'Kernoa', showing 2·4m above the red-and-white painted bullnose jetty, and the back marker, which is a 9m white lattice tower, also with a red top. These show F.R lights at night, the rear one intensified in the safe sector. The last half-mile of the 30m-wide channel is marked with buoys and perches of which the final green is lit. If arriving after dark without much water, note that this beacon is 70m off the transit and is in shallower water. The best depth lies in the middle of the marked channel.

Swing to port round the Jetée de Kernoa and make up for the lock. The gates open ±2½ hours HW springs, ±2 hours HW neaps. The lock-keeper listens on VHF Ch 9 at tide times. The berthing master is on ☎ 02 96 20 47 65. The lock works from 0600–2300 local time in season, 0700–2200 in winter.

Berthing
There are 300 pontoons and quayside berths inside Paimpol, of which 20 are reserved for visitors. The maximum length on fingers is 11m. The Quai Loti can deal with up to 15m, sometimes rafted up. More than 15m by discussion with the port officer – up to 50m can sometimes be accommodated. If there is room, the main visitors' berths are ahead of you as you come out of the lock. If you aren't met by the man in a dory, shape up for pontoon 'A'. If that is full, find what you can. Always report to the office (Quai Neuf) on the divide between the basins after berthing. Yachts may safely be left here for short periods.

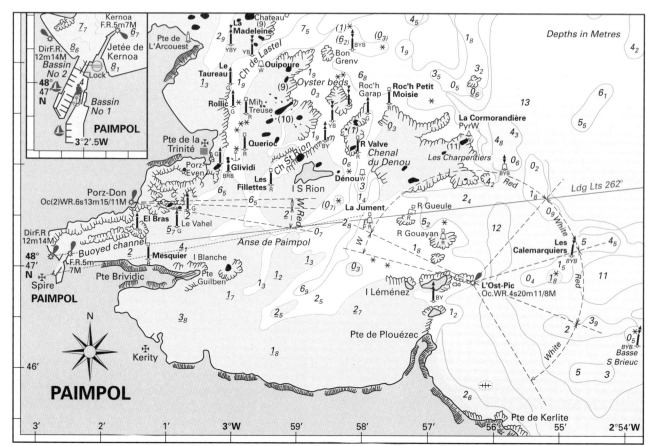

Paimpol approach

Paimpol

Anchorages

Off Porz-Even, with the isolated danger beacon (black/red/black, ⁑ topmark) bearing about 190° at around a cable distant, you can anchor in 2·7m just east of the moorings. This works well in suitable conditions. The whole of the Anse de Paimpol is potentially an anchorage, but you must look to your tide tables and read the chart carefully to discover the other good spots.

Facilities

Fresh water on pontoons. Fuel on the quay. Showers and heads (24 hours). Chandlery, yard facilities, sailmaker, *Camping Gaz* exchange and ice. Launderette at 4 Rue de la Benne. There is an excellent supermarket by Bassin No. 2 and all other town facilities, including the Librairie Maritime and restaurants to suit all tastes and bankrolls. L'Islandais serves an unusual menu whose wine list is sensibly salted with affordable bottles. You dine in surroundings of great interest beneath the ribs of an upturned *coque classique* under the velvet glove control of Madame herself. The bedrooms here are spectacular if you need a break from your cosy cabin.

Communications

Scenic bus-rides to neighbouring coastal towns. Rail branch line connecting to St Malo or Brest.

Ile de Bréhat

Tides

HW −0525 Dover

MHWS	MLWS	MHWN	MLWN
10·4m	1·1m	8·0m	3·6m

Depths

Variable, from drying to deep water at LW springs. For details, see plan and anchorage notes below.

General

Bréhat is a rocky archipelago, popular with owners of shoal-draught yachts, artists, and the day-trippers who arrive in vedettes with what Captain Coote described as the regularity of the Gosport ferry. The area is also loved by those fed up with motor cars – none are allowed on the islands.

Approach

Any navigation in the vicinity of Bréhat should be taken very seriously. Streams can run at up to 5 knots, and it is therefore axiomatic that you are continuously aware of your position.

From the north, shape for a point one mile east of Le Paon lighthouse, which is a yellow framework tower (F.WRG.11·8M) 12m high at 22m elevation. Leave the Plateau de la Horaine with its various markers to port and the north cardinal daymark *Petit Pen-Azen* well to starboard on 168°. This will place

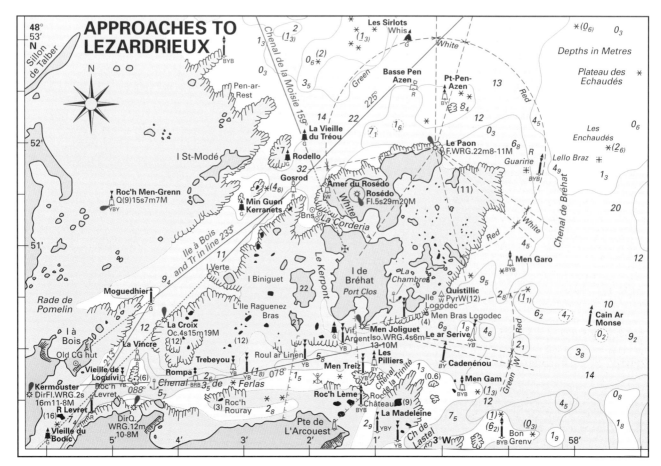

Ile de Bréhat. Port Clos looking south

you in the Chenal de Bréhat. Alter course if necessary to leave the unlit east cardinal buoy *Rc. Guarine* close to starboard and the east cardinal daymark *Men Garo* well to starboard. You now have the unlit north cardinal buoy *Cain-ar-Monse* ahead. 2 or 3 cables short of this, alter to a west-southwesterly heading to leave the south cardinal beacon *Lel-ar-Serive* to starboard. Now you can alter to 290° to pick up the south cardinal pillar due south of Ile Logodec for La Chambre, or to 278° for the west cardinal beacon *Men Joliguet*, bearing the sectored light at the southeast head of Port Clos.

The Chenal de Ferlas offers a further approach for craft coming out of Lézardrieux. In this case the west cardinal beacon *V. de Loguivy* is left well to port as you come onto a heading of 088° towards the isolated danger beacon (red/black/red, ⁑ topmark) *Rompa*. Leave *Rompa* to port and shape up on 078° to leave *Trebeyou* (south cardinal daymark) and the south cardinal beacon 1½ cables east-southeast of it to port. Continue on this track, leaving 3 south cardinal beacons at various distances as well as *Men Joliguet* to port and *Les Piliers* north cardinal daymark to starboard. You are now south of La Chambre.

Anchorages

La Chambre is marked with red and green perches with topmarks. There is deep water at the entrance if you can find room. Otherwise do your sums, then sound in. There is a dinghy landing.

Port Clos dries out to its entrance and is the vedette terminal.

La Corderie is approached from the main Pontrieux river channel until you see the white pyramid daymark, *Amer du Rosédo*, on the westernmost point of the north island. Head in for this until the green *Men Robin* beacon is spotted and leave this well to starboard, steering south-southeast. Now leave red beacons to port and green to starboard until you are into the mouth of the bay. There is deep water north of the *Kaler* green beacon, but in order to escape the tides you should tuck right inside. Halfway in, it dries about 2·5 metres; at neaps it is an excellent anchorage. Row ashore to the south island for a pleasant walk to Le Bourg.

Facilities

Basically, there aren't any, but the place is none the worse for this. Better, some would say. Don't expect paradise unfound, because of the visitors, but it is still a fine spot where peace may descend in due season.

Lézardrieux/Pontrieux

Tides

HW −0510 Dover
HW Pontrieux lock is approximately −0505 Dover and is the same as HW St Malo

MHWS	MLWS	MHWN	MLWN
10·55m	1·35m	8·05m	3·8m

Depths

Deep water all the way to Lézardrieux. For Pontrieux, see its own section.

General

Lézardrieux has the great benefit of being only a little over a tide from Guernsey. It can be entered in any weather at any state of tide. Berths are absolutely sheltered. The town is delightful and is reached by a short walk up an unchallenging hill.

Approach

Coming from east or southeast with a reasonable rise of tide, enter the river by passing south of Ile de Bréhat (See 'Ile de Bréhat' notes, above). From points north, after negotiating the Roches Douvres, Barnouic, or the rocks stretching seawards from the mouth of the Tréguier river, fix your position using Les Heaux de Bréhat (Oc(3)WRG.12s48m17/11M) and La Horaine (Fl(3)12s13m11M). The former is a 57m-high grey tower and the latter a black octagonal tower of some 20m. You will also see Rosédo lighthouse (Fl.5s29m20M). This is a 13m

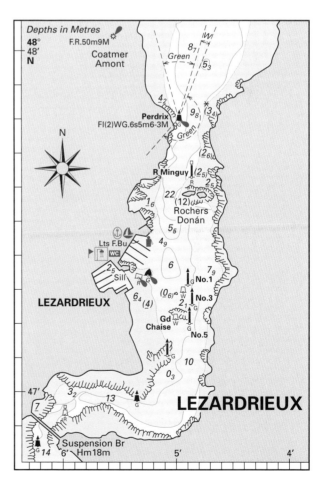

Trieux River looking upstream
Below Lézardrieux

Les Heaux lighthouse 57m high on rocks 2 miles offshore, midway between the mouths of the Tréguier and Pontrieux rivers

Le Paon lighthouse, a 12m high square yellow tower, 22m above the sea. It is the northernmost point of the Ile de Bréhat on the eastern side of the approach to the Pontrieux river

At the NW corner of Bréhat, near the entrance to La Corderie anchorage, stands the white Rosédo pyramid (A). La Moisie channel from the NW is in transit 159° with the Chapel of St Michael (B)

La Croix light beacon on the east side of the estuary. The fairway is when it is in transit with Bodic on 225°

Le Vincre red beacon ½ mile up-river from Le Croix

The *Vielle de Loguivy* marks the junction between the fairway to Lézardrieux and the Ferlas Channel to Port Clos

Conspicuous Bodic lighthouse overlooking the west bank of the river

tower at 29m elevation on the north part of Bréhat. The pyramid-shaped daymark (*l'Amer de Rosédo*) on the western extremity of the north part of Bréhat was demolished by an over-zealous German defender, but has now mercifully been rebuilt and painted white. If this lot seems complicated, don't worry. It isn't in practice. Just study the chart and be grateful for plenty of navigational aids.

Leave La Horaine a mile or so to port (watch for the *N Horaine* unlit north cardinal buoy) and steer 225°. If it is dark, the red sector of Les Heaux de Bréhat will now have turned white, indicating your approach to the runway, and you should now be picking up the leading lights of La Croix (DirOc.4s19M) beacon, a white tower with a flat, red top, and the DirQ.22M of Bodic, a squat white tower with a pyramid green roof on the skyline. These buildings are clearly visible in the daylight. The lights are intensified either side of 225°. As you pass La Croix tower a cable or so to port, pick up the second transit on 219°. This is defined by two white-gabled houses on the west bank. The front one is *Coatmer* (F.RG.9M) and the rear one is F.R. Both are narrow sectors, the front one ±25°, the back one ±22·5°. Along this transit you will pass various beacons (see plan), including the west cardinal daymark *V. de Loguivy*, which is left to port if you wish to enter the channel south of Bréhat.

After dark, steer for *Les Perdrix* (Fl(2)WG.6s) white sector on 198° before the transit has run you into Coatmer. If Perdrix turns green while you are still on the transit, you must alter sharply to port to

regain the white sector, then steer for the Perdrix light. By day, look at the chart and the beacons. Entry is straightforward. From Perdrix, shape up for the marina.

Berthing

Anchor at will off the fairway anywhere you feel is suitable, but watch for moorings. Lower down the channel is fine. You may well find a vacant mooring anywhere in the river, but these should be treated with suspicion. Optimists are known to have draggd them, so they cannot be guaranteed. The marina has room for 80 visitors in season, on pontoons with up to 2·5m at MLWS, and listens on VHF Ch 9 during office hours, ☎ 02 96 20 14 22. If you fail to make contact, tie up on No. 3 pontoon and await instructions. Note that there are no longer any fixed lights on the pontoon ends. Instead, the area has been lit with powerful arc lights which show what is what far more clearly.

Visitors may use vacant trot moorings opposite the marina. Fees are paid to the *capitainerie* and are not very much less than alongside, but it is a quiet berth if you have a good dinghy to beat the strong tides when coming ashore. Visitors sometimes use the inner marina by arrangement. This is entered via a sill which opens at a tide height of 6·15m to give 1·25m clearance. There is a depth gauge to report the rapidly deepening water thereafter.

Facilities

Fresh water and fuel on the marina. The fuel berth is inshore below the harbour office and has 1m at LW springs. Showers, heads and launderette at yacht club. There is a scrubbing grid at the Port de Commerce; also a chandler, repairs, *Camping Gaz* exchange, etc.

A pleasant *creperie*/restaurant and the Hotel du Port with decent restaurant, *La Marina*, will be found just beyond the boatyard. Otherwise, it's up the hill to the town, where you will discover a modest but agreeable choice of eating houses, as well as traditional food shops.

There is a launching ramp (dries 2m).

Pontrieux

Pontrieux offers a peaceful and agreeable diversion from the hurly-burly of the sea. There is plenty of berth space alongside, good restaurants, shops and even a torch-light procession on the third Sunday in July, with a funfair and other benefits. The Château de la Roche-Jagu hosts a programme of cultural events from 1 June through August.

There is a minimum of 18m under the viaduct, and although the river is not officially charted there is good water for a respectable-sized yacht to pass on a rising tide. Common-sense pilotage can be applied on bends in the river, where the outside looks and usually is steep-to and the inside is shoal and muddy.

Near the top of the flood there is about 4m at springs and 3m at neaps. If you arrive early for the lock there is a mooring (raft up if necessary) in deep water just below the château (see plan). Upstream of here, the bottom may be rocky and unsuitable for exploration before the tide is well up. The lock opens from 2 hours before to 1 hour after HW and the gates are 1 mile below the town. The river is buoyed for the approach to the lock. The sill is at 3·5m above chart datum. Do not be dismayed by the industry on your port hand soon after passing the lock. This is a 'one-off' and is soon forgotten.

Berth alongside the quay as far upstream as you can. The harbourmaster is on ☎ 02 96 95 64 66, also VHF Ch 12. The basin has all the usual yacht facilities, including fuel (from harbourmaster). Boats can be laid up here. Crane.

There are some good local cafés and restaurants, and much more in town, where all normal requirements will be met. The town is a pleasant, easy ½ mile walk from the berths.

Communications
Trains, with connections to Roscoff and St Malo for the ferries, or Paris for a good time.

Tréguier
HW −0540 Dover

MHWS	MLWS	MHWN	MLWN
9·8m	1·1m	7·5m	3·3m

Depths
Deep-water approaches. The river is also deep – at least 5m at MLWS – almost to the marina. The last 3 or 4 cables are dredged to 2m at LAT, but note that at MLWS this is 3·1m. The berths on the marina advertise at least 3m draught.

General
Tréguier is approachable by day and night in all weathers and at all states of tide. Its river is unusually lovely and offers anchorage in varied types of scenery. The town itself is a meandering medieval wonderland which contrives to be much less tourist-ridden than Vannes or Quimper in South Brittany, which have also retained their ancient buildings. It features a remarkable and ancient cathedral with a bizarre spire cut into hollows. It contains the tomb of St Yves, the patron saint of lawyers and, as a sideline, the protector of the poor. One day every May there is a procession in his honour, which would seem ideally timed for British yachtsmen, still on the ropes after paying their yard bills for the spring refit.

Tréguier river near low water

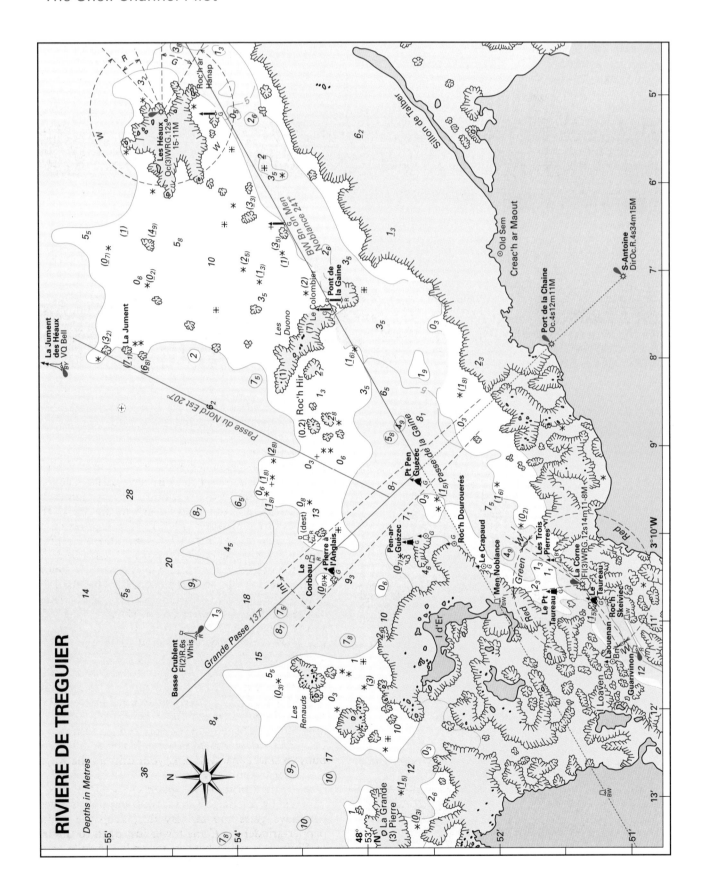

RIVIERE DE TREGUIER

Depths in Metres

Plougrescant church with its spire on the right-hand edge is a conspicuous mark by day when approaching from any direction

Tréguier river approach. Passe de la Gaine on 242° brings into transit (A) Men Noblance with (B) a white wall with black vertical stripe. (C) Plougrescant church well to the left

La Corne light beacon ½ miles upstream from Men Noblance is at the narrowest part of the channel

Roche Skeiviec ½ mile upstream from La Corne beacon

Approaches

By night, the various lighthouses are well charted and will provide good fixes in reasonable visibility. In thick weather this rock-bound coast cannot be recommended. Your landfall will ideally be at the brightly lit *Bs. Crublent* (Fl(2)R.6s) red pillar buoy, but you may arrive first at *La Jument* north cardinal with bell. Leave *Bs. Crublent* to port and shape up on 137° for the Grande Passe. This is easier by night, as the lights are a good sight clearer to see than the notoriously invisible daymarks at 3 miles' range. These are: front *Port de la Chaine* (Oc.4s 12m11M), a white-painted house, and rear *Ste Antoine* (Oc.R.4s34m 15M intensified ±3° on 137°), another white house, this time with a red roof.

If you don't spot the transit in the daytime, watch your back-bearing on *Bs. Crublent* until you identify the red buoy *Le Corbeau* (leave to port) and its green starboard-hand partner, the *Pierre à l'Anglais.* You must pass between these, and then continue on 137°, still on the transit, to leave *Pen ar Guezec* green buoy to starboard, watching your drift all the way.

At night, course is now altered to starboard to head for *La Corne*, whose green sector (Fl(3)WRG. 12s) will by this stage have turned white. If it is red, you have gone too far. By day, keep the white, pepper-grinder *La Corne* tower just open to the left of *Skeiviec*, a white beacon tower half a mile or so further in, heading in the order of 215°. You will pass various beacons (see plan) before reaching *La Corne*, which is left to port. The green channel buoy is left to starboard as you hitch onto 235° (in the southerly white sector of *La Corne* by night). Pass the Fl.R buoy *Le Guarivinou* to port, swing onto 210° for the next red, and so carry on up the lit

Tréguier Marina. Inner berths may dry. *Capitainerie* is the large building lower right

buoyed channel to your chosen anchoring spot or to the marina.

The last lit green buoy (*No.17*) is within 50m of the pontoons. The penultimate green buoy (unlit) marks Le Grand Rocher, which dries 3·7m; don't cut inside it!

There is also a 'daytime only' inshore channel into the river from the northeast, the Passe de la Gaine. This saves about 1½ miles if you are coming from Lézardrieux or points east. It passes over a 0·5m patch, within a cable of various drying rocks, and is generally tight, so it requires favourable weather, some rise of tide and good visibility.

Outward bound, the channel can be picked up at the *Pen ar Guezec* turning mark (green buoy), when you swing to starboard onto 062°, with the *Men Noblance* black and white daymark on a back transit with a white house and a black-and-white-painted wall 2 miles behind it. These carry you well beyond Les Héaux and past various self-explanatory beacons (see plan). With Les Héaux well abaft the beam you can come off the transit, after careful reference to the chart. Towards the end, you may require binoculars to see the transit.

Berthing

The river contains a number of moorings, and a suitable spare one can sometimes be picked up, subject to the usual international unwritten rules of lying to someone else's buoy. It is definitely preferable to anchor in this lovely river, and there are a number of sites which will appeal to the sharp-eyed mariner. On the west shore beneath the château ¾ mile north of the town is a good spot, where the compiler of *The Shell Channel Pilot* rode out Hurricane Charlie in 1986.

The marina maintains 100 visitors' berths. Tie up near the outside and report. Watch out for strong streams along berths.

Facilities

Fresh water, showers and toilets at the marina. Laundry in the Rue St André, up in town. Fuel on the pontoon. There is a launching ramp and a 30-ton crane on the quay, with 5m of water at MHWS. One of the best chandleries in Europe is situated just over the river bridge above the marina. Worth a visit just for the atmosphere, even if you don't buy anything. Boatyards, engineers, *Camping Gaz*, ice, etc.

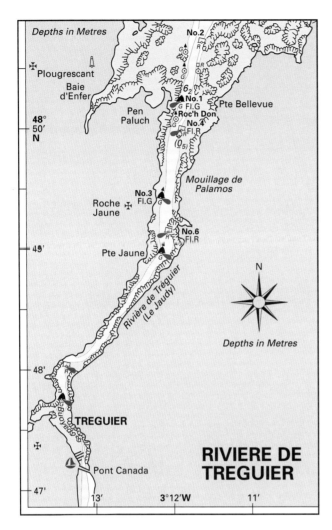

Depths in Metres

Plougrescant
Baie
d'Enfer
Pen
Paluch
**48°
50'
N**

No.2

No.1
G Fl.G
Roc'h Don
No.4
Fl.R
(0.5)

Pte Bellevue

Mouillage de
Palamos

No.3
Fl.G

Roche
Jaune

No.6
Fl.R

Pte Jaune

Rivière de Treguier
(Le Jaudy)

49'

48'

N

Depths in Metres

TREGUIER

47'

Pont Canada

**RIVIERE DE
TREGUIER**

13'   3°12'W   11'

There are bars and bistros down by the quay – the pizzeria is the best value – and a plethora of delights up in the town. Don't miss it, or the market once a week on Wednesdays where, as Captain Coote remarked, you could buy anything from 1-day-old chicks to 10-year-old Calvados. Lovely dinghy trips on the tide up-river to the charming little community of Roche Derrien. Nobody knows what an anchor is for here, so you can leave your dinghy with confidence and step ashore for a fine lunch. The passage takes something over an hour at 'seagull outboard speed'.

Port Blanc

Tides
HW −0550 Dover

MHWS	MLWS	MHWN	MLWN
9·4m	1·0m	7·0m	3·2m

Depths
Deep enough to anchor in the outer pool, even at LW springs, for any yacht small enough to be interested. At neaps shoal-draught yachts could get close enough in to stay the night – see plan. The quay, however, dries a staggering 9m.

General
Port Blanc is worth a visit, particularly a lunch-time stop in good weather, if only to marvel at the spectacular pink granite rocks. There is little ashore to tempt the fun-lover, but the sailor ridden with the guilt of his general excesses may find relief from his burden in the general *pardon* issued in the 16th-century century chapel on 8 September. Those

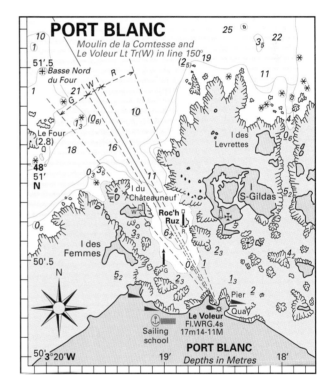

PORT BLANC
Moulin de la Comtesse and
Le Voleur Lt Tr(W) in line 150°

Basse Nord
du Four

Le Four
(2.8)

I des
Levrettes

I du
Châteauneuf

S-Gildas

Roc'h
Ruz

I des
Femmes

Pier
Quay

Le Voleur
Fl.WRG.4s
17m14-11M

Sailing
school

PORT BLANC
Depths in Metres

3°20'W   19'   18'

Tréguier. Commercial quay downstream from the marina. The cathedral has the tomb of St Yves, who is reputed to smile on the poor while looking after lawyers!

Port Blanc. (A) White daymark of Ile du Château Neuf guides approach from seaward on 150°. Deep-water anchorage off Run Glas on left

Protected, if drying, anchorage will be found north of the slipway of Ile St Gildas

Dried out alongside the quay at Port Blanc

choosing to stay overnight in what can obviously be a very exposed place may be disturbed by the manifestation of a local story which alleges the periodic arrival of a spectral woman at the head of a column of drowned sailors. All hands go ashore on the Ile St Gildas to water up, while their ships can be seen dimly riding in the offing.

Approach, entrance and Anchorage

Navigate with care to half a mile northeast of the *Guazer* red whistle buoy. You are now 1·2 miles to seaward of the harbour entrance on the entry transit of 150°. This is defined at night (not recommended) by the white sector of the Fl.WRG.4s light (Le Voleur) which also forms the front marker for the day transit. The rear mark is the Moulin de la Comtesse windmill a mile or so inland, which

appeared to have fallen down at the time of *The Shell Pilot's* most recent visit. Therefore, unless it has been re-established by an opportunist developer, keep the white tower of the light structure on 150°, treating the conspicuous white beacon tower on the Ile du Château Neuf as a starboard-hand marker. Thereafter, you have the red beacon *Rc. Ruz* off to port. By the time you reach the green beacon *Run Glas* on your starboard hand you will be thinking of anchoring, if you have not already done so. There are a number of visitors' moorings.

The adventurous bilgekeeler may be able to work into a fine berth and dry out amongst the rocks, but this would emphatically need to be arranged first at LW from the 'afloat' anchorage.

Facilities

Nothing is set up for visiting yachts in the way of facilities, but rudimentary assistance may be found ashore in the form of simple shops. There are also a couple of hotels.

If you have need of the harbour office, it is in the local sailing school, as are showers, toilets and fresh water by portage.

Perros Guirec

Tides
HW −0550 Dover

MHWS	MLWS	MHWN	MLWN
9·4m	1·25m	7·3m	3·5m

Depths
Channel dries 3·5m up to 1 mile from the marina. There is 2·5m inside.

General
Perros Guirec is a serious summer resort with wonderful beaches. Now that there is an artificial locked yacht harbour it has become a realistic possibility for the casual caller, who will find bars, discos and sports-gear shops in the marina area. The more traditional joys offered by hotels and restaurants tend to have stayed around the casino beside the north-facing beaches.

The bay dries to at least a mile offshore.

Approach and entrance
It is important before making a run in to Perros Guirec to establish that the sill will be open ready to receive you and that you have sufficient rise of tide to clear the drying shoals of the bay. In westerly weather you could wait for a while outside, but otherwise you will have an uneasy time of it hanging around in some very shoal and open water. The sill dries 3·5m and opening times, which immediately allow 3·5m depth inside the sill depend on the size of the tide. The 6-metre wide gate of the sill opens at springs from 2 hours before HW to 1½ hours after. At mean tides it opens from 1½ hours before to an hour after. At neaps it may only open for an hour before HW, and at dead neaps it may not open at all. If in doubt, call the harbourmaster on VHF Ch 9 (☎ 02 96 23 19 03).

There are two lines of approach, as follows.

From the northeast (Passe de l'Est) Leave the red can *Guazer* northwest of Port Blanc to port, and come onto a track of 224°. You now have 5 miles to go. As Ile Tomé comes abeam you should see the leading marks, Le Colombier in front (a white-gabled house 28m above the sea with an 15M light (Oc(4)12s) and, 1½ miles inland, the white Kerprigent tower, 79m up, carrying a quick flashing light intensified close to the course. By night, this transit will carry you right in until the end of the breakwater (Fl(2)G.6s) bears west less than a cable from you. Turn in to round it, watching for the lit red buoy

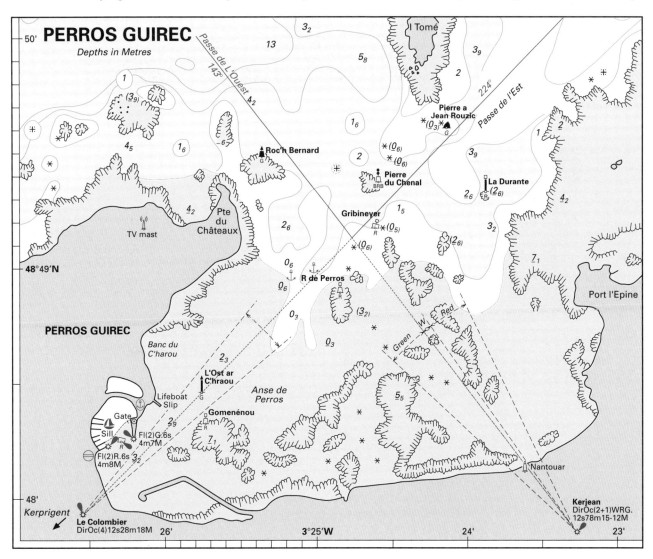

Perros Guirec

(Fl.R) which must be left to port on your way to the gate. By day the transit marks are clear, but if they are dimmed by poor visibility, pay due heed to the various marks on the plan. Leave reds to port, greens to starboard, with the large red and black *Pierre du Chenal* (ᢤ topmark) to starboard, and you will be fine.

From the northwest (Passe de l'Ouest) navigate into a position a cable or so southwest of the red daymark *Petit Bilzic*, on the end of the rock spit extending from Ile Tomé. If coming down from the north, be sure to leave the unlit west cardinal buoy *Les Couillons* to port. By night this position should put you in the narrow white sector of Kerjean (DirOc(2+1)WRG.12s78m15-12M). If it is red you must come to starboard, if green go to port. Follow this until you hit the leading lights for the Passe de l'Est, then swing onto them.

By day the pass is straightforward, leaving to starboard the *La Fronde* unlit green buoy and the *Roche Bernard* green daymark. When you are halfway from this to the *R. de Perros* red daymark you can swing round slowly to starboard, being sure to leave the green beacon *L'Ost C'hraou* to starboard before coming to the breakwater. Once inside, shape up for the northern-most pontoon.

Facilities
Fresh water on pontoons. Showers and toilets 24 hours a day (buy a token from the *capitainerie*). Laundry on the quay. There are various launching ramps and cranes from 7 to 20 tons. Scrubbing is possible on the west mole, but ask first for a suitable berth. Fuel from a pontoon inside the lock – open to coincide with the lock.

There is a chandlery, and light repairs can be arranged. *Camping Gaz* exchange and ice. The town proper, with its 12th-century church, is a mile or so uphill. The casino and the best beaches are a short cab-ride away for all but the fittest gamblers and sand-castle builders.

Communications
Bus to Lannion, where there is a railway station.

Ploumanac'h

Tides
HW −0550 Dover

MHWS	MLWS	MHWN	MLWN
9·0m	1·1m	7·1m	3·4m

Depths
Entrance dries 1·6m, and the sill dries 2·25m. The low water depth inside the basin is given as 1·5m, but the bottom is largely mud, so craft of greater draught can stay upright over low water. Greater depths have been reported inside.

General
Ploumanac'h is a rambly village with most small-town facilities. It is well equipped with bistros and bars, but has clearly been cleaned up from its days as a fishing community. It hides inside an entrance

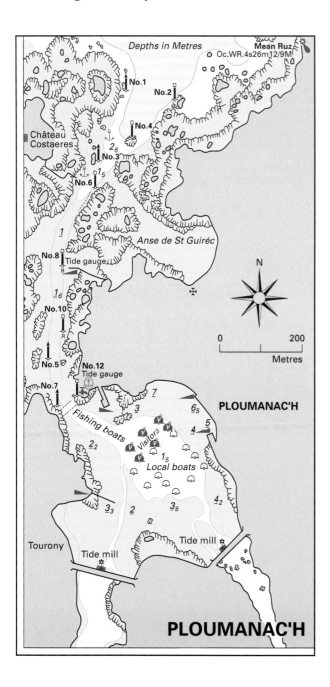

guarded on the east by outrageously sculptured rose granite rocks and on the west by the elegant Château de Costaérés, which has its own wooded rocky islet.

While its official size limit for the 20 visitors' berths is 10m, it has been known to extend a warm welcome to considerably larger vessels of the 'old gaffer' persuasion at times of *fête de mer*.

Shelter is excellent in all conditions, but entry may be unpleasant in strong northerlies and northwesterlies.

Approach
It is not recommended to make a first entrance in the dark. You will also have to calculate your necessary rise of tide for the sill (dries 2·25m). Having done this, the entrance is not complicated.

Identify the Pointe de Méan Ruz with its square pink light tower (Oc.WR.4s26m12/9M). Give Méan Ruz a healthy berth and shape up for the red (to port) and green (to starboard) unlit entry beacons, *Nos 2* and *1*. If coming from the northwest, steer for the light tower outside all dangers until the gap between the beacons bears about 165°, then turn in. Entry is now simply a matter of coming in between the beacons as per the plan. There are no nasty surprises, so long as you do not come too close to any of the beacons, some of which stand on ragged rocky bases. The sill is immediately after *Nos 7* (green) and *12* (red). The fourth port beacon (*No.8*) carries a tide gauge, and there is a depth indicator on the port-hand side of the sill, showing actual depth over the 'hump'.

If you need to wait for the tide, anchor near the mouth of the Anse de St Guirec by *No.6* red pile. A few visitors' moorings can be found here, in minimum depth 1·5m. This berth will only be of interest to those visitors awaiting water for the sill, unless you intend to take the ground in tight circumstances. In any event, take care because of the proximity of numerous rocks. The village here is now set up for tourism, but the beach is sandy and there is an excellent series of easy cliff paths to explore.

Ploumanac'h. Mean Ruz square pink light tower set on pink boulders 26m above the entrance

Ploumanac'h.

Ploumanac'h. Entrance on course 214° is well marked and not as alarming as it appears here. Château Costaérès and beacon *No.1* on starboard hand

Below Anse de St Guirec is an anchorage between beacons *6* and *8*

Berthing

Buoys consist of two fenders joined by aluminium rods. Pick one up by its pick-up line and secure alongside it. The outer row is for visitors, but the best water (2m) is at row C. The harbour office listens on VHF Ch 9 and 16, or ☎ 02 96 23 37 82.

Facilities

Dinghy landing near the sill after half-tide can be somewhat fraught. Seek a better alternative or wear your wellies and try the mud. Fresh water by cans from the Quai Bellevue. Showers and heads (24 hours) on the jetty by the sill. Laundry at the port. Launching slip on the Quai Bellevue. Chandlery and engineers available, but no major repairs. No *Camping Gaz* exchange or ice. There is an accommodating garage which does boat repairs.

There are spectacular cliff walks down numerous tracks in the direction of Guirec and beyond.

Trébeurden

Tides

HW −0600 Dover

MHWS	MLWS	MHWN	MLWN
9·1m	1·3m	7·2m	3·6m

Depths

Depths in the offing, which dries, appear to coincide with or be greater than the depth on the sill. This has a mobile gate which has an 'open' drying height of 2m. As soon as the sill opens, there is 1·6m depth over it, and this generally happens at HWS±3½hrs. At dead neaps it is almost always open. A floodlit tide gauge is helpfully sited at the sill and a green light is illuminated when there is 1·6m over the sill. The tide is swishing in at this point, and it is a good idea to wait for 15 minutes or so after it comes on for things to settle down.

Alongside depths vary from 3·5m on the outer jetty to 3m in the central basin. There are ten waiting buoys outside in a deep water pool just north of Ile Milliau. These are fine in quiet weather, but roll in anything of a swell, particularly towards HW. Further in and more sheltered are another set, which may well have enough depth to see smaller boats over LWN, but reduce to soundings to make sure near springs.

General

The coast from the Morlaix river to Perros-Guirec is some of the most spectacular in the Channel. It is also highly popular with French holiday-makers for its camping among the pine trees, pony-trekking and surfing or sailboarding from the fine, sandy beaches which lie between the rocky headlands. With only Lannion, Ploumanac'h and Plougasnou offering limited access to yachts, it is natural enough that a new marina should be built at Trébeurden, between two small jetties linked by a massive breakwater. The town is an up-market resort featuring 3-star hotels and an 18-hole golf course. The well run marina now offers an excellent stopover, as well as a safe place to leave a yacht for a while.

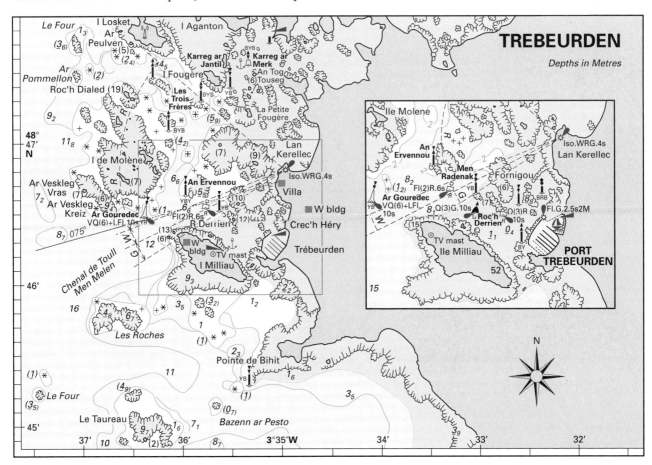

Trébeurden. Entrance to sill is hard by the breakwater end

Trébeurden. The sill at low water. Note profitable *pêche-à-pied* in progress and best water indicated clearly by beacons

Approach

This is possible by night or day, given a modest rise of tide. For details, see above ('Depths').

By day, work in so as to leave *Ar Gouredec* buoy (VQ+LFl) to port, then shape up on an easterly heading to pass between the first port-hand buoy and the northern extremity of Ile Milliau. This area is a good deep-water anchorage under the right conditions. Next, identify a green buoy on your starboard bow and a south cardinal beacon ahead or somewhat to port. Continue between these, then leave the next red buoy (*Roc'h Derrien*) to port. From here, take a heading for the end of the mole, where there are two green and one red unlit beacons close in. Take due action. On rounding the end of the mole, look for the green and red beacons (triangular and conical topmarks) indicating the position of the sill. Steer between these, according to the orders of the traffic lights, then make for the pontoon with blue pile tops, where you should tie up and report.

Beware of the fixed retaining sill (dries 3·5m), which is marked by beacons.

When approaching from the north, do not turn in onto *Ar Gouredec* too soon, as the rocks surrounding the tiny islands of Ar Veskieg Vraz and Ar Veskieg Kriez are notorious yacht-munchers.

By night, home in on the *Lan Kerellec* light (Iso. WRG.4s), situated approximately 4 cables to the north of the sill. The white sector (064°–069°) leads in past the *Ar Gouredec* lit south cardinal buoy and clears Ile Milliau. Once past here, look out for the lit red buoy (Fl(2)R.6s) near the edge of the green sector. Leave this to port and swing to starboard off the sectored light, heading to leave the next buoy (Q(3)G.10s) to starboard. A few degrees south of east from this is a red buoy (Q(3)R.10s) which is to be left to port. Now shape up to leave the end of the mole (Fl.G.2·5s) close to starboard, then proceed according to the daytime sailing directions.

Berthing and facilities

Contact the harbour office on VHF Ch 9 if at all possible between 0600 and midnight, or or ☎ 02 96 23 64 00 (*Fax* 02 96 15 40 87). There are 560 berths in all (maximum length 16m), of which a good number are for visitors.

There are showers and toilets ashore. Shore power, fuel (0800–2000) and fresh water are available, with a crane and a local boatyard for repairs. Laundry in the rue de Trozoul. Restaurants and shops at all prices abound nearby.

Lovely sandy beach. Town ten minutes' stroll. Bike hire.

Transport

Flights from Lannion airport. SNCF to Paris in 3 hours. Taxi on ☎ 02 96 47 48 49.

Lannion

Tides

HW −0605 Dover

MHWS	MLWS	MHWN	MLWN
9·1m	1·3m	7·2m	3·5m

Depths

Outside its narrow channel, the river dries up to 2·5m or more as far as the anchorage off Le Yaudet. Deep pools have been reported further upstream, where a carefully anchored yacht could float, even at LW. However, the bottom is reported as foul in parts, so the greatest care is required.

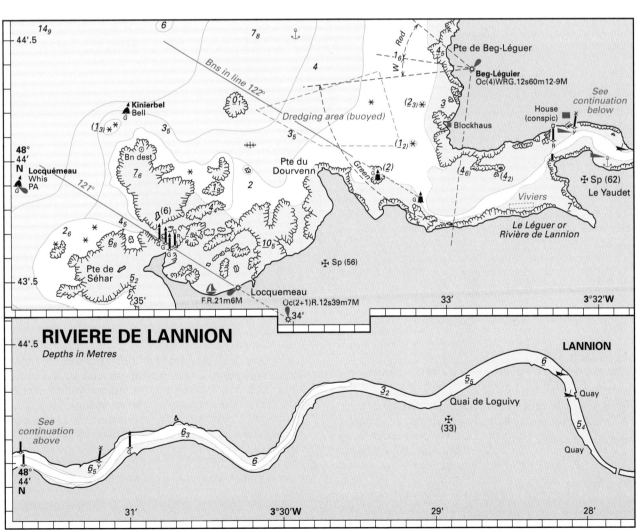

RIVIERE DE LANNION
Depths in Metres

Lannion. Le Yaudet

General

The pleasant country town of Lannion lies 4 miles up the Lannion river (or Le Léguer) at a modest elevation above the quays. The river is extremely pretty, but dries onto an often foul bottom. The quays are sadly no longer a serious proposition for cruising yachts to dry out, being either foul or taken over by fishing craft, though a trip on the tide in yacht or dinghy may remain an option.

The entrance is dangerous in west-northwest and northwest winds, particularly on the ebb. It seems reasonable to assume that it would also break in a big swell from the west under similar tide conditions.

Approach

Night approach not recommended. Nor is entry before half-tide or on the ebb. Navigate to a spot a couple of miles south of *Le Crapaud* unlit west cardinal buoy. Now try to locate the white house that is the Bec Léguer light structure (Oc(4)WRG.12s) just north of the entrance. It is not conspicuous by day, but it may help to know that it stands 60m above sea level. Steer towards this on about 095°, but if you cannot see it, sag south of the line to be sure of avoiding Le Taureau (dries 1·9m), and look instead for the unlit green buoy *Kinierbel*, 8 cables west-northwest of Pointe de Dourvin. The direct route from this to the entrance passes over a rock which dries 0·1m, so you are better off on the official route, but from half-tide on most yachts will cross this safely enough in calm conditions.

If you have identified Bec Léguer, keep in on 095° until the two green daymarks on the south side of the entrance come into line, then steer in on about 122°, keeping just to the north side of their transit. Give both 50m clearance to miss the surround rip-rap. Now keep in on 122° until close to the south bank, then sweep round to port and steer over towards the red beacon on the north shore. The rock pile on the north bank halfway to the beacon is readily distinguished by the small dry island (3m) near its outer end. From the red beacon, stay in the middle until you pass the slipway at Le Yaudet on the south side, then look for a vacant mooring.

Anchoring in 9ft (LAT) can be achieved, but is far safer at neaps, as boats have been know to swing out of the channel and dry out. Above here, the river shoals progressively and may dry as much as 6m.

The anchorage at Le Yaudet is well sheltered and the village is most interesting. Well off the tourist route, it is reached by a stiff but not 'cardiac' climb directly up from the tiny landing place. The church, which is open to casual callers as well as those looking for a quiet place to pray, has a fascinating tale to tell and a remarkable altar piece of seemingly unique importance. The church also boasts a number of unrestored 'votive ships' suspended from its rafters. A great rarity in these tidy times.

There are two hotels offering meals, the more up-market of which had the impertinence to advertise that it refused to serve Boeuf Anglais, and thus missed the custom of *The Shell Pilot*. The other was willing and able.

Primel

Tides

HW +0620 Dover

MHWS	MLWS	MHWN	MLWN
8·5m	1·2m	6·7m	3·0m

Depths

Deep water in the approaches, 1·5m in anchorage northeast of Roc'h an Trez Braz. Between 0 and 1m (LAT) in the 50m-wide dredged area behind the outer part of the breakwater. There is about 2m alongside the outer projection of the breakwater

Primel

PRIMEL-TREGASTEL

near the lighthouse. The rest dries, is foul, or is not available.

General

Primel is an almost natural harbour, completed by its breakwater. The entrance is fairly easy and readily identified. It is dangerous in strong onshore winds, however. There is some commercial fishing and some moorings for visiting yachts. The village is totally unspoilt and is in every respect a 'real' Breton fishing community.

Approach

By day, identify *Meloine*, the unlit west cardinal buoy marking Les Trepieds rocks. The entrance lies about 3 miles south from here. As you approach, pick up the conspicuous leading marks (white with red centrelines) on 152°. With Point de Primel abaft the beam you will pass Ar Zamegues rock to starboard, with a green patch painted on a white background, followed by a red and a green beacon. Keep on the line up to the breakwater.

By night, follow the leading lights in. Both are F.R and have a narrow visible sector.

Berthing

There are a number of visitors' moorings, some in fairly deep water, east of Roc'h an Trez Braz. There is plenty of room on these for small yachts. 40-footers (12m) would be OK, but larger than this may have to watch their extremities with care. If space permits, secure alongside the easternmost projection of the jetty (see 'Depths' above), but beware of fishing boats, which may appear at any time of day or night. Do not use the central projection of the jetty.

The moorings are moderately well sheltered, but some rolling may be experienced in strong westerly weather. Shelter is not ideal in onshore winds.

Facilities

Freshwater tap near fish market, where you can join the jolly Bretons filling their boots with *crustaces* and fresh fish of all sorts. There is a beach, an excellent chandlery in the fishing boat repair yard (where there is another fish shop), shops for simple provisions, a *crêperie* and a north-facing beach like a ghost seaside resort across the neck of land on the east side of the bay. You can land on either side, but for most purposes the 'pier' side is best. The Hotel de l'Abesse at the root of the bay has a public swimming pool, while the 'English Pub' with Guinness and 'jeux' will delight smokers exhausted by the excesses of the anti-smoking lobby, as they enter through a portal marked in large red letters, 'Bar Fumeurs'.

Morlaix

Tides

HW −0610 Dover

MHWS	MLWS	MHWN	MLWN
9·0m	1·3m	7·0m	3·5m

Note that low water figures may be variable

Depths

Deep-water approaches, fading out to a drying river (up to 5m drying heights). Depths inside the lock are billed as 2·5m, but are generally subject to silting which is cleared by periodic dredging.

Ile Louet and Château du Taureau seen from the southwest. The Grand Chenal passes between these two

The alternative channel (Tréguier) leaves Ile Noir tower clear to port before joining the main channel. Ile Stérec and the 1st red channel marker in the distance to the left

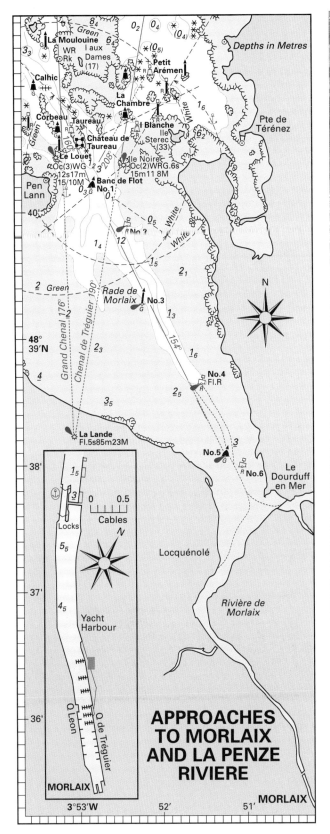

Morlaix town

General

Morlaix is a 16th-century town at the head of the river of the same name. A new bridge carrying the N12 autoroute spans the river below the lock, while above the basin an old viaduct above the town dominates the view. The locked yacht harbour is perfectly sheltered. The marina is not the world's most picturesque, but it is safe and can offer a convenient spot to leave a yacht or change crew, only 60 miles from the Chenal du Four. Morlaix is only 28km by fast road from Roscoff and the ferry.

The unlit approaches are not a proposition at night which is perhaps convenient, as the lock opens by day only.

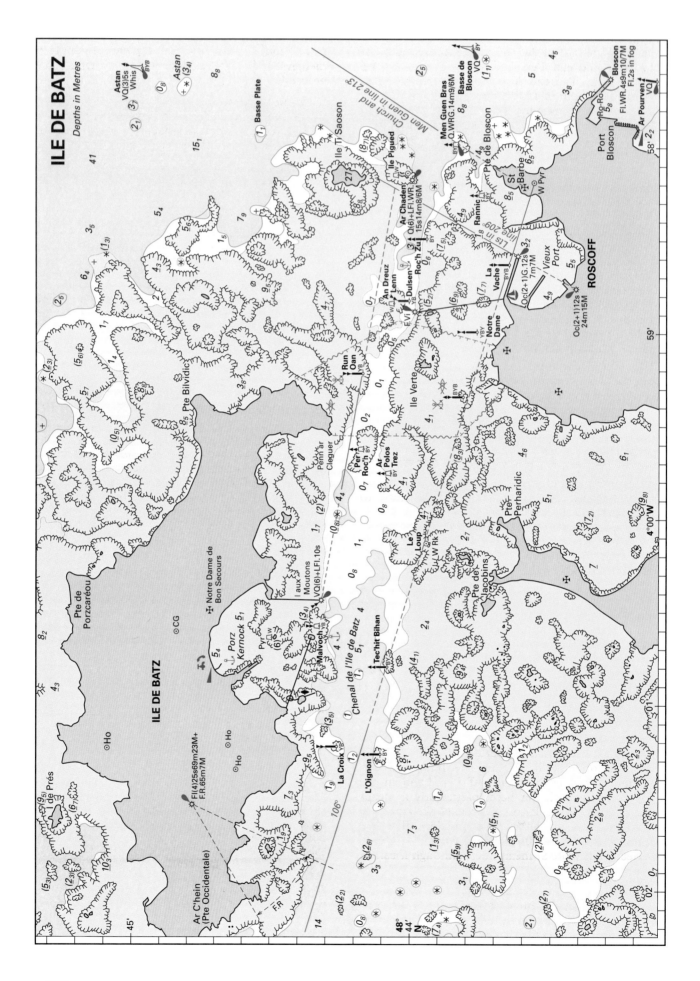

ILE DE BATZ

Depths in Metres

Approach

The trickiest part of the entrance is at the mouth of the river between Pen Lann and Barnénez. The Château du Taureau lies smack in the middle, having been built in 1542 to keep the Brits out, ten years after 600 marauders had been 'taken out' in their bivouacs just up-river. Once you are past this, there is a well-buoyed channel between the oyster beds to take you on to the river.

There are two main channels.

The Chenal de Tréguier starts effectively at the green beacon (*La Pierre Noire*) 2 miles west-southwest of Pointe de Primel. It is straightforward, leaving green beacons to starboard and reds to port (see plan), and joins the Grand Chenal after swinging to starboard onto a southwesterly heading with *La Chambre* green daymark to starboard. If in doubt, keep *La Chambre* on a back transit with the red *Petit Arémen* until you are near *No.1* buoy. Do not forget that this channel has one or two drying rocks of up to half a metre, so use it only with suitable rise of tide. Not recommended for strangers by night.

The Grande Chenal has a minimum of 3m of water and starts between the unlit red buoy *Stolvesen* and *La Vieille*, a green daymark, though care is needed in the offing to avoid the Plateau des Duons, further out to sea. The back marker for the leading line on 176° is the prominent square tower of La Lande (Fl.5s85m23M). The front mark is Ile Louet 1·7m square white tower with black top (Oc(3)WG.12s), sitting on its islet off Pen Lann. This line brings you safely between Ile Ricard, with its dangers, to starboard, and the various horrors to port.

When you have passed *Calhic* green daymark to starboard, swing onto about 160° to pass between *Le Corbeau* green daymark and its red opposite number just before the château. Once the château has been left to port, look for *No.1* green buoy, *La Banc de Flot*; leave it to starboard and proceed onwards between the buoys.

The channel, then the river, is well buoyed all the way with buoys and perches. When they finally run out ¾ mile from the locks stay in the middle.

The lock, (VHF Ch 9 and 16, ☎ 02 98 62 13 14). This opens 3 times: at 1½ hours before HW, at HW, and at one hour after. By these times there should be at least 2½m over the sill.

Berthing

In Morlaix itself, visitors' berths are to port as you lock in or on finger berths opposite. It is possible to anchor in various locations off Pen Lann in the approaches and shelter here, particularly at neaps can be pretty good. If you are looking for a passage anchorage as an alternative to Port Bloscon, consider the Penzé River where swinging room is perfectly adequate at mean tides, although it can be tight on a big spring.

Facilities

Fresh water on the quay, also diesel. Toilets and showers at the Bureau de Plaisance. All repairs, chandlery, *Camping Gaz* exchange and the rest. The city has the usual benefits common to all centres of population, but this one has a plentiful supply of medieval buildings to offset any gloom which may descend.

Communications

Buses and trains to Roscoff and the ferry, also to Brest and Paris. Trains connect to St Malo, but you have to change, so the experience is not speedy.

Roscoff - Port Bloscon

Tides

HW −0605 Dover

MHWS	MLWS	MHWN	MLWN
8·9m	1·3m	7·0m	3·45m

Depths

Roscoff dries out to about 3·2m along its north mole and to up to 5m on the inner harbour. The approaches also dry, but to a lesser extent.

Port Bloscon has deep water for a limited amount of anchorage.

General

Roscoff is known best today for its RoRo ferry terminal. In past times it was the point of departure for the Breton onion sellers whose striped shirts and bicycles festooned with strong onions were such a colourful part of British life. *The Shell Channel Pilot*, though it is technically none of its business, has not seen Johnny Breton in England these 30 years or more. Joyous to relate, however, 6 strings (excellent) were purchased by the compiler's wife in Downton, Wiltshire in 1998. The old port of Roscoff dries, but is well worth a visit nonetheless. It is pretty, with an agreeable aspect, a fine square and a number of points of interest, including the largest *vivier* in France, which you can visit.

The approaches to Roscoff can prove challenging, notably from the west, but Bloscon is comparatively easy of entry, and this roadstead, partly sheltered by the land, partly by the breakwater, gives a good lee in westerly weather. It is the ferry terminal, however, and yachts are only tolerated outside the swinging ground.

Approach

All approaches to Roscoff should be in the last 2 hours before HW.

Roscoff. Old lighthouse (A) on its transit with light on end of west breakwater. (B) Breakwater for Bassin de Vieux Port

Roscoff

From the west

From the west you have two choices. Either you pass outside Ile de Batz and award yourself an easy ride, or you save 3 miles and go for the Chenal de l'Ile de Batz, a rock-strewn, tide-scoured chamber of horrors which may yet be passed by day, given enough tide, fair weather and good visibility.

Inside To take the Chenal, first consult your tide tables, then keep the mighty tower of Ile de Batz lighthouse bearing about 070° until *Basse Plate*, a north cardinal daymark, bears about 100°. Steer to leave it about half a cable to starboard on a heading of around 106°. This will make good a transit of Le Loup, a steep rock with a white patch north of Pointe des Jacobins, and St Barbe, a distant white pyramid immediately to the right of a clump of trees. This transit carries you as far as *L'Oignon*, a north cardinal beacon to be left to starboard. You should now alter to a degree or two north of east and track east towards *Per Roc'h* north cardinal daymark.

Keep on this track until Ile aux Moutons ferry slip (lit south cardinal buoy off its end) a cable past *Malvoch* south cardinal daymark bears north. Now alter to 080° on Pen ar Cleguer, the right-hand edge of Ile de Batz. On this leg, the channel crosses a rock which dries 0·8m. Continue towards Pen ar Cleguer until *Run Oan* south cardinal beacon comes 'on'

with Ile Pigued white pyramid on 100°. Follow this transit, leaving *Per Roc'h* half a cable to starboard. When halfway between *Per Roc'h* and *Run Oan*, alter for the end of the Roscoff/Batz ferry pier (violet light), leaving this to starboard and *Duslen* south cardinal about 50m to port. *Run Oan* is also left to port by this course change. It is now safe to head for *Ar Chaden* south cardinal light tower a cable or so south of Ile Pigued, and thence to comparatively open water.

If you are headed for Roscoff, leave *Roc'h Zu* north cardinal beacon to starboard and continue with *Ar Chaden* on your port bow until the entry transit comes into line. This is the 7m white column (green top) on the end of the breakwater with the prominent square tower lighthouse (24m high) on the waterfront. The transit is 210°. For light characteristics, see plan.

Round the end of the breakwater and proceed to the inner, or Vieux Port.

Outside Give the Ile de Batz a comfortable berth to avoid its various off-lying dangers – 1½ miles clears all – until the lit east cardinal buoy *Bse Astan* bears southeast. You can then head to leave it to starboard in complete safety, so long as you monitor set and drift. From here, head south towards *Basse de Bloscon* lit north cardinal until the white pyramid north of *Duslen* south cardinal beacon is in transit with *Ar Chaden* south cardinal light tower on 277°. Now steer towards Roc'h Zu until the entry transit (see above) comes into line on 210°.

From the northeast
In order to keep off the Plateau des Duons, keep on a line joining *Men Guen Bras*, a 20m-high north cardinal light tower, with the bell tower of the church near the left-hand edge of the town. Come off the transit when *Ar Chaden* lines up with the white pyramid north of *Duslen* south cardinal beacon on 277°, as mentioned above ('Outside'). Then continue as per the 'Outside' instructions.

Bloscon
To enter Bloscon is a question of bearing in mind the information above, then steering round the end of the breakwater, paying sensible heed to the various buoys and beacons shown on the plan. Watch out for ferries, which have absolute right of way. Keep in the south part of the harbour, and steer somewhat south of east from the north cardinal buoy and sound in to the south of the breakwater. Shelter here is excellent in a strong westerly and, no doubt, in a southwesterly too.

Berthing
Anchor in Port Bloscon as described. As noted, a good passage berth in westerly weather, but a long walk to anywhere and not a place to visit ashore unless you have no option.

In Roscoff, dry out on the outer mole in the inner harbour. The outer harbour mole is much used by local commercial craft, whose skippers will tell you how things are.

Anchoring in Ile de Batz channel is a poor proposition on account of strong tides, but deepwater moorings have been sighted immediately west of Ar Charden at the east end of the channel which may be worth a try. Southeast Malvoch may look tempting and so it is, but should the wind come in westerly, as it once did on the compiler of *The Shell Channel Pilot*, a grisly time awaits you in the long, dark hours.

Facilities
Bloscon
Land on the small slipway at the root of the wall at the south end of the ferry-terminal car park. From here, it is 500m to the casino and the over-priced and poorly stocked tourist wine warehouse set up for road travellers bound home for Plymouth with empty tanks. Roscoff is ¾ mile.

Don't be tempted by the sign inviting you to patronise the supermarket up the road. *The Shell Pilot* walked a mile in the rain with no sightings, before retreating to the snug anchorage for cheddar cheese and paté imported by can from the UK.

Roscoff
Water from hydrants by arrangement, or tap in the toilets. Incredibly, no fuel is available in Roscoff. The 'de-taxing' of fishing boat diesel means honest yachtsmen are debarred from filling their tanks with

the French taxpayers' money. Municipal showers and toilets at the Gare Maritime on the Vieux Port – *jetons* for the showers from the Maison du Tourisme.

There is a chandler and a competent engineer, a sailmaker, etc., and various mobile cranes. *Camping Gaz* exchange and ice close by.

The town, as noted, is a winner, with good food and drink.

L'Aber-Wrac'h

Tides
HW +0347 Dover

MHWS	MLWS	MHWN	MLWN
7·8m	1·05m	6·1m	2·85m

Depths
Deep water past La Palue and well on up-river to Paluden, where a road bridge forms the head of yacht navigation. Water becomes shoal at LW springs just above the last bend to the south, but it is possible for a yacht drawing 8ft to lie just west of this bend to a short scope and a weighted cable, even at LW springs. Near the bend, in the mud, lie the dramatic remains of a Citroën which, *The Shell*

Ile Vierge lighthouse

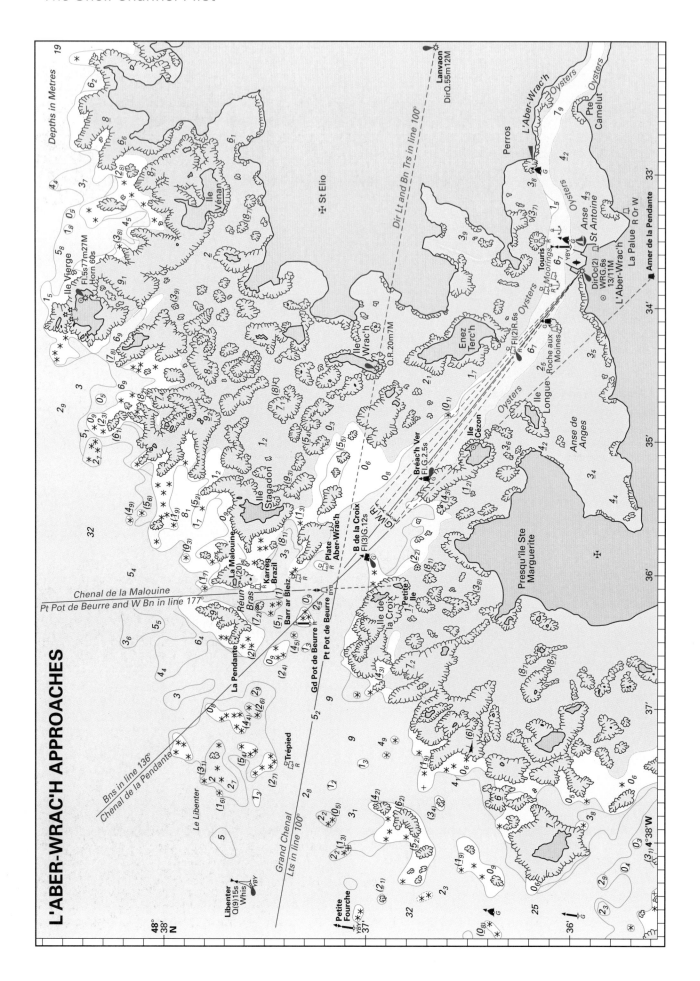

L'ABER-WRAC'H APPROACHES

Depths in Metres

48° 38' N

4° 38' W

L'Aber-Wrac'h approach. (A) Ile Wrac'h on 100° transit of Grand Chenal. (B) *Breac'h Ver* is a green tower beacon to be left to starboard. (C) L'Aber-Wrac'h. Chenal de la Pendante on 136° leaves *Grand Pot de Beurre* and *Petit Pot* (both red beacons) to starboard, Grand Chenal leaves both to port on 100°. (D) Chenal de la Malouine on 177° has the *Petit Pot* and a white pyramid on Petite Ile, immediately southeast of Iles de la Croix, in transit until it joins the other two channels

La Palue seen from the north bank, with (A) *Le Touris* port-hand beacon (B) lifeboat slip (C) boats stored ashore while pontoons are removed for the winter

Channel Pilot was once assured by a fisherman, was left there by a successful *suicé*. Perhaps this colourful wreck has now been cleared or, more likely, rotted away.

General

L'Aber-Wrac'h is famous for its strategic importance, good shelter and ready accessibility in all but strong northwesterly gales. Facilities are limited, but it makes an ideal place to gather one's wits for the Chenal du Four. Up-river, a pleasant soujourn can be passed in peace and tranquillity within easy reach of the raptures which await at Le Relais de l'Aber (see 'Facilities' below).

Approach and entrance

You simply cannot miss L'Aber-Wrac'h by day or night in decent visibility because of the colossal tower of Ile Vierge light (Fl.5s77m28M Horn 60s), 3 miles east-northeast of *Libenter* west cardinal buoy. Fog is not recommended for entering L'Aber-Wrac'h. It has been tried by sane and courageous navigators who have ended up amongst the rocks, saved only by kindly fishermen out stirring up the lobsters.

Grand Chenal This is by far the easiest entry, and the only option by night. Round *Libenter* lit west cardinal buoy on a southerly heading to be sure of missing the Libenter shoal and hold on until you pick up the transit on 100°. This consists of a white square tower with a gabled roof and a red top on Ile Wrac'h (Q.R.20m7M), and the conspicuous though distant Lanvaon light 2 miles inshore. This looks like a Venetian campanile, 27m high, square-sided, and 55m above sea level. The side you are interested in is white. (Q.12M intensified 090°–110°). Further on still, bang on the transit, stands Plouguernou belfry.

Should visibility obscure this transit, beware of cross-sets while buoy and cairn-hopping by maintaining a good lookout astern as well as ahead. If you can still see the marks, follow the transit as far as the *Petit Pot de Beurre*, a prominent east cardinal daymark. Leave this to port, then alter to 128°, leaving the green beacon *Breac'h Ver* (Fl.G.2·5s) to starboard and picking up the transit of two less than conspicuous red and white beacons in the vicinity of the lifeboat shed something over a mile ahead. By night you have an obvious sectored light to guide you in (white – straight ahead, green – turn to port, red – turn to starboard). By day, if you cannot make out the leading marks, do not worry. Following *Breac'h Ver*, you have a red buoy (*Ile d'Ehre*) to leave to port, then the green beacon *Roche aux Moines* to starboard. Immediately after this, leave the next unlit red to port and shape up for the moorings or the pontoon, leaving *Touris* red daymark to port.

Chenal de la Malouine lines up the *Petit Pot de Beurre* on 177° and a white pyramid on Petit Ile, immediately southeast of Iles de la Croix. The pass is very narrow and can easily pass over a 0·6m patch. It must therefore be treated with great respect and suitable tide rise. It can, however, save 3 miles, joining the Grand Chenal at the *Petit Pot de Beurre*. The channel is best spotted by looking south through the gap between the two large rocks, La Malouine and La Pendante. From the outside you will normally be approaching this channel from the east or northeast. Do not be dismayed if the white pyramid is slow to appear. Both features of the transit do not show themselves until you are almost on, and you should check them with a bearing (177°) to make sure you have got the right ones. The transit line takes you very close to the rocks immediately south of Réun Bras which may well be breaking. Stick rigidly to the transit and do not be alarmed.

Above La Palue, L'Aber-Wrac'h. Lifeboat slip lower left. Visitors' buoys above and to the right. *Below* Le Passage. Look for moorings when you see Beg an Toul green cairn. Left-hand white house (bottom right) is the Relais de l'Aber

Chenal de la Pendante passes northeast of the Libenter shoal. It lines up a white, target shaped beacon on Ile Cezon with a red, black and white beacon 3 cables south of La Palue lifeboat station on a heading of 136°, joining the main channel at the *Petit Pot de Beurre*.

Up-river

Follow channel markers as far as they go, then keep to the middle. When choosing an anchorage, watch out for moorings, of which there are many.

Berthing

On visitors' buoys off La Palue, or bows-to on the potentially uncomfortable summer-only pontoon (maximum LOA 12m). Mooring is expensive in La Palue, and the lad who comes for the money only takes cash, so be warned and hang onto your drinking vouchers. The buoys here are laid too close together. It's all fine on a summer's day, but they can give you an adventurous night with a gale blowing against a spring tide, as boats career around trying to do each other serious injury and owners hang fenders out more in hope than the promise of success. If you don't fancy it, go up-river and try your luck on the moorings. This section is probably off your chart, but fear not. Stay in the middle, be guided by the moorings and press on until you reach the green cairn *Beg an Toul*. Just downstream of this you will find 'dumbell' visitors moorings in 5m, with more of the same in 6m upstream of it. A landing place is established on the village side of the river with a 5-minute stroll to the action, such as it is. Sadly, anchoring in the river is now prohibited due to the oyster beds.

Facilities

These are better than you might imagine. La Palue still feels like a summer station rather than a year-round town, yet much can be achieved. Various hard-case bars await the bold, plus a couple of restaurants, of which La Palue right at the dock is excellent value and patronised by locals. There is also a useful chandlery, and meteo is posted at the dockmaster's office.

One mile up the hill is the charming little town of Landéda. Here is all you need to provision enjoyably, with a butcher, a *charcuterie*, a bakery/patisserie, and a supermarket well-stocked with properly priced decent wines. The locals are so friendly that on one occasion a passer-by took pity on the *Shell Pilot* who was staggering down the hill laden with heavy victuals, picked him up in his car and took him back to the dock.

The yacht club can provide showers at a price. Takeaway oysters from Belon des Abers.

If up the river, do not miss the opportunity of a meal at Le Relais de l'Aber, by the bridge. It isn't cheap, but for a proper French meal, unsullied by the word 'tourist', it cannot be beaten. Book early to avoid disappointment. The place is full of locals. . .

Appendix

I. Charts

ENGLISH COAST

Harbour	Admiralty	Admiralty Small craft folio	Imray
Ramsgate	1827, 1828	5605	C8
Sandwich	1827	5605	C8
Dover	1698	5605	C8
Folkestone	1991	5605	C8
Rye	1991	5605	C8
Eastbourne	2154	5605	C9
Newhaven	2154	5605	C9
Brighton	1991	5605	C9
Shoreham	2044	5605	C9
Littlehampton	1991	5605	C9
Chichester	3418	5600	C9, Y33
Langstone Harbour	3418	5600	C9, Y33
Portsmouth	2625, 2631	5600	C3, C9, C15
Bembridge	2022, 394, 2050	5600	C3, C15
Ryde	394	5600	C3, C15
Fishbourne	2022	5600	C3, C15
Cowes	2793	5600	C3, C15
Hamble River	2022	5600	C3, C15
Southampton	1905, 2041	5600	C3, C15
The Beaulieu River	2021	5600	C3, C15
Newtown River	2021	5600	C3, C15
Yarmouth Harbour	2021	5600	C3, C15
Lymington	2021	5600	C3, C15
Keyhaven	2021	5600	C3, C15
Christchurch	2219	5601	C4
Poole	2611	5601	C4, Y23
Swanage	2172	5601	C4
Lulworth Cove	2172	5601	C4

Harbour	Admiralty	Admiralty Small craft folio	Imray
Weymouth	2172, 2255, 2268	5601	C4
Portland Harbour	2255, 2268	5601	C4
Bridport	3315	5601	C5
Lyme Regis	3315	5601	C5
Axmouth and Beer	3315	5601	C5
Exmouth	2290	5601	C5, Y45, Y43
Teignmouth	26	5602	C5, Y43
Torquay	26	5602	C5, Y43
Brixham	26	5602	C5, Y43
Dartmouth	2253	5602	C5, Y47
Salcombe	28	5602	C6, Y48
River Yealm	1613		C6, C14
Plymouth	30, 1901, 1902, 1967	5602	C6, C14
Looe	147	5602	C6
Polperro	148	5602	C6
Fowey	31	5602	C6, Y52
Charlestown	31	5602	C6
Mevagissey	147	5602	C6
Falmouth	32, 154	5602	C6, Y58
Helford River	147	5602	C6, Y57
Coverack	154, 777	5603	C7
Mullion Cove	777, 2345	5603	C7
Porthleven	777, 2345	5603	C7
St Michael's Mount	2345	5603	C7
Penzance	2345	5603	C7
Newlyn	2345	5603	C7
Mousehole	2345	5603	C7
Isle of Scilly	34, 883	5603	C7

FRENCH COAST

Harbour	Admiralty	Imray	SHOM	Navicarte
Dunkerque	1350, 323	C30	7057	1010
Gravelines	1350, 323	C30	7057	
Calais	1351, 1892, 323	C8	7258	1010
Boulogne	438, 1892, 2451	C8, C31	7323, 7247, 7416	1010, 1011
Le Touquet/Etaples	2451	C31	7416	1011
Le Crotoy	2451	C31	7416	1011
St Valéry-sur-Somme	2451	C31	7416	1011
Le Tréport	1352, 2147, 2451	C31	7417, 7207, 6824	1011
Dieppe	2147, 2451	C31	7317, 7417	1011, 1012
St Valéry-en-Caux	2451	C31	7417	1012
Fécamp	1352	C31	7207, 7417	1012
Le Havre	2990, 2146, 2613	C31, C32	6796, 6683	526, 1012
Honfleur	2994, 2146, 2613	C31, C32	6796, 6683	526, 1012
Deauville/Trouville	1349, 2146, 2613	C32	7418	526

Harbour	Admiralty	Imray	SHOM	
Dives/Port Guillaume	2146	C32	7420	526
Ouistreham/Caen	1349, 2613	C32	7420, 6927, 7418	526
Courseulles	1349, 2613	C32	7420, 6927	526, 527
Port-en-Bessin	2613	C32	7056	527
Grandcamp Maisy	2613	C32	7056	527
Isigny-sur-Mer	2135	C32	7056	527
St Vaast-la-Hougue	1349	C32	7090	527, 528
Barfleur	1349, 2135	C32	7090	528
Cherbourg	2602	C32	7086, 7092	528
Alderney	60, 2845	C33A	6934	
Carteret	3655	C33A	7133	1014
Portbail	3655, 2669	C33A	7133, 6966, 7157	1014
Guernsey	807, 808, 3140, 3654	C33A	6903, 6904	1014
Jersey	3278, 1137, 3655	C33B	7160, 6938	1014
Iles Chausey	3656, 3659	C33B	7134, 7155, 7156	534
Granville	3672, 3656, 3659	C33B	7156, 6966	535
Cancale	3659	C33B	7131, 7155, 6966	535
St Malo/St Servan/Dinard	2700, 3659, 2669	C33B	7130, 7155, 6966,	535
La Rance	2700, 3659	C33B	7130, 7155, 6966	
St Briac	2700, 3659	C33B	4233, 7129, 7155	
St Cast	3659, 2669	C33B	7129, 7155	536
Dahouet	3674, 2669	C33B, C34	7129, 6966	536
Le Légué (St Brieuc)	3674, 2669	C34	7154, 7128	536
Binic	3674, 2669	C33B	7154, 7128	536
St Quay-Portrieux	3672, 3674, 2669, 2668	C33B, C34	7154, 7128	536
Paimpol	3673, 3670, 2668	C34	7127, 7152	537
Ile de Bréhat	3673, 3670	C34	7127	537
Lézardrieux/Pontrieux	3673, 3670, 2668	C34	7126, 7127	537
Tréguier	3672, 3670, 2668	C34	7126, 7152	537
Port Blanc	3672, 3670, 2668	C34	7126, 7152	537, 538
Perros Guirec	3672, 3670, 2668	C34	7125, 7152	537, 538
Ploumanac'h	3672, 3670, 2668	C34	7125, 7152	537, 538
Trébeurden	3669	C34	7124, 7151	538
Lannion	3669, 2668	C34	7124, 7151	538
Primel	2745, 3669	C34	7095, 7151	538
Morlaix	2745, 3669	C34, C35	7095, 7151	538
Roscoff – Port Bloscon	2745, 3669	C35	7095, 7151	538
L'Aber-Wrac'h	1432, 2644, 3668	C35	7094, 7150	539, 540

II. Distances

	Ramsgate	Brighton	Chichester	Portsmouth	Cowes	Lymington	Poole	Weymouth	Dartmouth	Salcombe	Plymouth	Fowey	Falmouth	Penzance

Distance table for passages between harbours on the south coast (in nautical miles)
The shortest navigable distances on the rhumb line between harbour entrances or bars

	Ramsgate	Brighton	Chichester	Portsmouth	Cowes	Lymington	Poole	Weymouth	Dartmouth	Salcombe	Plymouth	Fowey	Falmouth	Penzance
Ramsgate														
Brighton	78													
Chichester	112	34												
Portsmouth	119	41	7											
Cowes	125	47	15	8										
Lymington	132	56	24	17	9									
Poole	152	74	42	35	27	19								
Weymouth	173	97	64	57	49	40	27							
Dartmouth	212	135	107	100	92	84	70	52						
Salcombe	220	144	117	110	103	95	81	64	14					
Plymouth	241	165	135	132	123	115	98	82	35	17				
Fowey	255	178	152	144	139	129	116	96	48	36	20			
Falmouth	271	194	168	160	152	143	130	113	63	50	38	20		
Penzance	295	219	190	183	176	168	155	135	88	74	64	48	32	
Scilly	322	246	218	211	204	195	183	163	116	102	92	76	60	37

Distance tables for passages between principal headlands along the south coast (in nautical miles)
The shortest navigable distances on the rhumb line between safe distances off each headland

	N Foreland	Dungeness	Beachy Head	Owers	St Catherine's	Anvil Point	Portland Bill	Berry Head	Start Point	Bolt Head	Rame Head	Dodman	Lizard	Runnel Stone
N Foreland														
Dungeness	36													
Beachy Head	66	30												
Owers	101	65	35											
St Catherine's	125	89	59	24										
Anvil Point	150	114	84	49	25									
Portland Bill	170	134	104	69	45	20								
Berry Head	210	174	144	109	85	60	40							
Start Point	218	182	152	117	93	68	48	13						
Bolt Head	224	188	158	123	99	74	54	19	6					
Rame Head	242	206	176	141	117	92	72	36	23	17				
Dodman	263	227	197	162	138	113	93	57	45	39	24			
Lizard	282	246	215	181	156	132	111	75	62	56	44	22		
Runnel Stone	300	265	234	200	175	151	130	94	81	75	63	42	19	
Bishop Rock	330	294	263	229	204	180	159	123	111	105	93	71	48	32

Cross-Channel distances
Safe navigable routes between breakwaters and/or estuary entrances (in nautical miles)

	N Foreland	Dungeness	Beachy Head	Nab Tower	Needles	Anvil Point	Portland Bill	Berry Head	Rame Head	Lizard	Bishop Rock
Boulogne	39	25	51	97	125	137	157	196	227	269	318
Dieppe	90	58	58	91	115	126	144	182	211	246	294
Le Havre LtV	130	96	75	76	88	94	106	140	165	198	246
Grandcamp	158	122	94	78	80	82	89	116	140	175	223
Cherbourg	164	128	98	66	60	57	60	84	106	141	188
Alderney	180	144	114	74	61	53	49	65	85	118	167
St Peter Port	201	165	134	96	83	73	65	70	90	112	157
St Helier	219	183	151	113	101	94	87	94	108	130	173
St Malo	245	209	178	140	127	120	113	117	138	145	183
Lézardrieux	243	207	175	134	123	113	102	92	100	108	146
Morlaix	274	238	206	169	149	138	124	106	100	92	123
L'Aber-Wrac'h	300	264	231	195	171	159	146	117	103	84	104
Le Conquet	325	289	252	216	192	179	161	136	120	98	110
Brest	342	306	269	233	209	196	178	153	137	115	127

Safe navigable distances from breakwater to breakwater or fairway buoys (in nautical miles)

	Ramsgate	Dunkerque	Calais	Boulogne	Le Touquet/Etaples	St Valéry/Le Crotoy
Ramsgate						
Dunkerque	39					
Calais	27	20				
Boulogne	37	41	20			
Le Touquet/Etaples	48	51	32	12		
St Valéry/Le Crotoy	66	69	50	30	19	
Brighton	81	96	78	65	97	71

Safe navigable distances between yacht berths, outside Ile de Bréhat and Ile de Batz (in nautical miles)

	St Malo	Binic	Paimpol	Tréguier	Perros-Guirec	Morlaix	Roscoff	L'Aber-Wrac'h	Le Conquet
St Malo									
Binic	33								
Paimpol	38	19							
Tréguier	57	39	26						
Perros-Guirec	62	64	31	20					
Morlaix	92	71	59	48	32				
Roscoff	85	64	52	41	26	13			
L'Aber-Wrac'h	117	96	84	73	58	46	33		
Le Conquet	133	112	100	89	74	61	48	23	
Brest	150	129	117	106	91	78	65	40	17

Distances around the Channel Islands
Distances shown are safe navigable routes between breakwaters and/or estuary entrances (in nautical miles)

	Cherbourg	Alderney	St Peter Port	St Helier	Chausey (S)	Granville	St Malo
Cherbourg							
Alderney	21						
St Peter Port	41	23					
St Helier	57	40	26				
Chausey (S)	77	60	48	24			
Granville	83	66	53	29	9		
St Malo	83	66	52	30	15	21	
Lézardrieux	81	65	41	41	47	56	7

III. English–French Glossary

General
yes *oui*
no *non*
please *s'il vous plait*
thank you *merci*
excuse me *pardon*
it's nothing *de rien*
where? *où*
when? *quand?*
how? *comment?*
today *aujourd'hui*
tomorrow *demain*
left *à gauche*
right *à droite*
big *grand*
small *petit*
open *ouvert*
closed *fermé*
goodbye *au revoir*
good morning *bonjour*
good afternoon *bonjour*
good evening *bonsoir*
good night *bonne nuit*
I understand *je comprends*
I don't understand *je ne comprends pas*
OK *d'accord*
How are you *Comment allez-vous/Ça va?*
Fine, thanks *Très bien, merci*
Excuse me, do you speak English? *Pardon, Madame/Monsieur, vous parlez anglais?*
one *un*
two *deux*
three *trois*
four *quatre*
five *cinq*
six *six*
seven *sept*
eight *huit*
nine *neuf*
ten *dix*
twenty *vingt*
fifty *cinquante*
one hundred *cent*
one thousand *mille*

Sunday *dimanche*
Monday *lundi*
Tuesday *mardi*
Wednesday *mercredi*
Thursday *jeudi*
Friday *vendredi*
Saturday *samedi*

Shopping
apples *pommes*
apricots *abricot*
aubergine *aubergine*
bakery *boulangerie*
beans *haricots*
beef *boeuf*
biscuits *biscuits*
bread *pain*
butcher *boucher*
butter *beurre*
carrots *carottes*
cheese *fromage*
chicken *poulet*
chocolate *chocolat*
coffee *café*
cucumber *concombre*
eggs *oeufs*
fish *poisson*
flour *farine*
grocer *alimentation*
honey *miel*
jam *confiture*
lamb *agneau*
lemon *citron*
meat *viande*
melon *melon*
milk *lait*
oil *huile*
onions *oignons*
oranges *oranges*
peaches *pêches*
potatoes *pommes de terre*
rice *riz*
salt *sel*
sugar *sucre*
tea *thé*
tomatoes *tomates*
water *eau*
wine *vin*

French names and terms found on charts
anse bay, creek
avant port outer harbour
baie bay
balise beacon
banc bank
barre bar
basse shoal
bassin basin
blanc white
bouche mouth of river or channel
calanque fjord-like inlet
canal canal, channel
cap cape
capitainerie port/harbour office
château castle
chaussée causeway
chenal channel
col mountain pass
colline hill
côte coast
darse basin
digue mole
écueil shoal, reef
est east
étang lake, lagoon
fleuve river, stream
fosse ditch
golfe gulf
grand(e) great
grau channel
gros large
haut-fond shoal
île island
îlot islet
isthme isthmus
jetée jetty
lac lake
maison house
marais swamp
marine marine
mer sea
môle mole
mont mount, mountain
montagne mountain
mouillage anchorage
neuf(ve) new
noir(e) black
nord north
nouveau new

ouest west
passe channel
petit(e) small
pic peak
plage beach
plateau shoal
pointe point
pont bridge
port port
presqu'île peninsula
quai quay
quai d'accueil arrivals/reception quay
rade roadstead
rivière river
roche rock
rocher above-water rock
rouge red
sable sand
saline salt works
sommet summit
sud south
torrent stream, torrent
tour tower
vieux, vieil, vieille old

IALA SYSTEM A BUOYAGE

Lateral marks

Port hand
All red
Topmark (if any): can
Light (if any): red

Starboard hand
All green
Topmark (if any): cone
Light (if any): green

The direction of buoyage in estuaries and port approaches is generally from seaward.
In other areas around the British Isles the general direction of buoyage runs:
Northward along the W coasts and in the Irish Sea
Eastward through the English Channel
Northward through the North Sea
Where there is doubt buoyage direction is shown thus:

Lighted buoys are marked on charts by red pear-shaped flashes

Cardinal marks

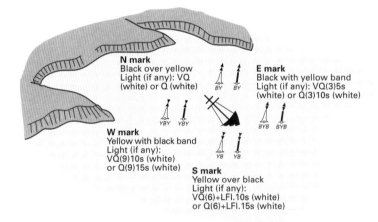

N mark
Black over yellow
Light (if any): VQ
(white) or Q (white)

E mark
Black with yellow band
Light (if any): VQ(3)5s
(white) or Q(3)10s (white)

W mark
Yellow with black band
Light (if any):
VQ(9)10s (white)
or Q(9)15s (white)

S mark
Yellow over black
Light (if any):
VQ(6)+LFl.10s (white)
or Q(6)+LFl.15s (white)

Isolated danger marks
(stationed over a danger with navigable water around)
Black with red band
Topmark: 2 black balls
Light (if any): Fl(2) (white)

Special Mark
Body shape optional, yellow
Topmark (if any): Yellow x
Light (if any): Fl.Y etc

Safe water marks
(mid-channel and landfall)
Red with white vertical stripes
Topmark (if any): red ball
Light (if any): Iso, Oc, LFl.10s or Mo(A) (white)

ABBREVIATIONS USED ON CHARTS

Bldg	building
Bn	beacon
Bu	blue
CG	coastguard station
conspic type	conspicuous (caption in bold type)
dest	destroyed
Dir	directional
Dk	dock
Dn	dolphin
dr	dries
ED	existence doubtful
FS	flagstaff
Ft	fort
G	green
h	hour
Ho	house
Ldg	leading
Lk	lock
LB	lifeboat station
Mag Varn	magnetic variation
M	sea mile(s)
m	metres
min	minutes
Obscd	obscured
Or	orange
PA	position approximate
R	red
Rk	Rock
Rep	reported
s	second(s)
SS	signal station
Stn	station
Vi	violet
vis	visible
W	white

Index